D1282911

ODYSSEY
Journey Through Black America

ODYSSEY

Journey Through Black America

by EARL and MIRIAM SELBY

G. P. Putnam's Sons
New York

301.451
S460

Copyright © 1971 by Earl and Miriam Selby

All rights reserved. This book, or parts thereof, may not be reproduced in any form without permission. Published simultaneously in Canada by Longmans Canada Limited, Toronto.

Library of Congress Catalog Card Number: 79-151216

PRINTED IN THE UNITED STATES OF AMERICA

But for These

WE THANK the men and women whose words —and lives—appear on these pages. We owe another debt to the hundreds of other black Americans who also gave of their time and insights to make this book the better. In truth, it belongs to all of them.

A special acknowledgment is due the READER'S DIGEST. There is no way we could have undertaken this work without the help, encouragement and support of its editors . . .

SEP 21 '71

HUNT LIBRARY
CARNEGIE-MELLON UNIVERSITY

Contents

ODYSSEY
Journey Through Black America

Why We Began

Odyssey

My wife and I are white, but this is not designed to be just another book in which white people are writing about blacks.

For two years we conducted a 46,500-mile journey through Black America, and what we did was listen, and what we heard from 300 men and women was the living testimony of the black experience.

Told by blacks, in their own words.

We began this journey in the fall of 1968, when we could see the shadows of Watts and Detroit and Chicago and a hundred other ghettos falling longer across the country. Polarization was pitting American against American. With the voices of protest and counterprotest, there was violence and upheaval.

As reporters who had spent years traveling this country, writing about people and their concerns, we knew some of this turmoil at first hand. I had, for example, been in every major ghetto. I wrote about the shattering impact of welfare on the people of Watts, the dead-end devastation of urban renewal in Cleveland's Hough area. I traveled the slums of Oakland's flatlands, the streets of Harlem, dismal Twelfth Street of Detroit's black belt.

But nothing in this background prepared me for Seattle.

Epitaph for Ed Pratt

In Seattle a black man talked about survival.

"It becomes little miracles," he said, "when one of us coming out of the slums is able to get through high school, into college, come out with a job, and not end up being an alcoholic or a dope addict."

Nine days later that black man ran out of miracles. Opening his front door to investigate a noise at nine o'clock one Sunday night in January, 1969, he was killed by a shotgun blast from his carport. Whoever fired it has never been found.

HUNT LIBRARY
CARNEGIE-MELLON UNIVERSITY

The dead man was Edwin T. Pratt, who had made it out of the slums of Miami, Florida, into college, through a master's degree at Atlanta University. For his last eight years, he directed the Seattle Urban League, and when a memorial service was held for him, the governor of Washington was there, and President Nixon sent a message to express his sadness.

Odyssey

I had come to Seattle because of Operation Equality, a program run by the SUL which bought run-down housing, rehabilitated it, and then sold it at bargain prices to poor whites and poor blacks, in the process quietly creating integrated neighborhoods. Here was a possible start—with an example of black and white working together. Perhaps if I went to stay for a time with a black family that had been helped, then with whites, I might get some clue to what each was feeling and thinking.

Pratt, who had helped shape the Seattle program, and Warren Thaxton, who was working on it day to day, listened to my proposal. Pratt sat in a straight-backed chair pulled out in front of his desk in the league office. He said he felt more comfortable when there were no barriers between people. In build, he was stocky, medium height. He had cropped hair and a mustache.

Ed Pratt

Yes, yes you could live with a black family we've moved into a white neighborhood. But in that area, you would still be white among whites, and the reaction to you would not be the same. You just can't start out in white adulthood and wrap yourself in a black skin. You cannot feel what this black family feels when they walk down the street in this white community or go to school or to the laundromat. You have to be black from birth.

Superficial acts won't get us immersed in racial understanding. We have Caucasians whose flirtations with black-and-white concerns are just that. Very few people in this country are serious about it. But always you take a white man at his word that he wants to learn and help, reserving, however, in your mind that you've been this route. He'll be around a couple of months and after he has been called honkie and black people have turned their backs on him, not appreciating all his "great efforts," he'll return to his white world.

Intellectually, you can know the rage of being black, but you can go home and look in the mirror and know you are white, and say, "Thank God I don't have to go through that again!"

Odyssey

The other black man in the room, Thaxton, thirty-seven, had only recently arrived from Washington, D.C. At one point I referred to the book *Black Rage*, in which the psychiatrist-authors said black children are admonished not to be "bad niggers." I asked Thaxton if this were true. He replied: "Let me ask you a question to answer yours. Do you know of any white families raising their children not to be, quote, unquote, bad honkies? Do you know some doing that? Same thing applies to the blacks."

Obviously, I irritated him. He went on: "You are going to have to start doing something about this problem. You come out here and sit with Ed and me, and say you're this and you're that, and that you are going to lose if the racial crisis isn't solved. Then you'll go away and try to find some way to wiggle out."

That night, when I returned to San Francisco, Miriam met me at the airport, curious about what kind of day I'd had. Lousy, I told her. We stayed up a long time, talking about the implications of Seattle and weighing them against our own backgrounds.

Earl Selby

My mother, a Swedish immigrant, was four months pregnant with me when my father died, leaving her with no money, and I was delivered as a charity case in the Cook County Hospital of Chicago. As soon as possible she put me in a day nursery while she worked as a waitress. Eventually she became a cashier, and the earliest picture I have of her is wearing a black dress with a white collar—her uniform.

I was about three when she was married again, to a house painter, also Swedish, and she quit her job. We lived in a basement flat, not far from the Union Stockyards. Later we moved to a bungalow, but with the Depression it was always a question of whether there would be enough to pay the mortgage. Early on, I learned the word "foreclosure" because we always seemed to be on the edge of losing our home. My stepfather was out of work for months at a time. One winter we lived mostly on the small savings I had accumulated from odd jobs and playing nickel blackjack with other kids. I had enough brown beans that year to last me the rest of my life. So when somebody says do I know what it is to be poor, I can say, "Yes, I do."

Miriam Selby

I never had to worry about having enough to eat or a place to stay. Mother and Dad graduated from Stanford University, she as an accredited schoolteacher, he as a lawyer. Dad, who was esteemed in his field, had a lucrative practice. For twenty-one years he also served as city attorney for Palo Alto, California.

We lived in a Spanish-style house with an enormous backyard that stretched down to a creek. We also had a walled-in patio, pond, and goldfish. In our home we had three bedrooms, plus quarters for the maid. We always had live-in help. I can remember going off to first grade and the Scandinavian maid we had then was putting on my new shoes. The date was September 1, 1939. I asked was this a big day. All she said was, "The war has started."

In our well-to-do suburban community I heard lots of talk about kikes and micks and niggers, as if anyone who wasn't white Anglo-Saxon Protestant were somehow distasteful. Consistently, I was reminded that I was a fifth-generation Californian. One day somebody who knew my family saw me throwing a football with some black boys on a playground. My mother got a call and drove over immediately to take me home. She said I was not to play with Negroes. This made me angry. I didn't see any reason for it.

Earl Selby

It never occurred to me that I would stay poor. I thought all I had to do was look for the door out, and for me that was professional baseball. By fourteen, however, I had to give that up, because I knew I would never make it. One of the deciding events was the afternoon I played with some blacks on a team made up of waiters and kitchen help from a hotel near where I occasionally caddied. I struck out, messed up a double play. I was bewildered by how much better they were. But I didn't wonder why they should be barred from the big leagues. As the product of an all-white enclave, not too far from where a mob in 1966 stoned Martin Luther King, I just accepted the discrimination. We had very little contact with blacks in our neighborhood. I knew that east and north of us there was a black belt, because we saw it when we rode the el train down to the Loop.

Once, as a high school reporter for a Chicago newspaper—journalism had succeeded baseball as my way out—I inadvertently identified two white basketball players as Negroes. And while the error was caught in time, an editor laced into me, saying it was hard to think of a more insulting mistake. Those were the days when a weekend's violence in the black area would be reported in a single paragraph under the heading: EIGHT NEGROES KILLED.

When I got to Northwestern University as a scholarship student in economics, I thought of myself as a New Deal liberal, one of the have-nots being put down by the haves. I could empathize with the poverty of blacks and, at least intellectually, argue it was wrong to lock them away in ghettos, to disqualify them from jobs because of color. This was quite strong in me until I transferred to the University of Texas at Austin.

First day I was there, a black man, probably no more than fifteen years older than I, stepped down from a sidewalk to let me pass. Impulsively, I followed him to the street, said I was a Northerner, and that there was no reason for him to do that. "White boy," he said, the pleading in his voice urgent, "please don't make no trouble for me." I got back on the walk, shook my head, and forgot him. If he didn't want my help, I wasn't going to force it on him. Exactly as Ed Pratt was to describe the situation thirty years later, I felt rejected. And that gave me my excuse to do nothing more.

Miriam Selby

While I was in a private girls' school in Palo Alto, I began playing tournament tennis. By my last year I was seeded fourth for the National Junior Girls competition. In 1950 I also played at Forest Hills. I received my degree from the University of California at Los Angeles, went to work on Wall Street, and became a broker. Then *Time* magazine offered me a job as a business researcher and I took it, even though it meant turning down the Fulbright grant I'd won for a year's study in India.

In 1960, after I was sent to Chicago as a correspondent, I did a business story about the Playboy Club, where I met a then-unknown black comedian and filed the first national report on Dick Gregory. Other blacks, including some who had been with the civil rights movement in the South, then began calling me to tell me what was happening. That is how I found out about Paul Crump, a black convicted of a payroll murder. While his case hung in the courts, he had been under the death penalty for nine years, during which, his friends insisted, he had become rehabilitated in jail. After interviewing him a number of times, I joined in the efforts to save his life. I helped bring in attorney Louis Nizer from New York to argue at the climactic hearing which led the then-Governor Otto Kerner to commute Crump's sentence.

In the next few years I reported on developments in religion, law and education. I also helped prepare the cover story on Dr. King as *Time*'s "Man of the Year."

Earl Selby

As a columnist and city editor for a Philadelphia newspaper I handled a number of stories which showed mistreatment of blacks. Some of the exposés brought changes in state law. However, I never felt any particular personal involvement, being motivated more than anything by the idea that in America everyone ought to have at least the semblance of a fair shake.

After going to the *Reader's Digest* as a roving editor, I did articles on welfare, unemployment and riots. I read books on what I then regarded as "the Negro question." I followed Congressional investigations, interviewed social scientists. And yet, as I realized when Miriam and I stayed up talking about Seattle, all along I had been seeing blacks as a *situation*, not as people. The fact that I was not too dissimilar from too many other "well-intentioned informed" whites didn't help any.

It was time—long overdue—for Miriam and me to seek out the *human beings* in Black America.

Odyssey

In the two years of our odyssey we went to twenty-one states and the District of Columbia. We were in big-city ghettos, night and day. We walked the treelined streets of Middle America's smaller towns. We drove the backcountry roads of the Deep South.

We used reporters' techniques in getting to people. We followed up on newspaper stories, sat in on public meetings. We went to churches, housing projects, business offices. We met those who quite simply have helped shape history in America. We saw the revolutionaries, as well as those who had praise for America. We heard voices of despair, triumph, determination, bitterness and compassion. We listened to nearly a million words of the voices of Black America.

We do not pretend that every conversation began in candor or without skepticism that whites could know what it is to be black. "You're white," said the wife of a PhD in Los Angeles. "What makes you think we blacks will tell you the truth?"

Indeed, occasionally blacks did exaggerate, such as the young man in New Orleans inflating his tough-guy, gang-oriented image by saying his mother was a prostitute. Then we talked with her and discovered she was a university graduate, with a high-paying, responsible job. "The black man is essentially cunning," a black dentist told us in Omaha, warning that blacks often tell whites only what they think whites want to hear. Uncle Tom, said a Harlem minister, "has been the means of getting us where we are today, saying one thing, meaning another."

But we weren't out talking to men from Mars. Besides, we had time and a commitment to *listen*. We weren't out to be instant experts on race, fleeing from meeting to meeting, going through a set piece of five quick questions. We had the opportunity for perspective, because we were fortunate enough to be able to spend hours with people, seeing them two, three and more times in the span of our odyssey. When we came to putting their stories on paper, it wasn't our words, it was their words describing what it felt like to be black in America, what blacks hope for, what blacks *really* want.

Within this book, there has been space to include fewer than one of every six blacks we talked with, so that our hardest job was in making the selection. We tried to avoid duplication. We wanted to present the greatest possible range. We aimed especially for those vignettes that give memorable pictures of the black condition.

In our travels we were occasionally exposed to honkie-hating rhetoric. In no way do we discount it, nor fail to understand the justification some blacks have for it. We only excuse the absence of more than a sampling of it here by saying whites are often prone to overestimate its importance. Some, fearing the hatred they have heard about or actually seen firsthand, wanted to know if we ever felt in any danger. The answer is an unequivocal no, even though we were in the roughest of urban slums, including what Malcolm X called the worst street in Harlem. Expecting no harm, we found none.

Except for Ed Pratt and Chicago's Black Panther leader Fred Hampton, who was also killed, all the major protagonists have authenticated the material associated with their names.

Our odyssey begins in the South, because that is the birthplace of America's black revolution.

The Reaping: Politics

In the Country . . .

Fayette

History sometimes chooses strange sites on which to leave its mark. Such a place is Fayette, Mississippi.

In 1969 two-thirds of its 1,700 people were on welfare. The average yearly income was $490. There was only one industry, a furniture plant with 75 workers. U.S. Highway 61 hardly widens as it goes through Fayette. About 65 percent of its people are black. Most live in dilapidated two- and three-room shacks, parked away in the woods, out of sight from the main road. Few of these blacks made their way through high school.

And yet this old town, tucked into the state's southwest corner, is important in the black revolution because here blacks proved they could take over a town from whites, not with guns, but in peace and with the vote. For in 1969 Charles Evers was elected the first black mayor of a biracial Mississippi town since Reconstruction.

As recently as 1961 John Doar, a black lawyer and former U.S. Justice Department civil rights chief, described Fayette as a being in "mean country." Ferd Allen, sixty-six, butcher, grocer and produce peddler, the NAACP chairman in Fayette, and one of the newly elected black aldermen, remembers how it was.

Ferd Allen

It took place in the late afternoon, down near the City Hall where they sold beer in back of the drugstore. And you know how it is when people get to drinking. Some disturbance came up, and a policeman went to the scene. He saw this one particular young black was involved, and he wanted to put him under arrest. But the young man told him No, and when the policeman pulled out his gun, the young man caught his wrists and held him.

That drawed the people, black and white. The young man just kept holding on to stop the policeman from shooting him. His mother come up and saw what was happening. She begun to cry. "Don't shoot my child, don't shoot my child," she said.

I was standing there, just close up, when this white man next to me said to another, "I believe you're going to have to shoot him." Just like that. This guy then drew a little automatic revolver and shot him. That weakened him, made the young man turn the policeman loose. Then the policeman shot at him. When he died, in me there wasn't no feeling. It was just a colored man got killed. That was the way life was then.

Odyssey

We first came on May 13, election day. It was hot. Dust was on the magnolias. Not much wind in the pecan trees. The wisteria was still in bloom. And in the county park, where U.S. 61 passes on its run south to the Mississippi River at Natchez, stood the inevitable relic of yesterday: the stone soldier of the Confederacy.

Fayette had never known a day like it. There were blacks and whites newly arrived from New York, Chicago, Washington, Atlanta: the national press, television and driving young men who once had been in Robert Kennedy's corps. For the blacks, the visitors were the heralds of a celebration. All seemed to know that the blacks were going to win that election. To Fayette that day had also come John Lewis, the young warrior of SNCC, who had led its voter registration drive in Mississippi five years earlier. We saw him sitting behind a table in the Evers headquarters, and later we asked him what he had been thinking.

John Lewis

It was just being there, reminding me of what I like to call the good old days. All this was coming back. We'd lost so many. To win one would be great.

I know what some people say: "Look at Fayette, it is so small, so isolated—what can it mean to be mayor of Fayette?" But it is important because it is so removed. Just a few years ago you didn't have any black people registered there. And here was a black man running for office. I had to think of what people had gone through to get that far.

That day in Fayette I saw some of the things we had hoped for, worked for, fought for—the whole idea of one man, one vote. And there in Fayette, I was seeing these elderly people, going down voting, actually participating, some of them for the first time in their lives.

It was a great moment.

Fayette

On election day, the cars, one by one, pulled into the parking lot next to the squat little fire station where Fayette votes, across from its neat, red-brick City Hall. Out from them came black people, the young helping the old and the crippled, going in to vote. In front of the polling place, the whites clustered at one end, the blacks at the other. The whites were grim-faced. They knew, seeing that progression of black voters, that power was slipping away. Things would never be the same again.

Over at their end Allen and two other black men—James Pierce and Marlo Thompson, also in their sixties—put the moment into their perspective.

James Pierce

I am an old man now, lived around Fayette all my life, just seeing about getting our cotton hoed and our corn plowed. Seven years ago I said, "I'm getting old, don't seem to take to field work like I used to." Children were grown, and there wasn't nobody but me and my wife. So we moved to town, bought a home, and now I take whatever I can do to make a living to justify myself.

We never knowed much about elections. Don't know how they kept them a secret, but they did. First time I voted was two years ago. Mr. Evers woke us up. Told us we was entitled to vote. Come as a great surprise, not only for me, but for every colored man here. "You're supposed to vote," he said. "Go down and put your name in the book!"

Until then we was boys. Now we feel we is free. We can walk in there and vote because the law say we can. I just now got to be a man.

Marlo Thompson

This election day is altogether different. Everything is peace and harmony. Nobody seems to be shaking. Everybody can go forward with a good spirit and that means a lot. It is like everybody know it is time for a change. Seems to me like the whites seen the fact that we have to work together. And that is the onliest way we is going to survive.

Ferd Allen

Tell you what this election shows blacks can do—it reminds me of the day the rabbits come together and said: "The dogs, the hounds, everything is against us. So there is nothing for us to do but go drown ourselves." And they all started down to the river, all joined up, to drown themselves. Along the way they run across some horses, and when the horses saw the rabbits were organized, the horses took off and disappeared. Then the rabbits run across some cattle, and when the cattle saw what was going on, they took off, too. So the rabbits said: "Wait a minute! We don't need to drown ourselves. All we got to do is stay organized."

Fayette

For the blacks of Fayette the rallying point is the Medgar Evers Shopping Center, built out on the road toward Natchez by Evers in memory of his slain brother. There is a café, a grocery and a small office-apartment for Evers. Upstairs there is a hall used for Fayette's Head Start program. The night of the election, campaign workers and supporters gathered there as the vote count came in. John Lewis was among them.

John Lewis

So much has happened in such a short time. All the sweat, the tears, violence and deaths that have gone into getting ready for this. You can see the progress, and you can say, "It can happen, even in Mississippi, in my lifetime. All is not in vain." I think that what we've had in Fayette is a great victory, not just for Fayette, but for the whole nation.

If Martin Luther King were with us, what would he be doing? He would have been down here. I had the feeling when we were singing "We Shall Overcome" that he would be walking in.

Odyssey

May 13: Charles Evers, six feet, bearlike, was tense, almost brooding. At age forty-six, Evers, Democratic national committeeman for Mississippi and NAACP state adviser, had fought segregationists in the South, tangled with the syndicate in the North. The three men closest to him, his brother, Medgar, Dr. King, and Robert Kennedy, all were assassinated. His life, he says, "hasn't been all rosy and great and humanitarian. I'm not bitter, though I have a right to be. But that won't solve the problem. Medgar and I vowed a long time ago to do all we could to try to make people, white and black, understand one another."

We talked to him that day and again in the summer and fall. We saw him in Fayette, his legal address, as well as in Jackson, where he lives. One time when he had to testify at a trial in Greenville, we flew him there in a small plane. The morning of the flight was dark, rainy, and both going and coming, the storm bounced the plane around. Throughout, no matter how much the turbulence, he sat stolidly in the back seat, showing neither fear nor concern. When we finally got back, he climbed out, touched one foot down, testing, then put both feet to guarantee he was really on the ground. "Goddamn!" he said. "I hate to fly."

That was typical Evers, gregarious, direct, seemingly unflappable in public. But privately very human. At the airport he called his wife, telling her he'd be home for lunch and to set more places at the table in their modern eight-room house. He is very proud and protective of his wife, Nan, a pretty, ebullient woman whom he met in college, and his four lively daughters. And he is absolutely the boss of the household. When the meal was ready, Mrs. Evers prepared his plate, placing steak, rice and okra on one platter, salad on another. Smilingly she told us, "Charles doesn't think it is dinner unless I serve him." Sheila, one of his teen-age daughters, added, "When Daddy calls and says he's coming home, there isn't anyone can cook for him but her."

Later as we talked in his comfortable den, Evers spoke of the morning's bumpy ride.

Charles Evers

You know, four years ago I never would have flown with you. Some nut might have been up there trying to force us down. And if you had come and sat in this room, every white racist in this town would have been here. Every cop would have been circling around like you were some kind of outlaw. When you come out, you would have gotten a ticket and been in jail before you could have gotten away from here to save your soul. That's how bad they were four years ago.

White people of this country have tolerated so much hate. But I don't look at these hatemongers as whites. I see them as poor, sick individuals who need to be cured. And you don't cure one pain by creating another. I couldn't tell my people, "Let's go out and arm ourselves and shoot honkies." Whites can have hatred, destruction, bigotry, distrust. I got to be strong enough to have love, devotion, respect. I got to live up to that because if I don't, the price paid by those I loved most of all will have been in vain. You got to be big enough to understand the worst hatemonger. I even understand the man who was charged with killing Medgar. I understand Ray, who killed Dr. King, Sirhan, who killed Bobby. These men, and the other murderers, like Oswald, felt free to kill because they knew that the silent whites of this country were going to remain silent, letting the bigots control the juries and the judges as the mayors and sheriffs backed them to the hilt. You don't know what it is like to see, as I get in my car each morning, my wife and children standing at the window, peeping out and wondering if, when I turn the ignition on, the car is going to blow up in a roar. It is a terrible thing. It tears you up, and unless you are strong, it eats away at you like cancer. This is the kind of thing that my people have suffered, and that's why White America must understand why Black America is beginning to hate.

Yet today, if we blacks can just hold our heads, we are closer to home than we have ever been. Whites are starting to rebel against each other. Right now if you look around, you'll see that it is not blacks who are really destroying this country; it is the young whites who are rebelling against their parents and their grandparents and their grandparents' grandparents, who made America what it is. So, if we blacks just keep moving in, be firm but fair, don't back up, don't become afraid—and don't be grinning and scratching—we are going to win.

Do you realize we took a town from a bunch of people who was known for beating and killing Negroes just for looking at them? And we did it without violence, without one black man being shot, without one hate campaign. But I don't want nobody to think that this is my thing. What you got to understand is that Martin and Medgar were the guys, along with us, all together, who really started to realize how wrong this country is. Martin said, "Let my people go." Medgar and others said, "Let my people become a part of it." They were the kind of guys who gave all of us courage. They never would send anybody else. They would always go themselves. We are only doing what they would have if they had been here, carrying out in a different way what they began—to try to make it a better place for all of us.

Odyssey

July 7: Under a sweltering sun, Charles Evers was sworn in as mayor of Fayette. Opera star Leontyne Price, who was born in Laurel, Mississippi, sang the national anthem. More than 500 local blacks were joined by such national figures as former U.S. Attorney General Ramsey Clark and Civil Rights Division chiefs Burke Marshall and John Doar. At the close of the ceremony a four-foot-tall marble monument dedicated to a civil rights martyr, Evers' brother, Medgar, was unveiled on the City Hall lawn, across from the county's Confederate memorial: "Born July 2, 1925, Decatur, Mississippi, assassinated July 12, 1963, Jackson, Mississippi." Engraved on it also is a quotation from Kenya's President Jomo Kenyatta: "One of the great affronts to human dignity which I have always opposed is that of racialism."

Charles Evers

Medgar and I were always very close. He was three years younger than I. When we were boys in Decatur, we used to go to the store on Sunday morning. Most Negroes in those days didn't have much money, so you'd buy from day to day. Whenever you

made fifty cents or a dollar, you'd go down and get food for breakfast, some sausage, some cheese, some grits. In these country stores,
there usually would be a bunch of red-necks, tobacco-chewing and
sitting around the little store. Whenever a Negro boy would go in
there, they'd make him dance, make him do something silly. I never
would dance. I remember one of them shoved me and said: "You
better dance!" I run all the way home—I knew my daddy would protect me, as he never was afraid of them. I was just a kid, but I told
Medgar: "Someday I'm going to have me a store and I'm going to
make the white folks dance."

There were four of us in the family, two boys and two girls. Our
parents had to get work from whites to make a living. Mother would
leave home early, five thirty or six o'clock, to be at the white folks'
home. She had to be there to get the children ready for school, washing them in the bathrooms that had hot and cold water, combing
their hair, dressing them, and fixing them a hot breakfast. But most
black kids had no bathroom. We'd draw water out of the well and
wash ourselves off on the back porch. We'd get on our overalls,
clean, but ragged; then we ate the cold food Mother left.

We'd start walking to school, about two miles on dusty roads.
Sometimes we had shoes, sometimes no shoes. But the white kids,
they had big shiny buses to go half a mile. The bus driver used to
come along and cut in at us black kids, make us jump into the ditch.
We'd come out wet and dirty. Other times the driver would slow
down, so the kids, some of them the very ones Mama had left us to
take care of, could spit on us and throw rocks.

These were things we went through as blacks. But my mother and
father always taught us not to hate. We were brought up in the Baptist Church, and we had the kind of religious background that made
us understand we was meant to care. Mama always liked to tell the
story of Christ who once came as a poor person and they turned
Him away. She'd say, "You never turn away anyone." Most tramps
in my day were white. We lived near the railroad, and they would
always come by begging for food. Mama would bring them in, sit
them down at the table, and feed them with what food we had. I
would say, "Mama, why you bring them in? We can't even go in the
white part of town." She would tell us, "Son, don't be mean to people. White people mean to us, but we got to be good."

Later on, when we wanted to go to high school, there was a white
lady, Mrs. Payne, who said, "I'll help you. You stay with me." She

was the kind of white person who kept us from really hating whites because she did things, not only for Medgar and me, but for other blacks. She lived in Newton, Mississippi, 10 miles away, and from the time I was twelve to about seventeen, I stayed with her during the week. She used to let us work in a little restaurant she had in the bus station to get spending money. When we'd come out front to pick up the dirty dishes, some of the whites, half drunk, would start calling us nigger. She'd get on them, saying, "Don't you call them that. Leave them alone, they're mine." If a white woman was for you, you didn't have to worry much, and so they shut up.

Mrs. Payne never looked down on us, never acted like she was afraid of us. She was always kind and nice. She used to tell us, "Look, you good as anybody. Just make sure you act like it." I would talk to her about wanting to have my own grocery. She'd say, "Son, just keep working and save your money, and someday you'll get one."

When we were young, my daddy did a variety of things. He was a lumber contractor. He worked on the railroad and for a time was in the funeral business with my uncle. But the two of them didn't get along so well, and Daddy got out. My uncle kept the business—and the money. Like most blacks, my daddy was a good moneymaker, but he didn't know how to handle it. I was about sixteen or seventeen years old when we lost most of the 20 acres we owned in Decatur on a deed of trust. I wanted to help my mama and daddy save our place—it was only $300 they owed—so I tried to go in the Army. I slipped off, changed my age, but somehow the Army found out and made me come home. In 1941 I was old enough, and they took me. At first I was getting $21 a month and I'd send $10 of each paycheck to my parents. Eventually we saved the land.

In the Army I did a lot of right things, a lot of wrong. I am not an all-good man. I was in the Pacific and always lucky enough. I never actually shot nobody, and nobody ever shot at me. I was in battalion headquarters, a couple of miles from the fighting, doing mostly administrative work. I became a sergeant major because I had the equivalent of a high school education at a time when most blacks had gone no further than about the fifth or sixth grade. While I was in the Philippines, I had prostitute houses, and I did a lot of black market. I would sell a truckload of tin, and then I would tell the policeman to go down and take the truck back again, and I'd resell the tin.

When I was stationed in Manila, I fell in love with a Filipino girl,

Felicia, whose daddy happened to be the mayor. I really loved her and wanted to marry her. I didn't because she was white. I couldn't come back to Mississippi and bring her, no way, not at any time. But while I was there, she was going to school at the University of Manila. And in order to be with her, I enrolled, studying government and business law. I began to learn something about elected officials and negotiable instruments and contracts. My eyes opened a little bit more and more about who was really responsible for mistreatment and hatred. And of course, it was the people at the top. I got interested in politics, and I wanted to vote.

I got out of the Army in 1946—though I was in the active reserve during Korea—as did Medgar, who had been in France. All the white soldiers was registering and voting without having to pay poll tax, and I thought we should be able to, too. But we had all kinds of problems in Decatur. They tried to prevent us from registering, denying us the right to vote. They stood in the door, blocked us with shotguns. We went in anyway and finally voted in Decatur itself. Very few of us did then. Yet Medgar and I kept on attempting to get our people registered. And we also started organizing NAACP branches all over Mississippi.

I had saved some money in the Army, and when I came home, I opened a little bit of a grocery store for my mama and daddy, a place where my folk could come in and ain't nobody calling them nigger or making them dance. The store kept growing, and now we have six. I also went to Alcorn College. It was the one school where they were giving the GI Bill of Rights. I'm supposed to have a degree, but it's just a degree on paper. It did not equip me. It's like I had no chemistry, no science, no physics and very little English. While I was in school, I helped my uncle manage his three Mississippi funeral parlors, in Mount Olive, Forrest and Philadelphia. We didn't always agree, so when I finished Alcorn, I bought out his Philadelphia operation. I began to spread out. I had a motel, restaurants, taxicabs, and was in the insurance business.

I also got into radio in Philadelphia. We had a program for the funeral parlor, and I wasn't pleased by the white fellow who was doing the announcing. I went out to the station raising hell and said, "I'm paying you so much a week for advertising, and the guy puts no emphasis on it. I could beat that." And so the owner says, "If you can beat that, then you do it." I agreed to. And just like that I started with my own program. He ended up giving me an hour. I started doing spirituals for my mortuary, then rock and roll, finally rhythm and blues. I did the news and special programs—we had a thing going. But always I would talk about how Negroes should get registered and about equality. And in 1954, with the Supreme Court decision on schools, I really pushed hard. The white people did not like it, and that's when the trouble began.

At the same time, Medgar was the first black to make application to the University of Mississippi law school. I was backing him financially, and the White Citizens Council, whose objective was to kill off Negroes economically and politically, knew this. I was making money, and I was vulnerable. They threatened the station with boycotts, demanding that it let me go. I didn't want to hurt the owner, so eventually I did leave. But meanwhile, they also went after me making all kinds of accusations. They set traps for me, and during 1956 and 1957 they broke me flat with lawsuits over automobile accidents that wasn't my fault.

But that day in court when they really got me—took $25,000 from me in one whop—I told that little old judge in that little old kangaroo court, "You broke me, but you can't beat me." And I said to Medgar, "You stay, I'm going to Chicago to make some money, so when I come back, we can finish the job we started in 1946." I was determined to be financially able to take all the abuse, the potshots, that I knew they was going to throw at me.

I left my family behind and went to Chicago. I got me three jobs, one at the Swift Packing Company, unloading trains and working in the hothouse where they cure all the hams and sausage, one at the Conrad Hilton Hotel as a washroom attendant. I put in fifteen hours a day. On weekends I worked as a bartender at a couple of taverns on the West Side. I was pretty bitter, no question about it.

A washroom attendant ain't nothing but a flunky, brush the whites down when they come in. So what I would do is take advantage of them, especially those Southerners. I'd be dusting a guy off, and if I had half a chance, I'd take everything he had. Sometimes they'd drop their wallet and I'd pocket the money before returning it. But this used to bother me, and I'd go home at night and say, "You shouldn't have done that." And after a while I just quit. I got a job in construction and as a physical education instructor in one of the schools in Robbins, Illinois. I didn't do anything but go to work, to church on Sunday, and to work.

But then I just wasn't making money fast enough. I had a friend who was in the policy business, and one day I went over and asked him for a job. He sat me down for about an hour and taught me all about policy, how to make out a book, drop books, write out numbers, and how to pick up. For two days he put me on a route with someone else. I went around with this guy, picking up policy, putting out policy, dodging the police, cutting corners. Then I got the route. I was out there for six months, and I decided, Why the hell should I pick up policy? I'll write my own. So I double-crossed my buddy, wrote my own book, kept on until I had my own wheel. This caused a little problem, but we worked it out by my taking one section of Chicago, his taking another. Naturally, one vice brings another, and I went into the jukebox business. I opened a tavern on the South Side, then a second on the West Side, and a third in Argo, Illinois. I got my own jukeboxes, was still in the policy business, and that's the way I was going. I've done all these things. No point in lying.

I brought my family up, and we moved into the basement of an old shack. It had four rooms, rats, roaches, filthy dirty. We stayed there for a couple of years. I wouldn't hardly spend nothing. I'd buy day-old bread, ten cents a loaf. We didn't have no pork chops, no steaks. We'd have neckbones. I'd send money down to Medgar and save the rest.

Medgar and I always would call each other. And I told him this one time that I was going to buy us a couple of buildings so that when I came back to Mississippi, we wouldn't have to worry about income. By this time I was in pretty good shape, and I went and bought one, an old converted building, about twenty-four units in it, and moved my family in on the first floor. I was ready to buy the second one when they shot Medgar.

Odyssey

Charles Evers talked about his late brother as if he were still alive. It was Medgar this, Medgar that, always the feeling that what they began, Charles must finish for them.

Charles Evers

It was on a Sunday, a week before he was killed, that I was telling him on the telephone about the trouble I was having with the syndicate. They wanted a cut on my jukeboxes and policy, and I wasn't going to give them any. They had threatened me, and I was carrying a gun. Well, Medgar and I got to talking about this, and he warned me: "You watch that damn syndicate. You know how dirty they are. They're whomping up trouble constantly."

I said, "No white man can take me—they won't get that close." For a moment we were just struck silent. I asked, "Are you there?" And he says, "Yes, I'm here. I'm just thinking. Suppose something did happen to you? What would I do?" I told him not to bother, to take no chances himself, and that I'd take care of them damn hoodlums up here.

The next week I was coming home from my Argo club, and it was about two o'clock in the morning. All the lights in my apartment building were on. I went in, and my neighbors were so solemn. My oldest daughter, Pat, had had some kind of sick spell, and I thought something had happened to her. I rushed to her room, and she wasn't there. She was in my room lying across the bed. I said to my wife, "What's the matter?" And Nan just turned. I knew right there what it was.

"What happened to Medgar?" I asked.

She said, "Sit down. They shot him. It's all over."

I said, "Aw, they can't kill us. We've been shot at before. They ain't but winged us. He'll make it. Don't worry."

"No, Charles, he's killed."

I just had a blackout. Nan tells me I said something about making me a reservation and started packing my clothes. I don't hardly remember getting on the plane and coming down here that morning. I left everything, my business, my building, my car. But I do remember when I got to the airport in Jackson, someone saying: "There's his *damn* brother."

I didn't really come to for a month. But I did tell the national office of the NAACP: "Don't look no further for somebody to take Medgar's job, because I am." The NAACP had used the hell out of him, and I would always be after him about it. They run him all over the country making these speeches, and he didn't hardly have enough money to get back home on. I'd say, "You're field secretary for the state of Mississippi, not for the whole damn country." Also, the NAACP had these big fine offices around, big desks and wall-to-wall carpeting. But Medgar, with what he was going through, didn't even have a file cabinet. Just old pasteboard boxes. He had an old raggedy chair that was wired together. No adding machines, just an old piece of a typewriter.

So after he was killed, I went into his office and threw everything out in the hall, that old chair, the boxes. And I ordered a complete new office: wall-to-wall carpeting, air conditioning, the whole thing. The bill came to something like $2,500, and I sent it to the NAACP in New York. I said, "You just go to hell." Medgar never would have done a thing like that.

He didn't want to hurt nobody's feelings. He was pleasant but firm. He was a diplomat, a humanitarian. He never gave up. He kept pushing, coming on. When he was alive, what was needed was an awakening of my people. He did that. During those times he made much more progress that I would have. After he was gone, it was my role to follow up, to put it through. It wasn't Medgar no more. It was Charles, somebody who was blunt, not too passionate, who really didn't give a damn except about getting the job done.

I knew Medgar's assassination wasn't going to change the minds of white people or to shame them. In fact, when I came back, I was determined to prove to them, more than ever, that killing one didn't stop nothing. That they only throwed a bucket of gasoline on the fire. It was going to be much closer now because I wasn't going to take the crap that Medgar took. I wasn't going to be as nice to them as he was. I was going after them for everything they had: to end discrimination and hatred and to stop reprisals, police brutality, hate groups—racists, bigots and businessmen—at all costs from taking advantage of my people. The way to do it was through boycotting and voter registration, shutting down businesses that discriminate against my folk, and ousting the racists from office. That means uniting communities and then using the economic and political power in a bloc to bring about change.

But to organize a community takes hard work, day in, day out. You've got to show leadership, that you are determined to do what's right and that you aren't afraid. You challenge the power structure, lead the marches, be willing to be gassed, beaten and go to jail. You go to the hospital with your people, to church with them, to funerals and be pallbearers. You're at the fish fries, be in their homes. Your actions got to speak your concern.

Three years ago we started what we call the NAACP Common

Sense meetings. In Fayette we have them every week. There's one thing about getting with somebody else. Until then you think, "Oh, God! I got the whole world sitting on me. I am in such bad shape." But when two of you get together, you see the other guy's troubles are like your own. We asked: "Why don't we have streets, fire protection, when all the whites have this? Why can't we patronize a store and the whites can?" And you tell your people: "That's wrong. You got a right to go down there. Just get in the habit of thinking you can." In our meetings we also talk about personal hygiene, how to wash your teeth, comb your hair, how to say just plain Yes and No. You got to keep driving, driving the idea that you are as good as you want to be.

We kept on working, telling people the importance of sticking together. If I've accomplished anything, it's because the community comes first. I organize for it, not for Charles Evers. And we've had three successful boycotts, in Natchez, Fayette and Port Gibson. In Natchez we really knocked it to them. We went in there four years ago and put on a crippling eight-month boycott until they hired Negroes in many of the stores, in the beer and bread companies; hired Negro salesmen and Negro policemen. We desegregated the hospital and the schools. And when we were through, we had the mayor singing "We Shall Overcome."

And we fought for the Voting Rights Act. In 1965, because of the rigid laws they had and the fact that the sheriffs and registrars was so violent against us, we had only 28,000 Negroes registered and no black elected officials in Mississippi. We got the law, and we proved that people who is together can't be beaten. Today we have 250,000 Negroes registered and 81 elected. We may not be able to select the governor, but we can sure defeat one. In twenty-nine counties we can beat almost anybody and lots of places where we can elect whom we want. Over in Port Gibson we have nine black officials. And in Jefferson County—Fayette is the seat—we've got twenty-one.

Odyssey

Evers had been mayor of Fayette four months when next we saw him. The memorial to his brother was still in place on the City

Hall lawn but had recently been assaulted by nightly egg-throwing parties. He was plainly annoyed.

Charles Evers

The white Mississippians can't stomach the fact that we got our own monument up there along with theirs. But we have been looking at their damn statue all our lives, a monument to the Old Confederacy, to slave drivers and slaveowners, which they take for granted but won't that slab of Medgar's. Medgar's represents freedom, and it drives them out of their minds. But wait until we take over the county. In that square we are going to put John Kennedy in one corner, Martin Luther King in another, Medgar Evers in one and Bobby in the other.

With it all, I think the white man in Mississippi is getting the message. The mere fact that I am mayor and haven't had my brains shot out is one example. For another, I have talked issues rather than race; this probably has done more to change some of the attitudes of whites than anything else. The reaction is one of wait and see. Nobody in Fayette has anything. This town is dead, and all the people are buried. So the whites say, "Hell, if he can do it, let's hope he does."

As the mayor I have reached one of those milestones Medgar and I always hoped to accomplish, a position of authority. If you use that power right, are really concerned about your fellowman, it can be so constructive. I tell my young black friends that in Fayette we are going to make a town into what every black has ever dreamed of: a place that is fair and just. At the same time, my folk, too, has to be educated to the point of taking on the responsibility of being free. Many of my people think that because I'm black, I will give them special privileges. But this is the kind of thing the white man has done, allowed people because they are white to do whatever they damn please to blacks. If I act like that, I am just as guilty. Blacks don't understand why as the judge I am so strict on speeders, why I don't allow them to get out on the streets and call people MF'ers and SOB's, why I won't let a young kid between the ages of six and eighteen walk the streets during school hours without picking him up. I got to do it, prove that as you become responsible, you have to have that kind of a community.

I'm tough on the one hand, but not so on the other. I'm not too hard on bootleggers. The average bootlegger is a poor white, poor black. I'm leaning a little, but the poor in the South just don't have a chance because of lack of education, lack of jobs. I try to understand the conditions. I know all those things I did in Chicago were wrong, but they forced me to do it. It was the only way I could make it. Had they not done to me what they did in Philadelphia, I'd still be making a living as an undertaker, running my funeral parlor and my hotel, going about my business. If there were plenty of jobs in Fayette, I'd be damn sure nobody did any wrong. But you just can't do that now. That's why I'm trying to get industry in here.

I could get a grant out of the government if I went hat in hand, scratching. Lay off Nixon, the administration when it does something wrong like trying to give the racists another twenty years to desegregate the schools. But I'm not going to be bought off. What I'm doing is going all over the country begging dollars, fifty-cent pieces and quarters, to get enough money for streets, sidewalks, an old folks' home in Fayette. We've got to rebuild this place, and you whites ain't going to respect us until we show you we can, right here in Mississippi.

I want to prove—even though it is said that this is the one state where it won't be done—that there can be justice, respect, freedom, and that, race relations wise, it can be one of the leading states in this country.

Mississippi is important to me. It's home.

Maynard Jackson

Ten years ago a black man would never have been allowed to run for the United States Senate from Georgia. He wouldn't have lived. But when I, a black man, went against Herman Talmadge, the most powerful political figure in this state, bar none, I shook hands with the Southern white man and asked for his vote. Many times I got a commitment for it. One Sunday morning a man describing himself as a "cracker from below Macon" called me to say: "When Herman Talmadge talks about the farmer, he doesn't mean the small farmer, he means the big one. Guy down here gets about $85,000 in subsidies, but we small farmers have to beg for one or two thousand. I ain't never lost no love for colored, but I have to admire somebody who can rise above that background. And we small farmers ain't got much money, but we are going to vote for you and send you what we can." Three days later, from a town in southwest Georgia, I got a check for around $39.

That campaign was an eye opener. You know the image of the so-called red-neck—the guy you see just standing around, a straw sticking from his mouth, and he is supposed to be the most rabid racist, the one who burns crosses on the lawn. But 13 to 14 percent of that image group voted for me. More than 30 percent of my total vote came from whites. I even carried the city of Atlanta by more than 6,000 votes. What all that said to me was that the mood has to be to get black men who will venture, who will take that step, who will try.

Odyssey

We went from the simple country crossroads of Fayette to the stone-steel-glass skyscrapers and the big jets and sophistication of Atlanta. This is a city that *aspires*. It calls itself the capital of the "new South," a city "too busy to hate." And even though that cliché is heard less and less, the fact is that Atlanta blacks have created a solid, enduring culture side by side with the white world. The Atlanta University complex has the world's greatest cluster of black colleges. Atlanta has been home for the emerging middle-class blacks, and they live in suburban-style settings, complete with barbecue rotisseries, swimming pools and the basement den with the built-in bar. There is a black Establishment, with traditions of leadership and accomplishment.

Maynard Jackson knows something about that. His father came from Dallas, Texas, to take over as pastor in the oldest black Baptist congregation in Atlanta. His mother earned her PhD from the University of Toulouse in France. His aunt was a star at the Metropolitan Opera. His grandfather, John Wesley Dobbs, was an Atlantan of distinction, who in the late 1940's founded the Georgia Voters League at a time when there were only 500 registered black voters in the entire state and who for years led the biggest black Masonic order in Georgia. Jackson himself was graduated—at eighteen—from Morehouse College in the Atlanta complex, and when he came out of North Carolina College's law school it was as a *cum laude* scholar and prizewinning debater.

By challenging Senator Talmadge in Georgia's 1968 Democratic primary, Jackson was daring to think about a day when whites could actually vote a black man into office. When he told us that, sitting in a little law office set up on a poverty grant to provide free legal help to Atlanta's poor, he was still only thirty-one, and there was no disappointment over having been beaten three to one. There was still time to look ahead, and as it turned out, he didn't have long to wait. In the fall of 1969 blacks and whites in Atlanta elected him the first black vice-mayor, giving him 58 percent of the vote in turning down a white businessman who was well regarded by blacks and who had seventeen years of service as a city alderman.

It was different from what it had been, twenty-four years earlier, when his father had run for the school board in Dallas, Texas.

Maynard Jackson

My father was a very passionate man, and he fought vigorously and openly for civil rights long before it was safe to do so. In

Dallas he was the first black man to offer himself for public office, by running for the board. And I remember, so clearly and distinctly, the night he was to go on the radio for the first time. He was in the bathtub when the telephone rang, and the caller said, "Is this where that nigger preacher lives?" And my mother said, "No. This is Reverend Jackson's home." The caller said, "Tell that nigger that if he even tries to go on to the radio station, we are going to kill him." My mother was shaken, but she didn't tell my father until she had called the chairman of the church board of deacons. And then the deacons and the trustees came to the house to give protection. My mother also called other friends, including some white people who stood to be ostracized if they chose the side of the Negro. But they didn't hesitate; they came, and one of them arranged for a police escort and even had a picture taken with my father.

Today, with all the problems we have, that may seem relatively unimportant, but in the context of that situation it was a hell of a big step. We children were spirited away that night to the home of a lady who sometimes kept us, and I can remember lying halfway under the covers in bed, listening to my father's voice on the radio. He made that speech, he completed his campaign, and even though he was not elected, many people say that what he dared to do made it possible later for blacks to be elected in Dallas.

Odyssey

Maynard Jackson, standing more than six three, weighing more than 200 pounds, had straight black hair, regular features. He was very light in color.

Maynard Jackson

We are black. We are very proud of being black. I am, however, the great-grandson of an Irish woman. Years ago my maternal great-grandfather was a porter in what used to be *the* downtown office building in Atlanta. The elevator operator there was an Irish immigrant, and this black porter and this young Irish woman fell in love and wanted to be married. But they knew that they could never live in safety in Georgia, so they ran away to be married—to Mississippi. Today that sounds strange. In those days it was possible. My grandmother, Thompson by birth, was born there in Columbus. She married John Wesley Dobbs, an unusual man who from the age of twelve had supported his mother. He was a master organizer and the orator supreme, and my father used to kid him by saying the only trouble with a self-made man is that he is always talking about the man who made him.

My father, who had some French and Spanish in his heritage, was himself sensitive about his color, because he continually found himself in situations where people never guessed he was black. He was an interesting-looking man, very admirable bearing, and he had a deep, mellifluous voice, no Southern accent at all. He had blue eyes, aquiline features. Italians took him to be Italian, Frenchmen for French, and Jews for Jewish. He was a proud man, and he never let any insults slide by. He always taught us—there were six children—never to be ashamed of being black. Both he and my grandfather Dobbs had studied black history, and we took pride in it. So all my life I have known that blackness doesn't relate just to skin color. It is an attitude, a way of life, and I am as black as if I were the color of my dark coat in the way I have been raised, in the effects of society upon me, and in the way that I think.

Odyssey

After Morehouse Jackson went to law school at Boston University but quit; still only eighteen, he didn't know what he really wanted to do. So he stayed in New England, selling encyclopedias for P. F. Collier. A top-ten salesman, he was directing a sixty-man field crew, even before he was twenty-two.

Maynard Jackson

I made a lot of money, but that's all. I cannot find satisfaction just from making money. I wanted something else. One hundred and four years ago my ancestor was selling for $2,000 and was not even regarded as human. I think that in the whole history of mankind America had the only slavery that sought to deny the slave's humanity. In wanting to help black people, I began to believe that through the courts meaningful changes could be made. So I went back to law school, this time in North Carolina, passed the bar in

Georgia, and was the first black lawyer assigned to the National Labor Relations Board in the South. I got married, left the NLRB to work with a neighborhood law office helping the poor. And then there was Martin Luther King.

Many people recognized Dr. King's tremendous leadership and motivational ability. But I don't think we fully appreciated—and I am not sure I can except myself from this—his real prophetic quality. It is only now that he is lionized among black people. He is as close to Jesus Christ as any human being of recent years can get. His effect on me was quite profound.

Our first child was to be born, almost any minute, when Dr. King was killed. I became very caught up in consideration of the life-death cycle. Our baby was born the day Dr. King was buried. I wanted to be at the funeral, so after the birth I marched part of the way on Auburn Avenue with the cortege, went back to check on my wife, then went to Morehouse to watch the service there from the third floor of the biology building. The assassination changed my life, because it gave me greater strength—not hopelessness. It made me think about the ways in which I could have a more immediate impact on the lives of black people.

A very interesting thing happened after that. A group of people asked me to stand for the Georgia House of Representatives, and while I didn't think I wanted to do it, I met with them. At the meeting one of the men said, "What you ought to do is run against Herman Talmadge—he's going up again without any opposition." We all kind of laughed, a half laugh, not because it was funny but because it was so almost ludicrous that I should run against Talmadge. So the meeting ended, and that night, June 4, 1968, I was watching television and I saw Bobby Kennedy killed. With King's assassination I had cried unashamedly, and I had wondered how in God's name could it happen in this country. That people are shot down because of what they believe? And then, that night, with Bobby murdered, I saw that these assassinations were not all accidental, that they were all related to racism. It came to me that they happen because there are people like Herman Talmadge committed to maintaining racism and who do things, or don't do things, the effect of which is to solidify racism in this country. That next day I got $3,000 from friends; with that, I qualified to run against Talmadge. I quit my position and went out to campaign.

That campaign showed me there is a very strong potential, even in Georgia, maybe across the whole South, for the weirdest coalition you ever saw—black voters and poor whites. The exploitation of poor whites is a story that needs to be told more and more. The poor white is just as raggedy, just as poorly educated, just as hungry. But he has been told, "That's okay, because you are white!" What does that do for a man when he looks across the table at his wife and even though she is only thirty she already looks sixty? Well, I think that now the answer is becoming more and more known. I remember those people telling me, "I never thought I'd vote for a nigra, but I am going to vote for you."

Ten years earlier I couldn't have gotten the kind of black support I did. Blacks were not registered in as big numbers as now. They were much more intimidated—turned away in elections by guns or threats of economic reprisal. But when I ran, people came out in communities where black people had never voted before. Poll watchers who had never ventured to stand openly in favor of a black candidate—or even a civil rights issue—stood in the little towns, openly handing out leaflets. It was precedent-shattering. In one place, when two black ministers went around telling black voters no one was running against Herman Talmadge, some of their own church members defied the ministers and walked in their tracks to tell about me, almost like a truth squad.

You know, there is a song, "Games People Play," and it goes:

> Peo-ple walk-in up to you,
> Sing-in' Glo-ry Hal-le-lu-jah!
> and they're try'n' to sock it to you
> In the name of the Lord.*

So that those ministers had sold out. Some well-known black people had gone to Lovejoy, Georgia, the site of the baronial estate of Senator Talmadge, to have breakfast with him. And the commitment was made there that they would do all they could to dissipate my vote, not opposing me openly, but working quietly to make sure there was not too much of a bandwagon on my behalf. I don't know who put out the money, but I have done some research and I happen to know that one man, a nationally known civil rights figure, was paid $30,000 to work in the rural areas, either to get the vote for Talmadge or to confuse the election. It is a fact that only about one-third

---

* Written by Joe South. Copyright © 1968 by Lowery Music Co. Inc., Atlanta. Used with permission.

of the registered black voters turned out. If all of them had voted, and if I had gotten all their vote, I would still have had only 440,000 against Talmadge's 697,000. But it would have been a different ball game. And even just the fact that I ran has made some changes. People can see that they don't have to expect a whipping or a lynching. Blacks can do something.

Odyssey

The job of vice-mayor in Atlanta has sometimes been defined as the mayor's stand-in at ribbon cuttings. But it does thrust the holder of it into political exposure because he serves as president of the Board of Aldermen and casts tie-breaking votes. He is also an ex officio member of the aldermanic committees and can vote on all issues when the mayor is not present . . .

Maynard Jackson

Clearly the emergence of the black elected official is one of the most significant developments of the last fifty years. I am aware that there is no single panacea that will bring black people our freedom—but the point is that *political power is attainable now!* As long as we have the American system, as long as one person's vote counts, where blacks have a numerical force, we can do something, not just talk about the lives we are leading.

For some unexplainable fact, black people have been more democratic than whites have ever been, and we have reacted on a higher moral plane in almost every given situation, compared with the reaction of the white power structure. We gave, for example, a greater emotional commitment to the campaign of Bobby Kennedy than whites gave to the election of Carl Stokes in Cleveland. What we have done is to look to the merits of the candidate.

I am not saying that black men are supermen. In the South you still have an awful lot of black people who believe that the only way is through accommodation with the whites or who don't have any conviction one way or the other, except insofar as money will help them into a belief. In politics I found this true to a frighteningly larger degree than I would have cared to think. During slavery there was the house slave and the field slave. The field slave prayed for fire to burn down the crops and for a strong wind to blow the fire toward the big house. The house slave, whose loyalty had been bought with little concessions, would pray for rain in case of fire. We have people today who are and have been house slaves, and that means they want to keep down anyone who would threaten their position, no matter what the cost. They are protecting their own things.

It is not going to do us any good to elect somebody just because he is black, if in fact he is going to sell out. Real freedom for blacks will come when we have a say-so, with tangible, visible power, in all things that affect us.

Thrust to Identity

A Bus Ride into History

Montgomery

To black Americans old enough to remember, the name Montgomery means bus boycott and Martin Luther King and a mass challenge to segregation. More than the 1954 Supreme Court school decision, Montgomery was the beginning of the black revolution because it was not whites creating change, it was blacks uniting in their own cause.

But by 1970 the terror and drama and triumph of Montgomery were already misted by fifteen years, and not everyone knew how tough had been the challenge. Especially was this true of one young black who came home to Montgomery from college in North Carolina. Attuned to revolution 1970 style. Proud to be black, contemptuous of whites, condescending to older blacks.

One day he met one of those older blacks, Edgar Daniel Nixon, whom he'd known all his life. "How you doing in school?" Nixon asked. "Fair," said the young man, "but not as good as I would if I had all black teachers." Nixon reminded him that "the law done away with having all black teachers, just like with having only white teachers."

"I don't pay no attention to the law," said the young man. "I set my own." Nixon said, "Sure you do—and the jails is filled with people like you. You driving your mama's car right now, and I bet you don't have a driver's license." True, said the young man. "That's wrong," said Nixon. There was no surprise in the young man. "I expected that from you," he said. "Because, generally, you is the biggest Uncle Tom in town."

"Listen," said Nixon. "I'm going to tell you something. If I hadn't been fighting for forty years, right up to now, and paved the way for you to walk on—you'd be in mud up to your neck!"

"Yesterdays," said the young man. "That don't mean anything to me. Only thing that matter is today."

Nixon shrugged.

Odyssey

When we came to E. D. Nixon he was in his seventieth year and six years retired as a Pullman porter. In our travels we had been hearing about "that porter in Montgomery without whom there might never have been a bus boycott," but few seemed to know if he were dead or alive.

E. D. Nixon is *alive,* all right. Six feet three, 208 pounds, he had no more than a stubble of gray hair. His hands were huge. He wore pearl-rim glasses, their size accentuated by the contrast with his black skin.

We met him first in the office he maintained to carry on the affairs of the twelve civil rights, political or community organizations he was working with. One block up the street from his office was the Dexter Avenue Baptist Church, where Dr. King was pastor when the boycott began. Across the square from the church is a symbol of White America, the Alabama State Capitol, where a hundred years ago Jefferson Davis took his oath as the first president of the Confederacy.

Five blocks away is the site of the house where E. D. Nixon was born. It has long since been torn down, but he still saw it, in his mind's eye.

E. D. Nixon

We had what was known as a four-room house. There were two or three Negro families on the block, white people living at each end of us. And we was all poor. In our family, I was one of seventeen children. We couldn't hardly have had any bread if all the boys didn't work. I've known many a time when me and another boy would go down to the slaughterhouse and get a cow head for a dime. It was so big we could hardly get home with it. My mother would clean it, get the tongue out, cook it. It was so good! Just shows how much things have changed. Today it would probably cost you $1 to $2 to buy that head. But the most important thing I remember was the gaslights. The company would put a meter in your place, and to turn on the gas, you had to put in a quarter. When the time was running out, I'd stand there and hold onto the quarter until the lights flickered down, getting the last second out of what we'd paid for.

Looking back now, I can't even tell you if I finished seventh grade. My mother passed when I was ten. But if she had lived, I would have been better prepared scholastically because she kept on saying she wanted me to be a doctor or a lawyer. I didn't have enough sense to know the value of education. I think maybe I just got grown too quick.

When I was real young, I didn't have no kind of feeling whites was pushing me around. We all used to play together. They was at our house, everybody eating and then laying down on the floor to sleep.

But when I went to work carrying bags down at the railroad station, it all broke up. Then I knowed blacks and whites was separate. I took that as the way of life everywhere. I was already into my twenties when I come to see it was the South holding onto segregation. In '23, I started with the Pullman Company and was running around the country, first one place, then another, and I could really see the changes in other places. In the South a colored person got on the train and he couldn't sit in the Pullman car, the same one I was working in. I saw them hang up a curtain to separate whites and colored when a colored person went into the dining car. I noticed in some Northern cities they actually had black policemen; some places even allowed blacks in the hotels. And like they had coaches for colored and coaches for whites in the South. In the North everybody could ride the same cars.

Once I went to St. Louis, and A. Philip Randolph, who later became president of the Brotherhood of Sleeping Car Porters, spoke, and I went to hear him, in the YMCA, I think it was. We didn't have a union at that time, and we were trying to get one. A. Philip Randolph was a good speaker, and the auditorium was loaded with people. He is about my size, but ten years older. He shook me up like nothing before. He made me conscious of the fact that the Negro needed to do something for himself, needed to stop accepting Jim Crow and how he ought to be fighting to eliminate this kind of thing. We porters were making $62.50 a month then. Mr. Randolph said, "If you stick with me, the day will come when I'll have you making $150 a month, and the day will come after that when that $150 will be tripled." Hearing him, I couldn't hardly believe him. And yet he proved it. Today porters are making around $500 a month.

After he shook me up, I kept watching and waiting to see what I could do. During the Depression I organized the Montgomery Welfare League to help poor people get on relief. A lot of them did. When the war come, there wasn't a lounge in the railroad station for the Negro soldiers, like the whites had, where they could relax, leave their bags, rest up. And they didn't have a USO club for Negro soldiers in all Montgomery. Of course, it was out of the question to think that we could go into the USO club for whites. We had the Negro Civic Improvement League then, and a committee went to find out why we didn't have a USO club for Negroes. So when this committee reported back that we couldn't have a club because we didn't have 1,000 Negro soldiers I said to the league president, "I don't know how, but I am going out lone-handed for a USO club." That night I told my wife, and she said, "That sounds just like you. If headaches was selling for a dollar a dozen, you'd walk into the drugstore and ask the man to give you a dozen!"

But I went in, lay on the bed, and the next morning, when I woke up, I told her I had the answer to my prayer. I was going to write Mrs. Roosevelt and tell her what we need. I generally gave someone my theory of what I wanted in a letter and some professor, principal or somebody would put it into a decent letter. I think it was Mrs. Rosa Parks, one of the most competent people you can come to and who was later in the NAACP with me, helped me write that letter to Mrs. Roosevelt. I wanted Mrs. Roosevelt to know what we was up against, and I told her I'd appreciate it if she'd direct my letter to the proper authority. About eight or nine days later my doorbell rung, and there was a little short, dark fellow saying, "I'm looking for E. D. Nixon."

I said I was E. D. Nixon, and he looked at me, up and down, and I said, "Is anything wrong?" He said, "Well, I don't reckon so. My name is James W. Geater and I just looked you to be sure I wasn't making a mistake. I been with the recreation department for fourteen years and I ain't never heard a Negro cry loud enough in the South that would make Mrs. Roosevelt send me down here to see what it was all about." In 120 days we opened a USO club. Then I started writing letters to people in Washington, and we did get to have a lounge in the station for Negro soldiers.

After all that, wasn't nothing but threats and so forth to me, with

people calling down to the Pullman Company and saying I was a or-
nery nigger who ought to be made "to want bread for a while." That's
the way whites usually retaliate, make you suffer by getting you out
of a job and everything. But it so happened that we had a union by
then, and the management couldn't fire you without cause. I was the
president of our local for twenty-five years, nobody ever even ran
against me, and I was one of those fighters who was going to fight to
the last inch. I knew the contract, and I knew my rights, and I stayed
within the contract so they couldn't put a finger on me. In those years
I had to represent the porters who was charged with something by the
company. I'm not bragging, but while I had men who were penalized
on charges, I never had one fired under me, and you can go ask Mr.
Randolph in New York. He'll tell you I am the only Southern local
president who got a white superintendent fired. This man kept violating our contract, and I filed a charge, and the company said they
couldn't go along with him mistreating people. They let him go.

All this time I was in the NAACP. I been Montgomery chairman
eight or ten times, running one, two or three years at a time. I fought
against police brutality and all that kind of stuff. It has been a long
and uphill fight, first one thing, then another. Mrs. Parks will tell you
this; her mother said the white folks was going to lynch us, her and
me both. Mrs. Parks and I were in the NAACP when other Negroes
were afraid to be seen with us.

Once a young lady, a Negro schoolgirl named Amanda Baker, was
found dead, and she had been raped and dropped on a neck of the
road out here. We couldn't get a thing done about it, so I decided to
go up and see the governor, man named Chauncey Sparks. That
morning I was walking to the Capitol I passed a church where the
Southern Conference for Human Welfare was having a meeting, talking about the terrible things going on. I went in for a little while and
was sitting in the back, when the chairman, elderly white woman, seen
me and said, "I see we got a new face here this morning, and I'm going to let the gentleman come up and identify himself." So I walked
up, and I said, "Good morning—I'm E. D. Nixon, president of the
NAACP, and I'm on my way up to Governor Sparks to ask for a reward for the arrest and conviction of the guilty party who committed
the crime against Amanda Baker, and all I want to ask is if there
is one man or woman here, white or black, that has the courage to
go with me, because if you do, I'd be glad to have you."

I stood there a few minutes, and not a word did I get out of them.

Finally I said, "Madam chairman, I'm sorry I've taken up your time, and I see now that nobody here really believes in what you are all talking about."

I got in to see the governor because it just so happen I knew his executive secretary. I come up on the train one day, and in Mobile a fellow said they had been trying to get a special delivery letter mailed and it was important and would I deliver it to a man in Montgomery? I said all right, and in Montgomery I did and this man said, "Nixon, my name is George Bliss Jones, I am executive secretary to Governor Sparks. I know you are active in Montgomery, and if there is any time we can do something, let me know." So he got me in to see the governor that day. The governor is sitting behind a desk, and it didn't have anything on it but a fountain pen and a telephone. He said good morning, and I told him I was there to ask him to offer a reward, and I said our organization would match it. He then pounded his hand on the desk and said, "The evening paper will have my answer." That night the paper said he was offering a $250 reward and that we were supposed to match it. So the paper said it was going to keep watch to see if Nixon would keep his promise. Next morning another man and me made a deposit of $250 in the Alabama National Bank, and I called the press to tell them the account number and that they could check it. Not a single line was ever printed that we had made the deposit. The money stayed there four years. Never found the guilty party.

You see, I like to have a reputation that if you come to me and say can you do such and such a thing, and I say I will do it, then you know I will. I want to have a reputation so that if you was 200 miles away and we was supposed to meet, you would say, "I got to get there because Nixon is going to be there." I live like that. My word is all I got, and I am going to do what's right, if I have to stand all by myself. I remember how I tried to register to vote for about ten years. They had a form with about twenty-one questions, and the governor himself couldn't have answered them if he had to do it real quick. So when you fill it out and hand it in, they say, "We'll let you know." But you never heard. Finally, about 1942, I filed a suit against them, and they claimed it was too late. So the next time I went to try to register, I told them if I don't hear from you in twenty-two days I'm going to file another suit, and it won't be too late this time. On the twenty-second morning I got my voting certificate.

It was somewhere along in there, in the early 1940's, that a col-

ored woman and a bus driver had a run-in on the bus here in Montgomery. You have to know something about the bus line. About 80
percent of the travel done on them was by colored. But the bus driver
could move colored people anywhere he wanted on the bus because
he was within his rights under a city ordinance. If a white person
came into the bus and sat 'way back in it, no Negro was permitted
to stand or sit between the motorman and that person.

Now I had an automobile, so I wasn't riding the buses, but most
people was. The point is that if I was riding the bus, I'd have to suffer the same things. As long as it was inflicted on all our people, that's
what we was concerned about.

So anyway, this woman had a run-in about a seat, and the police
arrested her. I went to court with a lawyer and he said he'd represent
her for $50, and I had the $50 in my hand and he was writing out a
receipt when he said the best thing we could do was go up there and
plead her guilty and get the lowest fine. "That's what you think?" I
said. "Yeah," he says. Then I said, "Well, I don't need you then because I can tell her to do that and save the $50." The court found her
guilty, and I told the judge I was going to file notice of appeal to take
on the segregation ordinance. I signed a bond to do that, and the case
just hung on and on until the woman died somewhere around 1951,
and in all that time the appeal case was never put on the court calendar.

Yet we still kept trying to get a good court case to test the ordinance. One girl was arrested who was a minister's daughter, and I
knowed that with the attitude her father would take we couldn't get
very far with it. He was one of those who believes in what the white
folks say. Another girl who was arrested was an expectant mother,
and I knowed they would have cut her to pieces. When a third girl
was arrested, I went to see her daddy. He was under the influence of
whiskey. The house was very poorly kept, four or five children. It
didn't have a privy or nothing in it, just a low type of home. If the
press had gone out there, we wouldn't have a leg to stand on.

So every time you didn't bow to the will of the bus driver, you
went to jail. In some instances, people was beat up. Whole lot of
times people stayed in jail a couple of days before anybody knew it.
And all those things, it just got to the place, like dropping water in a
bucket, that it finally got filled up. And at that time this thing happened to Mrs. Parks everybody was ready for it.

Rosa Parks

On the first of December, 1955, I was just going home from work. It was a routine day, but I can recall not feeling too well, physically, and I didn't feel particularly like standing on the bus, though you expected to. The first bus that come up at Court Square was very crowded, so I went across to the drugstore and made a couple of purchases. When I came out, I could see the next bus was quite empty. I felt that if I caught that one, I could probably get a seat. But by the time I got on, the last vacant seat was just in back of what was considered the lily-white section. *The seat I took was in the colored section.* By the third stop all the front seats were taken by the whites and there was one white man left standing. The driver looked around and asked the four of us in our row of the colored section to let him have the front seat. We knew he was talking about us getting up to accommodate this one white passenger. I didn't move. Didn't say anything. When he spoke a second time—"You-all make it light on yourselves" —the other three passengers in our row got up. He asked me, "Are you going to stand up?" I told him No, I didn't intend to. Then he said he was going to call the police, and I told him to call. I wasn't frightened, wasn't angry. I was thinking that the only way to let them know I felt I was being mistreated was to do just what I did—resist the order. You spend your whole lifetime in your occupation, actually, making life clever, easy and convenient for white people. But when you have to get transportation home, you are denied an equal accommodation. Our existence was for the white man's comfort and well-being; we had to accept being deprived of just being human.

Odyssey

In the black revolution's folklore, Rosa Parks is "the little heroine of Montgomery," but she left that city less than two years after the bus incident. We found her in Detroit, where since 1965 she has been a receptionist-clerk in the office of black Congressman John W. Conyers.

Everything about her is low-key—soft voice, unassuming dress, diffident manner. Gray hair tucked in braids over her head, jumper dress made at home. Speech slow and deliberate. When she listens to a question, she seems to plant it in the middle of her mind and then walk all around it. She began by being wary, and at the end she was still that way. As our talks went into the third and fourth hours, she wondered aloud why we wanted so much detail. "It just seems so much," she said. When we talked about her being history, she said, "I didn't feel I was making history that day. It was just another incident, more inconvenience and annoyance than anything else. Things like this had happened before."

Rosa Parks

The first school I attended was just a little one-room building located in Pine Level, Montgomery County, Alabama, with no windows, only wooden shutters, and if it was cold, the shutters had to be closed and so you couldn't see very well inside. Just a very short distance from where I lived in a very old house out in the country was a new school, a rather attractive building. It was without question for the white students. They had bus accommodations, and we never did when I was young. I'd see the bus pass my house every day. At one time I had to walk at least three miles to school. But to me, that was a way of life, and we had no choice but to accept what was the custom. The bus was among the first ways I realized there was a black world and a white world.

My unhappy experiences during that time was that the Ku Klux Klan was quite active, and through word of mouth or the newspapers we would hear of ransacking, burnings, an occasional lynching. There were mysterious deaths where people would be found murdered and no questions asked. The Ku Klux Klan was supposed to have killed a man not too far from where I was living. I remember it so well because we were constantly on guard in our house or in the church where my mother would teach. The doors were sometimes nailed shut, the faces were very tight, and my grandfather had one of those old shotguns he kept pretty close by. How well he could have gotten along if we had been attacked . . . but he just kept it.

I didn't think too much of white people, as a race, being an enemy, but I certainly thought the KKK was. At home the family would discuss in general the conditions under which we lived. The uppermost subject would not be integration and having the same opportunities and accommodations as other people, but actually just being able to survive, not getting into trouble by confrontation with white people who were not friendly to us.

We were regular churchgoers in the African Methodist Episcopal Church. All we ever did hear was the hereafter and heaven—spirituals on how when I get there, I'm going to put on *my* shoes and shout all over God's heaven. I guess it must have grown out of the times when slaves who went without shoes and proper clothing could think that while deprived here, there would be a heaven after death where they could enjoy all the wonderful things they didn't have. My maternal grandparents had both been born in slavery, and hearing them talk made it real to me. My grandmother told how where she was there were never any provisions for feeding the slave children except from a huge pot in the yard, where they poured it out like milk, just like it might be for feeding little pigs or chickens. My grandfather was the son of the slaveowner, but he was thrown out and treated very badly when his father died. Just the fact he existed must have angered some other members of the slaveowner's family. I think I recall him saying that he had never eaten any real food that was not stolen from the kitchen and slipped to him because, I guess, they were hoping he'd die. He became a cripple very young, would go without shoes in the winter, clothing too, and he was severely beaten by the overseer.

It really was something. I have often wondered how much we have overcome and how we have reached where we are, without things being worse. The only explanation I may have is that the most docile and accepting among us were permitted to survive. Occasionally there would be some who would retaliate, take a violent way of trying to express the resentment at being mistreated. He was called a bad nigger and was just killed outright and made an example of.

When I was very small, I read a book called *Is the Negro a Beast?* which said Negroes were an animal to be tamed and put to work for the white race. When I learned that we, *my* family, were Negroes, it caused me to think that throughout my life I'd have to prove myself as something other than a beast. I didn't have any idea that there would ever be a way to protest this. But in high school I read Negro history, about the accomplishments of people I had never heard of. I read everything I could, first in school and then later in magazines, and finally in December, 1943, I started working with the Montgomery Branch NAACP as the secretary.

The president then was Mr. Nixon, the sleeping car porter. He was considered the most militant man in Montgomery. He was the very first person who approached me about the need for trying to get registered. A few Negroes were registered, but very few. Mr. Nixon and a lawyer name of Arthur A. Madison, who came down to Montgomery to try to get people concerned about registration, organized the Voters League. I became a member. It was a pretty tough time for me to get registered. My husband never could. It took me three years to do it. The organization was small then, but it gave me some hope that if we were organized, we could appeal to the courts for doing away with legal segregation of the races. When we got the news of the 1954 decision outlawing school segregation, I felt that there might be still more possibility of not having to continue as we had.

All this took a good part of my life. It was a struggle—I don't know if you would call it that—just to be human, to be a citizen, to have the rights and privileges of any other person.

During those years I was working at various jobs. Sometimes domestic work or sewing at home. I also worked for a black insurance company as an agent, and I clerked in the office. I was forty-two years old and a tailor's assistant in a downtown department store when this thing happened on the bus.

I remember that when the driver went to get the police, a few black passengers got out, too. I suppose they didn't want to be inconvenienced while I was being arrested. The squad car came with two policemen. I got in the back seat. They didn't bother me at all, didn't use any profanity or call me names. My most uncomfortable feeling was when we got to the station and my throat was a bit dry. I felt like I wanted some water. But they wouldn't permit me to drink out of the fountain. It was for whites only.

The jailer wanted to know if I was drunk. I said No, I wasn't. They called the matron who put me in a cell with two other women. She seemed fairly kind. But I wasn't paying a great deal of attention.

After filling out a card, I was given permission to call home to let my husband and mother know I was in jail. Before he could come to get me, Mr. Nixon arrived. A woman who had been on the bus had gone over to the house of a friend of mine to tell her I was arrested. The friend dashed around to Mr. Nixon's house. She says she was too excited to use the telephone, so she ran three blocks. She went to the Nixon home because Mr. Nixon was the person people usually called on when they were in trouble.

E. D. Nixon

That afternoon I was at a meeting, but when I come back to the NAACP office, the tailor who had a place next to us came out and said, "Call your wife. I promised her I'd tell you soon as you came in." So I called her, and I say, "What's up?" She said, "They arrested Mrs. Parks." I said, "For what?" She said, "I don't know—but go get her." Just like I could go get her. I called down and asked the police what was the charges against Mrs. Parks. I told who I was to whoever was on the desk that night, and he wasn't too friendly, just said it was none of my damn business. I got ahold of a white lawyer named Clifford Durr. One of the most liberal lawyers, retired now. I told him what had happened and asked him to call the jail. He phoned back in a few minutes and said they'd got her charged with violating the segregation law. I said, "Well, I'm going down and make bond." He said, "Come by here and I'll go with you."

As I picked him up, his wife came running out, putting on her coat —it was cold that night—and the three of us went down there. We told them we wanted to make bond for Mrs. Parks. The man at the desk made out the papers and started to give them to Mr. Durr. Mr. Durr said, "No, Mr. Nixon is a property owner. He is going to sign." The desk man, a different person from the one I had talked to on the phone, let me and said, "Nixon, when do you want this case set? You can have it Saturday morning or Monday." I said, "I'll appreciate it if you set it for Monday the fifth of December, I'm going to be out of town over the weekend, and I'd like to be here for the trial." So he set it for Monday, and Mrs. Parks was let out of jail.

We all went home with her, and of course, we had coffee together. We hadn't planned on Mrs. Parks being a test case. We just stumbled on to it when she was arrested. There we was, all sitting around in Mrs. Parks' kitchen, and I said, "*This is the case!* We can boycott the bus lines with this and at the same time go to the Supreme Court." I said to Mrs. Parks, "With your permission we have the case to break down segregation on the bus." I knowed that if Mrs. Parks says Yes, hell could freeze, but she wouldn't change. And she was intelligent enough to take care of herself in court. She could come in this office right now and start reading the newspaper. She keeps a pencil in her hand, and you can see her pick out every word that is misspelled. But when I asked her about the case that night, she said she didn't know.

Finally, though, she said, "If you think it is all right, I'll go along with you."

That night I told my wife what we was going to do, and she told me again about those headaches I always kept buying for a dollar a dozen. She said, "Don't you know people ain't going to stay off the bus, cold as it is?" I said, "If they stay off one day while it is cold, I will know they are sincere." So that night on my tape recorder I recorded any number of names of ministers, schoolteachers, people to call. Next morning at five I began calling to tell people that we had the case we'd been looking for. But to go to court and boycott the buses, we had to have some form of organization. First one I called was the Reverend Ralph Abernathy. He was secretary of the Ministers' Alliance, and I wanted to get this to the ministers, so they could get it out in the churches on Sunday morning. That was one of the reasons I wanted the case against Mrs. Parks listed for Monday, to give us time.

Reverend Abernathy had worked with me on other cases; matter of fact, he had helped draft some of my letters. I expected him to go along. And he said, "Oh, yes, I think it is a good thing. I'm with you." Next I called the president of the Ministers' Alliance. He agreed. Third off, I called Reverend King, and he said, "Well, Nixon, let me think about it for a while and you call me back." By the time I got back to him and he accepted he became the eighteenth to do so. Everybody else except King had agreed right away. But he didn't know anything about me. Probably he had heard of me, but I had never met him to be friendly with.

The group of us set it up for a meeting that night. I had to make my train run, but before I left I talked with Joe Azbell at the Montgomery *Advertiser* newspaper and told him what we was planning to do.

Rosa Parks

The next day, Friday, Mr. Nixon called and asked if I could be at a meeting that evening in the Dexter Avenue Church after I got off work. I asked what was the meeting about? He said, "About this thing." I asked, "What thing?" He said, "You know—about your being arrested." I told him I'd come.

There must have been about fifty or more people at the meeting, ministers, faculty from the local college, some of the women in the community. Martin Luther King was there. He was the pastor of that church. I had to tell the people what had happened on the bus.

E. D. Nixon

On Sunday the ministers had a chance to say something. But we didn't dream we was going to get all the stuff we got in the *Advertiser*. Joe Azbell, the man I'd talked with on the newspaper, wrote a spread for the front page, and I think that did more to organize us than anything in the world. There were leaflets about the boycott around, and he used the part in them telling how the Negroes resented being pushed around on the buses and so forth.

With this thing in the paper, the commissioner of police had a slot on TV and radio. He said he wanted it understood there would be two police for every bus, "so if you want to ride the bus, get on it." Well, a lot of our people didn't hear that, and when they got out on Monday to catch the bus, they saw those two police. And figured some other way to get to work. The buses were empty, even before breakfast time.

That morning Mrs. Parks was tried and convicted. There were about 500 people around City Hall. Police standing out there with sawed-off shotguns and everything, looking like they was gonna kill somebody. There was a hall leading out of the courtroom, and when Mrs. Parks and I and one of the police came up it toward the city clerk's office for me to sign an appeal bond, the people outside on the steps saw us with the policeman. They crowded in so much we could hardly get in the office. It was the first time I had seen so much courage among our people! I told them, "Everything is all right, keep calm, because we don't want to do anything to make that man use the shotgun." After I signed the bond and released Mrs. Parks to her husband, I said to the men there, "Don't hang around, because all they want is some excuse to kill somebody." They could easy have done it.

I caught up with Abernathy and French, another minister, who was at the hearing. I said, "Reverend Abernathy, what's on the agenda for the meetings set up for this afternoon and tonight?" He said something like, "We're going to talk about boycott, ain't that what you wanted?" I said, "Yes, but we got to have a purpose—some recommendations, resolutions, a name for the group. We ought to have all that ready when we go into the meeting." My connection with organized labor and the NAACP had given me knowledge about organizing that was far superior to any of these people who were far superior to me in scholastic training. He said, "I hadn't thought of that," and I said, "C'mon up to my office." I had three resolutions all wrote out, and they was very mild. I tried to make them soft enough so the city commissioner would agree to what we was wanting done about the buses. Abernathy and French agreed to the recommendations. Then it came to a name, and I suggested the Citizens Coordinating Committee, but Abernathy said, "No, I don't like that name." French had some kind of name, and finally Abernathy said, "What about the Montgomery Improvement Association?" I said, "That sounds good. I believe I can go along with that," French could, too.

Next Abernathy said, "Brother Nixon, you going to serve as President, ain't you?" I said, "Not unlessen you don't accept the man I got in mind." He wanted to know, who was that? I said Reverend King. I had my reasons. King was a very intelligent man. He hadn't been in Montgomery long, and because he had a lot of intelligent people in his church, he didn't have to bow to the power structure. They couldn't get their hand on him nohow. So many ministers accept a handout, and then they owe their soul. I had only heard King talk once before, on the second Sunday in August, 1955, at the NAACP meeting. He was guest speaker. Wasn't talking about pie in the sky, he was talking about what people do in the community. I turned to the man sitting next to me and I said, "That fellow made a darn good speech; I don't know how, but some of these days I'm going to hang that guy to the stars." I thought about that when I put his name up. Abernathy and French accepted the idea.

We had an afternoon meeting to get ready for the big mass meeting that night. Was about twelve or fifteen of us, ministers and people. All the recommendations were accepted, and then we started talking about how to get the program over to the people in the big meeting. We could see there would be lots of white people there, police and everything, and somebody said we could mimeograph some forms telling about the resolutions and slip it to the people at the door so the white folks won't know what we was doing. I was disappointed in those ministers. They was talking about slipping around, didn't want the white folks to know, and I said, "How in hell are you going to have a protest without letting the white folks know?" I got pretty warm, and I used some language wasn't in the Sunday school books. I said: "What's the matter with you people? Here you have been living off the sweat of these washwomen all these years, and you have never done anything for them. Now you have a chance to pay them back. And you too damn scared to stand on your feet and be counted! The time has come when you men is going to have to learn to be grown men, or be scared boys."

I was angry. I had a right to be. We have all laughed about it since then, but if I hadn't stood up right there and then, we'd have missed opportunity, I believe, of being heard all over the world.

King jumped up and said, "Don't nobody call me a coward," and when he did, he was nominated as president of the Montgomery Improvement Association.

Odyssey

That night the blacks held a mass meeting and spoke their minds on what they planned to do. It is one of the footnotes of history that E. D. Nixon, as the association treasurer, collected so many contributions that he asked for—and received—a police escort home. Something new had happened in Montgomery.

Mrs. Parks had told us that she had felt no sense of history the night of her arrest, but, we asked, didn't she come to see that the implications went far beyond Montgomery? "Well, yes," she said. "It was one of those sudden changes in us as a people. Before, we had just been going along with the system as it was, and then this mass protest and resistance came up against the traditional way. Yes, to my mind it was quite a historic thing."

But at some price, to everyone. The shop where she'd been working closed. Her husband lost his job. There was real tension in Montgomery as whites came to see blacks were never going back to segregation on the buses. Dr. King's house was bombed. Three days later dynamite went off on the lawn of E. D. Nixon's home.

E. D. Nixon

I was on my run at the time, but when I come home, my wife met me with a letter postmarked, Alabama. Inside was a drawing of a casket with the grave all dug, and at the bottom it said, "Nigger, if you ain't left town by eight o'clock tonight, you going to be in a casket just like this."

Hard for me to tell you how that made me feel. I called the Department of Justice about the letter. Then I got more shells for every gun I had—a .30-.30 Winchester, a double-barreled shotgun, a .410 shotgun, a .22 rifle, a .32 special revolver, and a .38 Colt.

Up on the second floor of my home, I run up the venetian blinds. In this room looking out to the street I had a reclining chair, and I laid all the guns around me on the floor, cut the lights, and just sat there waiting. Finally a man went down the street, straining and looking. When he came back and stopped right at my door, I went down, throwed the door open, leveled the .30-.30 Winchester and said that if he didn't identify himself and do it fast, I'd kill him. He told me he was from the Justice Department and went to put a hand in his pocket. I said, "Pull it out easy because if you got anything shiny I'll blow your brains out." So he got out his identification card, and then he come inside to call the police to get me some bodyguards. The commissioner got me to get on the phone, and he said, "Nixon, I don't agree with what you and Dr. King doing, but I am going to send somebody out there to protect you." I said, "I don't give a damn what you doing, neither, but if you expects to send some white policemen here, keep them there with you because if anything starts, it just means I got two more to kill." So he sent out two Negro policemen, and for ten days and nights they sat out there. I didn't pay no attention to them.

Odyssey

The bus boycott went on for nearly a year, with the blacks steadfastly walking, hitching rides, organizing car pools—anything except riding the buses. But it was not the arrest of Mrs. Parks that finally got the buses desegregated.

E. D. Nixon

True, we did start out to take Mrs. Parks' case to the Supreme Court. But on the second Saturday in January, 1956, I called the Reverend King and Abernathy to come by the house for a cup of coffee.

When they came, I says, "Both of you boys—I can call you boys because I got a son old as either one of you—we all think we're going to the Supreme Court with Mrs. Parks' case." King says, "Isn't that what we are going to do?" I said No. I said that as long as the power structure knows we are depending on this case to go to the Supreme

Court, they'll never put it on the calendar. I reminded them of what had happened with that woman's case I'd filed the appeal on some years back. The power structure knew we had a good case on that one, so they never let it get on the docket.

King says, "Well, what *are* we going to do?" And I said, "We are going to find four or five people who will say they have been mistreated on the bus and we'll file a federal case right now." We got about seven people said they were discriminated against, that they paid fare like anybody else and yet were forced to stand while seats were vacant in the white section. And that was the case we won to have the right to go anywhere on the bus.

Mrs. Parks' case? We settled that in the court of appeals, and it ain't cost us but $51.

Odyssey

When Nixon talked about Mrs. Parks, he never used the name Rosa—always it was Mrs. Parks. There was a courtliness in his manner toward her and, also, a certain sense of sadness.

E. D. Nixon

Mrs. Parks stood up for the black community. But the community didn't stand up for her, not by a long shot. The whites wouldn't give her a job, and the Negroes wouldn't support her. One day I said to Reverend King, "With all the money we got here, Mrs. Parks ought to have a job—and we could give her $100 a month whether she got a job or not." He said, "I don't know, brother Nixon, we can't hardly do that."

But when they bombed the Reverend King's parsonage, the Montgomery Improvement Association paid a guard $30 a week to be in the door and read the funny papers every night until it was morning. I know, because as the treasurer I signed the checks. When Mrs. Parks finally left Montgomery, the MIA had about $400,000. They could have taken $100,000 and set up a trust fund for Mrs. Parks, and with the $5,000 a year interest she could have stayed here. But we done the same thing the white man wanted. After the whites made it hard for her to get a job, all the doors closed on her, and the Negroes kept them closed. The night before she left, when they had a Rosa Parks night, church crowded with folks, I said, "Here we forgot about this woman who's responsible for all that's happened in Montgomery and throughout the South and glorified a man who was made because of her." I said, "I don't care what nobody said, Mrs. Parks ought to have a place in the Montgomery Improvement Association —if nobody got nothing but her." I told the women, "At least I'd expect you to help fight to see that Mrs. Parks don't leave town." But everybody just forgot everything, went wild over King. I respect King, but I'm for Mrs. Parks, too. The point is that she should never have had to leave. But nobody would give a dime.

Rosa Parks

I wouldn't want to place any blame on the community, because I do feel it was my responsibility to do whatever I could for myself and not to look to the community or to Dr. King or anyone else for my support or livelihood. I felt as long as I was well and could move around, I should be on my own, rather than looking to anyone to reimburse me or reward me for what I might have done.

When the place where I had worked closed the shop, I had only sewing or doing some work with Mr. Nixon, but I didn't have a permanent job. I was living on what I could get as it came in. When the MIA learned I was going to leave Montgomery, the Reverend Abernathy, representing MIA, did offer me some employment, but since I had already made my plans, I felt the best thing for me was to leave. My brother and his family were living in Detroit. My mother, my husband and I were the last members of the family in Montgomery, and we didn't have any near relatives there, and I decided it was probably better for all of us to just move to Detroit. I don't seem to think I felt any bitterness or too much sadness. There wasn't any particular reason for me to remain.

Odyssey

As Mrs. Parks, looking so fragile, sat there in Congressman Conyer's office, reliving those last days in Montgomery, the pauses came longer between her words. Every so often she gave a little self-deprecating laugh, as if it were a moment in irony that she, Rosa Parks, should be able to say she was there, with history. "I felt it was just something I had to do," she said.

Rosa Parks

I don't seem to have any regrets over whatever I did. I don't know whether I could have been more effective as a worker for freedom in the South than I am here in Detroit. Really, the same thing that has occurred in the South is existing here to a certain degree. We do have the same problems. It seems to me that the establishment of white people and authority have a way of not seeing the progress or the good that our people want to do, but will antagonize and provoke violence. When the young people want to present themselves as human beings and come into their own as men, there is always something to cut them down. It was very upsetting in the Detroit riots in 1967 because we live right in the heart of the ghetto and could see a good bit of the looting and where some of the buildings were being set on fire. My husband was just beside himself; I had to spend most of my time trying to keep him as calm as possible. I was upset, too, because I couldn't see it was going to accomplish any good—but on the other hand, I could see it was the result of the resistance to change that was needed long beforehand.

Dr. King was criticized because he tried to bring about change through the nonviolent movement. It didn't accomplish what it should have because the white Establishment would not accept his philosophy of nonviolence and respond to it positively. When the resistance grew, it created a hostility and bitterness among the younger people, who worked with him in the early days, when there was some hope that change could be accomplished through his means. And of course when it didn't, they gave up the philosophy of nonviolence and Christianity as the answer to the problems.

Do I still believe in integration as a working rule? I have never been what you would call just an integrationist. I know I've been called that, but actually I was not trying to integrate the bus, I was only trying to go home. Integrating that bus wouldn't mean more equality. Even when there was segregation, there was plenty of integration in the South, but it was for the benefit and convenience of the white person, not us. So it is not just integration. What I am hoping for is that we can discontinue all forms of oppression against all those who are weak or oppressed. All people should be treated equal, and race or religion or nationality should not have any bearing on whether a person is exalted or oppressed.

E. D. Nixon

Just the other day I made a speech criticizing how people were not doing anything in Montgomery now. I said that what happened in Montgomery reminded me of a pilot light on a stove. I said, "Turn the switch on, and the gas goes on all around—but the pilot light stays the same." I said, "Montgomery set the world on fire, but Montgomery itself isn't moving. Our people are too complacent; professional people don't take part in anything."

Some time ago we had some kind of a meeting at the Holiday Inn motel, and a man said to me, "Brother Nick, I didn't think the day would ever come that we could sit down in a Holiday Inn and eat a steak without being humiliated." He made me so angry; he just happened to be one of those guys that had never done anything, but sit at home, look at TV. He wasn't there when folks got eat up by police dogs, or run over by a sheriff, beaten up by the police, drowned with water hoses, or stayed in jail all night. And I said, "Man, you ought to keep your damn mouth shut, because you ain't done nothing to bring it about."

My contention is this: Freedom is never free. It is something you have to continue to work for. And that is something I can't see today —all these youngsters walking the streets, won't work, won't go to school. And if a man does like that, he ain't got nothing in the world to look forward to but crawling on his belly for a handout, nothing to offer his children, no status in the community; his word don't mean nothing. I think a Negro has to be prepared, first with going to school, getting prepared for a good job, then working, buying homes, building a bank account. Then he becomes a solid citizen. You are earning your way in this society, and people respect you. You can't burn your way to freedom. There are some people call me Uncle Tom, but you know what I think about that? If I am the kind of a guy that people call Uncle Tom all across this country, then we need 10,000 Uncle Toms right here in this town.

One thing I can say. The day and hour that peoples are able to live together in a community like human beings is the day and hour that we are going to solve all our problems. Sometimes I do wonder if we can save America. I wonder is it worth it. But on the other hand, you do whatever you can to save it. Something has got to change. And we are going to have to try.

Sit-ins to Selma:
Nurturing a Revolution

John Lewis

Hundreds, mostly women and children, began gathering at about two o'clock. We met behind the Brown Chapel Church, in a playground for the nearby housing project. It was like going to a picnic, a sort of gay outing. We had no idea there would be any trouble. We were just going to march from Selma to Montgomery, to present our grievances to Governor Wallace.

The people, 600 strong, were very happy. We walked two abreast down Highway 80, out of Selma, across the Edmund Pettus Bridge. State troopers were waiting for us at the other end. One of them said, "I am Major Cloud. This is an unlawful assembly. You have three minutes to move, to disperse." But in a matter of just a flash he said, "Troopers, advance!" And they came at us, with billy clubs, pushing people around. Some fell down. But for the most part, the march stayed pretty much together and orderly. We passed the word back for everybody to bow down in a prayerful manner. Then the troopers came back at us again, this time with tear gas as well, and they started clubbing people. Sheriff Clark came in with a posse on horseback. They had whips and ropes they beat people with. It was just mass violence, a slaughter.

In the first rush they had just shoved me back. The second time I got hit on the head, while I was bowed on my knees, with my eyes closed, praying. I was saying to myself, "How could this happen?" I had fear. I really did. It was the tear gas, more than the pain from the stick, that made it just seem like it was my last breath. I was, like, saying, "It's here. It's finished. It's all over."

Odyssey

It was only ten years from Montgomery to the bridge at Selma, but for John Lewis it was a lifetime. *Time* magazine once said that he had a raw militancy, and all over the South, even today, there are police who remember him. They should. They jailed him forty times, clubbed him, split his head open, gassed him. But one thing they could not do: Stop him. He was there in the first wave of lunch-counter sit-ins, there with the original freedom riders, there amid the terrors of registering voters in Mississippi, there in the lead of the historic march at Selma. As the chairman of the Student Nonviolent Coordinating Committee (SNCC) during its greatest years, he became the symbol of the South's peaceful revolutionary blacks, totally committed to their cause, idealistic, compassionate and cool in the face of the gravest danger.

He was pointed out to us during the warm election day when he had come to Fayette to help Charles Evers. Very calm, thoughtful young man, short, alert, a very dark brown, seemingly untouched by the day's excitement. Lewis, neatly and conservatively dressed, was clearly someone from "the city." It was hard to equate this man, not quite thirty and so solemn, to the violence and controversy that had once engulfed him. Later, in Atlanta, where he heads the Voter Education Project, he reflected on his beginnings.

John Lewis

Growing up on a farm near Troy, Alabama, I was somewhat withdrawn. I have never been a violent type. On Saturdays and on Sunday afternoons my brothers and first cousins would be playing baseball or cowboy. I'd be reading the Bible or looking after the chickens. At a very, very early age, I fell in love with chickens. They were my responsibility to water, feed and see into the coop. I thought the chicken the most innocent creature, wouldn't harm a fly, just couldn't do anything wrong. I identified with them—I'd go into the coop and preach to them. They were my first congregation.

All along I had this inclination of becoming a minister. I don't know whether I believe in predestination, but I thought there were certain things that I was supposed to do, a certain role I was to play. When I was four, an uncle gave me a Bible for Christmas. My mother, who had gone through the eighth grade, taught me to read it. The first words I learned were: "In the beginning, God created the heaven and the earth." And another favorite of mine was: "Behold, the lamb of God which taketh away the sin of the earth." I didn't comprehend the full meaning of the words, but I recited them over and over again.

On the third Sunday of each month, the whole family would go to the Macedonia Baptist Church, about five miles away. I felt, even then, the possibility of a minister being a vehicle for doing good. But our minister came in just once a month, and I didn't see him doing anything for the community. People in that church for the most part were sharecroppers, and they were cheated. A man would make ten or fifteen bales of cotton, and at the end of the year he only got credit for four or five when he borrowed some money from the plantation owner. It became a system, call it a polite form of slavery, but the tenant farmer had to remain in it, on and on. Yet the minister never spoke out against this. He'd preach about an eye for an eye, a tooth for a tooth, your soul must be saved, just sort of by-and-by, pie in the sky, when you die. I became very disappointed with that type of sermon.

Then I heard Martin Luther King preach. All of the bitter criticism that I had with the old ministers—he changed for me. It was early 1955. I was fifteen, still in high school. There was this Montgomery black radio station, WRMA, which was very popular, especially on Sunday morning when they would have a local Negro minister preach. On this particular day, it was Dr. King. I was so impressed with his sermon that it has always stayed with me. He called it "Paul's Letter to the American Christian," and it was this whole thing on love. He made the Gospel alive. This was the first time I heard a minister come out and really appeal to people across the board to take an absolute position on love. He spoke of brotherhood that was for here, today, not for the tomorrow.

Later, when the Montgomery bus boycott started, I saw him as the most hopeful thing, emerging as the best symbol in my life of all that I thought a minister should be. And while I already had this desire to be a minister, there is no question but that Martin Luther King, his sermons and reading about him, had a terrific impact on me.

In February, 1956, I preached my trial sermon in the Macedonia Baptist Church. It was during the regular service before a congregation of about 200 people. It was about a mother wanting her son to be a man of moral courage. You know the emotions of the black church. People shout. And when a few people did during my sermon it was really a happy moment. I had a kind of vision of my life ahead. It was a strange feeling, for I did see myself involved as part of the beginning of a movement.

Odyssey

He was already an ordained minister when, at seventeen, he entered the American Baptist Seminary at Nashville. The religious feeling of a commitment to a moral courage grew stronger within him. He attended mass meetings, went to civil rights workshops, recruited other students for the movement. And then, in 1958, he heard about the beloved community.

John Lewis

That's when I started to understand integration. I had been going to workshops on nonviolence, led by the Reverend James Lawson, a young Methodist, one of the first black students in the Vanderbilt University Divinity School. Jim had traveled in India; he'd been with Dr. King at Montgomery. Before hearing him, I had always thought integration was a question of equality and certain rights. But when Jim talked about the beloved community as the Kingdom of God here on earth, I came to see it as the open society, a oneness of all.

During that period, Jim's workshops had about a dozen students from five colleges and universities. At first, we didn't talk about any practical application of nonviolence or direct action based on it. The meetings were mostly devoted to discipline and philosophy, beginning with the Old and New Testaments, the whole concept of love and resistance to evil, and into the entire history of Gandhi's struggle in India.

One day in the fall of 1959, somebody suggested we have a test sit-in. We asked to be served at the lunch counters in Nashville's two biggest department stores. When we were refused, we left. All we had wanted to do was establish in fact that the stores had a policy of not letting whites and blacks sit down and eat together. Some months after that, students in Greensboro, North Carolina, sat in at a lunch counter. Those of us in the Lawson workshops followed that by calling for a mass meeting of all students in Nashville to begin a series of sit-ins. On Saturday, February 27, 1960, I was arrested. There were ninety-seven of us that day. We had participated in a very, very nonviolent, peaceful demonstration. Everyone arrested had a copy of the rules I had prepared for us: "Do not strike back. Do not curse. Be orderly. Smile!" And in the end I wrote something like "The great teachers are Jesus, Gandhi and Martin Luther King. God bless you."

After I was charged with disorderly conduct and trespass, I spent the weekend in jail. I wrote a letter home explaining I had acted according to my conscience and that I could do no more. My mother's attitude was that I'd gone to college to get an education, and I shouldn't get involved with this mess. But my father's was: "Somebody's got to do it."

Soon hundreds of students were arrested. But in a matter of days, because the community got behind us, the lunch counters were desegregated. I know that today people say that's not important. But for students in 1960 and 1961, whether in Nashville or Greensboro or Atlanta, it was. If we had used guns or fists, we would have lost from the beginning. What we accomplished we did with nonviolence and our bodies.

Odyssey

Lewis was in Raleigh, North Carolina, when SNCC was born, Easter weekend, 1960, with the goal of integrating public facilities and pushing for voter registration. The next year, when the first thirteen freedom riders—seven blacks, six whites—were assembled by the Congress of Racial Equality (CORE) in Washington, Lewis was among them.

John Lewis

We bought on like any other passenger, splitting up so we rode in two buses. For the most part, we were paired, a black and a white, to get a seat near either the front or the back of the bus. The plan was that when we made our scheduled stops, we would go into the so-called white or so-called colored waiting room and integrate the facility.

My seatmate was an older guy from Cos Cob, Connecticut, name of Albert Bigelow. He was a pacifist with more experience than any of us. He had been the captain of a ship called *The Golden Rule* which attempted to enter the Pacific bomb detonating area in protest of nuclear tests. He and I got off the bus in Rock Hill, South Carolina, with the regular passengers and walked into the white waiting room. We were immediately attacked by some white guys and knocked to the ground. A police officer came up and asked if we wanted to press charges. We said No, walked over to the counter, and were served.

We went from the Rock Hill bus station to a small college to spend the night. It was there that the American Freedom Service Friendship Committee, with whom I'd applied for a two-year job in India, caught up with me. They wanted me to come to Philadelphia for an interview and examinations. So I got off the freedom ride and flew up there. This was on a Wednesday. I was supposed to rejoin the ride in Montgomery on Sunday. But first I returned to Nashville. And that's where I heard about the new violence.

In Anniston, Alabama, the Klan deflated the tires of one of the freedom riders' buses. They got on it and just beat up everybody. Then they burned it. In Birmingham the other bus used by the riders was attacked by another white mob. One white guy from New York was beaten very bad. At that point, CORE decided to drop the ride, and the people returned to their homes.

But in Nashville, those of us who belonged to SNCC wanted to continue the rides. So ten of us—eight black, two white—got on a bus there. We got to just outside Birmingham when a police officer got on the bus and asked, "Don't you have some freedom riders here?"

Well, there were two young guys, one black, the other white, sitting near the front. The policeman told them to get off. He then placed them under arrest for being together. The rest of us who were scattered throughout the bus remained on it. We arrived in Birmingham, where police started searching the tickets of the people to see where they got on and whether we were all going the same places.

So all of us that had tickets reading from Nashville to Birmingham, Montgomery, Jackson and New Orleans were identified as freedom riders and interrogated for a while. They kept us on the bus for three hours when more police officers came and made a kind of wedge or shelter as they shoved us into the so-called white waiting room. They closed the restaurant, closed the rest rooms. Everything was off limits. This happened around noon. There was another scheduled bus for

Montgomery at 5:45 P.M. We tried to get on it. The driver said, "I've got only one life to give, and I'm not giving it to CORE or the NAACP."

Although neither group was involved in this ride, they were symbolic of something in that driver's mind.

We just stayed there, waiting with our bags, trying to get to Montgomery, until Bull Connor, the police commissioner, walked up and said he was taking us into protective custody. He put the eight of us in a paddy wagon and carried us to the Birmingham city jail.

Friday morning, around one o'clock, Bull Connor and several police officers came to the jail and said, "If you promise you will not use means of public transportation for leaving the city, we will let you go." We refused. So they brought the police escort cars and literally picked us up and put us in them. They drove us back to the Tennessee-Alabama state line, where they let us out.

We went around searching for some black home in the nearest community so that when we called the Nashville student movement office, they'd know where to find us. Across the tracks, we found a home that belonged to an old man and woman. They had heard about the freedom ride, and they were very frightened and nervous about the whole thing. But the man went from store to store to buy food for us.

Someone from the Nashville office came and took us to Birmingham. By this time others joined us, so there were twenty-one of us on a bus when it started off to Montgomery. Only freedom riders were on board. The regular passengers were afraid to ride. A plane flew overhead, and every 15 miles or so you would see a state trooper car. We were all very quiet. Many people went to sleep.

In previous years I had traveled through Montgomery on my way to the seminary. So I knew the city. But this day there was just nothing in Montgomery as we came in. We didn't see a porter, didn't see any taxicabs. It was just eerie. As we stepped off the bus, the press came around. In a matter of seconds, white people came running from all over the place, hundreds of them, men and women and children, all organized by the Klan. They had stones, baseball bats, pipes, everything. And they beat the reporters down. When they finished with them, they turned on us. I was hit on the head and was unconscious forty-five minutes. I was taken to have stitches in my head. Then I went into hiding. We all did. Because even before we had left Birmingham, an Alabama circuit judge had issued an injunction saying whites and blacks couldn't ride together on the bus or the train or planes. We had violated that injunction, so the state officials were looking for us.

On Sunday night we all got together for a mass meeting in Dr. Abernathy's church. We didn't sit with the congregation. We went in the choir stand, hoping people would think we were singers, not freedom riders. There was a bandage on my head. It was shaped like a cross.

Dr. King had been in Atlanta, but he flew in to speak at the meeting. White people gathered in the park across from the church and marched on it, throwing rocks and stink bombs. It was then that Dr. King went into the basement of the church and called Bobby Kennedy. That's when the city of Montgomery was placed under martial law.

Montgomery

Alabama's Governor John Malcolm Patterson, calling Lewis and his fellow freedom riders "mobsters" and "trained agitators," said, "They have tried to change Southern traditions and ordinances on the streets instead of in the courts. The people of Alabama are peaceable. We have a right to expect visitors to come here and obey our laws."

The freedom riders spent that night in the church, and at five o'clock Monday morning they were taken to the home of a local black druggist. They stayed there until Wednesday, when, joined by hundreds of students and young ministers from both the South and the North, they resumed the ride from Montgomery to Jackson. Before Lewis left, he told reporters: "Each time I participate in a demonstration, I expect the worst. I love life. I don't want to die. But at the same time, if I must, this is the price I have to pay."

John Lewis

We got to Jackson, and 400 of us were arrested. We overfilled the city and county jails. About two o'clock one morning they put 45 of us, black and white, into a big van truck and took us to Parchman, the state maximum security penitentiary. We were very orderly, very peaceful. Nobody was saying a word. We walked into the prison, and they asked us to take off all of our clothes. They left us that way for about an hour while a guard stood with his gun pointed at us. Then, after being assigned to segregated cells, we were ordered to take showers—a guard still there with a gun. It was the most dehumanizing experience you could imagine.

Later they gave us Mississippi penitentiary underwear, shorts and a T-shirt. No shoes. That's what we wore for our whole stay there, forty days in most cases. Only things we had in the cell were bunks and a toilet. No face bowl. Oh, they did bring a Bible around. I didn't turn a page of it—I just wasn't in the mood.

Odyssey

In 1963, Lewis was elected chairman of SNCC, moved to Atlanta, and spent most of the summer preparing for the August 28 March on Washington, the largest civil rights demonstration in history. More than 200,000 Americans gathered before the Lincoln Memorial that hot summer's day, when King's "I Have a Dream" speech forecast a nation living up to the promise of all men being created equal. John Lewis also spoke.

John Lewis

In our very first meeting with John Kennedy, a week after I was elected chairman of SNCC, he told us he thought the march was a bad idea. He said it couldn't be controlled. A. Philip Randolph replied, "Mr. President, there will be a march. The question is, what type or form the march will take." Later when the administration saw that it was going to happen, they came in, got behind it. And the march became, in a sense, a part of the order of the day for Washington.

It was held on a Wednesday, and that Tuesday we all had to make advance copies of our speeches available to the press and to different sponsoring groups, the Catholic Church, the Protestant and Jewish churches, labor, etc. Late that night Bay Rustin, deputy director of the march, phoned me to come to a meeting to discuss my speech. He had received word that Washington's Archbishop Patrick O'Boyle, who was to give the invocation at the march, refused to appear unless I changed certain passages in my speech which he claimed were "inflammatory."

What seemed to concern him most was where I said, "The time may come when we were not going to confine our marching just on

Washington but we might be forced to march through the South, through the heart of Dixie the way Sherman did, pursuing our own policy and burn Jim Crow to the ground, nonviolently, splitting the South into thousand of pieces and putting it back together in the image of democracy."

Then, a number of the march's leaders were also upset with my comments on the administration's proposed civil rights bill. In my original text, I called it "too little and too late," saying we could not support it. Furthermore, based on our commitment to one man, one vote, I felt the clause in the bill saying only those with a sixth-grade education should be considered literate enough to register was unjust. If a state denied an individual a decent education, it could not also deprive him of the right to vote just because he didn't have it.

It was somewhat of a bitter meeting because other SNCC people heard about the objections and were questioning, as was I, what right had the archbishop, or Walter Reuther, or Roy Wilkins to speak for us. It was my feeling that these statements represented the interests of the people we were working with. For at that time we were, more than any other organization in the country, closer to, and more involved with, indigenous groups in some of the roughest places in the South.

But in the end, because, as Mr. Randolph said, "we have come this far together," I modified my speech.

After the march, I did a lot of speaking and fund raising around the country. I also had to represent SNCC at meetings with other civil rights groups. Our staff at one time was 250 people, and it was a full-time job.

In early 1964 we organized the Mississippi Freedom Democratic Party with a slate of black and white candidates. Its aim was to get seats in the National Democratic Convention that year. You had a situation in Mississippi where more than 450,000 black people were of voting age and only about 25,000 were registered. The white power structure in the state used all types of tactics, methods and means to keep people from registering. And they had the literacy tests, too. At the convention all the Democrats gave us was two "honorary" seats as guests of the convention.

People who had worked so hard on the job, given so much of themselves trying to get the people seated, became very, very bitter as they saw the essence of how the whole American political system worked. To them, what happened in Atlantic City was a slap in the face, not just for SNCC, but for the whole movement. One of those who felt that way was Stokely Carmichael.

In the latter part of 1964 and early 1965 SNCC's big push was in Selma, the center of Alabama's black belt. When my friend Bernard Lafayette and his wife had started a very small campaign to get people to register a year before, he was beaten up by whites. And he received very little support from the black community. Blacks were literally afraid to do anything. The city was strictly segregated, and out of its population of 30,000, over half were black, but only 300 of them were registered.

We were convinced that in a place like Selma we could put into action the whole idea of one man, one vote. On October 8, 1964, we held our first Freedom Day, had about 800 people just standing in line all day at the Dallas County Courthouse trying to register. Sheriff James Clark wouldn't even let people get food or water. And at the end of the day only five people had gotten in to register. Similar demonstrations continued.

As an organization SNCC went back into Selma full force, along with SCLC and Dr. King, in January, 1965. Dr. King had kept saying that the goal was to get Selma to write a Voting Rights Act of 1965 as Birmingham had written the Civil Rights Act of 1964. In Selma we had to really pull out everything that we had, to stay there until the country was aroused and the conscience of White America was pricked.

I remember the first time Dr. King came into Selma. It was January 18, 1965, and we went down on a mass march, hundreds of people, to the courthouse and stood in a very orderly fashion. Sheriff Clark met us, and he said to me: "John Lewis, you are nothing but an agitator. You're the lowest form of humanity."

A few minutes later we had all been arrested. We were released on our own recognizance, but in two or three days, we were back in jail again. It was a series of continual demonstrations with groups going down, standing in line trying to register, and getting arrested. This kept going on, and then hundreds of elementary and high school students, along with their teachers, got involved in the protests. We spread out into other towns and counties around Selma, to the most remote rural areas, knocking on doors, getting sharecroppers who had been scared to come into the city to register. They didn't know how the boss would react, whether they would be forced to leave the farms if they did. But in the end they made up their minds and they came. I felt we owed them something.

That is one of the main reasons why I supported the march from Selma to Montgomery. The people in the protests wanted to march. I also felt that it would be an education process to get the black people along U.S. Highway 80 involved. The idea of the march was suggested out of the clear blue by James Bevel, who was by then on the staff of SCLC. Other people started saying we should march. And SCLC scheduled it for Sunday, the seventh of March.

That morning, I met with Bevel, Andy Young and Hosea Williams —all from SCLC—at the Brown Chapel Church to discuss the final plans for the march that afternoon. Dr. King was in Atlanta. Several reasons were given. One, that he had received a call from Attorney General Katzenbach about a report that Dr. King would be assassinated if he went to Selma. Another was that he had to preach that Sunday in his own church. All I know is that I talked to him that Saturday, and as of then, he planned to be in Selma Sunday.

So the three SCLC people drew sticks to see who would lead the march, and it fell to Hosea's lot. Then they asked me to march with him. And I just felt that I should. You know what happened.

I think that the civil rights movement was at its finest hour in Selma, its best day in terms of a particular movement, a particular period. At Selma you had a large segment of the American population aroused, moving toward doing something good and progressive. You got almost the total religious community of America mobilized there, concerned with the bodies. The national climate was conducive to change. Out of what happened in Selma we got a Voting Rights Act.

Selma was the climax of a great deal of work by a great many people for many years. The signing of the act was perhaps the last, large, tangible result of the civil rights movement.

Something was born in Selma, but something died there also.

After that, we just got lost. The country became carried away, so involved, with the war in Vietnam, until so quickly Selma became something of the past. . . .

Odyssey

The last time that Miriam and I talked with Lewis, Selma was five years in the past. During that period in history, the black revolution he had come to symbolize had altered the course, gone off in different directions, sometimes abruptly and violently.

In May, 1966, Lewis was defeated by Stokely Carmichael for the SNCC chairmanship. Two months later Lewis resigned from SNCC. When he talked about leaving, it was without bitterness—only sadness, at the new antiwhite path it had chosen for itself. "I felt I could no longer relate to a good part of SNCC," Lewis said. "What Stokely espoused at that time didn't appear to me to be in keeping with the old SNCC, its oneness and unity, or with the philosophy and discipline of nonviolence. I had to be true to myself."

We wondered if all those years with the student movement had been worth it.

John Lewis

People today keep asking me if I think we pricked the conscience of White America. I answer, "Oh, yes, very definitely." I often think that a great deal of us tend to forget contemporary history, just shove it aside. But from 1955 to 1965 a nonviolent revolution did take place in this country, particularly in the South. It was *not* just breaking down the physical barriers. In some parts of the South during that period there was a whole change of attitudes on the part of both whites and blacks. For the first time, black people were standing up, going places where they had never been before, with a sense of dignity and a sense of pride.

I'm not sure I could do it all again. I feel I have passed this way before. Why should I go through this again? I've been involved all these many years—maybe it was just four or five, six or ten—but it seems like a lifetime. You know, I admired and loved Martin Luther King. I saw real hopes that the war was going to be solved and that he would emerge as much more of a leader. I thought his greatness was yet to come and that it would be on the international scene.

Then after his assassination, I said, "Well, we still have Robert Kennedy." I wasn't thinking so much of the movement, but of the world. I'd spent almost three months in Africa in the fall of 1964. And I was in Eastern Europe a bit. I saw the popularity of Robert Kennedy, how people loved him, especially the young. I kept saying to myself, "If we can get him elected President [and I disagreed with him on certain things] he is the one guy who can bring people together."

When he made his announcement for the Presidency, and with what was happening in this country because of the war, I took leave of absence from the Southern Regional Council and went out and campaigned with him.

Since his assassination, I've just sort of been wondering, I really have, that maybe it's bad to identify with causes or a movement, to have so much faith and trust in a particular person. Because it is very hurting when they take him away, just like that.

But all along it has been my conviction that the struggle was not to be short or temporary. I knew it would be long, hard and continuous. If you lost one battle, you just had to try again.

The Quiet Challenger

Odyssey

Gandhi loved a hymn which in part goes:

> I do not ask to see the distant scene,
> One step's enough for me. . . .

And when Andrew Young, as a nineteen-year-old senior in college trying to make sense of existence, first heard the words, it was with the sudden exaltation of discovery, pointing a direction never to be lost. "I knew I had to be living for something," he said. "I just accepted that, not knowing what I had been put here to do. But I figured that as long as I know the next step or the one I'm supposed to be taking now, I'm not worried about what I'll do next year or the year after that."

Ecclesiastes talks of "eternity in the heart," and at thirty-eight, Andrew Young, ordained minister, SCLC's executive vice-president, a leading figure in the nonviolent movement, had found it. There is about him an almost hypnotic calm. Nothing hurried, nothing worried. He has the grace of a man secure in himself. For SCLC, he has been both strategist and activist. In his quiet way, Young throughout the 1960's helped the movement mount its greatest challenges to racism—amid the dogs at Birmingham, the violence at Selma, the hostilities in Harlem, and the rock-throwing obscenities of Chicago's Gage Park. He was with King at Memphis. And when we first met Young, he was in Charleston, leading SCLC's fight on behalf of the striking hospital workers.

He is a lightish brown in color, medium height, no fat. He wears clothes with style, whether blue denims, as when we saw him in Charleston, or gray, Edwardian-cut suit, as when we were with him later at his SCLC office in Atlanta. On its walls was a graffito: "God

Is Not Dead—He's Bread!" A poster proclaimed: "They say the poor have it hard; well, the hardest thing they have is us." His office is a melange of pop art, slashes of color, signs, pictures, slogans, prayers, a distillation of confrontation—and of hope.

While Young believes in integration, he understands blacks who would polarize the races. "I see it as a kind of six- to eighteen-month phenomenon," he explained. "Most blacks always wanted to be white, and when they suddenly realize that that is not the answer to all their problems, they get mad with themselves. Then they get to be what I call superblack. It just takes some time to get over this, to go back to normal, where you can appreciate yourself and not have to knock anybody else."

Andrew Young

My childhood was not bitter. My upbringing was economically secure. I lived in a neighborhood in New Orleans where we probably were the only blacks. People for the most part were lower-working-class whites. In that environment, we were middle-class. The only basketball goal, for example, was in our backyard. That gave a kind of equality. At the same time I was kind of living in two worlds.

I was bused to a segregated school, and in it I had all the typical ghetto problems. My identity crisis came because I was in a Creole society in that part of New Orleans where most Negroes were *very* fair-skinned. They looked upon me as being quite dark. At school, I had to come to grips with that early by competing in athletics and by establishing that I was as smart—or smarter. Then it was a struggle. But now I think of it as a blessing. I was never protected or sheltered, and I took all of it in stride. There was, for example, nothing romantic about narcotics for us because they were around even in grammar school. You came to know that a junkie was just someone sick. There was no temptation to that because in our home and church we got a sense of right and wrong about everything.

I think my parents sent me to college on the American myth that the purpose of life is to make money, and going to school was good because it gave you an opportunity to make more of it. Although they may have felt that, they didn't live that way. My daddy was a dentist who never bothered to collect from patients if they were poor. He did half his work on neighborhood kids for free. That was in a time when Negro professionals were driving Cadillacs and trying to outdo each other with mansions. He never was interested in that, and he never drank or got caught in the middle-class social life. And he always went to church.

Odyssey

His father, Dr. Andrew Young, wanted us to share some strawberry ice cream when we came to New Orleans to visit him and his wife in their modest, but attractive, three-bedroom house. He laughed a little when we said it was hard to believe he had been born, as he said, in 1896. "Well," he answered, "I'm agreeable to your thinking that." His wife is ten years younger, a onetime schoolteacher, who maintains her contact with young people and the community through the church. She is gray-haired, slender, and somewhat more volatile than her husband.

The Youngs remembered their son Andrew as precocious. "Always asking questions," his mother said. "We would go out driving, and we would pass through the city park. There would be white children playing there, and Andy would ask, 'Why can't we be there? Aren't we as good as they are?' And where we were living then, some of our white neighbors were very prejudiced. There was an Irish boy that Andy used to play with. Then one day this boy's aunt promised Andy a quarter if he wouldn't play with her nephew anymore. Andy refused it. But when he came home and asked us about this, we had to tell him that these people were mean, although all white people were not that way."

Andrew Young

At fifteen I went to college in New Orleans, but in my sophomore year I transferred to Howard University in Washington. I don't think I was particularly interested in the black issue, certainly not as an active participant. Nobody was. My college years were in the Joe McCarthy era. I went to class, got caught up in the fraternities, was on the track and swimming teams. But I never really thought about what manhood was, what life was all about.

Then a very mundane thing happened to me. It was in the beginning of my senior year, when everybody was giving fraternity pins and talking about getting married. I gave mine. This made me realize, more than anything else, that I was no longer playing around. And while I didn't marry the girl, I had to think some things through. My daddy wanted me to be a dentist. I knew I didn't want to do that. But I just hadn't been pushed to see what I was about.

So for the rest of the year, I didn't date, didn't do anything except go through a stack of books. I sort of locked myself in my room, read everything I wanted to, and thought what I wanted to. And things began to awaken for me.

There were some people who got to me, too. There was Nicholas Hood, a young black guy, just out of Yale Divinity School, who'd become pastor of our church in New Orleans. He seemed very relevant. Then I met a young white guy, a missionary, who was taking his whole family to Africa in order to do something for black people there. This really bugged me. I wondered, "Why should he be more concerned about black people in Africa than I am?"

And I began thinking about the church, which is sort of ironic. Years before, when somebody in Sunday school had told me I wasn't supposed to question how Elijah could get to heaven on a flaming chariot, I just walked out. Never went back. But that last year at Howard I came to see that nobody except the church was trying to answer some of the basic questions I had about life. In my searching I found Gandhi. I read all the books you could get in this country about him and about nonviolence. I got hooked on his favorite hymn, not being bothered by not knowing all the ultimate answers in life. It was enough that I knew one step would lead to another. And so I just kept going.

From Howard I went to the Hartford Theological Seminary in Connecticut and from there to Georgia to take over as pastor of a little rural church in Thomasville for three years. Everybody, though, wants to try his wings with the Establishment, and I did that for the next four years, doing youth work with the National Council of Churches in New York. But it wasn't for me. I wanted to go back South. Since I wasn't a student, I didn't belong in the sit-ins. But in 1960 I was interested in the plans for SCLC's literacy project, training community leaders throughout the South to teach reading and writing to their neighbors. This was one way of helping people to qualify for registering to vote.

If you could teach people who would then be able to read about Negro history, about politics, about the kinds of things that would open their minds to new things, you'd have the basis for political groundwork. I asked my denomination, the United Church of Christ, whether they would agree to be the funnel for the money for the work. They said they would—if I directed the work. So I came back South again, still on the church's payroll. But I began to take on more and more duties with the movement, and finally, I went full time with SCLC.

Odyssey

Martin Luther King once wrote that in the black revolution, "The storm clouds did not release a 'gentle rain from Heaven'—but a whirlwind."

Andrew Young

Between 1955 and 1964 the movement was a struggle for social justice. We saw integration as the means of achieving that. Then it became a struggle for political justice, with George Wallace the symbol of that. After we had been in Birmingham, he was making the kind of venomous statements that almost gave the Ku Klux Klan a license to kill. The bombing of the church, killing those little girls in Birmingham, we attributed almost directly to Wallace racism. And we said to blacks, "You are not going to get permanent change in the South until you get politicians who will respect you and won't fan up the fears and anxieties of the rest of the community against you." We used Selma to dramatize that. Since then there has been turmoil. And more and more, the basic issues have turned on the economic challenges to the old order.

A strike, for example, is a nonviolent challenge. The hospital workers in Charleston proved that they weren't going to work unless they received respect and decent wages. By walking off their jobs in Charleston, they let everybody know there is a new Negro. Yet one of the paradoxes of nonviolence, however, is that while you don't deliberately provoke violence, you have to be willing to hold your ground in the face of it. In Charleston we marched up to the National Guard as they put on their gas masks and lowered their bayonets. We stood there for a while, then broke out singing and went away. There was no violence.

In my thinking, violence is irrelevant to the struggle today. The idea that it could make for a social change was only true as long as this country could experience a crisis in conscience, when people could still feel disgust at seeing the dogs and fire hoses put on human beings. But now this nation has absorbed and accepted such a level of violence—witness Vietnam—that we just seem immune. When the headlines tell of 730 killed in a single week, what difference does one more dead in Mississippi make? So anybody who embraces violence believing change will automatically follow is kind of naïve.

When we first started our work, people didn't generally identify segregation as the root of our problems, but after the 1954 Supreme Court decision outlawing segregation in the schools, the major newspapers, the liberal thought in America, spelled it out on what it was like and why it was bad. We in the South could know what that was. Not until the Kerner Commission in 1968, however, did you begin to get any kind of analysis of the big cities in the North. And it might be another five or ten years before the general public begins to understand the race situation.

In this country, the pattern of city government was developed for units of from 25,000 to 100,000. You have a constitution designed for one European ethnic group. Thirteen states, population of about 4,000,000, when it was ratified. Now, the structures of that constitution and that pattern of city government are being strained by the population explosion and technological change. You would probably be in trouble in the cities, even if there were no Negroes, just by virtue of the social changes.

Take Watts. You look at it as a struggle between the police and the Negro community. But the only reason those guys were out there on those corners—and hostile—was that there was no transportation service to take them into where the work was. All the things that should have been done in the 1950's—and we had the skills to build them in preparing our megalopolitan areas for the population immigration—weren't. The people hurt most by these structural inadequacies are the people who are on the fringe. It might have been whites, but as it turned out, blacks were there. So they are the ones hollering. Whites say, "Why isn't the Negro satisfied? What does he want?" They blame us, while we are only the symptoms of the problem. We say a slum is a result of a kind of domestic colonialism, where all the resources are drained out and nothing is drained in.

This situation has been masked in the North, because its cities have been so completely segregated geographically. Most black people don't know any whites, except on a formal basis—like the police. As a result, you have got a kind of neurotic black militancy. By and large, the Negroes have been cut off from their roots and caught up in this American consumer culture. On the other side, you have an alienated, lost white population, immigrants from Poland, Lithuania, Ireland, Italy, that never had any contact with blacks. Everybody becomes scared of everybody. Separation breeds distrust, hostility, suspicion. We met worse violence in Gage Park and Marquette Park in Chicago than we did in most Southern places.

I remember when SCLC was in St. Augustine, Florida, working on integrating public accommodations We were at a motel lounge. When we jumped into the pool, the guy who ran the place tried to throw acid on us. Yet one week later, when President Johnson signed the civil rights bill, we went back and the guy was totally changed. Seemed to me he was *relieved*. It was as though a terrible weight had been lifted—the weight of guilt. The white South has in some sense been Christian and I think many whites could never internally reconcile what they were doing with what they knew to be right. Once the law gave them an out, they bent over backwards to be nice, so much that I would rather go into Jackson, Mississippi, trying to get a hotel room without a reservation than I would in New York City.

Odyssey

We noticed that even though Young is a minister—and once looked to the church for direction—he made very few references to it.

Andrew Young

I gave up on the organized church as a leading force a long time ago. Basically, it has been a means of worshiping in the past, reciting the glories of what God *has* done, never making even an attempt to say what He *is* doing. I think of Jim Forman and his Black Manifesto.* And I imagine this is how it must have been with Amos and the priests and Levites of his day—a shaggy-headed prophet, very crude, didn't care about the worship and sacrifices and burnt offerings, just ranting and raving against the Establishment. The

---

* Forman interrupted Sunday services at New York City's Riverside Church in 1969 with a demand that white churches pay blacks $3 billion in "reparations" for racial injustices.

churches rejected Amos—as they did Forman. Never on the basis of what Forman was saying. They don't deny Riverside Church should feed the poor or argue it doesn't have tie-ins with South Africa. They say he shouldn't have disrupted the worship, just as was said about Amos.

As an institution, the church just can't seem to keep up to date. Somehow, we are unable to make the structure of local congregations relevant. That's why SCLC was made up of preachers. We got outside the church in order to perform that which it should be doing. Now we look upon it with nostalgia. When we get ready to retire, we'll go back to preaching every Sunday. We think of the church as kind of a rest home.

Odyssey

Some whites saw the manifesto as an indication of increasing racial polarization. But Young didn't believe whites and blacks were growing farther apart in the South.

Andrew Young

In Atlanta, blacks supported a poor white woman for election to the Board of Education. And she won. When SCLC had its march protesting the killings of blacks in Augusta, Georgia, and at Jackson State College in Mississippi, blacks and whites were in the line. Somebody carried a sign saying WELL, YOU FINALLY BROUGHT US TOGETHER, DICK.

What is happening in the South is that poor people, black and white, have become aware that they are in the same boat. The first strike SCLC got into here was with a group of firemen, most of them white. Nobody else would work with them. I went out, spoke with them, set up some meetings for them with Dr. King, then arranged for them to get with the aldermen. We did this because we saw it as basically a human struggle of poor people.

At another time, when black and white workers striking the Atlanta Sanitation Department had a meeting, some black nationalist students came in to say they'd help the blacks—but wanted to throw out the whites. Well, you know, we had to stop the black workers from beating up the students. The black workers were just infuriated by this kind of irrelevant ideology. I'm not saying there was any great love, blacks for whites or the reverse, but all of them knew that their survival was in unity. People may still be racists, but when you point out how much their prejudices are costing them, they usually give up in favor of the economic advantages. People enjoy their prejudices, but they don't want to pay for them.

Odyssey

In the spring of 1970 Young took a leave of absence from SCLC to go into politics, contending for the Democratic nomination to oppose Fletcher Thompson, Atlanta's white Republican Congressman.

Andrew Young

I see the potential for a new South. I know it is there, even though the South, perhaps more than the nation, has been victimized by the politics of assassination and accident. Ellis Arnall would have been governor of Georgia again but for accidents. In Alabama Wallace's nearest competitor in his first race was a young businessman, killed in an accident. Shep Morrison, the New Orleans mayor, was really a new breed of politician, but he was killed in Mexico. There was a whole generation of young political leadership who should be moving into position and power in the South now, except something *not* foreseen happened to all of them. And we were left with the Wallaces and the Maddoxes.

Nationally, we have been left with a leadership vacuum because of the assassinations of Dr. King, the Kennedys, and many others. But I think that the followers of those leaders have been growing steadily in the South and are looking for effective ways to come together. The black vote is awakening, being politicized, and that in turn is giving a new rallying point to the existing white liberal vote that has always been much stronger in the South than anybody gave it credit for. It was my feeling that this kind of coalition is possible and can be a very real stumbling block to the Nixon administration's Southern Strategy. That is what really hooked me into this.

I had never thought about going to Congress, but I worked in a dozen or more campaigns for other people. There is no better vehicle for changing attitudes, dealing with questions, educating a community. I think a lot of whites just don't know what is going on because many of their leaders don't want to run the risk of alienating them. They just charm and soothe them, don't take on the hard issues. But Robert Kennedy did. He didn't mind going to the University of Georgia or the universities of Mississippi and Alabama and talking about desegregation. I think people in the South respect you for disagreeing with them, not hedging and stating your position as logically as possible. So I regard the election I'm in* as a means of taking on gut issues, organizing people to see that quality, integrated education is the only kind of education that's worth having in this time. Or talking out about the danger in the Nixon's administration's concerted effort to emphasize the military as a consolidation of power on the right.

When you look at it, everything that is wrong with this country goes back to the imbalance of the democratic process in the southeastern states. And that's what we are at war with in a nonviolent way— against that coalition of rural, racist, militaristic forces. We said it in SCLC a long time ago, and we say it now: If we blacks can gain the right of the ballot, we can redeem the soul of America.

* After winning the Democratic nomination in a runoff with a white man, Young lost the November election to the incumbent Republican. He has since left SCLC to be a consultant on community relations.

The Gut Fighter

Howard Moore

I remember right up there at the Loew's Grand Theater here in Atlanta. It was December, 1939, and I was six years old. My aunt and I were standing outside watching this fantastic parade like I had never seen before. It was the premiere of *Gone with the Wind*. Being an impressionable kid, when the other people left the street and began to converge on the theater, I asked my aunt, "Why can't we go in there, too?" And she said, "Well, you just can't, you just can't. And—shut up!" Then she pulled me on down the street.

The law said I couldn't go into that theater. That law is gone now, off the books. This certainly removes some of the more odious or grossest forms of racism from my daily life. But is it sufficient to liberate me? *No, it isn't.*

Odyssey

In 1970, on a bright spring afternoon in Atlanta, we visited Howard Moore, Jr., attorney. We were to meet him in his office on the eleventh floor of the Citizens Trust Company Bank Building. We were unprepared for the man we encountered. We knew his reputation as an extremely able lawyer and gut fighter, who since 1962 has waged countless legal battles on behalf of SNCC. Among his clients: Brother-in-law Georgia State Representative Julian Bond and H. Rap Brown.

Moore's secretary led us into his simply furnished modern office, explaining he would be with us momentarily. Miriam was looking at his diplomas and pictures, including photographs of Muhammad Ali (Cassius Clay), W. E. B. DuBois, and Bond, the last bearing the inscription: "Counsel Moore, Fight on!" She had stopped to admire a picture of a pretty little girl, Moore's oldest daughter, Grace, age six, when in he strode. For some reason we expected he would be very black, short, stout, and cigar-smoking. We were wrong.

Noting Miriam standing before the picture of his daughter, Moore half joked, "She's beautiful—just like I am."

Well, he certainly was an impressive man, slim, about six feet two. His long angular face framed by a pointed beard and a somewhat out-of-control Afro which conveyed the impression of a head shaped like an inverted pyramid. Moore's whole bearing was pharaonic. His voice had a bell-like quality, muted by a slight Southern accent. While he could be joyous and amusing, as an advocate he was tough and deadly serious. We asked him if he thought the law an effective tool for social change. His answer was Yes—but with some reservations.

"The law has bent, but we, as black people, need it to break. In other words, there has to be a revolution, to break with this shit—the racist, capitalistic structure—on a worldwide basis and by any means necessary. The whole history of struggle since 1896, the year of *Plessy v. Ferguson** where white racism matured and established a definite *modus vivendi* by making Black America an alien nation inside of a nation, has been one of the law bending ever so slowly. I feel there is going to be more violence, of a sporadic and somewhat isolated and uncoordinated nature, for a good period of time."

Moore was born and reared in Atlanta by his mother, a practical nurse. His father, a tailor, had died when Moore was ten years old. Light of skin, Moore says, with some feeling, "I've always been black! I was taught to love myself by my parents and the people in my community, to have respect, to work hard, and to learn. I have never wanted to be white in my life. And I've been mad many times because I'm light. I remember a number of occasions, especially after I got to law school, when I'd go into a cafeteria and say, 'Give me a cup of coffee, black.' They would always ask you, 'With sugar and cream?' And I wanted to say to them, 'No, black like me, you motherfucker.' "

Howard Moore

I had what James Baldwin called "a full and complete life in my black school." It was a segregated one, but in my twelve years

* The U.S. Supreme Court decision approving "separate but equal" facilities.

there I didn't think it was inferior. We had some very able teachers who loved us dearly. There was no reason I couldn't run for office and be elected or be the editor of our school paper. And I did those kinds of things. I didn't have to say, "Well, will they vote for me in spite of my color?" They might not have voted for me because I was skinny or ugly or had a bad personality. But there never was a question of being passed over because I was black. I had a hell of a good time in school—I really enjoyed it. I didn't go around feeling sorry for myself or for my people. I guess I accepted things separated as a fact of life.

I tell you the kind of segregation that did bother me was in public accommodations, in restaurants and places like that. Being downtown and not able to pee. Or getting on the streetcar and having to sit at the back. That hurt the hell out of me. But I never felt that about my school. Don't get me wrong. I'm not advocating segregated schools. I don't want no segregation, period! It's a vestige of white racism. I may not want to be with white people, but I don't want them to segregate me, to have the power to force me into a particular school. Now, I prefer a black school, one that black people create, dominate and control. And that's a part of this revolutionary struggle that we are going to have to go into.

Odyssey

From the time Moore was very young he knew he was going to Morehouse College. "My family just programmed me to go there," he said. "My aunt was an educated woman and had gone to Atlanta University. My father had gone to Atlanta University high school and for about two years to what was then Atlanta University College. They were very much impressed with Morehouse. And that is the only school I ever remember hearing any discussions about." While in college, Moore decided to become a lawyer.

Howard Moore

It was in the summer of 1951 or 1952. I'd go hear Thurgood Marshall speak over here at the City Auditorium. I also used to see him going into a Jewish deli down on Auburn and Butler streets, where a bunch of us used to hang out. Thurgood would be visiting Colonel A. T. Walden, now deceased, an old-line lawyer who was admitted to practice in Bibb County, Georgia, in 1911, but was not allowed to go in a courtroom. Actually, the clerk would meet him in the hall and take his papers in to the judge, and sometimes the clerk would be illiterate and Colonel Walden would have to read them to him. Anyway, Thurgood seemed to be a rather human, ordinary kind of person. Most of the people who were educated that I knew were really righteous kind of people, didn't drink, didn't smoke, didn't run around with women or anything like that. I'm not saying Thurgood did all that—but, at least, I believed he did some of it. And I could identify with him.

After I heard him speak one time, I went home and told my mother, "Mama, I think I'm going to law school." She said, "Howard, what does it take to go to law school?" I said, "I don't know." And she said: "Why don't you go and ask the dean at Morehouse about it?" So the next day I went to see him, and the first thing he told me was that I had to pull up on my record. It's a good thing I had some determination because, you know, that kind of negative response would otherwise have frightened me away. But I pulled up on my record rather well.

I felt that law would be one way of living an intellectual life, reading, writing, and struggling. It also would allow me to be involved in social issues. And it was a vocation. I couldn't expect, in 1954, when I would be graduating from college, to go to work for, say, IBM or RCA. We could teach school or preach, be a doctor or a lawyer or . . . wait tables.

And as I understood the law then, it was an unbroken string of successes by the NAACP Legal Defense Fund, with Thurgood Marshall and Charlie Houston principally in the forefront. You'd hear of cases being won, but these things would be very distant. Up to 1954 and *Brown v. the Board of Education,** what chance did the black kid in the South see in his life through the law? None, whatsoever.

I remember the Monday when the school case got decided, and it was the first time I had ever seen white reporters out at Morehouse. They descended like flies on sugar, interviewed a lot of people, but not me. Then, when I was just walking down the street to go home, I was stopped by a reporter for a black paper. The guy knew me, and I had to give some response. I really hadn't gotten my thoughts together and just spoke off the top of my head. I told him that the deci-

* The 1954 U.S. Supreme Court decision outlawing segregation in public schools.

sion was "encouraging, but long overdue." But that now "the real struggle would begin, political and economic, and lead to subterfuge to avoid the decision."

Later, speakers came down to college and talked about *Brown*. And we had this one professor who involved many of us in his class by having us do a bibliography of all the books in the library dealing with race and with the legal question. At that time, we felt very much a part of the decision. It's ironic because *Brown* hasn't come to fruition yet in terms of enforcement.

Odyssey

Moore went off to Boston University law school. He chose it because, he explained, "it was taking in black people when most law schools weren't. In addition, I thought it would be a good place to go because I'd be exposed to the kinds of cultural contacts I had been deprived of in Atlanta." The city of Boston didn't disappoint him.

Howard Moore

To tell you the truth, I didn't like law school too much. But I stuck it out because I was always taught that when you start something, you finish it. And I didn't enter it to quit. Plus it wasn't very difficult. I spent most of my time doing nonlegal things, basically reading, going to plays, movies, particularly foreign ones. I felt that while I was there, I should participate in a cultural liberation. The one thing that I had to do was to live as fully an integrated life as I could because that was the thing I knew nothing about. And that's exactly what I did. During that time I had all the integration I'll probably need for the rest of my life.

I got out of law school, passed the Massachusetts bar, but it was kind of rough because nobody in Boston would hire me. I wanted to stay up North for about two years to get some experience practicing there because a lot of people had told me the level of professionalism was much higher than what it is in the South. Until I got a job, I supported myself by doing a little part-time work in a department store and playing poker.

One good thing about that period was that it made me understand the feeling of being unemployed, to be in a distant city with no job. I mean it is really a very, very hurting feeling. Everything seems so irrelevant to you because you have no wherewithal. Once, however, you are unemployed and go through that whole change, you then are emancipated from needing money, being dependent on it and on material comfort, because you know that you can't go any lower.

I finally got a job, and it was kind of funny. I was wandering around the Museum of Fine Arts, and this black lawyer who knew me came over and asked if I'd like to work for Federal Judge Charles Wyzanski.* I told the guy that I didn't have anything against that particular judge, and that, yeah, I'd consider it. And he said for me to come to his office. I did and he showed me how to do a résumé. He then took it to the judge. Apparently the judge wasn't around when he got there. This friend called me and said that the judge was away, would be gone for six or seven weeks, and that I would hear something from the judge when he got back.

So I said, "The same old bullshit! They ain't hiring no niggers." And I forgot about it.

Then one Tuesday about 11:20 A.M., early February, 1961, my phone rang. I usually answered the phone during that time, "Yeah, motherfucker." But on this particular morning, it would seem as though, as my mother would say, I had a premonition that something was going to happen. I just picked up the phone, and this very proper voice on the other end said, "I would like to speak to Mr. Howard Moore, Jr." And I said, "This is he, speaking." And the voice at the other end said, "This is Judge Wyzanski." I said, "Oh," and he told me his purpose for calling. He wanted me to come down that day to be interviewed. I had too much pride to go right then. I wouldn't let no son of a bitch know that I needed a job so badly that as soon as he called, I had to run out and be interviewed.

He didn't mean any harm. It was just his way, being efficient and expeditious. I understood that, didn't take any real offense to it. I did compromise, somewhat. I told him I would come any other day that week that he wanted me. He said, "Tomorrow at four thirty." I walked into his office the next day at four twenty-five. He was very gracious. We talked about law school and the intellectual environment there. He had just come back from Africa. I was then reading a lot about Lumumba and the Congo, and we talked about Africa for about an hour and fifteen minutes. It was very enjoyable.

He asked if I would take the job as his law clerk. I said, "Well,

* In April, 1969, Judge Wyzanski was the first federal judge to rule a conscientious objector need not justify his stand on strictly religious grounds.

look, when I came down here, I had made up my mind. My purpose on seeing you was to find out whether you wanted me." That brought a chuckle. He told me he'd let me know in a couple of days. A day later I got a letter telling me to start Monday. I worked for him eighteen months until I got ready to come back South. It was really a beautiful relationship. At that time he was—and is still—very bright, a genius. I don't think he needed me or anybody as a law clerk.

Odyssey

As the time Moore had set for himself to leave the North approached, he took the Georgia bar examinations. "What I figured was, well, if I go back home and take this bar and don't pass it, I don't have to explain that I'm dumb, that I don't know any Georgia law—which was true. I can just say they are prejudiced. What happened, this is September, 1961, I got down here in the General Assembly, the House of Representatives where they give the exam, and I saw all them crackers in there. I said, 'I'll be *damned* if I'm going to let any of them pass if I don't.' So I just sat down and wrote out a first-class paper. The hardest part about the exam was getting up on time and down there to take it. After all, I had gone to a very good law school; my professors were very erudite men. The hypotheticals we had in school were far more difficult than anything on the Georgia bar exam." He passed and in July, 1962, because there was "a real need for lawyers down here," Moore returned to Atlanta. That's when he became involved with SNCC.

Howard Moore

At first I didn't exactly know what SNCC was. It was just a group. I thought it was an arm of the NAACP or something. Then I found out about them and became very impressed. And I just felt that SNCC was the right thing for me to do. So I looked them up and told them I was interested in representing them in sit-in cases and would only charge $1 a case. This was sort of dishonest, because at that time there would be 100 cases a day. Then one thing led to another.

I discovered SNCC was more and more radicalizing me. At first I was sort of a retarding force, plodding along, saying the law says you have to do this, do that. Then I realized everything they did was working out regardless of whether there was a law or not. Like, for example, on the Vietnam War. My position had been that we shouldn't make a statement against it because it would cause a backlash. But the SNCC people went on and published it. John Lewis, who had already made known his own views, read it. SNCC was the first black, so-called civil rights group to speak out. It was really a clarion call to oppose not only the war, but also the draft. This was January 6, 1966.

My brother-in-law Julian Bond, a member of SNCC, had just been elected to the Georgia House of Representatives. When the legislature tried to deny him his seat because of his support of SNCC's anti-war stand, I had to defend him. I got a lot of books about the war, and the more I read, the more I, too, became opposed to it. The Julian Bond case was really one of the most significant and enriching experiences in my life.

Odyssey

Moore won it in the U.S. Supreme Court. Most of his practice continues to involve SNCC. "There are still cases hanging over around the courtry, like Rap's. That's from 1967." H. Rap Brown, Moore added, "doesn't go to court without me." *

After the Bond litigation, the next most meaningful event in the shaping of Howard Moore was his trip to Africa with SNCC's James Forman. It was in Africa, he said, "that I really understood imperialism. I'd, of course, read about it. But to walk down the streets and see the shops and all those goods designed for the white population and compare right there in the same setting the high level of material comfort for them with the low level for blacks is to know imperialism." Moore made it sound as if he were talking about the United States as well.

"Right, right! You see the struggle is indivisible. Conditions are the same. They may have a different setting. But it is all white oppression and exploitation of the black people of this earth. In Africa it is so visible that you can reach out and put your hands on it. You have to come back anti-imperialist. There are a lot of times when you were

* Moore was co-counsel with William Kunstler in the hearings for Brown's scheduled 1970 trial in Cambridge, Maryland. Brown did not appear for trial, and as of this writing his whereabouts are unknown. Moore subsequently became counsel for Angela Davis in her California trial on charges of kidnap, murder and conspiracy.

involved in something, worked closely with it, that you didn't see how it really looked. When you get away and can observe it from a distance, it's like going to the moon and seeing the earth, knowing it glows in outer space somewhat like the moon."

While travel expanded Moore's insights, refined his view of the law, he had the same basic feelings in 1970 that he did in his early years at Morehouse. "Each day, each hour, each minute, they become firmer. Each experience that I have, particularly with my people as I see them abused, my role becomes clearer and clearer."

Howard Moore

My liberation doesn't depend upon the white man's attitude. It depends upon mine. If I have a gun pointed at the white man, I don't give a damn what his attitude is as long as I have the gun, it's loaded, and I have the power to pull the trigger. Liberation of black people means self-reliance. That we make a decision and we enforce it, period! What the white man does is probably a fact or event of history. But what I have to act on is my ability to make change.

My role as a lawyer is to use the law in any way I can to protect my people. It is also my duty *not* to tell my people that the law is the only way. If I were to say, "Look to the courts," that's when I become a counterrevolutionary. There is nothing sacrosanct about courts. They are as full of bullshit and corruption as any other institution in American life. I ain't trying to program nobody into the courts. But on the other hand, if we have to deal with them, I want to be able to do so effectively.

Judges and court personnel down here are usually more courteous than those in the North. However, the courtesy is a substitute for recognizing the humanity in all people. The Southerners know, when it comes to the substance and real heart of the matter, that they are going to do you in because you are black. I think there is a lot of bullshitting in the North. White people there aren't blind. They are pretty well educated, and they know the shit they are running. I can't politicize anybody, tell white people, "Oh, look, this is all so awful and bad." They realize it because they made it that way. You know when you are screwing somebody. In a department store, you're aware that if you sell a suit with a two-piece crotch—not the standard one-piece—it's going to split. Shit! They know what they are doing to us.

Odyssey

I had to tell Howard Moore that the suit sellers had not only done it to blacks—they had done it to me. Just an hour before our meeting, I had bent over—and my pants split in the crotch. Howard Moore received that intelligence with the sober demeanor of one whose worst fears had been confirmed.

Howard Moore

One of the things that really hardened me was back in 1963. We were down in Americus, Georgia, about 140 miles south from here, and the police station was up over the fire station, a little, bitty old place, about the size of this office. And that's where the courtroom was. There were all these crackers sitting around watching as I was raising hell about the First Amendment rights of my client. So one old cracker up against the wall there, said, "Listen to that nigger lawyer from Atlanta giving them hell!"

If you really build a reputation for fighting, you get far more respect than you do from bullshitting and always being willing to compromise, afraid to challenge a man's word, go behind what he says and show him that he is stupid. The law is somewhat like Mao says, it's really a paper tiger. It can't deliver you, can't bring about the transformation of society that is required. Yet you can't ignore it. It has a very real consequence if you see it as a struggle for the use of violence.

The winner of any lawsuit has a right to call upon the state to employ violence to enforce that judgment—whether it is sending the troops to Little Rock or sending them to Oxford, Mississippi. No society however, is going to ultimately say that we'll use violence against ourselves. It's like Stokely raising the question from Camus: "Can a man condemn himself?" The answer, obviously, is No. And you can see now that is one of the reasons the courts are retrenching, and you get the Haynsworth-Carswell phenomena at the top level. That's the lesson of the legal struggle: It is cyclic. You have periods of liberation and reform; then you have periods of retrenchment and reaction. But the center of the circle remains white power, white domination, of the lives of black people.

The phase we are in now is very definitely counterrevolutionary.

Brown v. the Board of Education opened up new vistas of what was possible. It may have led to incorrect lines of struggle. But you had no Martin Luther Kings in the streets of the South before *Brown,* because segregation was not illegal. Then after *Brown,* you get the succession of events of the Montgomery boycott, the sit-ins and freedom rides. All pressing generally the same basic issue at new levels and in new aspects—that is, the elimination of racial separation in public life and places of public intercourse. This was progressive, because once people got there, they demanded other things. They said, "Well, what about poverty?" Before the ink was dry on the Civil Rights Act of 1964, people wanted their social-economic needs met and the political power to make the decisions and policies of government affecting them. And you got the Voting Rights Act of 1965.

Then the movement went into Chicago, and you can say "Goodbye!" White people were not about to give up their power to control the basic resources, the productive apparatus, of this country and the armed might to protect the decisions made about their uses. No matter what, it's still white people calling the shots. It's not liberation. Liberation means the right of black people to make the following choices and make them stick: (1) They may decide they want to become a part of the people of the United States; (2) they may decide to have a separate state or nation in part of the United States; and (3) some of them may decide they would like to go back to Africa or other parts of the world from which they originally came.

But there is not a liberated base in Africa, except, perhaps, for Tanzania. Black people would prefer the system of socialist construction of that country to the shit they have in the United States.

The people of the United States can only get to a people's democracy through a violent struggle. And the black people are the natural leaders of that struggle. For they are the most disadvantaged. And while white people are not going to give up power voluntarily, that doesn't mean that I'm impotent or that black people are.

So you tell me whites have the army, all the troops, the constabulary, the courts, and all of the economic power. Well, the only thing you are saying there is that it is a formidable task. Yet because *it is formidable* doesn't mean that I or black people should shy or shirk the responsibility of discharging the obligation that history has placed upon us. The only way we can reclaim our humanity is to engage this power. It is going to be an awesome, awful ordeal and struggle. But it's got to be. There's no way around it.

Black Women: A Gallery of Portraits

Life in Vine City . . .

Helen Howard

The people in authority, I don't think they know what is going on. And if they don't find out pretty soon—revolution!

When I used to hear people talking like that, I would say, "What the hell! What you talking about?" But now I know. I got involved in this Atlanta housing survey, down here in Vine City, and it was my luck to go into some of the worst houses, and I saw the rubbish the kids was playing in, the clothes they was in, and I would sit there and I couldn't move. The whole world was bearing down on me, and I couldn't override it. I was overwhelmed. You remember all the things you went through, things that had happened to you, and it just hits you: How can people live like this? Sometimes I wish I could call the White House and say, "Let's make an appointment to talk." Just get face to face, and I'd say, "Look, buddy, I feel you are not listening to the right people."

Odyssey

Vine City is a distinct community of 10,000 or so blacks, on the edge of Atlanta's downtown. It has narrow streets, frame houses, broken sidewalks, debris-splattered curbs. And Helen Howard knows it all.

She is short, about five feet five, weighs well over 200 pounds, has big breasts, keeps her gray hair cropped close. She is as quick to tears as to laughter. She wears out a cigarette in nervous puffs. Like a mother, she can be tough or tender, and, on occasion, both.

One afternoon two men were about to fight outside the Vine City Foundation, a ghetto self-help organization she directs. Both men had been working on an all-day cleanup sponsored by the foundation, and they were hot, tired, short-tempered. "I don't know what happened between them," Mrs. Howard said. "But somebody say they was about to fight. There is this man with a knife, biggest one I see in my life, and they say the other man have a gun. I know if we have a killing this day, when we all worked so hard for the cleanup, people on the outside would only think of the killing, not of all the work we done in the community. I run out and got the man with the gun, put my body between him and the other man, dragged him inside, shut the door, and then I sat on him, put my arms around him, held him, and there he was against me, crying. He didn't want to kill that other man, and I pleaded, I talked, did everything I could, and finally it cooled, and there wasn't no trouble."

Helen Howard has given at least seven years of her life to help cool Vine City. From two rickety side-by-side buildings on the ghetto's Magnolia Street, she runs the foundation, which has a nursery school, medical clinic, ceramics workshop, Bible class, scout troops, birth control center and counseling on the headaches of surviving in the slum. The foundation was born because she wanted to fight all the things that are wrong in Vine City. She has little illusion that she is going to win, "but it is just in me to try."

Sitting on a folding chair in the organization's meeting room, the street alive with the noise of passing trucks, the voices echoing from the bare walls, she talked about Vine City.

Helen Howard

There was me and my husband and the two girls and my mother in a duplex house in Vine City. Had three rooms on each side. We lived on one side. You had to go a block to carry the water back in buckets. For washing, you carried your tubs and your clothes up where the water come from a hydrant you turned on. Just a big pipe sitting above the ground, and you would turn the nozzle. Everybody trying to use the same faucet. We was all in such a close, cramped place. Out back, we had three johns, about ten families used them, and you had to line up and wait, and all that. Sometimes it was such a mess!

My mother grew up in a rural area in Florida. I was born in

Smyrna Beach, Florida. When I was a little girl, we used to go to a farm every summer, and there was a well we went to, it was in a kind of building, but it never seemed so bad as in Vine City. We had the freedom to run; we would go into the woods and pick flowers. In Jacksonville, we had a big house, and my mother was home with me every day, and I remember having Christmas trees, and it just seemed like we had more freedom then. I was ten when my father— he was a Pullman porter—got changed to Atlanta and we moved to Vine City. Three years later my parents separated, and that left my mother with the burden of supporting me and my sister. She was a domestic—a maid. She never was evicted from any place, because we always ran before the rent man came. It was just running place to place. I married at sixteen. Wasn't love; I was just escaping, like you run away from the hurricane. My husband was in construction, didn't make a heck of a lot, and I worked. We went to Florida for a while but come back to Atlanta when I was about twenty-five. We just naturally settled in Vine City. It was, like, home. I can remember going to the outside bathrooms, and it was cold, I used to talk to myself. Oh, my God! There must be a better way than this; it's got to be!

I had strong ideas about educating the two girls. I had to work, but I didn't leave them, like a lot of ghetto people. I would work at night while my mother was with the kids, and she would work in the day while I was with them. My husband didn't object to me being so strong for educating the girls, but he really didn't understand. I would do without almost anything to help them. When the twin boys came, it was like double trouble. I had no time for my husband. It was just like he wasn't there. One day he went to work and he just didn't come back. I was quite hurt, but not out of love for him. I really was still thinking about the kids—*How dare he do that to them?* Not, how dare he do that to me? Love didn't come into it. You don't have much time for that; it is hard to think about love when you are wondering if you are going to eat.

Odyssey

She herself never went past tenth grade; maybe that was the prod toward an education for her girls: "I never had anything, but I know today you got to prepare yourself, be ready to make a living." Her daughters did make it through college; "We did that on a nickel and a prayer," she says. It was while her youngest girl was in college, about 1963, that Helen Howard's horizon suddenly expanded.

Helen Howard

I'd married again, but we was still living in that two-by-four house. My daughter come home from college one day and told me the students were organizing a housing survey for Vine City. She said, "Mama, why don't you help in the survey? You're always griping about how changes should be made; why don't you do something about it?" Wasn't nothing but for me to go out with the kids. That's when I began to see, really see, Vine City. There were things that had been around me most of my life, but I had taught myself not to notice them. Going into those houses, seeing the kids, the people, all the troubles, made it seem like poverty was hurting so much more than I remembered when I was young. This really shook me up. I began to wonder what can a person do.

Well, there was a white man living down here, name of Hector Black, and with him eight of us organized the Vine City Council to do picketing and sit-ins. We didn't think the poverty program was doing service for the people, was just giving them a runaround, and we went down there and sat in. I don't know how much good that done, but right in the neighborhood there was a store where the food was lousy and the white man running it wasn't paying hardly anything to the black man working for him. We went picketing on the store, started eight o'clock in the morning, and I can tell you I used to pray for eight o'clock at night, because then the store shut and we could go home. I was so sick of picketing that damn place! But in three weeks the man working in the store got a $20 raise and the food got to be better. What we did there was a threat to other stores in the neighborhood, and we just had to go around and say, "Look!" and they would shape up, too. So then we was doing something.

One winter it was really cold in Atlanta. People in Vine City was freezing. We went all around, getting blankets from the Salvation Army, the air base, anywhere. I thought of the poverty program, and I called them and told them get off their tail and do something, too. Nothing was done. I called the top guy in the program. Then we got some help.

Later I went to work for the poverty program. Very first day the boss called me in. Turned out he was the guy I had told to get off his tail, and he said I wasn't supposed to go around calling the top man. I said, "Well, you didn't do nothing," and he told me I was supposed to go through channels. Hell! All I was thinking about was getting blankets. Channels didn't mean nothing to me. In the poverty program, I was on the carpet right from the start.

I was what you call an aide, go around talking to people, see what they need. We found people the poverty program hadn't helped, like this one old lady who ought to be in a nursing home. Welfare said they didn't have enough money for that, so I called my oldest daughter, who by this time was both a college graduate and a registered nurse. She told me how the Kerr-Mills Act has money for cases like this. When I told that to welfare, they didn't know what I was talking about. Then I got in touch with a guy from the state, and we got the woman into a home, using Kerr-Mills. Another time I was trying to help a woman whose daughter was retarded. Nothing was done for her. What you find in a job like this is there are so many gaps, so many services not available to poor people. This case really pissed me off. I raised such a stink we finally got the daughter to a psychiatric clinic.

Poverty program raised hell with me. They said I wasn't a social worker—I was just an aide. I guess they thought as an aide you're supposed to be stupid, not know anything! Just follow orders. I didn't like that. I don't think the higher-up people in the poverty program have any time for the poor. Social workers just go by the book, the rules, the regulations. Don't have no heart, no feelings. If you don't fit into some little eligibility crack, the workers ain't going to push for nothing. Most social workers are middle-class to start with and don't have any experience with the poor. They don't get involved. But they should—that is their job.

Odyssey

It was inevitable that Helen Howard, feeling as she did, wouldn't last long with the poverty program. But once having started helping the poor, she wasn't about to quit. With a group of blacks she formed the Vine City Foundation. She kept the door open for white participation, but she wanted it understood that this was one program that would be homegrown, with the blacks of Vine City deciding themselves how they could help one another. It was, as Mrs. Howard says, "the only self-help group around; we were the thing to get involved in." A foundation made two houses it owned in the ghetto available for $1 a year. A church donated $30,000. Nickels, dimes and dollars came in. The government gave the group an IRS number, meaning contributions were tax-deductible.

Typically, Mrs. Howard didn't begin with any huge master plan for saving Vine City. She and the others just tried to meet the everyday needs they saw in the community. Bail money. Evictions. Bread. And children, especially the children. As in ghettos the country over, the baby-sitters for the very young children of Vine City are often hardly more than babies themselves, six or seven years old, left in charge of their younger brothers and sisters. Nobody planned to have a nursery school, but the need was there to care for preschool children while mothers worked. The only available facility—an unheated church basement—was rented; five mornings a week, twenty-five children came. A fund campaign raised enough to buy a 60-foot house trailer, which was remodeled into one large room, an office and a kitchen. Now parked in the rear of the foundation's houses, the trailer is a beautiful little nursery school, supported by the $450 a month an affluent white church sends in to pay for a professional teacher and provide hot breakfasts and lunch for the children. When we were there, we pointed to a portrait of Dr. King on the wall and asked a three-year-old whose picture that was. "Martin Luther King," he said, and looked at us with the amazement of meeting someone dumb enough not to know that.

Four nights a week volunteer doctors and nurses run a medical clinic in the foundation. On the fifth, there is a planned parenthood meeting.

Helen Howard

There are black men in Vine City telling their women that the Pill is genocide. They say whites don't want black babies to be born because then black people would get to be a majority. Maybe the black man don't care too much about the Pill because having babies is a sign of his manhood. This been the only thing he got going for him. It's been a holdover from slavery. If he was a good stud, the man was well treated. But I tell you the women today are waking up about this. They're finding they don't need to have a baby to prove that they're a woman. I don't think that the black man will have anything to say about whether his wife takes the Pill, because even if he objects, she still takes the Pill, *as long as she has been educated toward taking it.*

We was making progress in the clinic until all this controversy come up about the Pill—is it safe or what? People maybe can't read, but they listen to radio and television, and they worry. Some nights only three or four women come to the clinic. Even my own husband thinks about the scare stuff. When this business come up, he was so glad! He said, "Now women will have babies like they supposed." But I tell him, "Man, grow up! A man has a baby and then he can't support it."

I know the white stereotype is that there is very little else to do in the ghettos. I agree it is a form of recreation, but I don't think we use it more than anybody else. We just have the things to show for it. White girl gets pregnant and she has an abortion. Black girl gets pregnant in the ghetto and she has the baby.

Odyssey

It is an Atlanta tradition that well-to-do whites and well-to-do blacks can get along in a genteel coexistence; we asked Mrs. Howard how much help she had had from the city's black Establishment. Her answer: None. "I think," she explained, "that the black power structure is waiting for us to fall on our face, because they think just a certain class of people supposed to be doing something. Poor ain't supposed to do anything for themselves! Only reason I get any recognition in the middle-class black world is that some middle-class whites have accepted me. The caste system in the black community can be as much as any place in the world."

Helen Howard

Black got to be thinking better about blacks. About two months ago I went to talk to some black women in what they call a literary club. Doctors' wives and all that. Oh, I got so damned mad! They kept saying "them" and "those people," talking about poor blacks. They didn't even want to be called black, wanted to be Negro. You know, their mama or their grandmama didn't have a damned thing. It really pissed me off to see black people turn like that.

The things I have been through in the last five years! White women making overtures to black men. I don't know if it is for the good or the bad. I was at a party one time and this upper-middle-class white lady, I have to say we was all drinking, she sat on my husband's lap. Oh, he was so scared! I didn't know what to do. He was so pitiful-looking I just had to go over. I said, "Oh, I don't like nobody to do that to my husband." I said it nicely. I did it for him. On the way home, he was still upset, but I just sat there and laughed and laughed, remembering how he had looked.

But people have to be aware of what is happening, not try to bury their head in the sand. Like I think poor whites and poor blacks are getting together. Right here, we made contact with poor whites on the Poor People's March on Washington. When we started out from Atlanta, it was kind of tense. Blacks with blacks, whites with whites. But it is an amazing thing—poor blacks are much more open, more friendly, and reach out to the poor white. When we made the first bus stop, we got some beer, exchanged it with the whites, and we started sitting together, and before we left Washington, we were cooking together, sleeping in the same tent, and it was just great. Up to then I had been afraid of poor whites. Was all Ku Klux Klansmen, far as I went. Red-neck crackers. But one day in Washington we had a meeting with Herman Talmadge. This white woman with us was trying to tell him how bad it was for her, she had had a heart attack and she had ten children and she couldn't get on welfare. He attacked her by saying she had too many babies because she stayed in the bed. When he attacked her, it was just like attacking me, and I said, "How the hell do you think you got here? You got here in the bed! You talk like birth control was something just started for poor people!" And he lashed out at me, and I said, "Bullshit!" I said this wasn't a black movement, this was whites and blacks together. He said he had something to do, and he left.

It is the class thing that you see now. Look at the strikes we been having. The people who are on the outside of the system aren't making enough to live, and they are going to rise up. I think class is going to overcome discrimination.

Odyssey

Mrs. Howard is often at the foundation before eight in the morning, and she is there three and four nights a week. And she has paid a price, as she knows.

Helen Howard

I am going to be very honest. I am quite sure I made some mistakes with my sons, and I think that one of the mistakes was being here in Vine City too much. When they were young, I was with them all the time, but in the last few years, my time in the foundation, I just wasn't attuned to them. I felt so sure I had given them all the things I could. Maybe there were things in these years that I didn't hear—that I should have.

The one boy I got troubles with is the brightest. I don't think the Negro high schools here prepare you for college, and for two summers we sent him to the government's skill studies program in Knoxville. Wasn't no giveaway thing, not a whole lot of money, but more than we can afford. But I wanted him to have it. It's just like black people are surrounded by a mesh wire, and every once in a while somebody squeezes through. The college education does that. But when my son come out of high school, he said he didn't want to go to college. And he was telling me things like nothing good can happen to black people unless there be a complete revolution. There has been a complete change in him. You don't see it coming on. It just hits. When he talked about revolution, I told him to cool it, he didn't know what he was saying. He told me that by trying to work in the system, like I am, I am doing more harm than good because the people here in Vine City just being piecemealed to death. And then he tells me, "Now why don't you come home like a nice old lady and let us young people do our thing?"

For two months I cried and cried. He turned down two scholarships—scholastic scholarships. Education didn't mean that much, he said. So I told him that if you are going to be a man, you got to take man's responsibilities—you got to get a job, because I won't let you just stay and tell me I am a useless person. He got a job, but in two months he said he was going to college. I was shocked. He went to school for about a year, and then all of a sudden I found out he wasn't in school. Plus he wasn't working. Plus the guys he was hanging around with was smoking pot. I have fought with him so many times that I am just weary. I tell him I think he is just copping out. My son is a black hippie! That is what I am trying to tell you. He is the closest to one I know anything about. I told him that if he joined the Black Panthers or any organization where there is something to work for, then I could feel something. But as it is, I just don't know.

When my older daughter was growing up, she believed, because I had told her it was so, that she could make it out of Vine City, get into a different class, get into the system, be included. I brought her up to think that you get whatever education is necessary and that black people then get to be middle-class. So she got the education, and she makes it with her own peer group, others like her and her husband, but they are all bitter because in a sense they were hoodwinked. They found out that even if you do pull yourself up by your bootstraps, you are still not included in the system. You are separate. Like my daughter found out that sometimes she got better qualifications to be upgraded in her job than white people—but white people got the job.

First off, she ignored the work I do down here. She moved out of Vine City, and after we have many fights in the family, she says, "Don't talk to me about Vine City!" She is caught in the middle. She don't want to be Vine City, and she is not accepted by the system.

I finally got her to work in the clinic because she is a nurse. But she says, "Let's not discuss it." I don't, and we can play pinochle all night and never mention it. It is a funny thing. Only a very small percentage of those who make it out come back. I am not making excuses, but I think they are afraid to. I don't think they even want to remember where they are from. They are running so damn hard just to stay where they are.

But my younger daughter, she don't care about being accepted in the system. She believes in what I am doing. She is down here all the time, trying to help me piecemeal it out.

Odyssey

In all we saw Helen Howard three times, twice in 1969, once in 1970. By then she and the Vine City Foundation had just come through a disillusioning period.

Helen Howard

We help everybody who come along. And these young guys come in and said they was from the Georgia Black Liberation Front, and I didn't know what the hell that was. We was so naïve. The guys was hungry and they didn't have any place to stay, and we put them up and fed them. For four, five months they was in and out. Sleep on the floor and anything. I even had them out to my house a couple of times and put on big spreads for them.

They came in, and they said they wanted to help us. We never turn that down. Like they were going to work with the ceramics shop we got. Get some artists, develop molds, sell the stuff. And they were going to get more and more black doctors involved here. And we sit back and hope they could do things we couldn't do.

Then we found out they weren't for real. Maybe it was my fault. Maybe I was gullible. They were selling the Black Panther paper, and they was talking about violence; some of that stuff they was spewing out! But we tried to keep it cool. Keep any confrontation out of it. We say, "Let them do their thing." But they didn't do nothing for us. I think most of the time they play games. I believe in change, but not to the degree they do. So they say we are just too slow, that we don't believe in violence. And they said we still dealing with white people, and they say you can't do that kind of thing, that you have to get on the opposite side from the white people, oh, the whole bag! It is just sickening. Finally I said, "Get the hell out!"

After that we were burglarized. Somebody even took the refrigerator out of the nursery school. Four-hundred-dollar refrigerator. Matched the stove. It hurts so bad! Two weeks ago somebody stole a typewriter out of the building here, and they took off every lock in the place. If they steal a typewriter, they just have to blow in one door and take it out, but every lock in the place was torn off.

Somebody had to hate us. You know, I have been used so much. By the right, by the left. For years, we have gone without any real money. I work my husband down here for nothing. I work my daughters down here for nothing. There is just so much blood you can give, so much to be done, until it seems like, oh, what's the use, you know? I feel like the people I have been trying to help don't realize what I have been through, and I don't think one person can change the damn system. I have problems of my own.

And I can't die for Vine City.

Ain't no way in hell I am going to die for nobody.

I am looking for an out.

HUNT LIBRARY
CARNEGIE-MELLON UNIVERSITY

Life in the Project . . .

Odyssey

The Perry Homes, far out on Atlanta's northwest side, in an ugly, tarnished, graceless public housing project. Built like a cluster of military barracks, it has more than 1,000 units, cast in a dreadful monotony.

People there tell of one woman who wanted to relieve the hopelessness of such living. Outside her door she planted a rose bush. But the project staff uprooted it, because a rule said nobody could do any private planting on the grounds.

In the early summer of 1969 Miriam and I went to Perry Homes to see a welfare mother named Mrs. Irene Martin, who was divorced and the mother of a ten-year-old son. A few days earlier we had gone to a meeting of Perry's tenants with the Atlanta Housing Authority and had noticed how articulate and outspoken she had been. Her apartment was on a circular drive named Drew Place. The first floor had a living room, dining area and kitchen; the second floor two bedrooms and a bath. The walls were faded green. Generally Perry floors are cement, but she had tried to break some of the regimentation by putting down asphalt tiles in the kitchen and hall. The screens didn't fit; the flies came and went. "Just try and get maintenance," Mrs. Martin said.

Irene Martin

I put in for this apartment with the idea I was going to have me a sanctuary, a home. But when I came out here, the neighbors helped to run me crazy, telling me that if I didn't do this or that, I'd be thrown out. In the nine years I've been here I have come to know that when you are living in a housing project, the manager is like the slave boss, and he's in his plantation and we is the slaves. Now me, I might like walls painted blue or some other color. What do we get here? Beige or green. That's it. You don't have nothing to say about it.

It bugs me the way if someone don't like me, she can call the manager and tell him I got a man sleeping in, and her word is accepted. I either have to go up to the office, or any time I am gone the staff can walk in and go through my closets to see if a man is staying with me. Whatever is found is reported to welfare.

Take like if your child don't show up in school. Truant people don't get in touch with you about that, they call the project. That doesn't do nothing, because the office isn't interested in whether your child is in class. We can't even fight in peace in Perry Homes. If my little boy and another boy get to fussing and his mother don't like it, she can go the manager, and then he comes to me about it.

Before any warrant or papers is served here, management is generally told you are in trouble. Sometimes the poverty program is notified. I don't know why, because they don't have the money to help you get a lawyer or anything. You'd think they would try to reach Legal Aid for you.

A while back a boy shot a man in the project. The boy went to jail, so he ain't no more danger in Perry. Even so the management told the boy's father he would have to move out. The father has been here for years and never did anything to warrant his being evicted. He's fighting it, and I am with him, because it just ain't right.

When you live in Perry Homes, nobody has to tell you that you are a ward of the state. All you got to do is look around and you get the message, loud and clear.

Odyssey

At forty, Mrs. Martin was well built, somewhat stocky. She wore a shapeless brown dress, moccasin-style slippers. She had a warm smile and lively eyes, but her hair was unruly. When she sat down, she did so slowly, explaining she was taped up and that it hurt her to move.

"Lots of nights," she said, "we can't get to sleep because of teenagers out on the street, cursing, talking loud, and the next morning we find glass where they broke their bottles. The police came into Perry two nights ago, and everybody was running out to see what was going on. The police started shooting it out with some kids, and naturally we all run the other direction. Somebody pushed me, and I fell down a hill. I was knocked out, yet I was lucky. I could have broke my neck. A friend took me home. I thought I was all right. Next morning I was hurting. Doctor found two ribs busted."

It was just another night in Perry Homes.

Irene Martin

You can get an idea of what it's like to live here, just from a washing machine. We don't have cars to take our clothes up to the laundromat in the shopping center. We don't have wagons to pull the load up and back. If you're a mother with a baby messing up the bed, the idea of maybe having a washing machine ain't a luxury; it's a necessity. But because we're on welfare, most of the big stores won't give us credit, and we can't take advantage of their prices. We got to deal with a guy who will let us have the machine on time, but what he does is buy the thing for like $100 from Sears and then resell it to us for $300 or $400.

I know about this kind of deal because I was paying $20 a month on a washer, but I only get $67 a month from welfare. And besides, I had all my teeth pulled out and I was trying to get my mouth fixed, so I couldn't meet the washer payments. I went to a lady lawyer at Legal Aid, and she wrote a letter to the store. They called her and said it was all right—I could keep the machine one more month. I suppose they thought I could wash all the clothes I'll ever need in that one month's time. It's a white man doing this to us, and you can see why we colored are sometimes sitting in judgment on whites.

Look at the television I have. I got to have one to keep my child happy, so he won't always be running to the neighbor's house. Way I bought it was that I saw an ad in the paper for a table model. When the white man come out here after I called, he wouldn't sell me that kind. He explained he had just sold the last one, and he claimed he was so sorry. All he had available was consoles. He offered me one on credit; I took it. Only way I could get a set. It ain't no good because the picture keeps rolling up and down, and I ain't paying no more. Now he is waiting for the first of the month to send his truck out here to pick it up. That is supposed to embarrass me, but we see the truck so often it don't embarrass nobody.

Odyssey

Just before visiting Mrs. Martin, we had been hearing denials that families on welfare were usually matriarchies. Even unmarried women, we had heard, deferred an important decision until their men friends came in to talk it over.

Irene Martin

People say things like that, but it ain't true. I don't know if I should say this, but I ain't ever been that interested in men. I have always had the idea that they are all right in their place, but I lost my respect for them real young. My mother, who separated from my father when I was about four, left me one night to get some food. She asked this friend of hers, not a boyfriend, just someone up from her hometown, to stay with me, and he tried fooling around with me. That upset me, did something to me. I couldn't tell my mother because she wouldn't believe me. Then, when I got big enough to realize what men were, the men in the neighborhood, well, I didn't have things like I wanted to wear, and they would have money in their pocket. They would persist to give you this money, and the only thing that would be on your mind was, I would like to have me a yellow blouse. . . .

I went to work at a hotel here in Atlanta when I was thirteen years old, waiting table, and the headwaiter was overly nice. He liked me because I didn't drink whiskey, but I had on enough makeup for everybody in town. He would paw me.

I had a stepdaddy, and I wasn't very fond of him. I upped and married a fellow because I thought it would mean I was going to leave home. Instead, he wanted to stay with my family. I didn't, and I wasn't ready to be married. I did the only thing I knew: I run away. There were colored people on every train that left Atlanta. I became one of them, went to New York, where my real daddy had a grocery store. I clerked for him, but I really didn't have to do anything. When I had been at home, I wanted loving so badly. Mama, though, would push me away when I walked up after she had kissed my brothers. I'd want to be kissed, too, and she would say, "Oh, you're my big girl," and she never would kiss me. My daddy would cuddle me, and when

I was in New York with him, I could just have been a lady, with nothing to do. But New York was a big dirty town. Atlanta was nice and clean. I came back to my husband.

One thing you will find in every colored man. They will either jump on you—fight you—or drink whiskey. I had a little more education than my husband, and regardless of what we would get to arguing about, this would come up, you know, him saying, "You think you're so smart because you been to high school. . . ." He would stay out all Friday night, and at first I used to call the hospital, the jails and things to see if he got hurt or was dead. One Friday night he came home at midnight and said he was going to a funeral. I laughed at him. Well, he jumped me, beat me up. I never called the jailhouse again, never called the police.

Odyssey

While we talked, some of Mrs. Martin's neighbors came in, a few with sleeping babies. Two women said they would clean the kitchen and get lunch ready. Others sat in the living room, listening, occasionally contributing to the conversation. A mother of six, Mrs. Rose Harper, who had reddish hair and very light skin, said that "when a man asks you to be his wife, you begin to feel he is going to provide for you. If he can't, and you have to go fend for yourself, then you are your own woman. This affects your relationship with the man, very bad. Sexually, mentally, physically and just about in every other way you want to put it. You think of him as a man, not your man."

Irene Martin

Black women are much more unforgiving than whites. They learn early they've got to take care of themselves. I went out and got me a boyfriend. One thing I used to say about me and my husband: If we got old and sat on the porch together, he ain't going to just grin at his past; I can grin at mine, too. The kettle couldn't call the pot black, because we had both been very busy.

I was building my ego, getting even with my husband. I didn't bother a thing about no long run. I was just intent on a good time. And this boyfriend was a man who would carry me to a nightclub, told me I had a beautiful dress, give me the money to get my hair fixed. This was the man who said no other woman in the world meant as much to him as I did. I never had any flowers until him. Never had anyone to send me a box of candy. I couldn't get this at home. This is why I enjoyed this man. I had all the things I ever wanted. He told me to get a divorce, that he would marry me. Maybe, if I had sense, I would have. I realized, however, that after he married me, he wouldn't do these things. I wouldn't get the candies no more, wouldn't get the flowers. I come to think that this man's wife was probably saying the same things about him I was saying about my husband. Besides, I went on a religious kick, and I thought I wasn't going to do that no more.

We didn't hardly have enough to live on. My husband was trying to make some extra money when they caught him with 75 gallons of corn whiskey, and he went to prison. What they say is that colored people don't stay together, but I was determined I was going to keep my marriage, and when he was released, I got pregnant. With that baby I like to have a nervous breakdown. Baby weighed three pounds two ounces, had to go in an incubator for two months. We didn't have no money at all. Finance company took back all our furniture. No place to stay. Nothing to eat. I left my husband and went home to my mama.

Then I come to the project, went on welfare. I had this young baby, and I didn't know how I was going to feed him because he was in a cast with a broken foot and I couldn't get nobody to take care of him if I went out and worked. Only furniture I had at the start was two old chairs my grandmother give me, so I had to buy things. When a guy saw me about selling furniture, I explained I only had a little money, told him I could pay him something on the fifteenth of the month because the check on the first went toward the rent. He gave me this long business about not turning the account over to no finance company—but that is what he did. First time I was in a bind and missed a payment the man from a loan outfit said to come and renew the account with him. While I was there, he said I could borrow money to pay off all my other bills, so I wouldn't owe nobody but him. I didn't understand how these things work, and I signed up. I got $400 and used it to pay off everything I owed to everybody except him.

Next, I got the flu and pneumonia, and I missed a payment with the finance company. Here comes two big detectives. I am not sure they was detectives; they could have been from the company. They have a routine. One talks real nice; the other talks to you like you are a dog. This gentleman called me a bitch, and he and I got to fighting. Everything my husband had ever done to me, everything every man had ever done, come up, and I took it all out on this man. When the police showed up, the only thing that kept me from going to jail was that I didn't have anybody to take care of the little boy. "She wasn't drinking, and she was in her own home," a policeman said. I still had to go to court, and that put something on my record.

Whites don't understand why colored feel they are defeated at every turn. I put in for a job at the post office and passed the examination. Then they said I couldn't be hired because I had this record. Everything goes in a bind. It was like I was losing my mind. When I got to hearing voices, I asked the county hospital for help, but a desk clerk explained to me that colored people don't get nervous breakdowns. That settled that. Made me feel real good. I even told it to whoever it was that I heard talking to me. Can't tell you how the voices stopped. They just did.

Can you see how all this starts? People don't have enough to live on. That's why a man don't represent anything but money to a colored woman. Nobody believes it, but this is actually what happen in the poor neighborhoods. Say, like you owe $80 and you only got $65. You know what a man is? He is a $15 deal. Take a case where you got $10 and the grocery bill is $9.95. You know good and well you have to have money for your light bill. Somebody come by and say, "I got $5," and you say, "My light bill is $5.35." You don't have time to be a lady; you have to grasp the money because you don't have enough to make ends meet.

Later the man might get to thinking he is running the household. Then we get into arguments. This is why colored people fight: The woman is independent, as she has to be, because she ain't never had anybody to cuddle her or love her. She's always had to get out and do things for herself. Black man ain't done that for her because he has always had to struggle to get everything he got his hands on, and he's tired, too, and he wants to be cuddled. So it is two very tired people trying to make out, and after an argument they do settle down. You say you want to call it love, I call it sexual sense to do this thing. Next thing you know, there you are, pregnant. You don't want the man that has got you that way, you can't work, you can't get rid of the baby, so you just run from one vicious cycle to another, all of the time.

Odyssey

Mrs. Martin said that she occasionally had worked as a domestic in the white world.

Irene Martin

When you work for them, whites will give you a few clothes or some leftover food, something they too scared to give to their own family. But try to understand you—they never bother about that!

Once I was working for a woman, and if her baby messed before I got to work in the morning, the baby would be sitting there, diaper on, waiting for me. If the baby had a stool at night, the stool was waiting for me to flush. She wasn't paying me but $25 a week, and yet when she would spend $30 on groceries, she would say to me, "Irene, I don't see how you can live on $25." That was just great to hear. She found out I wasn't with my husband, and she delivered an ultimatum that to keep the job, I would have to baby-sit at night. She would wait until just about time for me to go home and she'd say, "Oh, we're going out tonight." I had to come home, get a sitter for my own child. Cost me a dollar and a half. Bus fare back and forth at night would be another 50 cents. For baby-sitting I was paid $3, so you can see I didn't make but $1 clear for the whole night.

One morning her husband told me not to put his socks in the washing machine. Said they were wool and would stretch. He wanted them done by hand. I fairly hated that man. I nearly hit him. I was thinking how that morning I had left my sick baby at home, because I didn't have nobody to send to work for me, and I had to come. After telling me about the socks, he explained he was washing big light bulbs and that I would have to hold them while he heaped water on them. I just got so mad I took this man's socks out of the drawer and put them all in the dishwasher, turned it on, and went out and sat in the yard. The dishwasher shredded the socks and the woman asked me did I do it. I told her Yes, and I said, "My baby is home sick, and I called you for the day off, and you said you had to have somebody." I got my coat and left. Later they asked me a couple of times to work for them again, but I didn't. They had blackmailed me into keeping that job, and I just didn't want it anymore.

You work in a family and it is orders, all the time. It's "Irene, cook this," or, "Irene, love my child," and I would say, "Yes, ma'am," or whatever. But how do they know I didn't spit in the soup or beat the child when they was gone? But understand this: I am not just resenting the white man for what he has done. I am resenting the upper-class black ones, too. I am resenting society, period, for the bind they have put us all into.

Odyssey

What Mrs. Martin had been saying about working for whites was echoed by Mrs. Ann Davis, another neighbor. Small, with a sleek body and delicate features, she was in her early twenties, divorced, living with her three children and another child she was rearing for her sister.

Ann Davis

I love kids. Once, I was working in a home and this little white baby walk up to me and say, "Ann, what's a nigger?" He give me all the shock in the world. I looked at him, and I was going to say something very nasty, but he was so innocentlike, you know, he was saying to himself, "She'll tell me the truth." I looked at him again, and he was so cute, and he says, "Are you going to tell me?" And I say, "Oh, that's just a word people uses." He wants to know, "Why do they call people your color a nigger?" I told him, "A nigger is anyone who shows his ignorance." He went and told his mommy, "You're a good nigger, because you showed your ignorance." So she got so that she didn't want me around.

Another time I was worked in a different home, and when I would walk in, the mother would say, "Good morning, Ann, see you later," and she would leave me with the kid. The mother was eighteen, and I was eighteen, and she trusted me with this two-year-old kid. On my experience, I don't think whites are very good mothers. I'll say this, though: There used to be a time when only whites were bad, but that was just because the black woman couldn't do it the same way. But right today, I know some black women that have domestic help, and they are doing the same thing that whites do. You walk in and the black say, "Good morning—and good-bye, I'll see you!" Upper-class Negroes are a tragedy; well, not a tragedy, but they are not living right. They are just aping whites. Take dieting. Don't ask for no breakfast! For what? "I got to watch my figure," they say. Used to be a time when you put out the good grits, good bacon and eggs, and you would just fall into them.

This world is sure turning around. It is changing because the black woman is tired, tired of just being someone who all she can do is produce babies. You have to make the life you want, because no one will make it for you.

Odyssey

Mrs. Martin wanted us to know she hadn't just been sitting out there in Perry Homes, content with welfare or occasional domestic work. Although she had earned a high school diploma in her teens, she said she went back to class a few years ago to get a general equivalency degree, certifying her as having the equal of a high school course.

Irene Martin

You have to show a child. If my son sees me with a bottle, he'll follow me with a bottle. If he sees me with a book, he'll also follow me there. To live in this world, he's got to have an education. When he is grown, I feel like even the garbage collectors will have to have four years of college. If he gets an education, he might not have to go through some of the things I did.

Colored people today don't have enough incentive. Nearly everybody feels beaten down, disheartened. But all along I have been trying to fight this system, the way things are. Whites don't realize it, but life in the project can get to a point where you will do almost anything to get out.

I went to government training in MDTA.* Working with offset printing. I gave up everything for that course. My house was filthy. My child was in a nursery school, not getting the love he deserved. When I finished on the honor roll, I thought we'd get jobs. But the woman explained to me that I'd have to beat the pavements looking for one, myself. That made me mad. Wasn't no jobs for me.

I got into another training program. They give me problems like adding 2 and 3. I think the most I ever added was 33 and 11. And I said, "This ain't building my mentality; the little I have, it will take

* Manpower Development and Training Administration, a federal program.

before I leave." They were working on us to become file clerks. Wasn't no hope of that. These were older women. Their hair was looking like mine, spread all over, and they were larger than I am, and they had these run-over shoes. They know we're not going to get jobs as file clerks. We're colored! Least they could do was teach women how to dress, to make a good appearance. They would show us a film of somebody who had gotten a job, and it would be an auto mechanic or a domestic and cooking job. Colored people come into the world cooking! Teach us something we haven't had before.

In this program we spent a whole day at the Atlanta *Constitution,* looking at hot type, things like that. What I remember is that they had a little white girl, sixteen years old, making $2.10 an hour, showing us around. We also saw Virginia and Lester.* We seen the organ in their place working without anyone sitting there playing. We all seen player pianos before. Virginia don't have as much education as I got. None of us like Maddox. We heard somebody gave him a duck, and I couldn't understand why anyone wanted to bother with the man at all. The program took us out to see Willie B in Grant Park. He's a ape, named after a man who was mayor. They was showing us all the glories of the white man's world, but if they would give us a job to get off welfare, we could afford to see the zoo by ourselves. Besides, who wants to meet Willie B?

In class we had blocks to play with, like when you were a kid, and we had to get the square ones in a square hole, so they can find out how long it takes you. I did it, and the teacher said, "Brilliant!" Then I wired up a board for electricity, and they said, "Brilliant!" And I thought, "Great! I am about to get a job any minute." They gave me a cash register and play money. I got that right. Six weeks later I was still there, and they put me in the school workshop. Man says, "C'mon, sand this car!" I explained I didn't think anybody would hire me in a body and fender shop, and maybe it would be better if I learned a trade. In another room he let me sort out mismatched socks brought in by a store that paid $30 a week for you to match two and two. When I finished all that, I heard my counselor tell my instructor there wasn't any jobs. He said he didn't understand why all these people was out there because if we were over thirty, "They ought to be dead, anyway," on account anything they would give us would only be a stopgap until we died. But, you know, I do have training, and what I really want to do is go to work.

* Georgia's then Governor and Mrs. Maddox.

Odyssey

As we got up to leave that day in June, 1969, another woman, Mrs. Catherine Styles, said a little wistfully, "I do hope that when you come again, you can write about something they are doing *for* us, and not *to* us."

It was more than a year before we returned. In that time the world had turned around for some of those welfare mothers. Through a relative Mrs. Davis had been hired as a waitress in an exclusive private club. She voluntarily suggested to her caseworker that her check be cut by $50 a month and expressed the hope that she'd shortly be able to leave welfare completely. She began thinking about the house she had always wanted for her children. "I'm looking out in the suburbs," she said. "And I see my way clear to begin saving some money. I'm going to adult education classes in a couple of months. I always wanted to be a nurse. And I'm pretty sure that in about a year or so I'll be able to start my training. Sometimes, things take awhile to work out the way you want, but if you keep at them, and have some luck, it really can get to be a beautiful world."

Mrs. Martin, who had said she would fight the system, became a political doorbell ringer, part-time campaigner. She took an examination for a job in Atlanta's federal mint. Score: 98. Result: She was hired for a $6,400 job, ironically, to supervise the shredding of old money. She passed another examination, this one for a position with the Internal Revenue Service. While she was debating that possibility, the Urban League offered her $7,000 a year to help place MDTA graduates—the same program that had once infuriated her when no jobs were available. Some months before we saw her in 1970 she left welfare. "That feel so good," she said, "not to have to account for your money to nobody." Her income is above the level permitted in Perry Homes, and she was making plans to move. One of her Atlanta friends told us he had seen Mrs. Martin at a conference. "The real Irene Martin has finally had a chance to come out," he said. "What a pity, and what a loss, it had to take so long."

. . . *And in Peyton Forest*

Barbara Fouch

Some blacks have been saying that peddling birth control devices in the ghettos was "an attempt on the part of the white man to keep down the black population." While I'm in favor of birth control, like nobody else, I do see some merit in what is being said. Yet when you think about it, the next struggle won't be over just numbers; it will be in getting the black man ready for psychological warfare.

For years, the white man confused us, messed up our minds. Now we have to run the game on him, psych him, use against him what he's been doing to us.

Odyssey

Before we met Barbara Fouch, we had heard about her beauty, success, lovely home, devoted husband, but we were not expecting tough words. They didn't seem to go with her life-style. Yet as we spent more and more time with her, she made it plain that the black condition had given her certain insights and that she meant what she said, no matter how it might appear to contradict her obvious status.

She picked us up in her turquoise El Dorado Cadillac, in front of Atlanta's headquarters for the poverty program, where she had once worked. She had since become an established model: *Town & Country, Seventeen, Ebony* and *Elegant* magazines. She was taking us to her home in Peyton Forest, the black residential area in southwest Atlanta, and to an afternoon with her and her husband, Carl. She was then twenty-eight, exquisite, a lean five feet eight, light-skinned, with features almost Eurasian. Her shoulder-length hair wound like a crown. As we drove along, Miriam commented on her handsome yellow suit. She replied, "I always go in for high fashion clothes. I couldn't wear a twelve ninety-eight dress if it killed me."

The only thing Peyton Forest had in common with Vine City and Perry Homes was that Atlanta's blacks lived in all three areas. Peyton Forest's roads curved gently; the community's $40,000 homes were set in a profusion of pine, magnolia and dogwood trees. The Fouches', which they moved into on their wedding day, July 14, 1963, was a modern, eight-room, split-level brick house, with large lawns in front and back, a garden and many fruit trees. "My husband keeps up the garden," she explained. "He's been hung up on that community beautification stuff. Me, I never go outdoors."

She said the inside of their home represented "just something Carl and I put together, bits and pieces of things we like without regard to what the books or magazines say." The rooms were decorated in what she called "cool colors," relaxing shades of blue, green, lavender and purple. The walls throughout were covered with vibrant oil abstract paintings, all done by her husband. She had contributed one artwork: in the dining room, a large piece of black velveteen cloth stretched over a plain wooden frame, nothing else on it. Its meaning, she said, was: "Black is beautiful."

We finished touring her home just as her husband drove up in his gold Coupe de Ville Cadillac convertible. A good-looking man, age thirty-three, real estate broker, he is a trim six feet one, medium brown. She later joked about their colors: "Neither one of us is a good example of a nigger."

Barbara Fouch

We both grew up in Atlanta. Carl was the only boyfriend I ever had. I was fourteen going on fifteen, and he was a freshman at Morehouse College. He left the tennis court one day as I was leaving the library there. We didn't go out for some time, as I was too young then. But he just sort of came around the house until I was old enough to date. That's how we got started, and there's never been anybody else.

I was born on the West Side, and at that time it was the black bourgeoisie section. It has since run down terribly, but then it was very nice. There were seven of us children, and I am right in the middle. My father was among the first blacks to go to work for the post office. He started when I was one year old and remained there until his death two years ago. He was a very creative man, and he did interior decorating on the side. We were brought up in integrated situations because most of the people for whom he worked were white—blacks couldn't afford interior decorating. White people were in and out of our home.

Daddy really protected us. We just didn't know prejudice, although I'm sure it must have been right under our noses. We lived in a neighborhood where everybody knew everybody. When we went to a movie or into the stores, my daddy said that if "you find you haven't enough money or you lost it, you just tell them who your daddy is. Give them your address, and I'll send it around." He made us feel we could go anywhere. We were always more than welcome and comfortable on his job. I can look back now and think what all seven of us looked like flocking through the mostly white post office going to find our daddy.

I had little experience with segregation. Sure, there was our school bus which was all black kids. But I did not do too much riding public transportation. We had two cars in our family, and my daddy insisted by the age of twelve that we knew how to drive—girls, boys, and dogs, if they could.

Carl Fouch

My father was a barber who was born in Lincolnton, Georgia, about 100 miles from here. There were so few people that there was a lot of race mixing in the town. No more than two steps down in his pedigree was a white parent. This person's middle name was the same as this other one's last. They all lived in the same houses. But when they got to Atlanta, they went their separate ways, the white part of the family to the whites, the blacks to the blacks. Yet they still maintained a secret, unspoken contact.

Years ago, my father was always taking us into the "wrong" places. He was independent. Later, because of this, he became a deputy sheriff, very unusual for a black. He carried a gun and he was in every sense a man.

Barbara Fouch

My daddy was very much the boss, even though he had a tenth-grade education while my mother had attended three years at

Spelman College, a private black school in the Atlanta University complex. He would not let her work. She was to stay with us. She could, however, teach music in the home. Anything he said went. In fact, to a point which was just awful to us because if we asked her anything, we had to go to Daddy. He was the law. Nonetheless, they really loved each other. I never saw them either leave or come back home that they didn't kiss one another on the cheek.

The church was important to my mother. My daddy had his own form of religion. He didn't believe in many of the things that black preachers talked about. All of us played black gospel music. I sent myself through Clark College, in Atlanta, by performing in churches throughout the South. I studied psychology and English.

It was in the summer of 1959, the end of my freshman year, that I got my first modeling job. I'd gone up to New York to visit my brother who was a professional jazz musician and organist. He lived in a nice part of the Bedford-Stuyvesant area. There was this dress shop where he took me to buy me things. The owner, a white guy, was always persistent that I model. He'd tell me, you know, how I had the body build. I was pretty tall, skinny, and sort of like I am now. I didn't have any training, but I did some jobs for him that summer, and each of the next summers and holidays during college when I'd stay with my brother. I enjoyed modeling, but I didn't pursue it then. I always knew I was going back South and finish college

The Atlanta University complex was a great experience for me. I didn't know what was happening until I went there. Yes, I was very angry to know that a Rosa whatever-her-name-was was put off the bus because she would not move to the back or get up and give a man her seat. But while I was thinking this way about that specific incident, the attitude never carried over to the white people I felt I knew.

In college I got into a larger realm of young blacks who came from all over the United States and who were what I call the thinkers. They started telling me about and exposing me to another side of life. Something was rotten in the state of Denmark! I became involved in the sit-ins. We weren't part of SNCC. We didn't even have a name. Julian Bond and all of us just started getting things organized in Atlanta. We sat in at Woolworth's, Kresge's, and at H. L. Green. I'm not a marcher, and I don't feel comfortable on a line. I was never locked up, and the only violence I was subject to was being cussed, spit upon, soup or coffee dumped in my lap. Little things like that.

And still, with my upbringing, I asked myself, "What can I do to

show these people, young blacks and whites, that neither side is nec-
essarily right?" I can't see having to be all black or having to be an
Uncle Tom in order to do my thing.

Friends I had met in New York said I was dumb to stay in Atlanta.
But I graduated from Clark College in 1962, did some work towards
a master's degree while I taught English two years in the same black
high school I had attended. Then I was ready to move on. I heard
about an opening as assistant to the director of public relations for
Atlanta's poverty program. I applied and was accepted. During my
two years there, a local modeling agency, since defunct, asked me to
teach. I did this in my spare time. In 1968, I joined the theretofore
all-white Peachtree Center Model Agency as a model and then
became the director. The agency stages major shows throughout the
southeastern United States. It is the first one to receive a grant
through Model Cities to teach "self-improvement and motivation" in
four lower-income schools, working with black and white youths. I
supervise the program, also teach subjects ranging from personal hygiene to drugs.

To me, Atlanta is just the only place to live in terms of possibilities
for young blacks, allowing a lot of us to do what we want. The support we get from the white business sector, whether it is to keep us
from burning down their property or whether they have a genuine interest in what we are doing, is unique. You go North—and I travel a
lot—and you see people doing the same thing they were five years
ago while you have done five different things. In the North, you play
a lot of games. You go to each other's houses and the whole thing,
but the racial hangups are there. They just aren't as open.

Don't get me wrong. The underlying white racism is still here. Carl
and I have some friends who are white, and we think they are about
as genuine people as you can find. They are dedicated and have
proven themselves in trying to help the less fortunate. But there are
some things they don't understand, like us being what we call their
"show niggers." For the past couple of years it has been quite fashionable for whites to have black friends at their parties. We've had so
many invitations that if we accepted them all, we'd be hospital cases.
But we have gone to some to show their friends that *niggers don't
stink!*

Odyssey

We asked Barbara and Carl Fouch how they, with their backgrounds, could relate to the poor. He replied that the problem was more with the poor relating to them, mainly because "the old-guard black people who have made it on over have so long neglected the poor. This has, in turn, hurt Barbara and me a lot. Half the time lower-income blacks call us the booghies.* We have succeeded in the white man's world so they think we had to get in cahoots with him."

Barbara Fouch

The toughest job you have is convincing poor people that you are not some fat cat out there in Peyton Forest who has forgotten all about them. But over the years we have stood the test of time.

I go along with the words of Vernon Jordan, who was formerly with the Southern Regional Council and is now with the United Negro College Fund. Vernon made a beautiful speech to the VISTA workers one night in which he started out by saying, "I'm not up here to apologize for the carpet on my floor." The point was, if you are trying to bring people out of poverty, it is dumb and hypocritical to keep going around making excuses for what you might have accomplished or gained in life. Because people do want nicer things—whatever nicer is to them.

Some try to hide what they have, by saying, "No, I really don't like those things" in order to get along with the people in the ghetto. That's poor-mouthing and condescending. If you are for real, they will know your motives. They will not be concerned about what you drive up in or what you wear. I'd be a joke to walk into Perry Homes wearing a pair of blue jeans.

The poor people and the younger militants in this city know we live in Peyton Forest, know we drive big cars and all. But we have proven we are really, truly, concerned about them. When there is a choice between them and the Establishment, we side with them. For example, during the riots at Perry Homes in 1968, a white boss at the poverty program told me to use whatever influence I had to go out and tell the people, "Please don't riot." I said I wouldn't do that.

* The term applied to the middle-class black bourgeoisie.

I was *in favor* of what they were doing. The only objection I had was that they were not burning downtown Atlanta. In fact, I later said to some of the people in Perry Homes, "You ought to burn where it hurts somebody else."

LeRoi Jones says that to be conscious of being black during this period is to be militant. In a black area of Atlanta near Perry Homes, the people kept asking the city, "please give us a park for our thousands of kids to play in." Finally, after some rioting there, the city said, "Okay, we will." So you know what the city did? They put a park right next to a cemetery. Not only that, there is a creek that runs down behind it. Your kid isn't home at six, and you don't know whether she is drowned and floating in the water or not. You may wonder why those families accepted that park. Well, it's better than nothing.

Even so, I do have some hope for the future, a world in which people are color-blind. I want all ghettos eradicated and an end to war. I think that if women had more say-so in all our government, we could get there. And I believe we black women have a major role to perform, personally, as well as in relationship to our men and the world around us.

The white women, on the other hand, have been foolish, especially in the South, believing they were something on a pedestal. That's not true, never has been. Years ago the white man took to sleeping black almost all the time. So what was the good of being on a pedestal? In turn, the black woman got favors from the white man, things she couldn't get from her black man. She began leaning on the black, accusing him of not being able to support her, and the result was that she just castrated the black man. Everyone was against him—his woman and the white man.

But today it's the black women who are charging that the black man talks black but sleeps white, particularly a number of the activists. These men speak about the beauty in being black, and yet they pursue white women. They have this middle-class hangup that you haven't arrived unless you've got a white mate. It is part of the black paranoia in this country, being indoctrinated for so long to believe that white is right. To me, that's a lot of *nothing!*

Happily, the civil rights movement has helped to bring out a new black man, a new black woman. "Black is beautiful" is part of it: in the movement the black man was able to stand up and say what he believed and have somebody respect him for it, even if he had to get spat upon, beaten, thrown in jail and everything else. Women could see this process that the man was more than his stereotype—he thought, he had great ideas, but he had been blocked from implementing them. When he did succeed in getting some of them put into reality, women gain respect for what he was saying and doing—he was a man.

The new black woman that has evolved is sure of herself, but at the same time she is more aware of the needs of a black man. She doesn't overpower him. She purposely underplays herself, which is in complete contradiction to the women's liberation thing. I enjoy the extent of my independence. I go along with their "equal pay for equal work done," anything in the employment category. Beyond that I don't want any parts of that movement.

Black Belt

Faith on the Land

They have names like Choctaw and Wilcox and Lowndes and Pike, and they are Alabama counties, sixteen of them, stretched in a fat belt across the lower part of the state. Mostly they are black, and for hundreds of years they have borne the bitter fruit of slavery and segregation. One survey a few years back found that the average black family had an income of about $1,300 a year, 60 percent below the poverty line, 70 percent less than the average for whites. Among blacks twenty-five and older, the average education was fifth grade or less. Generally they lived on little tenant farm patches, out on the back roads.

Odyssey

A black Atlantan told us there was someone we should see in Alabama's black belt, and he called him Willie Harrison. The way he said it made the name come out like the stereotype of all the shiftless, faceless people in overalls you see on the country roads, who never get addressed as Mr. and who are known only by the nicknames the white man has given them.

But when we met Harrison, it was quickly obvious that he was not *Willie* but rather William—or, still more apropos, Mr. Harrison. He wore buckle shoes; his pants were creased sharp; his mustache was precision-trimmed, his hair kept short. Although he is small—135 pounds—he projected a strength and toughness that drew respect. There was nothing amiable about him; he answered the question, and that was that. Frequently he told us, "Let's face facts."

Harrison is manager of the Southwest Alabama Farmers Cooperative Association (SWAFCA), one of the country's largest black rural co-ops, with about 1,800 small-farm members in ten of the black belt counties. SWAFCA buys fertilizers and farming supplies in large lots, selling them to anyone, but mostly to members. It contracts to buy vegetable crops from its members at a fixed price and then distributes them in its own marketing setup. In the South there are about forty black rural co-ops. All have problems of some kind. They may be the black man's salvation from what Harrison calls economic exploitation. In SWAFCA's new offices, a short way out of Selma, Alabama, he talked.

William Harrison

You can interpret the co-op in a lot of ways—part of the system, outside the system. I interpret it as being the only way poor people are going to survive. A man learns he can't make it on his own; only way he can do it is through the cooperative movement.

SWAFCA was conceived out of necessity. Plantation owners in the area were taking advantage of the poor. Lot of people planted cotton, and if they were renters, they were never able to realize any profit. Always they owed back to the landowner. When the owner extended credit, he could charge what he wanted in interest. If you need credit bad enough, you'll pay 100 percent. The co-op came into being to break down that type of relationship.

In SWAFCA we can provide farm supplies cheaper than most people and in a wider area. We distribute in every one of the SWAFCA counties, not just in certain cities. On the average, our fertilizer is $5 a ton cheaper than anybody else. Two years ago one particular fertilizer, ammonium nitrate, was selling for $80 a ton. We were able to get it and price it, still not losing money, at $55 a ton. In 1970 alone, we hope to sell about $200,000 in supplies.

We're trying to get people away from cotton. It's a dying thing. We don't even handle it. There is a tremendous amount of money to be made in vegetables, with a very good chance that people who want to farm can make a good living. Example: Two, three years ago farmers would get three and a half cents a pound for their cucumbers. We're now offering eight cents a pound. Other people who buy produce from the farmers will have to compete with what we're paying—or they won't get any crops.

SWAFCA has helped in other ways. We have tended to make money much more relaxed in this area. Any SWAFCA member can borrow from the government on what we call a SWAFCA loan, without any collateral. You don't even have to own land. So far, 338 farmers have done it. The Agriculture Department has never done things like that. We've forced revolutionary changes. Director of the Farmers Home Administration in Washington indicated to me he'd see that all co-op members needing money would get what was adequate to farm with. Heretofore blacks were never able to.

People here may be uneducated, but they can know that they're part of a growing organization. That's important to the black man because he's never had a chance to express himself. Been completely isolated, nobody ever knew he existed. He was never part of anything that was an ongoing thing. But people all across the nation have tended to look to SWAFCA as one of the best, the biggest co-ops. The black man here can take pride in that.

There has been a real waste of people. SWAFCA has given some a chance to develop. Used to be they were doing things that had no relationship to their abilities. Take SWAFCA's office girls. Four years ago they were just typists; nobody gave them a chance. Now they are secretaries. They compose really good letters, just like college students. The potential for so many has been wasted. I see people on our board, some can't even read, and I see how in SWAFCA they have grown, how they can express themselves, and you wonder what would they be like if they'd had a chance for an education.

Odyssey

Harrison knows something about those people on the land. He was born on a two-acre rented farm at Lisman, Choctaw County, near the Mississippi border, in 1933. But he was one of the lucky ones. Education was part of his life.

William Harrison

There were nine of us, six boys. Most of us went to school wherever we could. But out of the nine, seven are college graduates. All my mother wanted us to do was get an education. She saw the advantages, didn't want us going through what she had. She worked hard, did washing, and she never kept us out of school to work. Not to pick cotton. We either picked it on Saturdays or after school, or we plowed in the early morning. I don't care what happened—we went to class! Might have been hungry, but we went. She died when I was fourteen, and since the only thing she wanted for us was schooling, that is probably what pushed us on to get it. We were close as a family, depending on each other. Oldest sent the next one to school; next one sent the next one.

One thing I wanted to be was a teacher. And after I finished at Alabama State College in Montgomery, I went back home to Lisman. But the white board wouldn't hire me. Said I was a bad nigger, accused me of being a Communist, just because I would say Yes and No to people, not Yes, sir or No, sir. That caused me some anguish, some bitterness. I stayed home, farmed a little, read a lot. Things run through your mind. One thing, more than anything else, I decided I liked Choctaw and I determined I wouldn't leave. Secondly, I determined I was going to be what I was. I wasn't going to change. I'd keep saying Yes or No.

Finally, there was a vacancy, and the board couldn't find anybody else, so they said, "Hell! We'll hire him and see what happens." I was in elementary school, then junior high, finally senior high. I was there fourteen years.

During that time we blacks in our area were all aware of injustices. But nobody knew exactly what to do. Let's face facts. We've all been scared, and a lot of things you wanted to do you just wouldn't. You have to mature, grow up. More than anything else the movement in Montgomery made people realize what could be done. If it happened there, in Montgomery, it could happen anywhere. We formed the Choctaw County Civic League, did voter registration, public accommodations. Boycotts, marching, the whole thing. We wanted to integrate the schools, but we didn't go at that, first off. We saw whites had school buses two years old, blacks had buses twenty years old. We went to court on that issue, and then I organized a school boycott, 98 percent effective, wouldn't let no blacks go to school until the court ruled. Right in the middle of the school term the court said the schools were unequal, the buses would have to be redivided. Next year we went back to court and charged overcrowding—which we had set up by arranging for 1,200 blacks to register in a school already filled with 1,000 whites—and the court ruled for us, and we got total integration, total desegregation. It was the first rural school in America to have anything like that.

One thing we never had in Lisman was violence. We let it be known that we didn't believe in nonviolence. Once when a black guy was running for road commissioner, we heard the Klansmen were coming to parade at his house. Nobody hit the cotton patches that day, and when the Klansmen started parading, we just turned loose and started shooting. We had no more Klansmen doing any parading.

Politics was another reason we got to forming SWAFCA. We found that black guys was selling votes to the white man. Black man sold it because he needed his food. The whites could threaten to throw him off the farm, or if he was paying for a truck, the whites could say, "If you vote the other way, we are going to foreclose on you." And you could get $5 for your vote. Anybody will sell a vote if he is hungry. You see, there was no economic stability, which meant that in a sense the guy was justified in selling his vote. We were not so much concerned about whom he voted for—we just wanted him to have a free choice!

Odyssey

One hot July day, en route to SWAFCA, we stopped in Selma to buy some supplies. I asked a white store clerk if things had changed much since the confrontation at the town's Pettus Bridge. "Not much," she said. I asked if black people could eat in any Selma restaurant. She gave me a queer look, as if maybe I wasn't as white as I seemed. "I guess they can," she said. "But it is only the uppity niggers that want to."

There was a time in Selma and in the country when black Americans could be dismissed that easily. But not William Harrison.

"When I was with the Alabama Council on Human Rights after leaving teaching," Harrison told us, "I spent two summers working to elect a black man as chairman of the Macon County Agricultural Stabilization and Conservation Service. That board handled more than $1.5 million a year in a county 51 percent black, yet the board had never had a black man. But we elected a black and got him as chairman. That was the first time in the whole country that any ACS board ever had a black as chairman. We did a few things that were quite illegal but that is the only way you can beat the system. It is illegal, so you got to do illegal things to beat it."

SWAFCA, born in 1967, almost died in controversy. Two Alabama governors, Lurleen Wallace and Albert Brewer, tried to veto poverty program grants for it, and twice Washington officials overruled them. Noting that one of SWAFCA's early coordinators was associated with the Black Panther political party started in Lowndes

County by Stokely Carmichael,* the Alabama legislature passed a joint resolution saying SWAFCA's federal funds "in reality will be spent to finance the lawless Black Panther movement, designed to overthrow the government of their country and particularly the governments of the southern states." When the Farmers Home Administration in Washington agreed to lend SWAFCA $852,000—bringing the total federal funds in the project to nearly $2,000,000—an Alabama Congressman asked the General Accounting Office to look at the co-op's books. GAO found accounting chaos: Moneys inexplicably missing, vanished records. SWAFCA's first manager was fired, and the co-op was in shambles.

Harrison, one of SWAFCA's pioneer directors, was drafted to take over. He brought in an accountant—a white man—to set up proper books and train the black staff. He reorganized the marketing system and beat such a trail through the countryside lining up new members that the staff took to calling him "the road runner." But his vital achievement was leading SWAFCA into developing a 13.5-acre site outside Selma into a $300,000 complex of air-conditioned offices, produce loading shed and platform, warehouse and machine shop. In contrast with SWAFCA's early spokesmen, he said very little about social and political reform. He concentrated on making money for SWAFCA members. He got the co-op into the gasoline business; it would be hard to think ill of anyone so American he pumps gasoline.

The result of Harrison's reforms: Governor Brewer, who had once tried to veto a poverty grant to SWAFCA, said in 1970 he had no objections to another one. And, he added, nobody in local government had voiced any objections, either. Harrison had understood the "system," had perceived why the heat had been put on SWAFCA, and had known what to do in calming the opposition.

William Harrison

They accused us of being Black Panther advocates, of being Communists, saying we weren't interested in making SWAFCA successful, we wanted to use the money for black revolution. They would have said anything else if they had felt it would hurt us. Part of the reason was that we were threatening the whites' established order. But more than anything we were handling a lot of money, and some

---

* Unrelated to the Black Panther Party organized in California.

others probably wanted to control it, get a chunk of it, you know. It's normal.

We are not having the opposition we did have. I think people have more or less interpreted us as a business, rather than some of the wilder accusations they made before. I think the fact that we have fixed capital is an indication to them that we are here. Probably people say, "Even though we fought them, they are still there, and hell, we might as well leave them alone."

We've had our ups and downs. SWAFCA as an organization is still not showing a degree of profit. A lot of people hope we do fail, which is why we are having such a damn hard time succeeding. Some people have fought it because they are not part of it. Others, because, just like the average American, they got to have somebody to exploit. And some people in government aren't so hot on the idea of a black cooperative. But why should the government, or anybody else, try to make us feel inferior by virtue of the fact that money has been given to us? For years the government subsidized the middle-class American cooperative movement. Government has subsidized railroads, General Motors, airlines. Why in hell shouldn't government make money available to low-income groups, black, white or whatsoever, so they can also have a chance to succeed in this environment?

Odyssey

It is an old populist dogma that eventually the poor, no matter how badly divided on the race issue, will unite in their common economic interests. Since SWAFCA was offering advantages to poor blacks, was it also appealing to poor whites?

William Harrison

Lot of people thought the poor would come together, thought it would happen in the co-op movement. It may happen, may not. I don't see any signs of it here. What I see is that the system has done a very good job of brainwashing folks. Black and white. System has made the poor white believe he is poor because of me, because of any black man. White got to hate somebody, so he ends up hating black. He can't bring himself to grips with the fact that he ain't poor because of blacks.

Put it this way: We're hoping to do a million dollars' worth of business in a year. We have done a lot for blacks, more for the membership than the organization itself. Why hasn't the white seen that? Why not, when the whites need the services we provide? I can look on the few occasions we get white people buying supplies from us. You know who does? The ones who can really save money through us, but don't need it any damn way! Just the other day a guy called and wanted 30 tons of ammonium nitrate, 30 tons of fertilizer, 3,300 pounds of cotton seeds. With his money he don't need us! Sure, we'll sell to him; we are in business to make money to be able to stay around and help our members. But poor whites don't see that idea of help because of brainwash prejudice.

I don't care how much education you got, don't care where you've been to school, if you are black, you are, in the eyes of the biggest segment of the population in America, still a black man. I don't think blacks and whites coming together is going to happen any time soon. Never in my lifetime, never in yours. I've done civil rights work much as anybody, and I have fought for integration as much as anybody, but you look around the last few years, and you wonder is that what we really need. Did we really want integration of the schools? I don't think blacks are going to be fully accepted in integrated schools, don't know whether integration is going to be helpful at this stage. Black pride has to be taught. That has to come out. Whites are going to have to be in a position to accept the black man as their equal. Until that, I think integration is never going to be a reality. I am not speaking as a separatist—just the plain realities. Ain't no way in the world you can accept me, as long as you feel you are better than I am.

When we were having troubles about funds in the bank, I went to see the banker. I don't think they had really handled the accounts the way they should have been. First thing he throwed at me was how smart he was. He had a law degree from so-and-so place, and I think he referred to me as "boy." But I took advantage of all the other stuff he told me, and when the time came, I really screwed him with it. I did everything I could to mess him up, took advantage of him, because, damn it, he thought he was smarter than I was. Now I can walk into his bank and he respects me. I've proven to him that, damn it, I am black, but I am smart as he is. I don't care if he does have a law degree. He's been deprived of a lot—including the fact of being black. I'm proud of being black. I feel I am as human as anybody else, and I am going to use whatever is available that I want. Whether *you* want me to or not. If they are available to the public, I am going to use them. I am not going to be deprived anymore. I am going to say what I want to say, just like any other normal American.

Martin Luther King's
Appointment in Samarra

Memphis

It rained in Memphis, Tennessee, the morning of January 31, 1968. There then unfolded a series of events that brought Dr. King to his own appointment in Samarra—death by assassin less than three months later.

The events came in this order:

With the rain, the white city officials in the public works department sent home the twenty-two black employees doing sewage work, all on hourly pay. This meant they got no wages that day. But whites doing the same work, and also on hourly pay, were kept on, and when the rain ended in about an hour, the whites were sent out on jobs. They were paid for a full day's work. The blacks objected. The city then agreed to give each man two hours' pay. Again the blacks objected.

This time they took their grievance to Memphis Local 1733 of the American Federation of State, County and Municipal Employees. The city had no bargaining contract with the local, refused to acknowledge it, but had agreed the men could pay dues into it and regard it as a "club" if they desired. The all-black local, without notifying the national union office, called a strike, and on February 13, a total of 1,375 public works employees, most in trash and garbage collection, stayed off the job.

The city gave no hint it would yield to the strikers, who appeared equally determined to stay out until they were recognized and collective bargaining was begun. As the siege lines hardened, the national union office asked one of its black organizers, Jesse Epps, later to be special assistant to the international president, to "run up to Memphis for a few days" to see if he could help the strikers. Seeking to mobilize public support for the strike, the union assigned a number of its people to Memphis.

Epps, Southern-born, thirty-three years old, but Northern-trained in unionism with the electrical workers in Syracuse, New York, was in the strategy planning group which thought pressure could be put on the city administration if national labor and civil rights leaders took up the Memphis cause. Among those appealed to was Dr. King, who agreed to interrupt his planning for the Poor People's March on Washington to go to Memphis.

Dr. King's charisma was high voltage. His first Memphis rally drew 15,000. A huge street demonstration was then planned. In the King tradition it was to be nonviolent, but when the march came off on March 28, violence was everywhere. The crowd swelled from curb to curb, beyond the sidewalks, jammed against storefront windows. There was a spattering of glass being broken, then confrontation between young blacks (who were not in the line of march) and police, and, finally, gunfire. When the melee was over, a sixteen-year-old boy lay dead, 60 people had been hurt, 280 had been arrested, 155 stores had broken windows.

In the wake of that came the bitter questions for King: Had nonviolence run its course? Was the movement that began in Montgomery to die in the bloody streets of Memphis? Dr. King tried to blunt the criticism by saying that his staff had played no part in planning the march and that his group had no knowledge before the demonstration that young blacks were talking of violence. And then he went back to Atlanta, vowing he would return to Memphis.

Jesse Epps

We knew we had to convince Dr. King of the great necessity for him not to give up on Memphis. But he told me, "Jesse, I would like to come back, but my staff is totally against it, and I think that perhaps they are right, because if I spend too much time in Memphis, I am not going to have anything for the Poor People's March. If you want me, you have to convince me and my staff that Memphis is the place we've got to come back to."

It had been planned that a Memphis minister would go with me to talk with Dr. King, but at the last minute he couldn't, so I went alone. It was Saturday morning, and Dr. King permitted me to sit in on the staff meeting. We argued there from nine o'clock in the morning until five in the afternoon. Dr. King was with us until noon, and then he came back at three o'clock. My argument was this: The press had done a very vicious job on Dr. King—which was wrong—saying he had run out. I said that impression had to be challenged. Dr. King asked for a review. Those against his return had their say. I said that Memphis was in a sense a miniature of Washington and that if you couldn't be successful in Memphis, the critics would say the Poor People's March would fail in Washington. When he spoke, Dr. King agreed—that this was going to be the criticism and that whether he wanted to or not, he had to go back to Memphis.

The next Tuesday he came back. We had a rally planned for Wednesday night, but that night it was raining so hard—if you listen to the tapes you can hear the thunder—and everybody thought: "My God! We are not going to have anybody at the rally, not even our own folk." So Dr. King asked his number two man, Dr. Abernathy, to speak in his place, but when Abernathy got there, he saw so many people he called Dr. King, and Dr. King said, "If the people are coming out, I'm coming over."

That was the night he made that speech.

Memphis

It was as though he were saying good-bye, in his own intensely personal style. He said:

"Well, I don't know what will happen now. We've got some difficult days ahead. But it really doesn't matter with me, now. Because I've been to the mountaintop. I won't mind.

"Like anybody, I would like to live a long life. Longevity has its place. But I'm not concerned about that now. I just want to do God's will. And He's allowed me to go up to the mountain. And I've looked over, and I've seen the promised land. I may not get there with you, but I want you to know tonight that as a people we will get to the promised land.

"So, I'm happy tonight. I'm not worried about anything. I'm not fearing any man. Mine eyes have seen the glory of the coming of the Lord. . . ."

Jesse Epps

The next night I was with him at the Lorraine Motel, planning for a mass meeting so we would work the community up for the march on Saturday. We were going to be sure we had discipline, and we were going to start everybody off in the march by making them pass through empty tractor trailers. By having them funneled like that, the marshals could keep everybody within the curb lines, and we would have control. He thought that was a good idea.

And I left, and twenty minutes later he was dead.

Memphis

At the Lorraine Motel a marble inscription marking the assassination says: "They said, one to the other, Behold, here comes the dreamer. Let us slay him, and see what will become of his dreams. . . ."—Genesis 37:19-20

Jesse Epps

There are times when I wonder if I was right, if I should have gone to persuade him to come back. I tell you, this has weighed very heavily on my mind at times. Once I said this to Mrs. King, and she said, had it not been there, that night in Memphis, it would have been some other place, in some other town. He *did* have an appointment in Samarra—somewhere. The thing is, it was not a Memphian killed him. It was the atmosphere of this country, just like it was the atmosphere in Dallas that killed Kennedy, not the man who pulled the trigger. It gave a license to anybody who made the President a target. This was her rationale, and it gave me, I don't know, a little more peace. Perhaps she is right. That really, in a sense, all of us in the American system are to blame, who sit idly by and do nothing about the evils in our community.

Odyssey

Jesse Epps is not a big man, but he has good shoulders, strong arms, narrow hips. He gestured constantly when talking to us, his face alive with sudden smiles, grimaces, frowns and bursts of laughter, some of it directed against himself. We saw him first at his union office, then later at his ten-room house in a suburban setting. The Epps family had just finished building on a new sunken living room, 35 feet long, decorated in Italian Provincial, with marble-topped tables, sofas done in avocado. Mrs. Epps, small, animated, did the decorating (with the drapes from Sears Roebuck) and told us she had always liked the Italian mode.

Epps sat one one of the new couches. At times he was bone erect; sometimes he slouched so far down that he almost seemed about to slip to the floor.

Jesse Epps

My father was a farmer, owned 120 acres in Dublin, Mississippi, about 75 miles from Memphis. Daddy told us once how a Negro had been dragged right through the streets of Dublin in the full play of everybody and was carried out on the edge of town and hung on a Saturday afternoon. And not a thing done about it. And another Negro was accused of approaching a white woman, just talking, and he was hunted down by a posse and killed.

Daddy, being a firm believer in the Scriptures, would say to us: "This is violence, this is wrong, not the way it ought to be. This is a sin, and God is going to judge the whites for it, and they are going to have to pay." This didn't seem right to me, just letting God take care of it. Once I said to my father, "What is there for us to do if God is going to do all these things?" And he said, "What we take unto ourselves, trying to do for ourselves; then God says there is a way to see right unto a man, and that as long as we love mercy and do justice, the Lord will work things out." That really wasn't a satisfactory answer, but I accepted it then.

I had three brothers who were in the armed services, and I shan't forget, even though I was only ten or eleven, when one of them came home and said to my mother, "I've been across the ocean to fight for this country, and then I come back to Mississippi and I can't even be treated as a human being." And then he went on, in words that have stayed with me, "I ain't going to pick no more cotton, I ain't going to pull no more corn, and if I catch the mule running away with the world, I am going to tell him, 'Go ahead on!' " And he left and went North.

Odyssey

Epps himself went North, he told us, because he needed work to support his wife and also wanted to get an education. In Syracuse, New York, he got a job in the General Electric plant by night and went days to the university. He was free of Mississippi, but there was, he said, still an anger in him.

Jesse Epps

At the university I was reading and reading, and I saw that all the things we were talking about—what was good for society, what was hailed to be American in character—none of these things were being done in actual fact. I read, with some sensitivity, and a sense of its real nobility, the Declaration of Independence. Also the Constitution. And yet, while at Syracuse, I could see the contrary of the democratic process being practiced.

I don't know that there is such a thing as true atheist, but I was about to dismiss the Scriptures as only theory, words that might have been practical for yesterday, but not for today. Then I began to really examine them in the light of ancient history. That was the turning point in my life. I saw for the first time that there ain't no difference between black folk and white folk. It says in the Bible that when Moses married an Ethiopian, a black woman, his sister and the rest of Israel condemned him, and God caused leprosy to come upon the land to show his displeasure with the feeling against Moses. When the Bible talked about the pharaohs of Egypt, I saw that if we look at the geography, the pharaohs were black folk! And they were hard task-masters on those who were white. So it was not always a white man that has had his heel of oppression on somebody else's neck. Black folk have had their heel on the white man's neck, too. It is not just a one-sided thing.

I began working with the International Union of Electrical Workers. At GE, where I was assigned, most of the other people were white farmers and they didn't articulate their problems. Not to the bosses. I was the one to speak up to the bosses. Even though the whites didn't like me too much, they made me the steward. That way I could complain, and if I got fired, that was all right with them because they weren't the one losing a job. After that I was elected a committeeman, giving me responsibility for supervising a group of stewards. Still later I was among those who helped to form a civil liberties group.

Friend of mine, George Wiley, was at Syracuse then—now he's executive director of the National Welfare Rights Organization—and headed the local CORE chapter. One day he said to me, "We got to do something about housing in Syracuse." He had been able to rally young people to stage sit-ins and lay-ins to stop constructions at urban renewal sites because there wasn't any decent relocation for the black people who'd been there. But the kids were carted off to jail, and we knew the city would beat down the protest unless we got some people with standing in the community or the backing of local organizations willing to get arrested. Since I was a vice-president of the NAACP chapter, I went to the board, asking them to participate, but they wouldn't. So the next afternoon I went down with the students and got arrested. It was the headline in the next morning's newspaper. The local union was caught in a bag. It couldn't publicly denounce my action, because it was within the confines of the policy and procedure of the international union. Well, the union had to support me, and the district attorney, who was a decent man, elected by labor, dropped the charges. And pressure was put on the mayor to negotiate with us on a good relocation system. Eventually we got that crisis behind us.

Odyssey

In the early sixties, Epps was on a leave of absence to organize an association for helping the black youth in his native Mississippi Delta country. On the surface, it was to be a recreational program, but Epps' real purpose was to teach reading and writing—as part of the program in teaching athletics.

"But," says Epps, "I wasn't going to get caught in that Mississippi trap. I wasn't going back there to live. I was going to have a local director for the program, and all I would do was go back and forth." It didn't work out that way. One Saturday in 1963 Epps was home in Syracuse looking at television with his son, Jesse, Junior, who was not quite four.

Jesse Epps

We were watching the news. It was on the violence in Birmingham. Jesse, Junior, who is a great lover of animals, saw the dogs being turned loose on the demonstrators. "Daddy," he said, "why they let dogs on the little boys and girls?" And I thought, that's something you can only really talk to adults about. But I wanted him to understand, so I said: "The problem, junior, is that the mamas and papas of these little boys and girls ought to be out there, and then the boys and girls wouldn't have to. But the mamas and the papas weren't brave enough, so the little boys and girls had to do it."

What this made me see, however, was that it's easy enough to stand up in New York and say a man ought to stand up in Mississippi and Alabama and be a man. But it is another thing to subject your family and yourself to the pressure of society within the context of battle.

I moved my family back to Mississippi.

Odyssey

He got a home in Clarksdale, not too far from Dublin. The recreation-and-education association he'd created became a part of the poverty program. When Mississippi got one of the first Head Start grants, Epps became assistant director of the county Child Development Project. Within a year, however, he began to see signs the power structure was moving to take over the association.

He later left the program, returned to union organizing, and was hired by Jerry Wurf, international president of the State, County and Municipal Employees.

Jesse Epps

It seemed to me Wurf told it like it was, in terms of the poor people, the blacks. Quite candidly, I thought: "Here's a smart Jew, saying all this, but not really believing it." But as he went on, I saw that his union was the real union of the poor. If you are discussing exploitation and the forgotten working Americans, here was where they really were.*

First thing I did in Mississippi was organize with the public works people in Pascagoula. That's where I always point as my example of black and white together. Very first meeting I went to the whites were on one side, the blacks on the other. We thought it best to lay the whole thing on the table—that the struggle was not between black and white, but between haves and have-nots, and that if we could be divided on the color line . . . well, just forget it! But if they were committed to fight because it was right, then we'd stick with them. In the meetings that followed they were pretty well integrated, and it be-

---

* Since we talked with Epps, he has resigned his union position.

came a group working together. They demonstrated their sincerity when the predominantly white membership elected a black man as treasurer. The amazing thing is that when you have whites giving the black power salute, black power in the sense of deliverance, you have poor whites who know their whole salvation is tied to the success of the group. So we had our strike in Pascagoula, and I had to be there for two months. We'd just negotiated the contract when I got the call to go to Memphis.

Memphis

The Memphis sanitation workers' strike in 1968 lasted sixty-five days. When it was settled in mid-April, the city recognized the union, agreed to a pay raise for the sanitation people, and approved a checkoff system for paying union dues.

Jesse Epps

Memphis has given new meaning to the working poor, new hope to the hopeless. The sanitation man in Memphis was symbolic of those who have given up, who regard themselves as totally unidentified and unidentifiable in this society. But when you saw how it was during the violence in Dr. King's last march, the tanks on the street, the soldiers with bayonets, and there came a little man walking along, with a sign saying I AM A MAN!, when you could see that, no matter where you were, you could take hope. People could say, if the men of Memphis can do it, we can too. This is why I say that Dr. King did not die in vain.

Close-up: Turmoil
in South Carolina

The View from the Campus

Odyssey

Ernest Carson just sat there in the living room of his family's home. He was muscular, biceps and chest straining at his white cotton T-shirt. He was reciting horror, but in a dead calm, as if numbed by what he was remembering. For he had survived what Black America knows as the Orangeburg Massacre.

It took place the week of February 5, 1968, in the little town of Orangeburg, the center of black college education in South Carolina. Students from the community's South Carolina State and Claflin College attempted to integrate a bowling alley/snack bar which refused to serve blacks. What followed from that small, modest goal became the hallmark of police-student confrontations: arrests, resistance, rock throwing, glass breaking, billy clubs and, finally, gunfire. At Orangeburg, state highway patrolmen fired pistols, rifles and shotguns, killing three black students, seventeen and eighteen years old, and wounding at least twenty-seven others. The gunfire lasted less than half a minute, perhaps as little as ten seconds. But it marked the bloodiest outbreak of racial violence in South Carolina's modern times.

Ernest Carson was then seventeen, and a freshman at South Carolina State.

Ernest Carson

We students had been conversing around campus, talking about Orangeburg, thinking the separation of blacks and whites shouldn't be. According to the population, the majority here is black, but we still had segregated places, holding the blacks out. The idea was to integrate these places to get blacks and whites together. The owner of the only bowling alley in Orangeburg said he was running a private club, and we couldn't get in. February 5 I had heard that students were going down there, so I went. Other students had arrived before me, and they had forced their way inside. The patrolmen told them to leave. The students said they wouldn't until the whites did. Next, everybody was asked to leave. The whites waited around on the outside, figuring the blacks would go and then they could go back in. We stayed until they drove off, and then we returned to campus.

Tuesday night we went back to the bowling. Patrolmen was waiting on us. We forced our way in. This time I was on the inside. The patrolmen didn't ask any white people to leave. They told us to or be placed under arrest. It was about thirty of us. They placed us under arrest and were getting patrol cars to carry us down to the jail. They didn't want to carry too many patrol cars there, so they said, "If you don't want to be arrested, you can leave now." The students remained. They still didn't get enough patrol cars, and some of us were not taken to jail.

There was some incident outside, rowdiness, and when the students in the bowling alley came on the outside, they found the dean talking to the chief of police or whoever had authority over the patrolmen. A fire engine came down there, and I imagine they planned to heap water on us. The students gathered around the truck and were making statements like "We were wet before, you know!" Students had been sprayed with water some years ago. This time the truck was ordered out of there, and then a few students started back to the alley. As we did, someone broke a window. Patrolmen came rushing over, and they grabbed one fellow, figuring he did it. They took him to jail. And they pushed the students back with their billy clubs. I really don't know what happened to get them rowdier. I was somewhat like in the number two rank, or file, in the crowd, and when they were swinging the billy clubs, a fellow in front of me got hit. I saw where a girl was hit with a club. The crowd was running and stumbling over each other, trying to get away from the police. I myself hopped over the edge of a car and was just missed by a patrolman with a club.

It was about a quarter of a mile to campus, and as we were running to it, we were met by other patrolmen trying to drive us back to the police at the bowling alley. Students were sprayed in the face with tear gas. There was a whole lot of gassing and billy club swinging. I saw one student where he was hit in the face with gas, and he was holding his stomach like he had been hit with a fist or club or something. He could barely make it. After all this happened the students began to pick up rocks. We didn't see why we were being hit and gassed. So out of frustration we broke windows. And I was in this number. When we got back to campus, students threw bricks and bottles at cars passing by the college, but later that night everything settled down.

Wednesday I was on campus all day. There were some students in the center playing cards or shooting pool, but it wasn't no meeting or nothing.

Thursday night there was a meeting at Claflin College—just a fence separates it from State—but an important factor was that the person who was supposed to talk didn't show up. So I went to a room in Claflin, was playing cards when I heard some shots. Student came running from State and said something had happened there. We went running over, but we didn't see anything. We built a bonfire on the road, on the edge of campus, just below this little hill that runs to the highway. There was some wood already there, and we also took wood from the house next door to the campus. Molotov cocktails were thrown on it, and it was lit. I was sitting there on the edge of the hill when a fire truck came, with patrolmen and state troopers and national guardsmen. When they came, the students started to run to the inner part of the campus because the policemen were all coming at us. All I saw on them was billy clubs. I hesitated awhile, but when they came within 30 yards of me, I started to run.

The fire truck was out there working on the fire, and the students came back again toward the edge of campus where the patrolmen were. The students got louder and louder, and I imagine this brought some fright to the patrolmen or guardsmen or whoever did the shooting. About 40 yards from the policemen the students stopped. There was some noise, and I turned my head for a split-second to look back at the students behind me. There was firing from where the patrolmen were. It was shotgun fire. Also sounded like automatic weapons. I was hit while I was standing there, hit in my legs, near the kneecap. I tried to run. I took about three steps and fell down. While I was on my knees, trying to crawl away, I was hit from the back, in my thigh. I knew I couldn't progress toward the inner part of the campus, so I just stayed flat. The shooting was so low that I got hit in my left heel bone, directly from the rear because I was facing away from them. Being hit in the heel really pained me. I could feel some funny strains going up my leg, and it was numbed completely. I just gave up. I knew that since they shot, they were going to complete it, continue firing until they got quite a few of us, killed us. So I just lied down there, hoping they would stop but feeling they weren't going to. And I was hit again in the left arm at the wrist. All told I was hit eight times before the shooting stopped.

I managed to hop up on my right leg and get over to a lawn nearby before I fell down again. Two students came up to me and said, "Here's one that was hit." They put my arms around their necks and started to carry me to the infirmary. I was like so exhausted my arms could hardly hold on to them. It was like they were dragging me. Then they picked up my legs, and I was toted the rest of the way to the infirmary.

I lied there on a couch in the infirmary about fifteen minutes before they got me a ride to the hospital by another student who had his car. At the door of the hospital the patrolman said, "Those who aren't injured, don't come in." To the students who were injured they made statements like "If you were able to go out there and get shot, then you're able to come in here on your own." One student had been shot in the buttocks, and the patrolman didn't think he was and said for him to be taken out of the hospital. The student showed him where he was shot, and he remained in. He was the one who helped me to the waiting room where they gave me a pain-killing shot that didn't relieve the pain at all. I suppose the loss of all that blood just causes people to be thirsty for cold water because everybody in that room was thirsty.

Later on my brother, who teaches high school, came to the hospital entrance door. He looked at me first; then he asked one of the patrolmen, "Why did you shoot my brother?" They grabbed him and took him outside, where, he later told me, he was hit on the head with a billy club. They were wheeling me around to the X-ray room when I saw him again. He was bleeding, and they had brought him in to have stitches. I didn't get a chance to talk with him then.

They took two pellets out of me. Some had gone right through, but I still have one in my left heel bone and maybe one or two in one of my knees. I have a lump there and it gets stiff.

Orangeburg

The official explanation at the time was that police opened fire in response to sniper shots. But nobody found any weapons or spent cartridges that could be traced to students. Nobody saw any students with guns. No police were shot. And while, as Carson said, there had been some unexplained gunfire earlier that night, police never did arrest anyone as a sniper or produce any evidence to support the claim.

The tragic irony of Orangeburg is that it took killings to accomplish what might have been done without bloodshed. Two days after the shootings the U.S. Justice Department went into court to desegregate the bowling alley. Less than three weeks later black men bowled there for the first time. The department also tried to get a local grand jury to indict policemen for murder. The jury refused. The department then brought nine of the state patrolmen to trial on charges of violating the students' civil rights by inflicting summary punishment without due process of law.

A jury found all nine patrolmen innocent.

Odyssey

Carson was talking to us on the eve of his appearance as a government witness in the trial of the nine, yet he showed no desire for revenge. He even thought there was some good in the fact the trial was being held: "I do not see any winning, but it will like be a start, so the same thing will not happen again."

Ernest Carson

I try to think deep, to ask, "Now why did this happen?" And when I see the white people in incidents like this, I know that they have the slave bit or supremacy instilled in their minds. From their great-grandparents and their ancestors they feel the blacks are supposed to be the underdogs, and this is what caused them to act this way. And some black people, without deep thinking, would underdog the white man, feel down on him, saying that if one of them is like this, then all is like this. This is not my feeling. I'm not down on anybody—nobody!

I classify myself as an integrationist. Because all that we did, the

Monday through Thursday of that week, all my thoughts and feelings was for integration—which is the freedom for all men to walk the streets, with no prejudices against them, no distinguishing characteristics between people because of color. People wouldn't have the fear. A white man wouldn't have to worry about a white hater hitting him aside the head, or a black man wouldn't have to worry about a black hater hitting him.

Odyssey

There are seven children in the Carson family. When we saw them in spring, 1969, two of them had already graduated and three were in college—although Ernest Carson later withdrew. Their father was a carpenter who traveled as far north as Philadelphia, Pennsylvania, coming home every two or three weeks, to make the kind of money he needed to support his family.

Ernest Carson

If I could make the kind of world I want to live in, it would be a world of integration. I feel Orangeburg's schools will be integrated after a while, when they redistrict, so that there will be white children, starting from kindergarten, in a predominantly black school and blacks in a predominantly white one. Whites got to know that blacks can think like whites can; blacks have the tongue to speak. It's only a skin difference, is all. Young people spend a majority of their time in school, and if things were right, parents wouldn't be able to plant segregation in their children. Start with integration and it is going to stay there because the child grows up with it, just like he does with his arm, or his head, or his teeth. It is just there. And with this feeling, there is nothing that parents can do to change their children, white or black.

Odyssey

On the second anniversary of the Orangeburg killings, the student newspaper at the University of South Carolina editorialized:

We know that nothing like that will ever happen to us, because we are white, we are middle class, we are cautious liberals, and we are at the big university, not at State. But when one, or 28, get shot in the night, can others, even though popular or safe at the time, be safe for long?

For the rest of White America the answer came in less than three months. Four young whites observing a protest against the Indochina war were shot and killed by national guardsmen at Kent State University in Ohio.

The View from the Streets

Isaiah Bennett

Let me tell you about the song "We Shall Overcome." Hear it all over the world. That song was originated right here in Charleston, South Carolina, over on that corner across the street from here, at the American Tobacco plant in the strike of 1945. It was so hard. Company was doing everything it could to break the strike. Locking people up. Had scabs going through the picket lines. Finally, the whites in the union with the blacks went back to work. What that said was: "Some white people you can't trust. You think they are really with you, and then they cave in." Then some blacks went back. In every race you have traitors. Only people staying out was black. Were on the picket lines for months. Everything was against them. Out there on the streets, in the picket lines, people began to sing. Didn't write down the words, just made them up. And what they sang was what we call "We Shall Overcome." *

Charleston

In legend it is a city of quiet grace, with porticoed mansions, cool green gardens, handsome iron lacework, vaulting churches; a city of serenity, content with its traditions. In fact, it is a seaport, with a huge Navy base, the home of steel and tobacco and fertilizer plants, and when the wind is right, you can smell the paperworks from 10 or 15 miles, flying in at 4,000 feet. With more than 60,000 people, something less than half are black. With isolated exceptions—the 1945 strike, for one—the blacks accommodated themselves to a social order in which they were forever second. It was *the Charleston way.* The only nobility ever established on American soil was

* Adapted from a Baptist hymn, "Ah'll Overcome, Someday."

founded here; Charleston's first settler, Anthony Ashley Cooper (in England, the Earl of Shaftesbury), set up a society, with barons, dukes and earls. It didn't last, but its spirit did, and the slavery nurtured on the great rice plantations was venerated as the Lord's work. And the first shot of the Civil War was fired in Charleston, with the barrage against Fort Sumter.

Odyssey

It was the kind of bar where Faulkner's Popeye might have dragged Temple Drake as part of the ordeals in *Sanctuary*. There was a brutal directness about everything. Couple of tables. In the corner an old radio. Well-used old bar. An air conditioner's fan clanking its halfhearted fight with the sweat-drenched air. Not much light. It was the barroom for an old union hall near Charleston's riverfront. And Isaiah Bennett, sitting there with us at a table, talking about his role in Charleston's great hospital strike of 1969, was as direct and harsh as the setting.

Isaiah Bennett

White man can never lose the prejudice to black people. That is like a disease that he have. So a lot of them don't understand what we are doing here. This is an antiunion state; this is an antiblack state. They believe that a black man must remain in slavery at all times. They don't believe in a black man saying, "Since I am working for you, let's sit down and talk, and let me tell you how much I think I am worth." White man say, "No, you not supposed to tell me; I am supposed to tell you." That's why they don't want the union in this hospital strike. They don't want anybody to dictate to them; they want to do the dictating. The whole thing here is decency and respect for human beings. I am telling you fact. I just can't see it no other way. I am living here too long.

Charleston

In the beginning it seemed no more than an obscure little labor dispute, tucked away in a Southern town, involving no great principles, just some black women who did things like empty bedpans, sweep floors, serve meals and all the other menial chores of a hospital. But before that dispute reached its climax, it generated a tide that swept far beyond the streets of Charleston. It engulfed the governor of South Carolina, invaded the editorial pages of the New York *Times,* brought together such implausible bedfellows as Walter Reuther and George Meany, embroiled Cabinet officers and the United States Senate, and in the end reached into the White House itself.

Isaiah Bennett

Why are they interested in Charleston? Because the nation is ashamed. This is a freedom movement for black people, and it has taken hold at the hospital, taken on the whole city, the whole state, because people want to be free. We are rooting out discrimination, all the stuff that is going on. People now rebel against that! That is why I say that Charleston will never be the same, South Carolina will never be the same.

This is my home. I am forty-two years old. My father had ten head of kids; that's why I had to quit high school in the tenth grade, go to work at American Tobacco to help put the others through school. My mother worked on and off, but she had a lot of kids, things were hard. When I first started with the tobacco plant, I was making about $15 a week. That was 34 cents an hour. Seems like I been organizing for labor unions all my life. Union was Local 15, Retail, Wholesale and Department Union Workers, AFL-CIO. I was already on the board of it when I went into the service in 1944. But I was in communication with the people here; they write me what was happening, so I know all about the strike in 1945. When I came out in 1946, I wanted to leave South Carolina, but one man, S. B. Graham—he was the local's chairman and in the tobacco plant—persuaded me to stay. I went back to the plant and to the union. We used to open the local's meetings singing "We Shall Overcome." From the strike in 1945 we had a contract, but we knew things should have been better. They said the law said there had to be separate cafeterias for black and white, separate rest rooms, separate drinking fountains. We said that was wrong! We were working for the same company, going into the same building. Why should the company put up two fountains in the same department, *white only* and *colored?* That is a disgrace! An insult! That was saying we were hardly not a human being. Then federal laws came, and the plant got to be integrated. Blacks started working on the whites' floors, whites on the blacks'. All this time I was working for the union. I felt I needed some more basic education, so I went back to school nights and on weekends. I got my GED.* In time I got to be vice-president of the local.

We organized a chemical company, got the food stores under contract, signed up a baking company. Only way I know to help my people is to unify them, let them know they can fight for justice. If you have a feeling for people, you know when they are in trouble. You listen to them talk about where they work, how they are treated on the job. One night in early 1968 two men came to see me about five black women, practical nurses and nurses' aides, at the state's Medical College Hospital in Charleston. In the hospital there is a pattern where before you go to work, you go to the nurse in charge and get a reading on each patient so you know what the medication is. On one particular night, I was told, the white nurse in charge said, "We are not going to take a reading on the patients tonight." So the black practical nurse asked why. The white nurse said, "Do as you are told, or go home." The black nurse said, "I am not going to endanger the life of nobody, so I think I better go home, because if I don't know what to give my patients, there is no sense I work." So the five black women got together, and when one walked out, they all walked out. This is the key that started the hospital union.

The two men who came to see me were not in my union, just friends of mine. "Where can we go to get justice?" was their question. We met with the five nurses and someone from HEW. His finding was that the nurse in charge had done wrong. I don't think he threatened the hospital one way or the other, but the five women were reinstated. They didn't get back the job they were doing. They got a job, but with less authority. I started calling meetings with them to find out what was going on. I told them to bring 5 more, and the 10 became 15, became 25, and so on. We organized, underground, until we had about 200 coming to the meetings, looking at problems, listening to grievances. They were all nonprofessional help. All black. And anything in the book of grievances and mistreatment that you can name—they had it. White people calling them "Hey, you" or "Hey, so-and-so." Don't even know your name. Talk back to the supervisor, and when evaluation time comes, you don't get the raise. If you get sick in the hospital, don't have no doctor for you, no medical care, have to go over to the county hospital. Making only $1.15. Right

* General equivalency degree, tantamount to a high school diploma.

next door at the Veterans Hospital same kind of help make $1.60 an hour. Come time for vacation the Medical College people tell you when to start, when to come back. You don't have no defense to any charges. And they come to feel that they cannot get self-respect, dignity, unless they have a union to speak for them. So because we didn't have any hospital local yet, we worked with them in Local 15A, which still represents the tobacco workers.

Sure, the hospital knew what was going on. They have spies. When we had about 300 workers, we notified the hospital in September, 1968, we were ready to sit down and talk. We claimed a majority and said we respectfully requested a conference to talk about the workers' problems and needs. The hospital sent out a letter, a very strong one, signed by Dr. William McCord, the president of the medical college hospital. I got it right here. It says:

> . . . I want to make our position crystal clear. We do not want a union here at Medical College. It is our sincere belief that this union has nothing worthwhile or constructive to offer to any of you. This union is interested in one thing only. That's money, your money. This union plans to charge you initiation fee, dues, fines and assessments. They would hope to collect approximately four to six dollars in dues alone from each of you, each month. This union is like a business. It is out to make a profit. Its profit would come from the money they plan to collect from you. . . . It is up to you whether you want to give them some of your hard-earned money but make no mistake about it—it is your money they are after. We of course consider this union matter to be extremely serious. It will affect both you and your family. It could affect you and your job here at Medical College. For this reason it is our intention to resist this union in its attempt to get in here with every legal means at our disposal. Make no mistake about that.

That is what started the ball rolling. We called that a very insulting letter to the people, that he could tell us what organization or union to belong to. It was none of their business. We got the people into Local 1199B of the hospital workers, which has the same international as the tobacco workers. On the seventeenth of March, 1969, we had a meeting set up with the mayor and with Dr. McCord and several workers. But it was postponed. That afternoon at three o'clock Dr. McCord fired 12 people, said he didn't need them anymore. One of them was Mary Moultrie. Workers said they wanted her as their president. Our people said that unless the 12 went back, nobody was going back. An injury to one is an injury to all—that was the pledge we took. We sent a telegram asking that the 12 be reinstated. When the hospital said No, we didn't go to work on March 20. The picketing started on the streets and sidewalks. Next week they got an injunction against us, limiting the picketing to 10 people, 20 yards apart. Some people defied the injunction. More than 100 got arrested. On March 28 the nonprofessional workers at the Charleston County Hospital joined the strike. We wanted to let the nation know what is happening in South Carolina. So we called in SCLC to mobilize the community, make this the whole community's fight.

Charleston

The shadow of Memphis and the martyrdom of Martin Luther King fell on Charleston on April 3. When it became known that the Reverend Abernathy, Dr. King's successor in SCLC, was coming to address a hospital workers' rally that night, the parallels with Memphis—the joining of civil rights and a labor dispute—were too obvious. Charleston was tense. Governor Robert E. McNair ordered a National Guard unit on standby alert, and the men took the call so seriously they practiced bayonet drill for hours. That night Abernathy told a crowd of 1,500 that he was committed to fight war, racism and poverty. "If you need me," he said, "I'll be back. I've been to jail twenty-three times, and I'm just itching to make it twenty-four." He did. Later that month, with the state and county frozen in their refusal to recognize the union, Abernathy came back to lead 500 picketers, or 490 beyond the limit set in the court injunction. When at least 40 of them broke through the police lines to sit down on the Medical College Hospital steps, the National Guard was brought in. Abernathy and a crowd of others were arrested, and for the next several days Charleston was in turmoil. More than 350 were arrested; a state of emergency was declared; 300 state troopers and 700 national guardsmen ranged the streets; a 9 P.M. curfew was ordered. Congressmen petitioned President Nixon to intervene; he directed Justice Department observers be sent to the city. "Charleston," said Dr. King's widow in a national appeal to fulfill "my husband's dream," is "an armed camp. Armored carriers rumble through the streets. National guardsmen encircle the black community with fixed bayonets. Helmeted state troopers are everywhere. . . .

Charleston, like Selma and Memphis, has become a national test. . . ."

With Abernathy in jail, his executive vice-president, Andrew Young, directed SCLC's tactics at Charleston.

Andrew Young

We really anticipated a very quick strike. The hospital workers were asking for so little we thought anybody in their right minds would give in, because it was obvious that the strike issue was going to get bigger as it went along. But the state and the hospital administration didn't see it this way.

We came in to back the hospital workers because the federal government doesn't give any legal underpinning. Ordinarily, workers are protected against being replaced; laws govern the conducting of strikes; there are certain rules for arbitration. None of these apply to hospital workers, who don't even get covered by the minimum wage laws. So the only thing to do was develop community support. That starts out as a moral suasion, but pretty soon it has to develop into political and economic power. If you have enough votes in the community to put pressure on the political structure, that helps—but if not, as in Charleston, you almost always have to turn toward the economic structure. And SCLC's experience in the South has been that the decisions are made by the people with the money, anyway. So our moral logic was that if the community is making over 600 hospital workers (the number the strike ultimately involved) suffer and do without jobs, then we will support them by spreading the suffering around. We organized the community to stop shopping downtown— where most of the trade is Negro—on the theory the merchants would learn that until the poor did better, nobody would.

At first we didn't have to do much with the boycott. Troopers and guardsmen did it for us. There were so many of them in the Negro community that everybody was really afraid to shop. We used that time to pass out maybe a couple hundred thousand handbills in the suburban shopping centers telling about the boycott, and when we came to using it, we think it was pretty effective. Plus, while the Guard was here, conventions were canceled—four in the first week alone. They figure an average meeting has about 200, and that a conventioneer here spends about $110 a visit. So to a convention city like Charleston that was a pretty big blow. The businessmen came around and put on some pressure, first on the mayor, then the governor. Basically, in a state like this, politicians are much too vulnerable to make creative decisions, whereas a group of businessmen isn't vulnerable to that kind of public opinion. As a matter of form we tried to talk with the governor, but we thought it was much more important to talk with the merchants, the bankers, the men in real estate and insurance. This is what kept the pressure on, the progress coming. The state took the national guard out, they eased and then lifted the curfew, and we were able to keep the negotiating meetings going.

The hospital director, Dr. McCord, is the son of a missionary who grew up in South Africa. What that says about him I don't know, but he is a good old Southern Scotch Presbyterian, and that Calvinist notion of right and wrong, good and evil, is just very hard to deal with. And he is probably past the age where he can be flexible. He was once quoted as saying, "I am not about to turn a $25 million complex over to a bunch of people who don't have a grammar school education." So all these things contributed to making this a race issue, as well as a labor issue.

It is a touchy thing when you get a mixture of race and poverty. Personally, I have no trouble talking with the bankers or the hospital board chairman, but for months they refused to talk with Mary Moultrie, the workers' president, because she is poor, she is uneducated, she is black. Ironically, she is also very, very intelligent, and in the times they attempted to talk with her she has surprised them with her intellectual aptitude. It was so ridiculous that at one time they were willing to settle if they just didn't have to deal with her. There was even informal talk of trading her off for Dr. McCord, letting him retire if we got rid of her. It was just too much for some folk to bear that poor blacks were rising up and really speaking as equals, learning they *are* equals and demanding respect and dignity.

If it hadn't been for race, the workers wouldn't have organized in the first place. As a nurse's aide, Mary Moultrie, who had done that work for six years in New York, started in Charleston at $1.30 an hour. Now she makes more—$1.33. So she teaches a white girl what to do in the job. Black folk look at checks, and she notices the white girl is making $1.60 or $1.75. As they began to look at one another's checks, as they began to see who was promoted, they sensed the dual treatment at the hospital. Had they been white, the clear injustice in classification would have been remedied, probably as soon as they complained. But because they were black, no corrections were made, and attempts were made to fire the women who did the complaining.

In most of our struggles, SCLC went in with maybe a handful of sensitive or dedicated Negro leaders, plus the kids and the preachers. But here we started with a corps of 600 hospital workers, which meant a link to just about every family or neighborhood in Charleston. Just the size of the city is important. Basically you've got one little island, and everybody is right down in here together, and you can walk to almost any place in Charleston. Geographically there is such a tremendous grapevine that I can walk out and say to somebody on the street that we want to have a mass meeting at eight o'clock, and folks will start talking, and the word will spread. Another thing: People know each other. You have blacks and whites going back through three generations of acquaintance. If you look around, blacks and whites live side by side. There have been some very interesting exchanges between the hospital workers and the local police. One lady told me that when a policeman got very mad at one of the workers, another woman said to him, "If you put her in jail, I'm going to tell your wife that you used to go with my sister." And even though they finally got arrested, he used to come by and see them all in jail, bring them candy, cigarettes and things.

Isaiah Bennett

This country don't understand nothing but force. The strong survive. But this is wrong to believe—shouldn't use power to enslave people, to kill them. During the war I was over in the Philippines, and that changed the heart of me, to walk and see poor people who have nothing, not even a hut, cooking outside, and all they have is one big plate, and everybody put their hand into it. One white sailor was driving a truck where poor people was sitting beside the road with their kids, all eating out of the pan. You know what he done? He pulled the truck off the road, and these people had to pull the kids back into the ditch, and the sailor drove off and laughed. I said to him later, "Why you do that?" And he said, "They is the ones cause me to be away from my family." I said, "These people didn't call you in the Navy; don't do that, not to human beings!" Then when I come back to the United States, they do me the same way, would run over me the same way. When they shot down the people in Orangeburg, everybody laughed. Governor said he was sorry, but he commended the troopers, said they did a good job. It was law and order. What does that mean? It means shoot me, shoot the black man. That is what I feel about the whole government of the United States. They are controlled by whites. The white world is together in terms of the race issue. The blacks are not. First thing is for blacks to come together. Everything included—do it together. Right or wrong, fight together, register together, vote together, march together and, if necessary, die together. The blacks don't know it, but if they could get together throughout the world, they would be worse than any atomic bomb you could have. That could be the worst holocaust you could ever sit on.

Blacks are just now beginning to see how the whites have divided blacks. Black preachers are preaching white nationalism. Everything is white. Jesus Christ, the Madonna, Santa Claus. I told my kid, "Don't you never think of Santa Claus as white!" No Christmas tree in my house, no, never. I believe in God, but I don't believe that after I am dead, I am going to rise again. Nobody got no proof. What I want the white man to say is that I am a human being *now,* and I don't have to die to prove I am a human being. So give me what belong to me, now, and don't tell me to go to church every Sunday.

Andrew Young

The basic questions have been economic. The struggle has never been so firmly symbolized as at Charleston. More than Memphis, even. It was Dr. King's death that dominated Memphis; people didn't really understand the issues as such. In Charleston you've got a whole town with a per capita income of about $2,500 a year, and that's partially because South Carolina is the lowest state of the union in labor organizing. I think the two go together. The labor movement has been dead as far as the poor—and the poor blacks—are concerned, but here in Charleston we have an issue that labor can identify with. The New York Labor Council—the workers here are in the same union as the hospital workers there—said it was treating the Charleston strike as a New York strike. Walter Reuther comes in here and brings $10,000. George Meany gives $25,000. Longshoremen were asked to close down the port here, and the textile workers are saying this looks like a strike somebody can win in South Carolina. Several busloads of white textile workers came over from Florence, South Carolina; some even went to jail with us. We basically think that is a pretty good thing, and we encourage it, because we don't like the idea of racial polarization and because it means additional support in building a larger political force.

This is going to help organizing possibilities all across the state. United Auto Workers began trying to organize a new plant. District 65 of the Mine Workers started talking to the garbage workers. We've never had so much support—it is getting to a point where it is more than that; they're taking over the struggle from us. We don't mind, because it should have been their struggle all along. So, if we can motivate labor, motivate a reawakening of the liberal-to-moderate politics, motivate the registering of 20,000 more black voters, not only will this district change, but, potentially, the whole state. And if it goes on long enough, you've got the Nixon administration in a bind it can't really get out of. They almost have to do something.

Charleston is ideally suited to start the pressure on them. For one, this is Strom Thurmond country, so you have a natural tie-in with the Nixon administration on the best possible battleground for dealing with them. You're not dealing with the sophisticated Republicans you'd meet in Illinois or Ohio or Pennsylvania. Here you've got good, old-fashioned, the worst kind, of right-wingers. The other thing is that this is Mendel Rivers' Congressional district—a person who keeps the poor, poor. The racists are located here and are symbolized no better than by Thurmond and Rivers. Almost every week you get a documentation of the military-industrial complex's excesses, and it's always Mendel Rivers [now deceased] in the forefront defending it.

Charleston

Senator Thurmond and Congressman Rivers almost had enough muscle to block a settlement of the strike. The union, with representatives from SCLC and the community, had been chipping away at the negotiating obstacles, and had prompted the state to boost the minimum wage from $1.30 to $1.60 an hour. And the federal Health, Education, and Welfare Department, after the union had complained about the firing of Mrs. Moultrie and the other 11 workers, investigated as part of a long-range look at whether Dr. McCord's hospital was discriminating against blacks. Opinion: It was. Significance: The hospital could lose about $12,000,000 in federal funds, unless the objectionable practices were eliminated. On June 5 the hospital and the union reached agreement, under which the 12 would be re-hired. But suddenly Dr. McCord reneged on the rehiring. On the same day he did that, Rivers and Thurmond were announcing in Washington that HEW's then Secretary, Robert Finch, was "restudying" the threat to cut off federal moneys. "They really don't want to cross Thurmond," Young said, "but at the same time they've got the Democrats breathing down their neck, so if the Nixon administration gives in to Thurmond, it creates a big national issue."

Within days the Nixon people had done all the studying necessary. A call from the White House told the hospital people in South Carolina that Mr. Nixon wanted that strike settled. And, 100 days after it began, the walkout ended at the state's Medical College Hospital, with everybody rehired, wages set at a minimum of $1.60 per hour. Thirteen days later the county hospital strike ended, with an agreement to rehire 64 of the 89 nonprofessionals who had struck . . .

Andrew Young

That increase to $1.60 an hour in South Carolina for the state hospital workers didn't just affect them. It applies across the board to about 20,000 state workers. Gives them about $12 more a week. As far as I am concerned, that is the war on poverty—if you can get a decent salary for the working force, you lift the bottom of the economy.

The Civil War was started in Charleston, and we say it is probably where the second one begins, too—a new civil war to unite the nation economically and create the one America the Kerner Commission talked so much about.

The Ditch

Fannie Lou Hamer

A white girl who was down here once said to me that I should take a trip on LSD. And I told her: "Hell, I'm having enough trouble with the trip I'm already on." Sunflower County, Mississippi, is the ruralest of the ruralest, the poorest of the poorest, U.S.A. This county is Senator James O. Eastland's. Six miles from my home here in Ruleville, he's got 5,800 acres of land that he has been paid one-quarter of a million dollars in two years to waste while people on his plantation suffer malnutrition. The government calls that money subsidy; for black folks it would be welfare.

No, I'm not carrying a hate about it. But what I am saying is that from here on following, we won't stand for it.

Odyssey

It was a chilly but clear November morning when we arrived in Ruleville to see Fannie Lou Hamer. She was living then in what she referred to as her "raggedy old house," two bedrooms and a kitchen, no real indoor plumbing. As we approached the sloping wooden steps to her porch, we met her coming out. She was bundled in a heavy tweed coat and wool scarf. All we could see of her was that she was short and heavy set, with a very black face. She had an errand in town and said for us to go in and make ourselves comfortable; she'd be right back.

We pushed open the creaky door, which led directly into the front bedroom. Three neighborhood women were sitting there around a glowing gas heater. Otherwise it was a dreary, dimly lit room, the only bit of color being a row of freshly starched and ironed little girls' dresses on a makeshift clothesline above a double bed in the corner. The dresses, we learned, belonged to Mrs. Hamer's two granddaughters.

The room was very quiet. There was little talk among the women. They were just there, waiting until Mrs. Hamer returned.

She burst into the room, talking and gesturing as she came through the door. Untying her scarf, she exclaimed, to no one in particular, "I just saw the mayor, and he suggested we sit down and talk about federal funds for housing on the land we've got optioned. Who would have thought he would have said this, even two years ago? Why, he wouldn't even speak to me! This is the same mayor that I caught hell from starting in 1962."

When she says hell, she really belts it. Her husky, powerful voice ranges through outrage, resignation and hope. Her entire demeanor suggests great strength, although, in fact, she walks with a pronounced limp. In childhood she'd fallen, and because there was no doctor available, her hip never healed properly.

Fannie Lou Hamer

I grew up on a plantation right here in Sunflower County. My parents were sharecroppers. It was a very small family, six girls and fourteen boys, all from my mother and father. I was the twentieth child. My mother was about fifty-eight years older than me. I remember nobody believed I was her child. As a little kid when I'd be going somewhere with her, people would say: "This your grandchild?" And she'd say, "No, this is my baby." And they would look at Mama real funny.

I can safely start remembering my life when I was around six. My parents would carry me to the fields with them, and I would just run up and down the rows and play. I'll never forget the day the landowner drove up and asked me could I pick cotton. I told him I didn't know. He said that if I picked 30 pounds of cotton that week, his commissary store on his plantation would give me sardines, crackers, cheese and gingerbread called Daddy Wide-legs. Daddy Wide-legs was a real dark ginger cake of a slim brown boy, with a big mouth painted white, standing there with his legs spread out. It was about eight inches high and didn't cost but a nickel. We didn't have a nickel, so I thought that his offer was truly fantastic. With a family like we had we didn't get a chance for this kind of food. In fact, we never knowed what fruit was until Christmas, when my parents would have saved up enough to buy some oranges.

I told my parents what the man had said. They was very honest people—wouldn't have given me one bowl of cotton—and they said for me to earn it, to pick that 30 pounds. I did and I got the food. Then the landowner bet that I could not pick 60 pounds in the next week. That's how I started to work. After I got older and thought about it, I knew the man tricked me. But you know, it was a kind of challenge to me. By the time I was thirteen years old, a man couldn't hardly beat me picking cotton.

Odyssey

Mrs. Hamer spent thirty-eight of her fifty-two years in the fields. For a child growing up on a Mississippi plantation, school went only from December through March, when there wasn't cotton to be picked. Even then, she said, "If the man had some cornstalks to cut or logs to pile, you'd have to stay home and work. I might go to school two months one year, and the next I might not get to go at all." Emotionally, she added, "I just loved school. I went every chance I could, until I was practically grown. And yet I didn't even finish elementary."

The weather during those four months, Mrs. Hamer said, "was unbelievable. We wouldn't have shoes, and we'd walk four miles over a gravel road to school. It was nothing but a room in a church. There would be maybe seventy-five to a hundred of us in there with just a little potbellied stove to warm us. But the teacher put in a lot of time. Before the run of the day, she would have had every child to that blackboard. Not only did she teach us our alphabet, but you had to learn to say it forwards, then backwards. Once you did that, nobody could ever fool you about an *A*, nowhere in the world."

Mrs. Hamer learned her numbers equally well. "I remember one of my teachers was taking some kind of extension course in arithmetic, and she would have me doing a lot of her work for her. Once I saw somebody else do something, I always felt I could, too. It was a challenge."

Twice within a few minutes, Mrs. Hamer had spoken of responding to challenge. We wondered if any one member in her family had set the example for this.

Fannie Lou Hamer

It's really just all of them. I never met my grandfather on my papa's side but they say he was really something. If the white folks was going to people's houses to search for something, they would never go in his because he'd tell them, "Now you know I'm not doing nothing wrong and you are not going to come into my home." And they didn't.

My daddy was a man that would speak out, too. He had a dispute with a white man, told him he was wrong about something. And that white man sent one of our own color back to poison all of our livestock. But that didn't stop my daddy from speaking his mind.

All of my mother's people was kind of aggressive. I had an uncle, and one time a white man jumped on him. He told my uncle, "If I had my gun, I'd kill you." My uncle said: "I didn't know you didn't have your gun. Because if I'd knowed that, I'd have beat the hell out of you!" Then my uncle went ahead and beat that man up pretty bad.

But my mother, she was a beautiful, smart, black woman. She never really talked about nobody bad, but if she had to challenge a white man, she'd do it anywhere. I remember when I was young, a little thing that happened that made me very proud of her. This niece of mine, Pauline—we was raised up together—who had married and was living on a different plantation, got into some kind of argument with her husband and had come back to us. The same man owned both plantations. And this one day he come riding up on his horse and told my mama, "Aunty"—you know they call you aunty before they would ever say Mrs.—"I'm going to tear Pauline up this morning and make her go back home."

Well, my mama stood and braced that man on the horse and said: "Mr. Brandon, if you get down off that horse, I'll knock you to hell and back this morning before hell could scorch a feather."

I perked up. I always pictured hell as just a lot of fire and I knowed that if she go down and back with him before a feather is scorched he was going to be really traveling. He said she was crazy. But it was just the kind of thing she would do. She was a brave soul.

Once I asked her how come we wasn't white. White people had something to eat, they wasn't working, and we slaved and never had nothing. It looked like to me that if we had been white, we wouldn't have to suffer so. And she told me, "There is nothing wrong with you being black" and that if I lived to be a hundred years old, I was going to be black. It wasn't going to change my color. She said, "Number one, you have to respect yourself as a black child. And as you get older, you respect yourself as a black woman." First black doll I ever seen in my life my mother bought it for me. Through her, I learned very early that black power and black dignity was self-respect. I said to myself that if I ever got the chance, I was going to do something about what she was talking about.

She wanted her daughters to be as nice and intelligent as anybody's. I'd look at her sometimes when she'd be out in the fields, and her clothing would just be patched, mended over and over, and I'd think about all she had done for us, trying to teach us the right way. I'd vow that if I ever live and get grown, I'd never see her wearing nothing patched again. The last ten years of her life were in my house, and she never did.

In the meantime I was just working in the fields, raising hell when I knew it was necessary. I was keeping up with all the cotton weight, every pound picked, because I had learned to figure with a pencil and nobody could take that from me. And what would make me mad on this plantation is that we was out in the country and they would hire people from town. They would want to, like, give the town people $3 a hundred pounds, but we who was living on the plantation, they wanted to give us $2. I was the only one out there who spoke up. I said, "Look, if you don't pay us $3 like you are paying the other folks, we ain't going to pick no more cotton." I was always saying something like that. I was what you call a bad nigger. I said to my people: "You know these white folks don't give a damn about us! They don't care. I just hope I live long enough to do something about it."

This is how I became involved in 1962. Until then I'd never heard of Dr. King, sit-ins or freedom rides. Nothing! I knew absolutely, positively nothing! First thing, we didn't have television, period. What happened out where we was living, you went to the fields about four o'clock in the morning, and when you got back at seven thirty or eight o'clock that night, even if you had a radio, you was too tired to play it. So we didn't know anything about no civil rights.

Yet there was something that happened early in 1962 that gave me pause. When I wasn't in the fields, I would work at the white woman's house. As I'd be doing the ironing, I would watch her television and she didn't do anything about it. This day while I was watching it, I saw troopers, I guess they was, pick up a man and put him in what they called a paddy wagon. He was singing "We Shall Overcome." And I never will forget it. I just stood there, froze. It was something about what was happening there, and I wanted to know more about it. But in the middle of this the woman told her daughter to cut it off. I asked her why didn't she put it back on because I'd like to see it. She said: "Oh, that ain't nothing."

But to me, it was.

Odyssey

The isolation of blacks living in the rural Deep South was almost total, with the church the only meeting ground. The church had special meaning for Mrs. Hamer, whose father was a minister, as were three of her brothers. She has an unshakable belief in God, and when we asked that if God is love, why did He let such misery be visited on black people, she shrugged her broad shoulders. "I think that each person is on earth for a purpose," she said. "Some of us suffer more. You know, I get a great kick out the Psalms of David, the Twenty-third Psalm," and with little prompting she recited it to us.

In the summer of 1962, at the Williams Chapel Baptist Church, little, wood-framed, in the town of Ruleville, Mrs. Hamer first really heard about the movement.

Fannie Lou Hamer

The fourth Sunday in August, I come to church as usual. But this particular time, the pastor announced there was going to be a *mass* meeting at the church that Monday night. He said, "I don't think you should miss this because it is going to benefit Negro people." And it just rang a bell.

So that night my husband, Perry, carried me to the meeting. Jim Forman and Bob Moses from SNCC, Dave Dennis from CORE and James Bevel was there. James Bevel preached from the twelfth chapter of St. Luke, fifty-fourth verse, which is about discerning the signs of time and how a man could look out and see a cloud, predict the rain, and it would become so. Then Jim Forman talked about voter registration and how it was our constitutional right. And you know, that was the best thing I'd ever heard!

They next wanted to know how many people would go down to Indianola, the county seat, and register. I was one of the bunch that held up my hand. A group of us, eighteen, went to register. Bob Moses was with us, and a black guy from over in Bolivar County that had an old school bus carried us there. We sang all the way—and I love singing. But when we got off the bus, we was very quiet and orderly. We went into the county registrar's office, and there was a strange bunch of white folks there. They had guns; they was watching us like we had done some kind of crime.

A clerk asked, "What do you-all want?"

Nobody else didn't say anything, and so I said, "We're down here to register."

And he said, "All of you get out of here except two."

I stood there because I knowed what I was going to do. And a young man, Ernest Davis, stayed there, too. So we taken this literacy test, like "Write the date of this application. What is your full name? By whom are you employed?"—that meant you'd be fired by the time you got back home—"Where's your place of residence in the district? If there is more than one person of the same name, by which name do you wish to be called?" That meant your name would be given to the Klan and the White Citizens Council.

Then the registrar brought out this big black book which was the constitution of the state of Mississippi. He opened it and pointed out to me the sixteenth section dealing with *de facto* laws. He told me to copy it—and I did—and to give a reasonable interpretation of it. Quite naturally I couldn't. Because I knowed as much about a *de facto* law as a horse knows about New Year's!

Once you'd taken this literacy test it would be thirty days before you could check it out to see whether you'd passed. During that time they'd run your name in the paper so many days and you was catching hell from everybody.

When I got home that evening, my oldest daughter met me and said that the plantation owner, Mr. Marlow, was already raising almighty hell. She said, "Mama, I don't know what's going to happen." Then the landowner come up and said: "I was called three times today and they told me you was down there to register. Fannie Lou, you got a choice. Either you go back and withdraw your registration or you leave."

You see, they didn't care how grown you were, and even though I was older than this man, I was supposed to have obeyed him. But I told him, "Mr. Marlow, I didn't go down there to register for you today; I went down there to register for me." He said, "I'm looking for an answer, yea or nay. You're going to have to leave this place if you don't go back."

I knowed I wasn't going back, so I didn't have no other alternative but to leave. That night my husband brought me and our two girls into Ruleville to Mr. and Mrs. Tuckers'. Then the next morning Mr. Marlow talked to my husband and said that it was a damn good thing that I left. At that point my husband said to him, "I want to be with my wife and the kids. If she can't stay, I'll just have to leave, too." Mr. Marlow told him he couldn't get our belongings if he didn't stay on the plantation and help to harvest in the bean crop and cotton. So my husband had to stay.

Then one night he came out to the Tuckers' and said he felt it would be safer if I went to my niece's in Tallahatchie County. "I was in the office," he said, "and I saw some buckshots, plastic shells with buckshot. And I know that these people ain't hunting rabbits at this time of year." He carried me to my niece's. And it wasn't but a few days later, on the tenth of September, 1962, that night riders shot into the Tuckers' house sixteen times.

I stayed at my niece's until Saturday after the third Sunday in October, when I quit out at the field and told them, "I'm going home!" Everybody was real upset. But I said, "I'm not a criminal, and I'm going back home." When I come back to Ruleville, I went to my sister's to live and started looking for a house. On a Sunday, the third of December, Perry, the girls and I moved into this raggedy old house.

On the fourth of December I went right back to that county courthouse, and the man said, "What do you want?"

I said: "Well, this is Mrs. Hamer, and I haven't been here since the thirty-first of August. You are quite aware of what happened. But you can't have me fired no more because I'm already fired. I won't be forced to move because I'm not living in a white person's house. And I just want you to know that I'm coming down here every thirty days until I pass that literacy test. Because if I live, I'm going to register to vote in Sunflower County, Mississippi."

Again he gave me the test. This time it was the forty-ninth section of the Mississippi constitution dealing with the House of Representatives and the two-thirds vote. I went back a month later and found I'd passed.

And then did we have harassments! An early morning in February my husband had gotten up and gone to use the little stool—it's not a bathroom; it's an old, leaky commode. When he come out, there was a knock at the door. He went to see who it was, and two white guys, guns in one hand, lights in the other, walked in. One of the men was the brother of a man who was charged with helping lynch the little kid Emmett Till. Emmett was fourteen years old. He come down here from Chicago in 1955, whistled when a white woman passed, and was lynched. Anyway, these two men wanted to know what my husband was doing up at that time of the morning. They ain't done a thing with us, but that was just to let us know they was around.

One day I got a water bill charging us for using 9,000 gallons. And there wasn't no running water in the house! I went up to the mayor and I told him, "I'm going to pay you this time, but I want you to know you ain't fooling me."

Actually, they done some of everything. They'd call me up and tell me they was going to put me in the river. You just excuse me, but I'm going to tell you the kind of talk they used. I'd answer the phone and a guy would say, "Nigger bitch?" Uh-huh. "We're going to kill you, nigger bitch." Then there'd be a funny sound in the phone, like someone was blowing bubbles.

"You hear that sound, nigger bitch?"

I'd say, "I'm listening."

"That's me, and I've got my ass up to this telephone and I'm farting in your face."

And I'd say, "Well, have you ever thought that you were deformed? Because if you got your ass up to the phone and your mouth at the same time, you are in *bad* shape."

So they'd hang up, you know.

Nobody would hire me to do nothing. That was one way they was in a sense punishing me, by putting "this nigger" in her place. My husband had just as much trouble getting a job. They knowed if he got one, I would eat. Somehow or another we staggered through it, hungry a lot of times, but you'd have never knowed it because I always walked with my head up. And there is a God, just like in the Twenty-third Psalm. For He did prepare a table before me in Ruleville in the presence of my enemies, when people desired to see me starve.

I got to making contact with people, and not only was I able to feed myself, I began to get where I could bring foods in for other people. And I kept working on voter registration.

Odyssey

In 1963 Mrs. Hamer started crisscrossing the state making appeals. She surprised even herself. "You know, I would never have dreamed that I could have spoken to an audience," she told us. "I'd be telling Bob Moses, SNCC's project director in Mississippi, about all the frustrations and the things that I'd seen happen to me and to my kids and to everybody else's—whether they was white or black. And Bob would say, 'Don't tell it to me. When you go to church, you let them know what you think.' So I did. And after I started talking and saying what I felt, people wanted me to come to other communities and talk out. And that's the way I move all around the state and the country now."

In 1963, on a picket line in Hattiesburg, Mississippi, with fifty-two out-of-state ministers, she asked if they could send in clothing and food for helping the poor. "Those kids in Sunflower County," she explained, "were going to school raggedy as a jar of kraut. You ever seen sauerkraut? It's in pieces. That's the way their clothes looked. I started getting clothes for them. But I didn't just help black people. If I got the chance, I slipped things out to the white folks, too."

That didn't impress the white power structure, which continued to pressure her. But the more they pushed, the harder she worked to get people registered. "Me and my husband as a team," she said, "have carried more people to register than any two in the county." In 1962 there were less than 10 black people registered in Sunflower County. By 1970 there were more than 8,000 out of a potential of about 15,000 black voters. "We already now is in a majority. But we're still going to try to get that huge majority. The vote is an important way out for black people. If it wasn't, we wouldn't have caught this much hell trying to get it."

In June, 1963, Mrs. Hamer was arrested in Winona, Mississippi.

Fannie Lou Hamer

I had been to a voter registration meeting in Charleston, South Carolina, and was riding a Continental Trailways bus back to Ruleville. When we got to Winona, I remained on the bus while some of the people went in the terminal on the "white side" to get food and use the washroom. Suddenly Mrs. Annell Ponder, then SCLC southwest supervisor, came rushing out. I got off to see what was wrong.

She said, "There's a chief inside tapping people on the shoulders with billy clubs and telling us to get out."

I said, "Well, Mrs. Ponder, this is Mississippi." And I got back on the bus. Just as I was sitting down to look out the window, I saw a patrolman putting the people in his car. So I got off the bus again, and as I did, this patrolman, pointing to me, screamed, "Get that one there!"

A plainsclothesman in another car turned to me and said I was under arrest. There were five people in the first car, and I was in a second one with two white men. As they carried me to the county jail, they would curse, asking me what was we trying to do. I told them that we wasn't really doing nothing. It wasn't no demonstration or anything. When we got to jail, they charged us with disorderly conduct and resisting arrest. As I came into the booking room behind the five other people, one of the tall policemen—he must have been six eight—was jumping on the feet of this young black guy, James West, who was with us. Then they began to put us in cells. And I'll never forget the sounds and screams from the booking room. I could hear a body hit the concrete floor. Then I heard somebody say to Mrs. Ponder:

"Can't you say, *Yes, sir,* nigger bitch?"

She said, "Yes, I can say, *Yes, sir.*"

"Say it!"

"I don't know you well enough," she said.

Next, they passed me carrying a fifteen-year-old girl to another cell. She had a hole in her head, and the blood was running down over her bosom. Finally, three white men, one of them a state highway patrolman—I saw his name and badge—came and asked me where I was from. I told him and he said, "We're going to check on this."

Naturally when they called Ruleville, they'd would be told I was one of *them Niggers* doing voter registration. The patrolman came back and said: "You're from Ruleville, all right. We are going to make you wish you was dead!"

And the three white men led me into another cell where they had two black prisoners, neither of them from our group. The patrolman ordered me to lie facedown on a bunk. I was flat on my stomach, and he gave one of the prisoners a blackjack. The prisoner asked: "Do you want me to beat her with this?"

He was told, "If you don't, you know what we'll do to you."

The prisoner began beating me with this long leather thing full of some kind of metal. I tried to protect my back with my hands, but my body kept getting harder and harder. He beat me until he was exhausted.

When the prisoner couldn't even raise up his arm to hit me one more time, the patrolman ordered the second prisoner to take the blackjack and beat me while the first one sat on my feet. During that time my clothes worked up real high and so I went to smooth my dress down. At that point, one of the white men walked over, took my dress, and pulled it up over my shoulders, leaving my body exposed to five men. While the second prisoner was hitting me on that same hardness, it got to be just too much. I got to where I couldn't stop hollering and screaming. I remember burying my face in the cot to kind of muffle out the sounds as they beat me on the head. I don't know how long that lasted.

But I finally raised my head, and a patrolman was cussing me, telling me to get up. My body then was as hard as metal. I couldn't hardly bend my knees, and my hands were navy blue. They told me to go back to my cell. I wasn't able to walk, so they had to carry me.

It was about this time that one of our group who had remained on the bus, a SNCC field worker, came to the jail to see what was happening to us. They arrested him, carried him to a different jail, where they beat him. They took his privates out and tried to burn them off. They opened the jail cell where he was, giving him a chance to escape so they could shoot him. He refused.

They also opened our cell doors. But I couldn't have escaped if I had wanted to. Then they got me up one night, trying to get me to write a statement saying *how nice* they'd been to me. The white folks thought we was really that dumb!

So I said to myself, "I'm going to trick you." They gave me this paper and pencil and began dictating. I just marked up that piece of paper ridiculous. I wrote over and over the same line. The white man said: "Do you know what you are writing?"

I said, "I'm trying to write what you tell me."

He said, "Can you read it?"

"No, sir," I said.

He looked at me and shouted, "Give me that paper. You are so stupid!"

I wasn't going to sign no nothing that he had been nice to me. Later—and this was funny—when I was getting ready to get out of jail, I really shook this man up. I'd stayed in jail from the ninth of June until the twelfth, when I was bonded out by James Bevel and Andy Young. This man was standing there as I signed my bond. He thought he was going to be able to show the world how dumb I was.

But I wrote my name and wrote it right quick. I looked at him as I walked out, and he was just standing there with his mouth hanging open.

Nobody was brought to trial for beating us. The Justice Department had a little something going, but it never came off. And when we was tried, I was convicted of disorderly conduct, but not for resisting arrest. A black woman doctor—she was later run out of the state—who examined me after my release testified that I couldn't possibly have been dragged off to jail. I had no scratches. My body was hard because I'd been beaten.

There is always a reason why the anger is there with the young blacks. A lot of people don't know, but when Stokely was here in Mississippi, he went to jail twenty-six times. In the summertime when they put you in jail, with the temperature 100 and something, they'd put the heat on. In the wintertime, they had the air conditioning on. There is a lot of us that know what they mean when they say "law and order." It's nothing healthy for us.

On the morning of June 12, 1963, I hadn't walked but six feet away from that jail when they told me Medgar Evers had been assassinated.

Mississippi

In the eyes of the nation, violence in Mississippi was at its rawest during the voter registration 1964 summer project. It began June 21 in Philadelphia, Mississippi, with the disappearance of three young civil rights workers, Andrew Goodman and Michael Schwerner, both white, from New York, and James Chaney, black, from Meridian, Mississippi. They had gone to investigate the burning of a black church and beatings of some of its members. The charred hulk of their abandoned station wagon was found a few days later.

That summer of violence ended August 4 with the discovery of their bodies, buried in a shallow red clay dam. All had been shot; Chaney had been severely beaten as well. During that summer, at least fifteen black churches where workers were either conducting voter education classes or freedom schools were burned or bombed. Among those earliest hit had been the Williams Chapel Church in Ruleville, where two years before, Mrs. Hamer had learned that voting was her constitutional right.

Mrs. Hamer's brutal Winona experience had neither discouraged nor embittered her. She ran for Congress in the Democratic primary in the spring of 1964, collecting 388 votes. She hadn't expected to win. "I didn't have a chance. There wasn't nobody registered. We wanted to get people involved with what was going on in this state." When the summer project volunteers arrived in Ruleville, after twenty-four-hour bus rides from the program's orientation quarters in Oxford, Ohio, the cheerful figure welcoming them was Mrs. Hamer. She'd tell them, "The first thing we'll do is find every last one of you a place to sleep. We'll start at my home." And throughout the summer the workers would meet to map out various strategies under the big old pecan tree in her front yard.

The kids, she said, "was all over here. The police told me, 'You are going to have to keep your people from coming across the white folks' places, and if you don't, you are going to pay for it.' So I said, 'Look, kids, you-all stay on our side of the track. But when we get ready to go downtown, we are going downtown. We are going across town and wherever we want to go.' So throwing bottles and shooting and all that kind of stuff didn't stop us."

What she remembers most about that summer was the courage of the young people. Speaking almost in a whisper, she recalled, "It was friends, you know. Friends like Andy Goodman who I met in Washington at a civil rights hearing. Then I had been with Andy, Michael Schwerner and James Chaney the Sunday before they went to their orientation meeting in Oxford. I know that a lot of my people have been killed, but I would never change my attitude—I have to fight for black and white. As one of the Scriptures in the Bible says, 'Greater love has no man than the one who is willing to lay down his life for his friend.' And Andy and Michael and James, they died, not only for my freedom, but for yours, too. No man is an island, and until I'm free here in Mississippi, you aren't free no matter where you are."

This was the same message she had brought to the Credentials Committee of the 1964 Democratic National Convention in Atlantic City. As a member of the Mississippi Freedom Democratic Party delegation challenging the regulars, she was chosen by her group to argue its cause. Millions of Americans saw her on television as she vividly and movingly described the beatings, jailings, and harassments they had gone through trying to register people.

September after the convention, Mrs. Hamer tried to run in the general Congressional election as an independent. They wouldn't put her name on the ballot. "You know"—she chuckled—"if they had just let us loose and told us to go ahead, I'd probably have dropped it. But I knowed as bad as they didn't want us to have it, I would just as sure has have to have it."

Fannie Lou Hamer

So the Mississippi Freedom Democratic Party made our own ballots, set up voting booths, and had a mock election. We included the white candidates just like we did the black ones. I was running from the Second District, Mrs. Annie Devine from the Third, and Mrs. Virginia Gray from the Fifth. In this election I got 33,009 votes and my opponent got 49—49, not 49,000. The other ladies won big, too. On the fourth of January, 1965, we went before the door of Congress to challenge the Democratic Representatives from Mississippi because we had the ballots to prove that if black folks had a chance to vote, things would be different. For the folks that voted with the Freedom Democratic Party would have registered, if they had been allowed. We didn't want Congress to seat us, but until we could prepare a proper challenge, we didn't want the regulars seated, either. They didn't let us in at that time.

Then we went running all over the country asking lawyers to come down here and people for donations to help pay them. And there was about 125 lawyers from California, Chicago and New York City, from everywhere, started taking depositions, and that's how we got 15,000 pages of evidence to prove that the five Mississippi Congressmen shouldn't be in Washington, D.C.

That September I got a telegram from the Speaker of the House telling us we were supposed to be in Washington on the thirteenth, when they was going to discuss dismissing our challenge. We went before the subcommittee on elections, and it was really disgusting!

All the Congressmen that were from Mississippi, they sat in big chairs at the table, and they didn't want us to sit up there with them. And Kunstler, the guy who was for the Seven,* objected. He said, "This is not right. These women have a right to sit in some of the nicer seats and sit at the table because it is their challenge."

The subcommittee told us, "We won't say you Negroes are not right. But if you get away with this kind of challenge, they'll be doing

---

* William Kunstler, attorney for the eight—later seven—defendants in the Chicago conspiracy trial growing out of the 1968 Democratic Convention. He previously represented the Mississippi Freedom Democratic Party.

it all over the South." Well, Rita Schwerner, Michael's widow, had done a lot of research for us, and she found this guy named John R. Lynch had placed the same type of challenge almost 100 years ago and succeeded. And this was 100 years later, and we was failing! So we brought that up. And the folks, they just left us. They really didn't dismiss the hearing. They simply got up and walked out.

Four days later we went to listen for the challenge to come on the floor. We was met across from the White House by Congressmen John Conyers, August Hawkins, black, Don Edwards and William Fitts Ryan, white. They escorted us up into the gallery. When they called for our challenge, we went down to go on the floor. We got there, and they had people to block our entrance, not really throw us out, but to try to convince us that we didn't have no business on the floor. In talking about the challenge and how we didn't supposed to go on the floor, Congressman Powell told us that if we got in, we would be the first Negro women that walked on the floor of Congress in the history of this country.

And I said, "Well, you can get your pen out and start writing because we are going to make history!"

We went in, sat on the floor of Congress and watched the reactions to the kind of count that was carried on. One hundred and forty-three voted for us, over 200 against. I sure learned a lot about politics that day. It was the kind of hypocrisy that the young people is bugged about today.

Odyssey

After the vote Mrs. Hamer, standing in front of the House wing of the Capitol, told reporters: "We won't stop the fight. We will come back year after year until we are allowed our rights as citizens. With God's help, without violence, I'll keep on fighting until the Constitution means more than a piece of paper."

And she did. At the 1968 Democratic National Convention in Chicago, Mrs. Hamer was among the forty-four-member delegation, an integrated coalition which called itself the Loyal Democrats of Mississippi, which ousted the regulars. But she was far from satisfied. She was especially unhappy about what happened to young whites on the streets of Chicago during the convention, noting at that time, "You don't build anything with fixed bayonets." Remembering that, she said, "You know, I had them laughing up there. I told them that

that was one time I was glad, like the white folks was, to hear 'I Wish I Was in Dixie.' And I really did wish I was back in Mississippi."

As we got up to leave, Mrs. Hamer came out on her porch with us and pointed across a very wide field to a group of modern brick houses. "See over there, the one with a carport, that's mine. Ministers, kids, just people from the community, helped build it. The folks are there right now putting in the heat. It has seven rooms. First time in my life I'll be living in a house that's got a bathroom and running water."

When we came back to see Mrs. Hamer in early April, 1970, she was in her spacious new house. Contributions to the Fannie Lou Hamer Fund, set up by a group of Southern *white* churches, had paid for the furniture. We talked with her in the den, the walls of which are lined with a dozen or so plaques paying tribute to her. There is also a framed color photograph of her, wearing a mortarboard and gown, taken in 1969 when she received an honorary LLD degree from Shaw University in Raleigh, North Carolina. As we sat in this pleasant room, we reminded her that on our first visit, she had offhandedly commented that when she was fixing up the house, the white folks had just looked at her "like I was something from outer space."

Fannie Lou Hamer

This house was a kind of puzzlement to them. They'd come by and ask to come in. I'd say, "Come on in." And they'd say, "Oh, this is nice." See, a lot of people never thought a grass-roots person like me would have such a place. They look down on grass-root persons, but if all poor people had a chance, they would like to live decent. They want a place where their kids won't be ashamed to be. They desire the same kind of education for them as anybody else. I'm fifty-two now, and I don't have a chance at an education.

Since 1963, I've been running all over the country talking to church groups, speaking on college campuses, trying to get things for poor people, like food stamps. In the fall of 1968, when I was on the East Coast, I told Miss Dorothy Haight, head of the National Council of Negro Women, "What we need is meat; let the kids, at least, have it." She got in contact with a white man from Mississippi from Prentice Institute, near Jackson, who deals in livestock. He brought fifty female pigs and five males into Sunflower County. And we started our pig-bank program, which is part of our Freedom Farms Co-op project.

Right off we give a family a pig. Everybody that gets one has to sign an agreement that they won't sell the first pig or trade it, but will keep it. And when it has a litter, they give two little pigs back to the bank. The rest they keep to fatten up for their own slaughter. When the pigs in the bank get big enough, a whole new set of families gets one—and we've given them to white folks, too.

Odyssey

Easter Sunday, 1970, was Fannie Lou Hamer Day in Ruleville. Hundreds of people, young and old, black and white, from all across the state, gathered in the local school auditorium to honor her. The mayor who wouldn't even speak to her two years ago had sent a letter. "It really takes a man to say the things he put in it," she told us. "He said that he appreciated the community and the citizens for setting aside this day because I had earned it. 'Many people,' he wrote, 'had been decorated for battles won that they hadn't faced anything in.' He said that I had faced the opposition, 'the enemy, and I had gone straight through their camp,' that I was 'making things better and the results were coming in year after year.' "

Fannie Lou Hamer

If you just stand there and don't lash back, you can find a real human being in a lot of people. I don't never write nobody off. All this time I've been part of a nonviolent revolution. My policy is to do unto others as you would have them do unto you. I'd tell the white powers that I ain't trying to take nothing from them. I'm trying to make Mississippi a better place for all of us. And I'd say, "What you don't understand is that as long as you stand with your feet on my neck, you got to stand in a ditch, too. But if you move, I'm coming out. I want to get us both out of the ditch." I'm not saying that I can't get angry sometimes. Oh, yes, I do. And when I do, I'll walk up to any of these folks and say: "Look, now we are going to do something about this. Number one, you can write your dates on the calendar because you ain't getting back in office because we'll vote you out!" And they know we mean it.

I've always believed that one day, even if I didn't live to see it, this country would be different. It would be a place for all people to live, where they could be without the hangings and the lynchings and the killings and the bombings. We are our brother's keeper whether he is black, white, brown, red or yellow. As the Bible tells us, God has made of one blood all nations.

In 1965, about the time the kids was getting beaten in Selma and we had 1,000 of them in jail in Jackson, I went up to Washington, D.C., and really let them have it about what was going on. I stood in front of Lafayette Park and told President Johnson to bring the troops home from Vietnam. I said that the war was wrong, morally and everything else.

That really wasn't nice to say in 1965.

The thing that dawned on me was if Senators Eastland and Stennis had something to do with the war, it had to be wrong. Papers wrote me up, called me something like a demagogue. I thought, "God! What in the world is a demagogue?"

But think how many people was in the moratorium on the fifteenth day of November, 1969. This showed that one man's feet can't walk across the land. But if two and two and fifty make a million, we'll see that day come around. That's what we have to do. I don't give up because I know I'm right.

My mother used to sing a hymn, "Should earth against my soul engage, and fire at me be hurled, but I can smile at Satan's rage and face this frowning world." I can smile and do my work, go out and tell you and tell the folks what's happening. I refuse to hate you because you hate me. Hate to me is something like a cancer.

I really think this country has a chance, that it is not *too* late for it to straighten up. But what's happening in it now is terrible. You are almost afraid to say "justice." What is justice when they say a judge has the authority to bind and gag people in court! Not only that, think about the kind of laws that's being passed, like the no-knock law where a person can just come in your house and search it without knocking. If somebody don't do something, the kids will.

I think these young people today, black and white, is the most fantastic thing that has ever happened to America. I've talked to millions of them throughout the country. Universities, chaplains, students groups, bring me in. I've been known to go into these areas where they have very troubled spots and I don't have one minute's trouble communicating with the young. These kids that folks call "extremists," well, you have to know them to understand them. They are beautiful.

This generation is selfless, 100 percent, and they really want this to be a better world. These kids are very honest, and they are saying:

"You haven't told us the truth; things has been wrong." Everybody better look at what they're saying because these youngsters happen to be right.

At this point, I say America is sick and man is on the critical list. What I'm trying to do is to cure it, to heal some of the sickness before it's too late for all of us.

Fire on the Campus

San Francisco

When the soft gray fog rolls in, there is a dreamlike cast over the bay, and the compelling beauty of that scene has given San Francisco the illusion of nirvana: beautiful people on their timeless hills.

But the nonviolent revolution begun in Montgomery, Alabama, altered that imagined tranquillity. In less than ten years the planted seeds of change, but mutated in a new form, erupted in the San Francisco Bay Area. They were carried there by many of the young people who had gone South for the sit-ins and freedom rides, later SNCC's Mississippi summer project, and who, upon their return North to home and campus, concluded that racism knew no geographical boundaries.

These young people came back in a different mood. Integration was irrelevant. The goal in the North was: Liberation, self-determination NOW!

At the University of California in Berkeley the revolution was expressed by young whites in the Free Speech Movement, latterly by the strung-out hippies in San Francisco's Haight-Ashbury district. At Oakland's Merritt Junior College two young black men, Huey P. Newton and Bobby Seale, began a journey which led them into that city's ghetto with a rallying cry: "All power to the people!" Their vehicle was the Black Panther Party. At San Francisco State College, it was the founding of the Black Students Union (BSU).

On November 6, 1968, the BSU shut down the campus at State, demanding a meaningful black studies program under the direction of Dr. Nathan Hare. What followed was the longest student strike on record—four months. State was also the first college to be occupied by police on a continuous basis, with 200 to 600 of them there each day. There were 731 arrests, in the course of which 80 students and 32 officers were hurt. A dozen bombs exploded on campus, a major fire was set in a vice-president's office, and smaller fires were counted in the scores. It was, says a report for the President's Commission on Violence, "one of the most distressing episodes in American history . . . a scene of violence unmatched in higher education."

Nathan Hare

I endorse violence as one of many social tactics. From the time Martin Luther King came on the scene, I thought his nonviolent approach was ridiculous. I was taught violence from the cradle by my mother, who told us, "Someone hit you, white or black, you fight back. But you had better win, or else when you get home, you are going to get another whipping from me." Nonviolence is not only antithetical to America, but also to human nature; Thomas Paine called it masochistic, abnormal.

There is a reason for our saying that when whites—or their Negro lackeys, so-called nonmilitants—tell us to turn the other cheek, what they do is to kick us on the two cheeks. After the U.S. Supreme Court in 1954 gave the stamp of "supreme" authority to assimilation as an ideal, Dr. King came with his movement of nonviolence, later picked up in a more direct and intensified form by college students. This was given lip service by the liberal, moderate Establishment and the mass media. Everything was: "Integration is good: nonviolence is good." But what I could see, beginning in the late 1950's, was that we were becoming more assimilated than integrated, more integrated than elevated. And because of this, the nonviolent strategy was failing.

As this happened, people naturally turned to something else. In 1964 you got the Harlem riots by people who were not middle-class, who didn't have the money to go to the coffee shop, stay at the Hilton, ride the Pullman car or send their kids across town to the white folks' schools. And for these people in their frustration, having no microphones or television or the press, the only way to communicate discontent was by mass, a sort of desperate, exploding. And they did it. Next came Watts. That marked the turning point in the approach toward violence.

We do not live in a reasonable society. We've cried and prayed and begged for all these decades and centuries for justice from the people who oppress us. The white man has held us down, hurt us economically, psychologically, sociologically, physiologically. We've been taught that it is not "reasonable" to be bitter, or do violence. But if someone sticks a pin in you and you don't yell out, then there is something wrong with you.

Odyssey

Miriam and I were in San Francisco the winter of 1968-69, while the strike was on, and it almost seemed as if Hare had tenure on the front pages. Then thirty-five, director of State's black studies department, member of the Black Students Union's Central Committee, he was forever pictured as malcontent, irrational, a verbal bomb thrower. Dr. S. I. Hayakawa, then State's acting president, consistently blamed him as the obstructionist to the strike's settlement. "Actually," said Hayakawa on one occasion, "I don't see the worst of the disrupters as communists . . . or anarchists. They are just plain nasty." And there was frequent mention of Hare's having been fired as a teacher at Washington's Howard University for plunging that school into similar chaos.

In July, 1969, when we telephoned Hare, the strike was over, and Hayakawa had announced he was going to fire Hare. We said to Hare that we had *read* much about him, but *knew* little. He agreed to see us, telling us to come to a little cubbyhole office the college had temporarily allotted him.

He wasn't the firebrand, honkie-hating revolutionary of his press clippings. He was quiet, fatalistic about what he regarded as his implausible situation. When we offered him a peppermint Life Saver, he declined, saying: "What I need is a real one."

Over the next several hours his words came tumbling out, staccato, racing to keep up with his thoughts. Not tall, but very muscular, onetime professional boxer—and former Golden Gloves welterweight state champion—he often slipped into imagery from the ring. To him, the role of the social activist was like that of the fighter going from "jabjabjab to punchpunchpunch," constantly changing tactics. He was someone whose inner ear still heard the thud of fists. He clenched and unclenched his hands, once or twice cocking his arms to illustrate his ability to go into an instant alert.

"I'm not a leader, not a rallier," he said, "although sometimes by default I've had to become that kind of person. It will take many minds to come up with the ideology for a reconstructed America. What I have to offer is my commitment and a special sensitivity, an exposure to life in more different and intimate ways than a great many others."

He paused. "Besides," he said, smiling, "I can always go back to Oklahoma, where I was the best cotton picker in Creek County."

Nathan Hare

I was born, one of six children on a sharecropper's farm three miles from the little town of Slick. In those days, you weaned kids from the breast of their mother by taking them to a friend or relative. I was sent to my aunt in Oklahoma City, stayed there until I was three. I had all the toys a child could want, but when I returned home, they got broken. My father ran over my tricycle with his wagon. And nothing was ever replaced. Very early, I had the notion that when I grew up, I was going to be rich: big farm, painted white, with two teams of fat horses. At that time our houses weren't painted, and our horses were what you'd call razorbacks. My younger brother and I would go gathering berries, and I would draw him pictures in the dirt of how things would look when I was rich. Boxing, I thought then, was a means of getting there.

I learned to read as a four-year-old. I also started picking cotton. We'd work in the fields three days one week, two the next, go to school in between. I was in a classroom that went from kindergarten through second grade. All the teacher would do is give you a page a day to read. Once when she had to work on something else, she turned the class over to a junior high girl, saying, "They do as much as they can." I went through this whole book, and they didn't quite know what to do with me. I'd done all the white "Dick and Jane" stuff so they gave me some "Negro" books. In one of them was a passage I still remember: "Tick tock/say the clock./ It is day/Johnny May./ Out of bed/sleepy head./ Up, up/and away." It was really just a variation on the white theme, but with black faces.

Next, I got the story of Booker T. Washington, going in, rushing where he was not supposed to, where it was not safe, saying good-bye, putting on his clothes, handkerchief on a stick, and going into the world, they said, to become a great man. But, as we later learned, it was to become a great Uncle Tom.

Education was always very important to my mother. She'd gone through the eighth grade, wanted to go further, but her father, son of a slave master, said that she was such a strong, good worker—she could pick more cotton than most men—that she ought to help the family make a living. We kids admired her. She was much stronger than my father. One time the justice of the peace, who also owned the place we were renting, came out to talk to him. "Seddie, Seddie!" he shouted, and when my father didn't immediately come out of the shed, he yelled, "Nigger! Where *are* you?" My father came out, grinning. I was embarrassed. Had it been my mother, she'd have run that white man off the place.

A white bus driver hit me one day—I was six or seven—and my sister who saw it happen went home and told my mother. Mother was doing clothes with a washing stick. My father, knowing her, hid the pistol, but she put a razor at the end of her stick, walked into town, and when she found that bus driver, she ran him all over the place, right out of town. Next day they arrested my father for the assault. They couldn't bring themselves to accept the fact that a 125-pound black woman had done that to a white man.

She was always able to cope with any situation. Years afterwards, when all of us left, she was still on the farm, with only my sister's boy with her. She was working in the yard, digging up weeds with a butcher knife. When that job was done, she went into the chicken coop to get eggs, reached down, and a rattlesnake bit her. First thing she did was to use her knife to stab the snake to death. Then she cut the finger where the snake had struck her, did the blood thing, and ran down the road to find someone to take her to the hospital. They kept her in the hospital for a week or so. But after that, she decided to move to Kansas City, Kansas, where her sister and brother live.

Odyssey

We later visited Mrs. Hare in Kansas City, where she had an apartment in a public housing project. Like her son, she is proud in bearing, black, with features more American Indian than African. Laughing about "that damn snake," she spoke of her son with real affection. "Nathan always took after me," she said. "You couldn't keep him down. Never a complainer. He became the man in the family at age nine, when my husband just disappeared."

Nathan Hare

I came home from school one day to find that my father and all the other deacons of the church had been arrested for bootlegging.

The farm surplus thing had just come into being, and we, with only 40 acres of cotton, were told to plow under all but 1½ acres, which meant we had to make money other ways. My father went to jail for two months for brewing illegal whiskey. Soon after that he left to go out bootlegging religion. He never had a church of his own, but he preached in Phoenix, Arizona, and Seattle, Washington, before he died.

During World War II, mother took us to San Diego, California, where she worked in a defense plant for two years. I was twelve years old, and it was the first time I had been in an integrated school. There was a white guy who was considered the toughest, and I challenged him to fight. He refused. I guess he was afraid he might get shown up.

There were only about 20 blacks in this school of 1,500. In some ways it was like a nightmare in which I'd wake, be caught in an integrated class, and punished by the police or something. I remember when the teacher was reading from *The Yearling,* a best seller then, and got to the part which said, "The little raccoon's paw looked like a little nigger baby's hand." All the kids turned and looked at me.

I wanted to major in foreign languages, but my teacher would only recommend me for courses in woodshop. You had to buy your own wood. My mother didn't have the money for it. So I just sat in class and watched the others make stuff.

When my mother brought us back to Slick, I was offered more than woodshop in the all-black high school. I graduated and enrolled in Langston University. It's a small, all-Negro school in an all-Negro Oklahoma town, named after John Mercer Langston, the first Negro elected to public office in the country. Most people don't know this, but Langston was one of the twenty-five towns set up after the Civil War when they wanted to make Oklahoma an all-Negro state.

Until recently, blacks didn't have any history. The white educational system, the whole American culture, has kept so much from not only blacks, but whites as well. Just take something as modern as the student movement in the South. I know kids, six to seventeen years old, who were sitting in in Oklahoma City in 1958. I've still got the New York *Times* clip on it. Story was buried back near advertising, losing out to the *big* issues of the day: Sputnik and Governor Faubus' refusal to open up Little Rock, integrated. Then in 1960, in the dead of winter, when there is nothing except a basketball game going on, four college students sit in at Greensboro, North Carolina, and it's quote, unquote, the beginning of the student movement.

At Langston I boxed, winning the Golden Gloves welterweight championship. When I got a Danforth Fellowship for graduate study at the University of Chicago, I figured I'd just combine the scholarship with boxing. I did better in the ring—made the finals for amateurs in Chicago—than I did with Danforth. I discovered it was an attempt to marry teaching with spiritual searching. As a child I had prayed, did believe there was a God. But by this time I had pretty much given up on religion. The last of it went after He didn't immediately answer my prayers when I thought I had lost something that was very important to me.

Odyssey

Hare leaned back, clasped his hands behind his head, and said: "I lost a girlfriend, and I felt God should get her back for me." No one can know what divine help finally intervened, but Hare did get the girl. Her name then was Julia Reed, and since his early days at the University of Chicago she has been his wife.

Once we met her, we could understand Hare's consternation at the thought of losing her. She was beautiful, with sculpted features, regal lines. She wore her hair in soft Afro style. She had a master's degree in musical education, was once named "Educator of the Year" in Washington, D.C.

Hare turned back his Danforth Fellowship—"I could not, in good conscience, take the money because I had become a committed atheist"—and in 1958 dropped out of the university. He did six months in the Army Reserves.

Nathan Hare

I had made it clear I wouldn't fight any nonwhites for them. If the country went to war, I'd be picking off my fellow white soldiers out of the foxholes every chance I got.

After the Army, I was hung up on boxing, but when people began telling me how it would get to your brain I concentrated on college again. Ultimately, with scholarships and a job as a research assistant, I finished my PhD in sociology at the University of Chicago. I had this exaggerated notion of a doctorate's value. I thought it would get students to listen, to be influenced, and that magazines and journals would give more credence to what I had to say. It didn't work out that way.

In 1961 I accepted a teaching post at Howard University at a lower salary than I could have gotten on other offers. Yet I wanted to be part of a Negro school in order to help make black students aware and concerned. Howard was middle-class in orientation. When I started talking to my students about violence in self-defense, they weren't ready for it. They thought I was crazy. The kids were scared even to be in the room. As I spoke, you could hear a pin drop.

Then I turned to humor as a teaching device. I'd read a book, *The Psychology of Laughter,* which said, mainly, that you can exaggerate reality into the ludicrous, but so long as you were trying to put across the truth, people could identify with it. I would tell about the Mississippi guy who took a Howard speech program called "How to Lose Your Negro Dialect." Back home at Christmas he fell in with his old buddies at this store where they had pickled pigs' feet, and the guys would say, "Give me one of them feet." But now that this fellow had been educated at Howard he said, ultra-politely, very long *A*'s, "Please may I have one of those fibula tibias?"

That story had meaning for me. I grew up with the uneducated, relatives and friends. My speech is not pretentious; in fact, it's barely speech at all, although I do okay in public because of the human thing, I guess, rather than how I say it. At Howard, I, too, took speech lessons, and the more I had, the worse I got. I stopped them.

The important thing was in communicating with the students. By 1963 I was a little better, and by 1965 I was getting good. Me a farm boy, teaching urban sociology! As an assistant professor I built up courses which the head of the department said were advantageous for passing the graduate record exam.

I was always very concerned about making sure the students got the basic concepts. From the very beginning I told them that we blacks were following the wrong path. Segregation, I said, was just like a wall—blacks on one side, whites on the other. And the whites were thought by blacks to have the better terrain: Sun shines over there, rains over here. Blacks keep trying to get over there by climbing up, one by one, on the shoulders of one another. And I'd tell my students, once blacks get up there on the wall, the whites push them down until finally, whites, getting tired, say, "Okay, we'll let one or two of you come over here if you be nice, go slow, don't raise hell."

But then the whites add, "We don't have a lot of slots. You've got to be qualified to exist here." What the whites do next is make that kind of Negro a gatekeeper, to help the whites knock down the blacks who keep coming on. What we should do, I said, was to turn within ourselves, develop an *esprit de corps* by building a ramrod to batter that wall down.

All along I was saying black power. One of my Howard students was Stokely Carmichael. I advocated what I called "total civil disobedience." All black folks would just not go to work. Elevators wouldn't run; cars, taxicabs, buses and all would be abandoned on the streets. I felt there would be chaos, and either this white man's whole system would get straight or it would be destroyed.

In those days I kind of wished the blacks had taken the road of the American Indian: Have a showdown; get it over with. But I realized there was no such thing as instant victory. All your waking hours you have to go on struggling against racism, to bring the oppressor down.

Odyssey

In 1965 Hare's book *The Black Anglo-Saxons*—about blacks who want to be whiter than white—was published . . .

Nathan Hare

Many of the persons at Howard recognized themselves in it. The chairman of my department told me that if I wanted to stay around there and get promoted, I'd better not make any more public pronouncements, at least, through the fall of 1966, which marked Howard's centennial. I said okay, because I wanted to devote more time to writing anyhow. But on September 3, 1966, a story appeared in the Washington *Post* quoting Howard's president, James Nabrit, as saying he wanted to make the college 60 percent white by 1970. I wrote a letter to the campus newspaper, mocking the idea. I said there were enough universities around for whites. The school said, "Does this mean you disapprove of our policy?" And I said, "I do." So they called me to a hearing, threatened to fire me. The chairman was hounding me, because, he said, the dean was hounding him. But the other members of the department voted to keep me.

In the winter of 1967 the Students Rights Organization was formed by the then liberal, quote, unquote, militants, who took their heroes from SNCC but styled themselves after CORE. They were big on rallies and petitions. After they walked out on a speech by UN Ambassador Arthur Goldberg supporting Johnson on Vietnam, they were patting themselves on the back for this act of protest. Myself, I was appalled at their moderation.

But there was a group of eleven freshmen, not top scholars, football players, or anything else to distinguish them, except . . . they were dedicated to change. They came to me asking if I'd help them launch a Black Power Committee. I said I would. Meanwhile, they managed to break up a campus appearance by the then Selective Service Director General Hershey. People, on and off the campus, were horrified. South Carolina's Congressman L. Mendel Rivers exclaimed, "My God! What are we coming to?"

Odyssey

The answer came in a few days with publication by the Black Power Committee, Hare as spokesman, of a black manifesto for Negro education. "For full many a decade," the statement said, "America has suffered the failure of the Negro college. We stand opposed to that pathetic and shameless trend. Our aims are: 1. The overthrow of the Negro college with white innards. 2. To raise in its place a militant black university which will counteract the whitewashing black students now receive in 'Negro' and white institutions. We are working to bring the black college and the black community together as one invincible army to fight our common enemy. . . ."

For Howard, it was too much. Hare was fired. Students were suspended. However, a federal court later ordered them readmitted pending administrative hearings. As a party to the court appeal Hare could have pressed his claim for reinstatement. Instead, he announced he was leaving "this slave plantation," Howard, and going back to boxing.*

Nathan Hare

It is really kind of funny. I had the attitude of most blacks that when you got fired at college, you were blacklisted—or whitelisted—and I wouldn't be able to get another university job. So I told

---

* Hare, in his early years at Howard, had turned professional, winning three of his four fights.

them in the press about my cotton picking and how, if it ever came to that, I'd burn my doctorate and go back to the fields. Ironically, I got more offers to teach: City College of New York, University of Tulsa, Colorado State, University of Illinois and San Francisco State. At first I said No to all of them. I was disillusioned with college life.

Yet my wife was anxious to leave Washington because of my general image as a "black militant." She was having a hard time because of me. Whites she was working with would say, "We didn't invite you to our party because we felt your husband wouldn't want to come." Neighbors were giving her pressure, too, always talking about my "not working." They would see me hanging around the house a lot. I'd go out in the morning, run around for roadwork, maybe go to the gym and then come back and write. Other times they'd watch me leave the house in the middle of the morning and not be home by seven o'clock. They didn't know that in that period I'd flown to Atlanta to make a speech. While I was getting money for this, enough for us to get along on, they thought I was just fooling around.

So when San Francisco State contacted me a second time, I reconsidered the university scene. Jimmy Garrett, founder of the Black Students Union, a former SNCC worker in both the South and the North and an articulate persuader, asked me to come out to assemble and direct the black studies department they were trying to put together. Although I was ambivalent, I said Yes. Somebody had to do it.

I had promised myself I would never teach at another Negro college. A black university, yes. But there aren't any. It represents a hoped-for ideal. It is very important to distinguish between Negro and black. "Negro" is a derogatory term, describing a person who is thought to have some black ancestry but who would just as soon be white. He identifies with the oppressor, longs for intergration; he is an assimilationist and a conformist. I have often said that it would be an irony if the oppressors used segregation to hold us down in the first half of the twentieth century and then used integration to keep us back in the second half. Segregation, integration, they are irrelevant today. What we need is elevation and empowerment. And it does not much matter whether we achieve these goals apart from, or with, the white group.

The black person is nationalistic or, at least, pluralistic. He has his own standards, values, and he rejects assimilation in and of itself. San Francisco State, at the initiative of the Black Students Union, was seeking a genuine black studies curriculum. As such, it was the first to do so. The proposed program was uniquely designed to meet the awakening appetites of black college students for more black-oriented courses and was to be structured in such a way that the community could take part in it.

Before I gave my final okay to taking the job, I received absolute assurances that black students—unlike the kids at Howard—would back me to the hilt. And in my interview with State's vice-president for academic affairs, I was led to believe the administration and faculty would do everything in their power to see a black studies department come into fruition, controlled and taught by blacks.

Odyssey

In spring, 1968, Hare went West, hopeful that in this school with an enrollment of 18,000, about 5 percent black, he could build a program that would be a model for the rest of the country. Instead, he found, like Alice, that he had accepted an invitation to the Mad Hatter's tea party.

State had had seven different presidents since 1960. Hare dealt with three in less than six months of 1968. The campus, located in the midst of a white middle-class neighborhood, was but a few minutes away from three of the city's worst slums, with all the problems of urban America. Students, like their counterparts in many other colleges, were in an uproar over the Vietnam War. Before Hare arrived, racial issues had begun to surface. Young blacks had invaded the school's newspaper office, beat up its white editor, charging the publication was "racist" for, among other things, referring to the heavyweight champion as Cassius Clay, not Muhammad Ali. A number of blacks had been suspended for participating in the melee, including the intense, expressive George Mason Murray, a graduate student at State, part-time English teacher, coordinator of the student-run ghetto tutorial program and, as subsequently noted, minister of education for the Black Panther Party.

Murray was readmitted, went to Cuba for a visit, and was quoted as saying there that every time the Vietcong killed an American, there was "one aggressor less" to deal with at home. Murray's return to campus, greeted by demands from the university's trustees for his transfer to a nonteaching position, about coincided with Hare's presentation of a black studies curriculum. Later that fall, Murray was reported by a newspaperman—who admitted he was not present at the time—to have said in State's cafeteria that black and brown students "should carry guns to protect ourselves from racist administrators." Again Murray was suspended.

The Black Students Union, already pressing for greater autonomy in black studies, called a strike, adding Murray's status to its grievances. On the walkout's first day, an estimated 70 to 90 percent of all students stayed out of class. The Third World Liberation Front, composed of some blacks, but mostly students of Asian, Mexican and Latin descent, and the American Federation of Teachers participated, later joined by Students for a Democratic Society (SDS).

The Black Students Union had a list of ten "nonnegotiable" demands, including: Hare was to be made a full professor, with commensurate salary; all black studies at State were to be channeled through him; Hare, his faculty and staff were to be given sole power to hire and fire in the department. The BSU also wanted State opened that fall to any black who wanted admission. At the bottom of the list was the reinstatement of Murray.

Three weeks after the strike began—with no end in sight—Hayakawa, part-time professor, noted semanticist and already a hard-line critic of the walkout, was named State's acting president. In his own words, his performance made him a "folk hero." He told a study team for the President's Commission on Violence that one day when students were using a sound truck: "I sort of blew my top and climbed the sound truck and pulled out all those wires, and it just happened that all the media were there. And so, like any symbolic figure, you're good copy, you're always news just because you're there."

But in the violence that followed that day's incident, nine were hurt, thirty-nine were arrested, and while Hayakawa "regretted" the ruckus, nevertheless, he said, "It was the most exciting day of my life since my tenth birthday, when I rode a roller coaster for the first time."

Nathan Hare

Hayakawa kept telling the public the reason the strike continued was that I refused to submit a report on the planned black studies program. Actually, I had turned in two before the strike began. Afterward I got word he wanted a more precise description of the courses and the teachers. I had this in hand, but I did not give it to him. To have done so, while the teachers and white student leaders were still pressing their demands, would have made the BSU strikebreakers. But the press never would print that Hayakawa was trying to make me a black scab.

So we kept on, and there was a day when 457 of us were arrested, charged with unlawful assembly on the campus. But the police had surrounded us, and we couldn't have dispersed if we had wanted to. The next day Hayakawa had a faculty meeting called, and the prepublicity was that he'd make some important announcement about the black studies department. It was to be a nationally televised press conference as well. In the meeting, there were about twenty-five cameras arrayed around him so that the small audience of about 200 had to sit way in the back of the auditorium in order to see him. He started right off joking about going "fishing the other day and catching 457 fish in a net." With that, three of us took off and went up on the stage, figuring that if he had his say, so should we. We were so frustrated at not being able to get our story across that we seized his forum—nonviolently. We shouted, "Hayakawa has no power! Hayakawa has no power!" And he was left sputtering, "Get that man Hare! Get him!" The guards came and took us off the stage for disturbing the peace.

But there wasn't any peace anyway.

Hayakawa rushed to fire me, although he couldn't in a court of law do so on the basis of that incident. His excuse was that I hadn't turned in my report. I was cleared of all charges—the report thing and going on stage—by his own handpicked, lily-white faculty panel, the grievance and disciplinary committee of the Academic Senate.

Odyssey

When the Black Students Union and the administration finally reached an agreement in March, 1969, to end the strike, the college promised to meet some BSU demands, but refused to consider rehiring either Hare or Murray—the latter having gone to jail for six months on charges of violating an earlier parole. Hare had already told the press he would be back as head of black studies, with or without Hayakawa's blessing. He admitted, however, his contract had not been renewed. The BSU had issued a public warning it would do "whatever is necessary to ensure Hare's return. He is the choice of the black community, and the black students. We stand firmly behind him against the fascist, racist Hayakawa." In those early days of summer, when we saw Hare, the BSU believed it had the muscle to make that stick.

Through Hare's intercession, we arranged to meet BSU's minister of information, Wade Woods, who, like Hare, was a member of the Central Committee. On a very warm and sunny afternoon we drove to meet him in the Fillmore district, a narrow, low-income mixed-minority group neighborhood of nineteenth-century wooden buildings. Of this area a report for the President's Violence Commission had observed:

> Middle-aged and elderly black men lounge around the signposts and building corners throughout the day, some drunk, others just idle. Toward the middle of the afternoon, one of the city's largest inter-racial prostitution operations swings into action, supplying a variety of girls . . . until well past dawn, volunteering a variety of services to anyone who does not look like a plainclothes cop.

The San Francisco office of the Black Panthers is in Fillmore; the BSU is there, too. This is a community where, as the commission report noted, "the language and attitudes students bring from there to the campus reflect the violence that is a basic part of ghetto life in every city. . . ."

Wade Woods and three other State students were living that summer in one of the district's two-story houses. We climbed the stairs to his place, rang the bell, knocked, and got no response. We turned to leave, then noticed two young men coming nonchalantly up the street. Both seemed to be looking right through us. The one in the lead, about five ten, slender, a light brown, wild Afro, wearing bermuda shorts and tennis shoes, carrying a can of beer, barely nodded as he passed us going up those stairs. No introductions were necessary. It was Wade Woods.

The youth behind him, very dark, expressionless, short cropped natural, wearing a black leather jacket, tapered black slacks, later and with reluctance, identified himself as Warren Tucker, twenty-one, a junior at State. We asked: "Member of the BSU?" "Friend of all the people," was his reply.

Woods, then twenty-three, led us down a hall, past a high-ceilinged living room with little furniture but hundreds of books on makeshift shelves and into a kitchen in back, motioning us to sit at a table in one corner. Coming from the grimness of the street, we were surprised to find ourselves facing out on a colorful garden.

Woods was born in San Francisco, raised in Fillmore. Oldest of five children, parents separated, mother on welfare. We asked if he knew his father well, liked him. "Yeah," he said. "My childhood was happy in the sense we were all together. A struggle to live. Everyone in the neighborhood was going through the same thing: Getting enough food to exist."

Wade Woods

When Malcolm X died, I really didn't know what was going on. Then I began listening to his record album and to read him. While I already knew the things he was saying, the point is, nobody had said them before. Through Malcolm, I understood there was something I needed to do in terms of helping black people, being humanitarian. What I did was look around on who is helping black people. Weren't but two things happening when I got a chance to go to State—Black Panther Party and Black Students Union. So I was like going to college and went into the BSU. If I hadn't been, I'd have joined the Panthers.

I had some tough time getting to State. Like most black kids here, I went to Polytechnic High, where basically they steered you into industrial arts, woodshop, metalshop, all that. It was just luck I didn't drop out because I wasn't really interested in those things, though I did well in sports, got the nickname of Speedy as a track man. Still, I came out of Poly with a B-plus average, passed all the college tests. But the counselor I had—a white guy—didn't even talk to me about going to State. Place for black kids was San Francisco City College, junior college, just two years of making time to nowhere! Girls waiting to get married, guys to get drafted or a job in the post office.

So I went to City College. Just because it was there to go to. I would have dropped out, but I got drafted first. And the onliest reason I got drafted was that I was ignorant of the draft laws. I could have got a deferment. As a result, I have lately been like helping people learn the laws through what we call the Black Draft Counsel Union. You know, there are black people in the Army today got drafted when they were taking care of ten kids. Anyway, I went to Vietnam. I didn't relate too much to the Army. I was just there doing my thing—statistical analysis of cargoes. In my Army experience I saw how bad the United States treated the Vietnamese in terms of second-class citizenship. Black guys on the garbage detail told me how they were ordered to throw out food rather than give it to the hungry. Reason: Free food would hurt the economy.

I got out in '67. Here I had almost two years at City College, this Army experience, and when I went to the unemployment office, run down my training, this white chick sent me to a packinghouse to unload fish! Well, I wasn't going to do that, but I didn't dig City, either. Then some friends told me about the black arts and culture program started by the BSU at State; it was like the only one around.

That's how I got to State, involved with the BSU and, ultimately, the strike. In that, we just addressed ourselves to the issues, laid it all out!

What happened at State was the first time you had a black-led student strike in which whites participated but were not out there in front. We changed the whole idea of a strike, moving it to a higher plane than, like sit-ins, which are temporary, to a more active role in trying to halt the whole institution until it changed. Before, you had like 200 taking over an administration building, and the next day the police or whoever move you out. While everybody is trying to get bail bond money, everything else is like going on normal in that administration building. The BSU showed that students do have some type of power in closing the institution down, per se, on an overall, prolonged basis.

Odyssey

We talked with Woods again in June, 1970. He was about to graduate, but he said, "I'm not certain what I'm going to do. Right now, there ain't nobody knows what is going to happen."

Wade Woods

You know, we probably couldn't pull a strike today like we did. Most people feel the fight for black studies at State is foolishness, because they will never let us have the authority we want. People don't want to stand out there and get beat for nothing. So they say: "Hell! Move the black studies off the campus!" That's what we are working on now—building a community college, starting from scratch. We got to do it.

Ain't just rhetoric no more. It's a whole lot more serious. I think that what we did at State was get black students in this country to start looking at the educational system they were in. It heightens the contradictions for them. As you go around now, you see how the black students have come out of the fraternity bag they were in. They are beginning to address themselves to the issues.

Odyssey

The Black Students Union never pressed its "warning" that Hare had to be rehired. And in the early fall of 1969 Hare announced he was publishing *The Black Scholar,* a monthly journal born, he said, "out of the struggle of black scholars, intellectuals, leaders—all black people—for education that will provide meaningful definitions of black existence."

During the 1969-70 winter he was arrested and put on probation after police said they found a gun in his car.

One spring night in 1970 we took the Hares to dinner at a Ghirardelli Square restaurant, but the white *maître d'* barred us, briskly explaining that Hare's dashiki didn't meet the house rule of tie and jacket. Hare shrugged and then invited us to a restaurant in the Fillmore district where nobody challenged our attire.

Nathan Hare

Personally, that whole episode at State hurt me, psychologically, possibly physiologically. There was always a fear of getting killed. Crank phone calls, letters. At the same time, there were people with praise. I even got a plaque as "Community Leader of America." I sent that to my mother. We were not successful at State. The kids were not ready. It's obvious we have to do our homework. This is a time to reflect, to prepare.

Eventually, it is going to be confrontation, violent or otherwise. Yet we should not let it be an end in itself, unless you do something dramatic like taking up guns, as they did at Cornell. I guess the kids there were more middle-class than we were. With the history of conflict at State, the police would have shot us if we had had guns like that. They knew we would have used them.

We are headed in the direction of a civil war of some sort. Though the black issue will be prominent, this war will not be between blacks and whites, but rather, radicals and conservatives, left and right. In this coming confrontation everyone will have to choose up sides. People will be forced to fight who ordinarily wouldn't. One doesn't welcome polarization, yet it is just like having to see the dentist or the doctor—necessary. A surgeon can't nurse the body back to health until he cuts out the cancers, the sores. He has to be destructive in order to be reconstructive, destroy a part to save the rest. I can't tell you when the revolution is coming, two years, two decades. It is building all the time. I am afraid the die is cast.

The Subtle Savagery

Mary Henry

We have been told for generations that the only way to be accepted in society is to get an education. Get a good job. Pay your dues, salute God and country, salute the flag, and you're home free, right? But when we got educated, put on ties and white shirts, got our hair trimmed and fixed, they still closed the doors they had said we could come into.

This is why I say that America is one of the goddamn lyingest nations on the face of the earth, to have made promises, starting with the damn Declaration of Independence—what are those things they say? Life and liberty—what's that? And the pursuit of happiness? Promises and commitments and lies, and then more promises and commitments and more lies. I am getting more bitter by the day, and I don't want to be bitter. I am getting more frustrated by the day, and I am too old to be frustrated every day.

For God's sake, America, stop lying!

Odyssey

For most of her forty-one years, Mrs. Mary Henry, director of a VISTA project, named a "Woman of the Year" by the Los Angeles *Times,* member of the Urban Coalition, had lived with her "hope and dream that white racism would one day be overcome." But by the summer of 1969, sitting in a Los Angeles ghetto settlement house, she no longer felt that way.

Mary Henry

I have reached the point of believing there is a subtle savagery among white people that will never, ever make them ready to accept people of color. I don't say the Pledge of Allegiance anymore, and when I see red, white and blue I feel like upchucking.

I think of black people in this country generally like our hands and feet are tied. And White America unties our feet only enough to go where it would lead us, unties our hands only to have us take what it would give us. But if you do that to me, you must also bind my mind and my eyes, plug my ears. Because unless you do, I can see other people in good jobs, moving into decent homes, and I can hear them negotiating on whether my children get into a good school, debating about the voting laws that affect me. America has to put up or shut up.

A number of years ago I believed that one of these days there would be total brotherhood, peace on earth among all men. Well, I don't think that anymore. I now know white people for what they truly are. Some are in pathetic little groups talking about brotherhood. But others are the most dastardly, evil, corrupt, sinister and conniving, who plan day by day for the destruction of the souls and minds and dreams of minority people in this country. Chiefs of police do it. Some educators do it. There are scientists doing it. And they are all going at it vigorously! They plan with material things like tanks and concentration camps. But they also work with subtle stuff, like saying, "That black kid is no good, his mind is not up to a white kid's," as part of their brainwash into thinking we are not even human beings.

The more I have become involved in our struggle, the more I see the needs of the low-income people, the power of the Establishment, and how the two never come together. Last week, I met a youngster, sixteen years old, who was so obviously ready to give up his life for the emancipation of other blacks, prepared to kill whites if that would be of any help. And my despair is that I know his little life doesn't matter a damn to a George Wallace, a Bull Connor, a Sam Yorty or a Richard Nixon!

Odyssey

The Avalon-Carver Community Center, where we had arranged to meet Mrs. Henry, is in a south-central Los Angeles area that she wryly called "Watts North" as if, somehow, it were the suburb you always wanted to move to. She had a voice you have to respect. The voice is in keeping with her: large. Her hair overflows in a superfull natural cut. When she talks, her expressive brown eyes supply the exclamation points.

Mary Henry

I was born in Kansas, but we moved to Gary, Indiana, while I was a baby. We had a home in what was then considered a fairly decent neighborhood. My father, who was from Kansas and had been educated in Wisconsin, taught at the Roosevelt High School. My mother was from Georgia, and with five of us in the house she didn't go out to work. I had a pretty good life, but nothing fancy. The community was almost all black; so were the schools, and the teachers.

Within that context it was part of my birthright to know there was such a thing as a white world and a black world. No one had to tell you. You learn it, know there is a difference. It has been the same for my children. They didn't wake up one morning and suddenly find there are white people who are antiblack. They know that white racism is as much a part of their lives as their food is or their prayers at bedtime. This understanding isn't exclusive to them, as it wasn't to me.

But when I was growing up, I still had hope, however, that white racism was not going to prevail. And I went along with the system. I went to school at Marquette University in Wisconsin, then to the University of Indiana, studying psychology. I did that for three years. I got married to a man I'd grown up with. He was a welder, and one day he said he wanted to live in Los Angeles. He'd been here once before and it was a grass-being-greener situation. It was his decision, which I accepted. Of course, southern California was greener than the steel mills of Gary. But he couldn't get work. He took sick, and then one day he just dropped dead at my feet of a heart attack. I was unemployed, living in public housing, had to go on welfare.

In a way, that's why I didn't have any hesitation to take on the Establishment. I had nothing to lose. The city decided it was going to close the playground that served the housing project, and our kids wouldn't have any place to play. I organized a group of parents, got a lot of petitions, went downtown, fought the closing, and finally we won. A part of the agreement was that somebody from the community be hired to keep the playground going, and they put me in the job. I think they were trying to appease me. Their reasoning must have been: If we hire her, then she becomes a part of us, and she won't make that much of a battle anymore. It didn't work that way. I kept screaming and fighting, and they would hire me for new jobs. Finally, I got into a VISTA project, organizing adults around community education, tutoring, things like that.

Odyssey

In Los Angeles the white Establishment began asking her to speak at various meetings. The school board put her on its advisory council. "I guess," she said, "I was the first black woman who didn't sing or dance named an LA *Times* 'Woman of the Year.'" And the Urban Coalition, White America's attempt to unify a community in fighting ghetto problems, appointed her to its executive committee.

Mary Henry

I am what you would call upset by that coalition. It has so many people with skills and knowledge, everything necessary to effect change, but they have changed absolutely nothing. They have talked and talked, month upon month. And they have not even come close to accomplishing anything for the ghetto. They have influence over the whole system of this city, but when the time came to take a position on police brutality, they turned their backs totally. They refused for one reason or another to ever take a position on some stupid law-and-order concepts people dumped in their laps. I have never seen so many people with power suddenly become powerless.

The test of whether an organization is viable is in the number of people who have been helped. And nobody has, other than those who have been hired for the staff. The people who run the coalition control employment in this city. But knowing that ghetto men need jobs and believing that they ought to have them are two different things. When these large corporations get boards of directors who want to deal with people's minds and hearts and souls, rather than statistics, then you'll have ghetto men trained and hired for jobs.

I think you have to get into the system in order to change it. We can put the Mary Henrys on the boards to yell and scream and knock down, verbally, all the barriers we can. And if the country doesn't start listening to people in my generation, the moderates who have been begging peacefully for action, there is another kind of pressure that comes from youngsters who are willing to sacrifice much more than I am. They have a fearlessness and commitment which allows a sixteen-year-old to say, "I'm going out there, and if they shoot me down—okay!"

Only when men are threatened off of their pedestals, out of their neat little compartments, do they begin to do something. The church, for example, didn't even begin to address itself to the needs of the black community until James Forman issued the Black Manifesto. It is no longer enough to send white missionaries into the ghetto every time there is a Watts or a Newark or a Detroit; by working with blacks only, the white liberal faction is really finking out. Those whites who are convinced that minority Americans are human beings must take the time and energy to turn around other whites who are of unlike belief.

Now, you sitting here with me, I'm not too bothered about that. In a one-to-one relationship, there is very little harm you can do me. It is in masses, as a group, that you white people hurt us, saying I can't have this position, or live in this house, or do this or that. If I were to come to you about a job, would you go to bat for me? Would you risk the impact of white racism on you? I don't know. I tell my kids: "If I deliberately knock over a vase of flowers, it's broken; if I accidentally do, it's still broken!" Overt racism, or just tolerating it, doesn't make any distinction. Both oppress people. And when you tell me that a young black man has been elected mayor of Gary, I say that if he could be elected mayor, he could be elected President, if it weren't for the prejudice.

Racism is destroying a part of this country, destroying black people who long believed in justice for all but don't see it happening, at least in their lifetime. I am myself a casualty of racism, because hope has been stripped from my heart.

Maybe you have just caught me on a bad day.

Odyssey

One year later we came back to the settlement house. Walking around the building, we noticed on one wall a childish drawing depicting two astronauts in white suits hanging from the moon—upside down. The lettering beneath asked: "They went—BUT WHY?"

We mentioned the picture to Mrs. Henry, and she laughed quietly, savoring the irony in a black child's seeing White America's most vaunted symbols of triumph as upside-down adventurers, pursuing silly, quixotic goals.

In the year since we saw her Mrs. Henry had become director of the center, which, in addition to being home base for the VISTA project, has a group-work program, serving preschoolers, teen-agers and adults. She still had her anger, her determination, but the bitterness and frustration had gone.

Mary Henry

I spent four months, nearly half a year, despairing over why we couldn't bring whites and blacks together to move in the direction we ought to be taking. I cried a lot, was nervous and unhappy, feeling there is no hope, that I didn't have any contribution to make. There was no way to fight racism, I thought. I backed off from everything, looked around me, looked at myself, and then it came to me: "Mary Henry! What the hell! You're sitting on the sidelines, copping out, crying, doing nothing but bleeding."

So I quit bleeding, at least in the same way. This whole business of blackness and black pride replaced whatever faith I had lost in White America. For me it was a reestablishing of values that were brainwashed out of me from the time I was a little girl. And now I do not see the need to be involved with anybody white. I am satisfied with the fact that there are always going to be blacks with blacks, whites with whites. At this time I look upon this as a positive, not negative, thing. Here, in this center, I have seen that you can make things happen to improve your community, and when you do that, you don't have a chance to dwell on the negatives. For example, I used to despair that this was the only settlement house in this community. Now I say, how horrible it would be if there were none. You know, it is better to light the one candle.

I find myself spending less time outside this area because there isn't a lot that I believe will happen with the black cause until we get blacks together, mobilize them out of concern and respect, make them aware of the fact that we have been tricked, through political chicanery and games, into not being benevolent with each other.

I have such a strong feeling and commitment to do things within the black community that I find I am uncomfortable now when I am not working in it. Not too long ago I was at one of those Assistance League tea-and-crumpet sort of things which I used to take some pleasure in. There we were, sitting around, drinking tea, wearing pretty hats and smiling so charmingly at each other, while I knew there were kids hungry and unclothed out here. I have reassessed my priorities.

For me there is no pleasure in going to meetings at the Chamber of Commerce or the Urban Coalition, which is still doing nothing, unless they relate to something beneficial to the black community. I still prod the coalition, but if they don't respond, I say: "Move out of the way!" I am in a position now where I have a staff at our center that I can channel into things that need to be done, here.

I have a running fight on with the United Way, which funds us; their pattern of allotting money is so ridiculous! It is probably the first time that an agency head has dared to bite the hand that feeds it. But the United Way can talk and talk and talk, until, in a moment of weariness, you might believe that they really do care. But when you go back to your center, they keep on manipulating the money just like they did before you went to them, and you say to yourself: "While I was there for three hours, talking, I could have helped a child to read or a mother to feed her family."

What we are confronted with is that whole legacy from the white missionary syndrome: Let us do it for you, and then we can control you. And while I am responsible to my own board, which is separate, autonomous, free, the United Way might withdraw its funds. I hope they do not, but in a sense we in the black community have to start depending on each other for our survival. Like my paycheck—every week I put a portion of it into this community. Whether it is to the preschool program to buy that extra book, the new globe of the world, or to some youngster who's saving to go to college, or to a mother needing medical help for her baby. Just as I pay taxes to the government, so do I tax myself to assist people here. And sooner or later, I think we will get many more black folk feeling this way, and then we'll be able to pull it all together, do our funding for our own projects in the community.

I have never had the tenacity of blackness that I now have. It is pleasing. I am sure I will never be any other way. And I am happy that my four boys, ages eleven to eighteen, will never be caught in that transition of wanting integration. They are very black, and they are proud of it. They don't particularly see the need for any interaction with anybody white. Neither do they reject it. They know black men are rising on their own, realize that kings of African tribes were

dragged to America to be denigrated by the dregs of society. Those
people who came over on the *Mayflower* were not the pillars of recti-
tude as they have been pictured. So my kids are asserting themselves
as human beings. They don't even know what an inferiority complex
is.

They still get a great kick out of seeing the flag. This is their country. I want them to feel they have a stake in it, should work for its
betterment, change it, fight for their rights. I say to them: "See that
wall? On the other side is where you have to go. And if they don't
open the door for you, then you will have to knock the whole wall
down, to move over there, where peace and freedom are."

Fortunately, my children are not isolated, living the life of the average ghetto dweller. Our home is in Compton, a nice community the
other side of Watts. They are in predominantly black schools where
the teachers show interest and concern for them. They spend a great
deal of time with me here at the center. Education is still important,
but they know their prime responsibility is to be of some service to
the black community.

I hope very strongly they marry black women. I feel sorry for some
of my black friends who have white wives. I think they got them during the time when it was the thing to do. It is very strange. All this
blackness, and you look behind a guy and there is a white wife. Some
time I am going to get up enough nerve to ask one of my militant
peers: "Hey, fellow! Where did you get her?"

There was a point in my life when, were it not for my children, I
felt like committing suicide, that I just ought to go to sleep, never
wake up. Now, though, I am looking forward to their being grown
and doing things ten, twenty, thirty years from now. The difference
between myself today and the way I was a few months ago is that
each night, I go home in peace.

. . . *And from the Hills*

Odyssey

Richard Allen knows what it is to be black and poor. His first Los Angeles home after leaving the slums of Indianapolis was public housing in the Watts ghetto. He was able to do something about the poverty, using his skills as an entrepreneur to develop a business grossing more than $1,000,000 a year. He sent his son to school in Switzerland, acquired a 280-SL Mercedes (trading in his Lincoln Continental Mark III), and bought property in the hills over Los Angeles. What he has never been able to do anything about is being black.

Richard Allen

It is possible to be born poor in this country and to amass money, just by using the system. The secret is in learning how to work within it. Once you do that and are successful, then the system gives you new opportunities, including a chance to change some of the things around you.

But if you are black, you can only come out of the ghetto to a certain degree, like moving from one end to the other, winding up, you might say, in a golden ghetto—but one that is no less a ghetto. As long as we are in America, we are not free of the inequities heaped upon black people. You can be a PhD or a successful businessman, whatever, and you are still black. If a brilliant doctor, for example, happens to stand next to a pimp, a white American driving by just thinks of it as two niggers togther.

Odyssey

Richard Allen suggested we see him at his office, go with him on a "little errand" as he put it, and then ride over to his home for steak and talk. When we met him, it was almost 5 in the afternoon, but there was a crispness about him, although he had been at work since 10 A.M. in the sound tape duplicating business he and a friend built up from a $1,000 investment. His pink and hand-tailored shirt was wrinkle-free, his electric-blue slacks were unruffled, and his black ankle boots had the sheen of fine leather. Then just thirty-nine, he carried himself with a fluid ease, the mark of a man priding himself on his body. He wasn't "about" six feet two; he was, he said, *exactly* six feet one and three-quarters. He didn't weigh about 188; he was precisely 187½. His "errand" that night proved he did more than talk about being "in shape." Some friends in the Japanese colony were holding a festival, and he had promised to appear in a judo exhibition.

Allen, a "black belt" man, worked out with a teen-ager who at first was politely ritualistic but then went at Allen in earnest. Allen instantly turned tiger, lithe, quick, stalking, confident, and he won the exhibition, but with a sportsmanship that brought no shame to the youngster.

When we later got back into Allen's Mark III he said he wanted to show us his neighborhood, which includes a section called View Park. Mostly black, it is an area of moneyed people and Allen pointed to mini-estates he valued at $180,000 and up. He singled out the home of Ray Charles, offhandedly noting the blind entertainer was a "pretty clever guy . . . excellent chessplayer." From the hillside where Allen has bought a site for a new home, we could look down on the lights of Los Angeles, dimmed and tinted blue in the valley's early evening smog.

"Never see this on television," Allen said. "I don't want to paint the picture that all the brothers are living in affluency, but I don't think we should always make it seem everything connected with black people is limited to the view from a Chicago tenement." He didn't say it complainingly. He recalled that camera crews on assignment from the State Department had spent three days at his company, "but they never showed the film in this country, only in South America."

Allen's home, three-level, painted a light green, picture window opening onto the street, is built so that we went directly from the garage into an entertainment room, with stereo, television, stand-up bar, and a game table, all harmonized in deep mahogany. To announce our arrival to his wife, Rose, he used the intercom.

Richard Allen

All we have ever had in this country is an integration lasting from nine to five. When a plant closes, the black people go back into their area, the Mexicans into East Los Angeles, the Jews into Beverly Hills, the Okies into Torrance. And it is this way not only in Los Angeles. It is true in any city. Historically, America has never been a melting pot, but there is a difference in the conditions for blacks and for whites. By choice, whites have been able to be separatist, to colonize by ethnic groups until they want to spread into the wider community. But for blacks, color is the lock, so that we are segregated without ever having any choice about it. When we moved into these hills, the neighborhood was 70 percent white. Six years later it is 90 percent black. What that says to me is that no matter what degree of wealth, position and achievement blacks attain, it is just automatic that when the black man comes, the white man leaves.

I can explain it with a story. The most prejudiced person ever made in Alabama can meet you, a black man, in Italy, and he'll call out, "Hey! Ain't you an American?" Actually happened to me. Fellow invited me to sit down and have lunch with him and his wife. Probably was the first time he ever related to a black man as an American. Back home, I'd just be "boy" to him. In Italy he wasn't hung up on the institutional racism we have in this country. He had a different perspective over there, so that he was glad to see you.

It is like someone has been in the smog all the time, and when he goes to the country, he just stands and breathes, because he didn't know fresh air could feel so good. But when he goes home, back into the smog, he doesn't want to tolerate you. Institutionally, it has been ingrained in the minds of white people that they are superior in this country. So, how can blacks, the least acceptable of Americans, have any reason to believe that they can make integration work?

Odyssey

The intercom buzzed. Allen listened to his wife saying dinner was almost ready and told her we would be along. "For seventeen years," he said, "I've had a very pleasant marriage, with never any problems." He explained that he had once taken a course in marriage and family planning at Los Angeles State College. "Most valuable," he said. "Broadened my scope in how to deal with people, how to respond, how to compromise. Played a tremendous role in my marriage."

In a few minutes he led us up the stairs to the dining room, which was furnished in a Spanish mode. When Mrs. Allen came into the room, she was so light in complexion that Miriam asked if she was black. Yes, she said, adding that she had "never measured" what part of her background was white. She came from a New Orleans Creole family, and, as she said, "I have known families there with children that ranged from totally black to completely white." For dinner we had a Creole-style rice with sirloin lightly braised in an onion sauce. Mrs. Allen, as quiet as her husband is forceful, mentioned she'd heard of a white family moving into the area because the mother wanted her children growing up in an integrated community.

Richard Allen

Okay. That's one. But there is no longer any responsibility by black people to prove themselves to whites. It is the whites who have to prove that they are willing to take a position in correcting all the wrongs that have been perpetrated on black people and brown people and people with Spanish surnames for all these years.

I'll tell you something. The white community is not thinking, baby! It has not realized there is a time bomb ticking away. The President and the Vice President, for instance, don't know the seriousness of what they are flirting with. Whites say, "Well, it is twenty-five million of them, one hundred and eighty million of us, so if they bother us, we'll put them down!

What they forget is that of the civilizations that have fallen, nearly every one did because of internal rebellion. Blacks know that if you can spend $24 billion to put a man on the moon, if you can take housewives who could hardly pick up an ashtray and teach them to rivet ships—as you did in 1941—you can do anything. We know slums could be totally eradicated; only White America is not willing. I was all over New York and Washington trying to get industries into Watts. White America would rather die than let a black American become an equal part of society.

And yet, with all these wrong things, I still believe this country is worth salvaging. To those who would burn it down I say: "To replace it with what?" Ever notice how that question always goes unanswered. To those who say we should leave, I say: "To go where?" I have traveled much of this world, and I know from experience that no other place offers us the potential we have here. Provided, that is, we work to break down the barriers that are destroying the fiber of this nation. And why should a black man do that? I think a man has to look at his sons and say, "I don't want them to walk in the same shadows I had!" He must love his family enough to want to make the country a little better for them, for the next generation.

That means being practical about what it is we are going to do. Look at it this way: Once the restaurants were open to everybody, many of those who had picketed to get them open couldn't go in. They didn't have the money. Personally, I am not particularly concerned about ever eating in a restaurant that doesn't want me. What I am concerned about is working to make it possible in this country so that if we blacks do our homework, if we plan intelligently, within two years we could open our own restaurant, and it probably will be better!

Odyssey

After the pecan pie and fruit, Mrs. Allen led us into a large living room, which had deep-pile avocado carpet, fireplace, sofas in L arrangements, several Impressionistic oil paintings. Allen served some brandy.

Richard Allen

I suppose if my father had worked in the post office, I might have been a schoolteacher. But my father never worked for anybody; he was always in business for himself, and looking back now, it seems that from my earliest days in Indianapolis I was grooved to go into business. At one time he had seven or eight companies going: trucking, taxi, record shop, restaurant, hotel, moving van, fish and poultry store. He was a black conglomerate, even though we didn't use the word then.

He was a father of that generation, and everyone in the family respected him as the chief breadwinner. But the point to remember is that even with his abilities, his successes, we still came up in the ghetto. Every day, going to school, I had to pass a junkyard. One day the place caught fire, and a brick fell off the building and hit my sister in the back. We tried to sue, couldn't get any money. In one way, Vice President Agnew was right: See one ghetto, you've seen them all. Later, in Watts, I noticed that right next to the housing project I lived in was a junkyard.

In Indianapolis I went to work doing chores out of school hours when I was twelve. By fourteen I had my own business. My father let me drive one of his trucks, and whenever I used it, maybe going to play basketball, I'd leave a sign on it, with my home phone and offering light delivery, quick service. People seeing the truck would call me on jobs. Sometimes I'd use my friends as helpers. That gave me my first experience in hiring people. It was kind of a thrill because I realized I was more or less the supervisor. Though they did most of the work, the bulk of dollars went to me.

What I was learning was that it was possible to work within the system. Same as for a Jewish lad who comes up in a family where the father might own a delicatessen, and the son works after school, on the weekends. His experience tells him something of what business is all about, and that prepares him, so that with his later training he can operate on a more sophisticated level.

Basically, with only rare exceptions, businesses have been foreign to the black community. Not until the civil rights boycotts was it brought home to us how important business is to White America.

After coming out of high school in Indianapolis, I went for a semester to Indiana University. That really wasn't for me, and when my sister, who was living in the Watts housing project, told me about the glories of going West I did what White America did—I went. Besides, I had heard that I could get quite a decent deal playing basketball with one of the junior colleges. I stayed with her and went looking for a job.

In Hollywood I got one with a health club. I came to know everyone there, all the customers, and when Benny Goodman's manager bought the place, he asked me to take it over while he was on the road. Our deal was that he paid the rent, I paid for the sheets and gas, which is quite an item in a health club. When he'd be away two, three months at a time, I ran it totally. We had some of the big names —Mickey Cohen, Vincent Price, Willie Shoemaker—that came in. Place was clean, open all the time. For the orthodox Jews we had a guy who gave Russian platzus, a bath with eucalyptus oil and a technique of spinning heat into your body. I think you spell that p-l-a-tz-u-s. I am not sure. What I do know is that it brought in the customers.

Meanwhile, I was also going to college and playing basketball. Later on, I went semipro, but always I was figuring how much the gate was and how the guy operating the league was making out. Because I wasn't running the game, I didn't feel too comfortable. I started looking for other things to do. This was the time tape recorders were coming in big, so I took a job in a company's quality control section for tapes, then went to school to learn electronic designing. That made me ready to go in with a fellow who had a small firm dealing in prerecorded sound tapes; there was only me and another guy and the owner. Eventually we got that up to 60 people, and a white conglomerate took it over.

About a year after that, Warren Gray, another black working for the same company, and I did some thinking. We realized that if we could make money for the man, we could make it for ourselves. We went to a bank for a loan to start our own company, duplicating tapes. The banker asked asinine questions. His philosophy was that he wasn't going to waste good white money on a business run by blacks.

So Warren and I each put up $500 to start American Tape Duplicators. I wasn't worried about whether White America would accept us, because I knew that if the money is right, White America will deal with you. And I knew at that time we could put out a product cheaper and better than the competition. As long as the white man can save 5 percent, he doesn't care if I am darker than a thousand midnights. I could cut that 5 percent because I was smarter than other people in the business. Coming up in the ghetto, you learn how to hustle. Some of our greatest salesmen in America are in the ghettos. Nine, ten years old, and they are out hustling their sister, marijuana, every conceivable thing. Kids, out there conning. And that's all sales is: the super con.

Besides, we weren't reinventing the wheel. We were only doing what White America has done for centuries. We worked. Sometimes twenty-five, thirty hours at a stretch. In the beginning, I sold, packed, duplicated. Everything. Warren sold, packed, duplicated, everything. Within four years we were doing upwards of $1,000,000 a year in sales. We started a tape club, have three facilities, even make our own electronic consoles for producing the tapes.

In this country we've got to get more and more young black people exposed to businesses run by black men. The youth going into a big company can't really relate to it, but when he sees an American Tape Duplicators controlled by blacks he can say, "Well, they made it, and so can I." The sooner we get black men succeeding in business, the sooner we end the drain of good black minds out of our community into the big white corporations, those outfits that need the right image today and hire show niggers. Draining our people into that just perpetuates the oreos, who talk like White America, think like White America, wear the shirts and ties of White America. Speak of chitterlings to one of them and he says, "I don't eat those—nooooo!" He really digs Aretha Franklin, but he hides that when he goes to the opera. He's comfortable with rock and roll or jazz, but if he's got it on the car radio, he has to keep the windows up, or the volume down, because publicly he has to identify with the white community and never look back at the black brothers trying to survive in Watts.

Watts

The stranger coming upon the community of Watts is always struck by its contrast with the tenement ghettos of the East and Middle West. Most of the homes are single-family. There are trees, grass, some open space. But for all that, Watts is as much a ghetto as Harlem, if you measure by the unemployed, the welfare rolls, the hopelessness of spirit in those who have been locked in or, as some might say, locked out.

For years Black America knew Watts as its "port of entry" to Los Angeles, the first, sometimes the last stop on the way West. If White America knew Watts at all, it was only as the site for a curious, compelling sculpture, the Watts Tower, painstakingly erected year after year by a Mexican-American laborer using pieces of colored glass and broken porcelain embedded in concrete. Standing there, in the middle of a rotting slum, the tower was one man's lonely search for beauty.

But in the summer of 1965 Watts became something more: a part of the language. When the poor, the black, the alienated of Watts rose up that August in a week of rioting, 34 persons were killed, 1,032 injured, 3,952 arrested, and the damage from arson and looting ran to $40,000,000.

And ever since, Watts has been the enduring symbol of the powerful forces that can be turned loose in urban violence.

Richard Allen

The plight of black people is that they don't run their own communities. And if the blacks who can help to bring them control don't work for it, blacks will never get it. Whites have never shown they will willingly give it up.

The key is an economic base. The Jews of Beverly Hills have about 99 percent of the business there, which gives them the say in the economics and politics of their area. But in Watts about 98 percent of the business is run by whites, who siphon the money out, so it doesn't recirculate at all. Result: The blacks have no economic base, therefore no power. They cannot direct the appearance of their community, and they cannot demand better public services because they can't control their politics.

In this vacuum some people talk about black capitalism—but that is the most ridiculous term in the world. When we started American Tape Duplicators, we didn't start a black business; we have a business that is out there competing in the mainstream. If you want to say that black capitalism exists, then it must exist in the black banks of this country. But those banks have only about 1 percent of the assets of the Bank of America. What's more, in the early 1930's there were more than 100 black banks. Now there are about 25. By no stretch of the imagination do I want to perpetuate black capitalism.

Some white banks and insurance companies are talking of the money they have made available for risk capital in the black community. Let's do some analyzing. A major insurance company with assets in the billions is going to make $1,000,000 available to blacks. A million? When this country spends $92,000,000 to send a monkey around the earth, and then the monkey dies! I know that when you are dealing with masses of people $1,000,000 won't buy anything today. But still the banks and insurance companies go on segregating their money, saying things like "We got a million down there in a special bank for you people."

Business can help the ghetto, as long as it understands the ghetto is no different from any other area that needs economic rebuilding. If a technique works for White America it will work for Black America. Simple as that. In Los Angeles we're proving it.

The Democratic administration in the late sixties realized it had made a serious mistake with its poverty program. None of it was successful because the money went to the preachers, the teachers, the sociologists. And the people got nothing. Then Washington said, "Let's go to the people who make economics operate—businessmen." They brought nine of us together out here, gave us $9,500,000, and told us to go! We created the Economic Resources Corporation (ERC); I was chosen to be president. And in eight months we did more for the Watts area than had been done since the 1965 riots.

With Lockheed as our first tenant, we started the Watts Industrial Park. We have plans so that eventually there will be 2,400 people working in various plants in the park, which in turn means another 3,600 satellite jobs in businesses around us. That's a payroll of $44,000,000* and that money stays in the community.

Some people have noticed that of the nine ERC board members, seven are white. No other way to do this. Just as I went to the Japanese to learn judo, so did ERC go to White America, because there is where the business expertise of this country is. Black America doesn't know how to build an industrial park. Not because we're stupid; we just never had the opportunity to learn. The reason nothing was accomplished in our community is that not until ERC was there a way to get committed white businessmen active in our problems. Example: We tried to raise $400,000 of equity capital for one of our projects by going to the black lawyers, doctors, anybody with money. Couldn't do it. But one of the members on ERC's board made the phone call that cleared a $2,000,000 loan. You bet we better have rich white businessmen working with us!

To build our staff, we have raided White America for good white —and black—minds. They are college graduates who don't hate America, don't want to burn it down, and they don't walk around the office in dashikis or have a beard. Can you imagine a militant, or a politician, or a preacher sitting down with Lockheed's lawyers and negotiating a twenty-five-year lease? But our staff could do it, because there was no communications gap.

We were approached by one company that wanted to bring needlework into the park. We said No. We want industries that are orientated to the black male in the ghetto, because we know that for the

---

* By mid-1970 the park had not developed as fast as anticipated. Lockheed had about 200 men working in its plant, building parts for the L-1011 Air Bus, but two other major industrial firms caught in the business slowdown delayed their building plans.

first time he must assume the role of being the household head, to help his son and daughter grow up respecting a masculine image in the family. I can see the mother spending more time in the home, becoming more active in the PTA to make schools more relevant. I can picture a man's discipline returning to the family. In fact, I see a whole restructuring of life, because the male can get a job making $140 a week when before he couldn't make more than $1.40 an hour washing cars. And the youngster who is now being incited by the militants to drop out of school will be stimulated to stay, because he can feel the pride of what is happening.

It won't all come by tomorrow or the day after that. But it is coming. And the lesson from it all, at least for me, is that you don't give up. One man might not be able to make that much difference but he can make things a little bit better.

Mr. Phillips Goes to Washington

Channing Phillips

Inadvertently the black man discovered the most potent weapon he has is violence. With our compacted urban areas, fifty guys can turn a city upside down. What happened in Detroit or right here in the District of Columbia has a fascination for the have-nots. It gives them a power that cannot be denied, and what's more, it is immediately available. The alternative is to find ways into less violent arenas, such as politics or economics. If blacks can't get entrée to those, you can expect them to use the muscle they have to disrupt the city.

Odyssey

On the night of August 28, 1968, something new took place in America: The name of a black man was offered in nomination to be the Democratic Party's Presidential candidate. And while the convention chose Hubert Humphrey, the record still shows that on the first ballot in Chicago the Reverend Channing E. Phillips, black minister from Washington, D.C., got 67½ votes.

About eight months later Phillips got an Orwellian chill in looking through an encyclopedia's 1968 yearbook: there wasn't one word about his candidacy, even though it was a historic first in any major party. "Just like that," Phillips said to us in Washington, "they wiped me out of their history. You could say that a funny thing had happened to me on my way to the White House."

He told the story without rancor. "The black man's struggle has been going on since he put foot in this country, but the problem is that our histories haven't portrayed that."

Channing Phillips

White people are just discovering, and some blacks rediscovering, the Nat Turners and the Denmark Veseys, who used militant, sometimes military, moves in their thrust for freedom. Black people have always had a strong sense of pride, but there is not much you can do with that unless you have some viable weapons and tools to negotiate with White America as peers and not as its slaves.

In Washington, for example, proposals for housing projects were rejected by the Federal Housing Administration and the insuring people, who said there was no money. But after the 1968 riots they called us back, and we discovered that money was indeed available. What that said to us was nothing new. We have always known about the white man's game playing, hypocrisies, and his lying.

As a matter of fact, if you want to see sophisticated dissent, look at the role of the black man in this country, beginning right back in slavery. He always structures his conduct on the assumption that in the white man the beast will dominate the best. To survive, we have had to know the man, which gives us the advantage, because we know both the black and the white world. We understand the white arena because we work in it, and we bring the knowledge of it back to become a part of the black community's lore. For instance: The black man doesn't pay one bit of attention to the white talk about illegitimacy in the ghettos. From my own experience I can explain. For a number of summers I waited tables and did room service at hotels in Cape May and Ocean City, New Jersey. I saw too much junk going on in those rooms for anybody to be able to make a case to me about the blacks being immoral. I have no problems with a white man going to bed with his mistress in a hotel. I just have problems when he tells me that I can't do it. All blacks know that the white man has one standard for himself and one for us.

Odyssey

During the 1968 Chicago convention White America's televiewers got their first sustained look at Phillips: six feet four, light brown, a long face, rail-thin, with patient eyes and, even in the tumult of that violence-drenched scene, an enduring calmness.

Over the next eighteen months we talked with him several times, and always he exhibited the same ease. When we first saw him in the Washington office of a nonprofit housing development corporation he serves as president, he was forty-one but looked younger. He wore the kind of conservative dark-gray suit you see in bankers' boardrooms, with white shirt and subdued tie. Everything about him was quiet. He could talk about America needing "a nigger class to exploit," making it seem only a statement every logical person should be considering. And he frequently talked about God, remarking at one point, "He has a bias for the underdog."

Channing Phillips

My father is a minister who was president of New York City's Baptist Conference for a number of years, and his influence clearly pervaded the family. Three of my brothers are ministers; my sister married a minister. My father was born in North Carolina but left, and even though he later had some very good offers to return, he never would, because of the segregated patterns. My mother, college-educated, a schoolteacher, Northern-oriented, happens to look as though she were white, and on one train trip South the conductor wanted to move her out of the car set aside for blacks. After that incident, she would never again go into the South.

My first home was in the Bedford-Stuyvesant area of Brooklyn. There were six of us children, and we had a strict family life, very pious sentiment in the house. We were not allowed to see a movie, go to a dance. Still, we didn't find that extremely uncomfortable, because our association was with each other. The family was our gang.

Bedford-Stuyvesant had been a very nice residential community, but when I was about nine years old my father came to a decision he had to get us out of there because he didn't want his kids subjected to the new influences that were coming. The neighborhood was getting overpopulated, and with that came all the social ills of people who have been turned by the system into serious problems. You can see the impact of this in any ghetto; the deterioration in Bedford-Stuyvesant since I lived there is really dramatic. But I didn't know anything about those conditions then. To me, Dad was simply taking another church when he moved us into the East Liberty section of Pittsburgh.

There, for the first time, I saw the separation between the races. Blacks were restricted to ghettos. In the midst of all that, however, my father always retained for himself—and therefore, for us—his approach to human values. I'd call him bourgeoisie, a Puritan. To this day I have a great deal of respect for his steadily maintained conservative values. And I think his community does, too. I have seen him walking the streets, always wearing his collar, and the drunks and junkies and so forth holler at him, but with a kind of respect.

He raised all of us to have a strong sense of personal worth, which was not diminished in contact with whites. I saw my father in some very defiant positions with the white man, standing up, telling him a thing or two, so I was never caught in that white-superior black-inferior bit. Schools are usually the place where that issue is highlighted, driven home to black youngsters in comparing their progress with that of the whites. But in our home it was just naturally assumed we would do well and that we would go on to college, and because I did get good grades, I never had any problems with thinking the white man was smarter.

When I graduated from Pittsburgh's Westinghouse High, the Army took me, sent me to study electrical engineering at the University of Utah. It was about this time that I came to have radically different ideas from my father about the true nature of the human being we call man. At home, there had been constant preachment as to what man ought to be doing. There was a naïve, I think now, assumption that he is basically good and that you could expect he will care about his fellows. In the Army I saw the competition that takes place on the adult level, when people are bucking for promotion or driving for more power. Then men no longer relate to each other in a cooperative way. They use each other for their own ends, and the kinds of injustices that people levy against one another give you a totally different view of man. I saw that while he has the capacity to do good, if left to himself, he won't. I was beginning to shape my own anthropology.

After leaving the Army, I was in sociology at Virginia Union University, and I didn't have any thoughts of going into the ministry. Then during my last months before graduating I took a look at the skills I thought I had: relating to people; being able to see their needs; the desire to do something to help. All these abilities seemed to give me some peculiar aptness for the ministry, and that fall I enrolled at Colgate-Rochester's divinity school in New York. In my sophomore year I was ordained as a minister in the National Baptist Church. The insights that I had developed in the Army were sharpened by my studies into a theological framework, giving me an understanding that has always stayed with me. I felt that what we needed was a theology of the powerless, founded on the premise that society has to be structured to protect them from man's baser instincts.

At that time I didn't take any call to the pulpit because my teachers persuaded me that with my work in Greek and Hebrew I should consider going for my PhD and teaching. Drew University in Madison, New Jersey, made that possible by designating me a graduate fellow. I never got the doctorate. The family I was living with in Madison had a daughter going to a girls' school in Pennsylvania, and when she wrote home that her closest friend there needed a date for the senior prom, I drew the assignment. It wasn't a blind date because I had already seen the friend, and it was on my mind that I might want to marry her. Six months after the prom I did.

I accepted an offer to teach the New Testament at Howard University in Washington. I was there two years, but really, it was tame. I kept getting the feeling too many of my students only wanted what you might call a union card, a certificate to teach or something else for a job, and that they weren't there for an education. Probably just because it was offered to me, I went into the ministry, serving as the director of education for my brother-in-law, who was senior minister in the Grace Congregational Church in Harlem. Some things came clear to me in that experience. One, in the ministry, wherever your brothers are, you go. Two, the church and ministry basically means an opportunity to move into people's communities and be free enough to work for change.

In 1961 I accepted the senior ministership at Lincoln Temple, United Church of Christ, in Washington. I came really hoping to effectuate change. What I found was that this is a town that is basically bourgeoisie. Washington, of course, is a colony. It has no self-government, it does not have the kinds of radical action necessary to get it. There is a real timidity about striking out, simply because the federal government is here. From all this, an agony developed for me: How do you stiffen the backbones of people who have been in despair for so long?

Odyssey

We asked if this was the style of ministry practiced by his father. "Hardly," said Phillips. "And we argue theology all the time."

Channing Phillips

For me there was a need to go beyond the church itself. I became a member of a variety of organizations. Stokely Carmichael was in Washington at that time, working on inner-city programs from a church right across the street, and I got to know him. Later I worked with him during the Cambridge, Maryland, situation, when our church was used to train people in nonviolence for the demonstrations there. Then came the terrible beatings on the bridge at Selma. I went to Alabama with other members in the religious community. My wife was one of those picketing Lyndon Johnson's White House in wondering how he could send troops to Vietnam but none to Selma. After that, about forty civil rights organizations came together in Washington to form the Coalition of Conscience, in which we started out to help the people of Selma but then began focusing on the problems in the District of Columbia.

It is only historical truth to recognize—now—that the civil rights movement of the South was itself a cause of despair in the Northern ghettos, when people thought about how much had been given in blood and sweat and how little the results had been. It was ineffective in Harlem or wherever it was tried in the North, because you couldn't ferret out the enemy. There was no Bull Connor to hang it all on. How do you personalize the fact that the real enemy in the North is the capitalistic system which needs a nigger class to exploit?

What the North did was to create an economic form of slavery. Instead of keeping blacks on plantations where the master had to care for the slaves during the nonproductive years at each end of the lifecycle, the Northern system was to put the blacks in ghettos, calling them out as the labor market demanded, but having no responsibility for them. I think that much of what we have been seeing in the last few years—what is variously termed the rebellion or the riots—is the result of this kind of isolation and letting blacks out only when they can be exploited.

Because ghetto people have had no way to escape from this, things began to explode. Then blacks discovered that this in itself was a weapon. All the pleas for help got nowhere until the cities started burning. In the same context, real focus on the issue of police brutality began only after the Black United Front labeled the killing of a white policeman justifiable homicide in the same sense police are allowed to kill black people and call it the same thing. I signed the statement because I recognized that its language made it one way of opening a dialogue on the system which invites such violence.

But in Washington today I think that the black community is discovering that rhetoric alone won't rebuild any of the shopping centers

or buildings burned out in 1968's riots. The depletion of housing resources, continued deterioration of services, are making blacks see
the need for capital and economic development. And that you don't
get out of rhetoric. At the same time the white community is discovering that no matter how much capital it has, if it wants domestic
tranquillity, it will have to pay much more serious attention to the
things that produce the explosions. Thus, with whites and blacks irre-
trievably interlinked for mutual survival, the time may be here to
begin moving in new directions.

I believe that people—and I mean all of us—are searching for
some kind of uniting force that can move us ahead as a nation. Not in
the same bag as before, whites leading, blacks following. The need
now is for a cooperative leadership, a cultural pluralism, in which a
cohesive black community using the political majorities it is now at-
taining in the cities can deal as equals with the whites, each doing his
own thing, but understanding the necessity for all the country to go in
the same general direction.

To me, it is the only way to end the arteriosclerosis that has come
upon our American system.

Odyssey

Implicit in his approach was one word: politics. How had he
made the move into that?

Channing Phillips

I was never directly involved in politics until 1968, when some
people from Bobby Kennedy's office, knowing of my opposition to
the Vietnam War, asked if I would give leadership to his campaign to
elect convention delegates favorable to his cause. The assumption was
that if we could beat the Lyndon Johnson supporters running for the
delegation in his own backyard, we would give other areas of the country nerve enough to take him on over the peace issue. That made
sense to me. And of the twenty-three delegates elected, 21 were pro-
Bobby. Among the Johnson people defeated was the Democratic national committeeman for the district. I was elected to replace him,
which meant I led the delegation to the convention.

When Bobby was assassinated, we met with Gene McCarthy, but
he did an excellent job of offending most of the people in the

delegation, as is his wont. Mr. Humphrey decided not to meet with us. Realizing that all the cards were not on the table, we decided to go to the convention with the favorite son strategy, using me as the stalking horse in trying to have some bargaining power. Of course, we weren't thinking about winning. What we really wanted was fifteen minutes of prime TV time to talk about issues that probably would not be floored at the convention: the role of the black man in politics, the status of the district as a colony without self-government, and the peace question. We had planned to put my name in nomination just as a delegate from the District. When the convention's black caucus of about 300 delegates approved my candidacy, we broadened our base to get Mayor Hatcher of Gary and Congressman Conyers of Detroit to make seconding speeches.

As the convention developed, I had no particular sense that this was historic or anything like that, partly because of the sheer fatigue, partly because of what was happening outside the hall with Mayor Daley's people and the white protestors. The full meaning of what had taken place didn't really come to me until about a week later, when CBS sent me a complete tape recording of my name being presented to the convention, together with five condensed versions for each of my kids, and that suggested that somehow posterity was involved.

Odyssey

The convention over, Phillips did not give up politics. Despite his differences with Humphrey on the war issue, he campaigned for him in a number of cities, a decision he justified by saying, "I look at the options that are available, and having reviewed what has happened under the Nixon administration, I think it was right to be for Humphrey, and we should have worked even harder." For Phillips, Humphrey's defeat was not a total loss.

Channing Phillips

We were living in the parsonage. It seemed to me it was time to be moving on. We looked all over Washington. With the tight money market we couldn't buy anything. Then it occurred to me that many of the people who'd gone out with the Johnson-Humphrey administration were leaving Washington, so I started tracing out where they lived. I knew they'd have big mortgages, written at a time when you could get good rates, and we finally bought the home that had belonged to Humphrey's press man. It's in the District's Chevy Chase section, probably worth about $45,000 or $50,000. We have, would you believe, seven bedrooms, about right for a family with five young kids and one St. Bernard.

In the months before we moved I had been an increasing symbol of controversy in my church. I had gone off salary, and was serving as senior minister on a volunteer basis, supporting my family on my salary at the housing corporation, because I wanted church funds used to hire more staff in helping the ghetto people. But the church didn't do that, and the only reason it has been operating in the black is that it didn't spend the money that had been paid to me. In addition, as I became more active in politics, some of the church people were seeing a hidden agenda in everything I did. So in May, 1970, I resigned altogether and am now full time in the housing field.

I have become convinced that the church cannot be the instrument of radical change required by these times. Churchism is kept alive by people whose basic physical needs are being met. But the people who are sorely frustrated in their lives haven't found their way into the churches because the churches have turned them off.

There is an old psalm that teaches "Give me Jesus, and you can take the world." That is the kind of foolishness white missionaries have taught blacks. But it is not the case anymore. Blacks still have a good deal of faith in Jesus, but they have changed the second line to read, "I'll take as much of the world as you've got." And I don't find that incompatible, at all.

On Growing Up

In the Country, Long Ago

Odyssey

Bayard Rustin wanted to be sure the restaurant had fresh crabmeat, and then he asked for it to be sautéed, spaghetti on the side, and he drank scotch sours, all of it done with some elegance: fastidious, just the right amount of offbeat flourish. The restaurant responded with a beautiful dinner, and he sent his compliments to the chef.

We had met him late that day in CBS' New York studios, where he had taped an appearance on a panel show, but it had not gone well. Rustin said he thought it "dreadfully difficult" to get into a subject when three or four people were all having a go at it. Having said that, he almost seemed physically to push the thought away, and we got the feeling that in his life, programmed hour to hour, from breakfast to bed, the gears are always shifting.

Rustin is a tough man for a quick-and-easy identification. The usual approach is to say that he did a brilliant job in organizing 1963's March on Washington. He has also been Quaker, socialist, draft resister. He worked with Communists, then broke with them. In SCLC's early years he was secretary to Dr. King. He organized school boycotts in New York City, and he voices "heretical" views on black studies: "What in hell are soul courses worth in the real world?" He helped Hubert Humphrey corral delegates to the 1968 Democratic Convention. As the director of the A. Philip Randolph Institute, created mostly to give him an umbrella for his activities, he serves labor as thinker and needler, the speaker-writer whose remarks always raise some blood pressures. In the usual sense, he is not a leader. He has no great following. What he does have is influence, because he is recognized as an intellectual whose articulated thoughts have spawned numerous black strategies.

West Chester

It is a little country town, the seat of Chester County, about 22 miles out of Philadelphia, and all around it is the mark of history. To the north is Valley Forge; to the south, the scene of the Battle of the Brandywine, where Howe outwitted George Washington and advanced to take Philadelphia. For anyone who has ever lived in this area, it remains forever some of the most beautifully tranquil land in America, with swelling hills, long green fields, clumps of oak and maple along the creeks.

Bayard Rustin

When I was growing up in West Chester we had a ten-room house, which belonged to an Italian fellow who was a member of the Elks Club, where my grandfather was the caterer. It was in an Italian neighborhood, and it had an enormous yard with a garden. Here I got my original interest in art, because in this garden there were a number of statues, copies of famous things, in the way Italians will have. It was truly an enormous house, always filled with people, always very joyful, and there was no indication that I was other than a complete member of the family.

I was born in March, 1910, illegitimate. Now, I understand the whole syndrome in the ghetto that leads to illegitimacy, the breakup of families, the ugliness. To counterbalance this, I have a very beautiful feeling: I was taken in, I was loved, I was never brutalized. If years go by before you know you are illegitimate, that is a magnificent testimony to the people in the town.

Until I was about twelve, I thought of my mother as my sister. My grandmother had nine children, and I made the tenth. I called her Mama, and all my uncles and aunts were regarded by me as my brothers and sisters. I called my mother Florence, and in this extended family she just got lost, had no significance for me whatsoever.

Unquestionably, my grandmother was the dominant one in the family. She happened to be, as I am, reared as a Quaker, in the home of the Quaker General Smedley D. Butler. She attended the West Chester Quaker Secondary School, which in those days was equivalent to a college education. My grandfather had come out of Maryland, had less than a third-grade education. He had taught himself to read and write. He was content to make the money for the family, and while he was a very strong man, his attitude was: "Mama knows best!" Which was very common in those days.

My grandmother and grandfather were never known in West Chester as Julia or Janifer. Every white person called them Mrs. Rustin or Mr. Rustin. At one time she was president of the Garden Club of the county, and that was a big exclusive group to which the country-club set belonged. Because of his catering, my grandfather was known in most of the aristocrats' homes, and this gave me a great advantage over most blacks in the town. There was scarcely a home where I wasn't welcome, because I was a Rustin.

The catering business had very interesting effects on our family. It meant that all of us became rather good cooks, because we had to help. As a boy of seven or eight, even later, I took huge turtles—I imagine they were purchased in Philadelphia—and tediously stripped them out of their shells for real green turtle soup. Very often, when the affairs were over, the people would say to my grandfather, "Mr. Rustin, you take the food home." And so while we might not have enough milk, we would have all kinds of tidbits in our icebox. There would be a huge pot of *pâté de foie gras* or maybe some lobster Newburg, all of it made by him. Neighborhood kids used to love to come by and sample the various types of food. At that time I discovered children really do not like what they have not had before; while they came to test these various things, what they really wanted was the ice cream.

My grandmother was very active in the NAACP. As a quite small child I met Dean Pickens, who was one of the important men in the NAACP. From my earliest days, I presume that the three words I remember the most, and which have made an impression on me, are "discrimination," "segregation" and "NAACP," all taught me by my grandmother.

In our home, personal pride was something you grew up with. For example, when I was a youngster, Henry O. Tanner, whose paintings hang in the Louvre and all over, came to our home for dinner. Du Bois came. And I just did not know any white people who were so eminent as these worldwide figures, so I never had the feeling we as a people were inferior or couldn't hope to achieve.

Across the street from us was a white guy named Paschal Dubunda. We had fruit trees in our yard, and the Dubundas had tomatoes and other things in theirs. My grandmother and Mrs. Dubunda were very dear friends. When Mrs. Dubunda made tomato paste, she would bring some of it to us; if there was any small fish left over from his catering, my grandfather would send it to them, because they were very fond of fish. Just for fun, we stole tomatoes from the Dubundas and Paschal stole fruit from us. My first real sort of shattering experience came when Paschal and I got into an argument and he called me a "black nigger." I don't think anyone had ever called me a nigger, but I knew it meant disrespect. Well, I came home very dashed and told my grandmother I just didn't feel up to dinner. She said, "What is the matter?" and I said after a bit of hesitation, "Paschal Dubunda called me a nigger."

What happened then was, I think, the greatest lesson I ever learned. She pulled me very close to her, and she said, "Oh, Bayard! Do you know what Paschal is doing now?" I said No, and she said, "He is home, eating his spaghetti and meatballs. He will go to bed, little aware that he has been unkind. Why don't you tell him tomorrow what he did? But if you are not up to that, don't let him give you ulcers because he was not nice. Don't go to bed hungry. That's silly." And I thought about that, and I said to myself, "She is so right."

The next day I spoke with Paschal, and he said he didn't mean it. I said, "It is easy for you to say that, but you shouldn't do what you know is going to hurt people." "What do you want me to do?" he asked. I said, "I think you should pledge yourself never to say that kind of thing again." He said, "Why don't you call me a wop and then we'll be even?" When I said I wasn't going to do that, he burst out crying, which made me realize he knew he had been trying to be rude.

There was another incident in which, while older, I behaved less maturely. In a mass meeting, Dean Pickens was telling about a lynching which had taken place in Mississippi. I held my hands over my ears, began to cry, and I made such a racket that my grandmother had to take me out. That was when I first understood that people could be cruel because they were white. This description of the lynching, talking about what happens to black people in Mississippi, went beyond being mean. What it said was that just because of his color, the white man was compelled to be cruel to people who had done nothing to him. And that terrified me.

Odyssey

Rustin is six feet three. A vigorous stand of gray hair flares aggressively, up and out. High cheekbones. Light-brown skin. Voice cast in the British mode: somewhat high-pitched, words clipped.

Bayard Rustin

I am not at all sure there was any deep love between my father and my mother. I think I was just the result of an older man's ability to take advantage of a girl who was not yet sixteen. There was never even any question about my being given his name. I was seven or eight before I even saw him. On my way to school one day I noticed a parked moving van, with a pile of blankets, some furniture, and a man was standing up in it. Another man with him was giggling in a silly way, some joke between them. The boy I was with pointed to the man standing up and said, "There is your father." How he knew, I don't know, but I suppose mothers talk; people love to engage in the immorality of others, while obscuring their own.

However, I did recognize this man as looking like me. When he called out to me, I said, "What do you want?" He said he wanted to shake my hand and say hello. I asked, "Why?" He said, "Maybe we are relatives." I told him I had never seen him before, and he said, "You don't always see your relatives." I shrugged and waved good-bye, but there was something in the way he saluted me that let me know we were related. Still, I don't think I mentioned the incident to anybody. It didn't seem that important.

Through one of my high school teachers I later got a job at the Green Tree, an old English-type inn, with a courtyard where the horses could be brought. There was one enormous green pine tree, plus some of the most elegant trees I think I have ever seen. Working in the place was someone who was acquainted with my father. One Sunday morning this man asked me if I would like to meet some people, and when I said I would, he took me upstairs where the help lived. There were two women, two men in the room, and I immediately recognized that one was the man I had seen on the moving truck. We had an absolute resemblance, he and I. We all had a very pleasant afternoon before I had to go back to work in the pantry. He never said anything about being my father.

I got a note from him just before graduation from high school. I had won speaking contests, played football, was on the track team, won a state tennis championship, took first in the essay contest. Some of these honors were going to be cited at the convocation, and my father, having heard about that, wrote me, identifying himself for the first time. He said that despite his not having done what he should have for me, I was his son, and he wondered if I would be interested in getting him a ticket to attend the graduation. I asked my grandmother what to do. She said that since I was getting out of high school, I was at an age to make some decisions for myself. I said, "Well, he is my father, and he did ask me to come." So I offered him a ticket. He came. And I think he was very moved.

After his appearance at the graduation, showing that I knew of our relationship, people figured that there was no longer any reason to hide anything about him, and I was told he had become a drunkard. One day, drunk in Philadelphia, he was arguing with another fellow when he fell down a pair of steps and broke his head wide open. He died that way. When I heard, my reaction was one of deep sorrow, as it would be for any human being who ends up in some tragic death, which is so common in the black community.

Odyssey

Rustin went to college, but only because of his grandmother's intervention.

Bayard Rustin

Even though I had won all those honors in a completely integrated high school I was notified that no scholarships would be available to me: The colleges giving them did not accept Negroes. My grandmother said, "We are not going to endure this indignity." Going to see the superintendent of schools, she told him he had to do something. "But, Mrs. Rustin," he said, "I don't know what I can do." She said, "Until something is done, I am not leaving this office." He was very distressed. I think he knew they were not behaving justly. In about five hours he raised $100, making it possible for me to go to

Wilberforce University, which was operated in Ohio by the African Methodist Episcopal Church.

At Wilberforce, my ability to sing—two white professors at West Chester State Teachers College had given me a musical education for free—enabled me to do a lot of traveling. I was in the college choir which went all around the country, giving concerts at AME churches to raise money for the college. For me it was a very broadening experience, the beginning of my real understanding of the racial problem. As we went into Mississippi, Georgia, Alabama, I came to see racism. The incidents weren't dramatic; in fact, they were very undramatic. We'd be in an automobile and need to go to the toilet, but place after place, maybe as many as a dozen in a row, would all tell us that "ten miles down the road" there was a place Negroes could use. Or, if you were downtown and wanted a drink of water, you'd be told that if you went to a college, clear across town, there'd be a fountain for Negroes. You'd wait twenty-five minutes to be served in a diner, and if you complained, you'd be told, "We don't want niggers in here, anyhow." One night, when a boy with us got sick, we went with him to two hospitals in this one town, and both said it was the next town that had the Negro doctor. It was all just tedious and irksome, wearing away at one's sense of Christianhood.

I determined that someday I was going to come back to fight that racism. There was no single moment of reaching this idea, it was just a growing conviction that people ought not to endure this, which led to the feeling that if people should not endure it, what was I going to do about it?

I left Wilberforce, went to a teachers college, and then to New York to attend City College. My purpose, though, was not to finish it. I wanted to have a legitimate base within the university system to carry on political activities which would work at striking down racism. I was a Quaker, but the Quakers were not involved in the cases of that time, such as Scottsboro.* But the Communist Party was in all these things, so I joined the Young Communist League. In doing that, I don't think I was rejecting the Quakers' approach of nonviolence as much as I was rejecting the inactivity of those who said they believed in it.

I can remember the exact moment I decided I had to break with

---

* Convicted of rape, eight of the teen-age "Scottsboro boys" were sentenced to death, the ninth to seventy-five years in prison in Alabama. The fight to save them was a legal *cause célèbre* in the 1930's. Ultimately they all were released.

the Communist Party. In the CP I had been authorized to set up a committee against discrimination in the armed forces, something that wasn't hard for the Communists to do, because this was when they were calling it Roosevelt's imperialistic war. But when Hitler moved against the Soviet Union, the party called me in to say, "Okay, you must destroy your committee. We must have a United Front. This is now a people's war." I was really distressed. I realized that even though the Quakers had not lived up to everything I thought they believed in, at least they were not playing the Communists' kind of game.

I got back into the pacifist movement, worked with the American Friends Service Committee, then with the War Resisters' League. As a conscientious objector I refused induction, and I was in Lewisburg Penitentiary for twenty-eight months. My grandmother said, "I hate to think of your being in jail, but I would hate more to think of you being someplace else, despising yourself for what you did not have the courage to do."

Finally, a man is only the degree of integrity he can express, and integrity can be defined as a consistency between belief and action. If I hadn't resisted the draft, I might not have had the strength to do what I have done since then. My supply of capital for standing up would have been eaten away.

I don't want to be showy about it, but I feel I have gotten a great many advantages out of this society and that I have a great deal of responsibility to put something back in. I don't, you know, look upon myself as being brutalized. But I owe my brothers, regardless of their color, some effort to make this a better place, where we can all have some peace.

Once, when our West Chester football team went over to Norristown to play a game, they didn't want to let Negroes eat there with the whites. My coach, whose name was Zimmerman, said, "All right, we're not interested in playing this game." So I feel I owe Mr. Zimmerman something. He stood up, and he fought back.

In the Ghetto, Now

Sonny Zoo

It's like a jungle, man. I don't know how the outside world is, but I know this ghetto, and if you can survive here, you got to be able to survive anywhere. People go through four, five years in Vietnam and don't nothing happen to them. They come back to the ghetto and get killed. That is something to think about, man. A ghetto is a very dangerous place.

Odyssey

At the time he said that Sonny Zoo was twenty-one, just over six feet, rangy. His black face was dominated by large brown eyes that stared out, direct. He was living then in West Philadelphia, in what was for him a tight little island embracing a few blocks running south on Thirty-ninth Street from the Pennsylvania Railroad tracks. The heart of the area was the intersection of Thirty-ninth and Aspen, the geographical identification for the street gang he ran with. On its four corners were a steak place, a grocery, a house with boarded-up first-floor windows and a barbershop. Radiating in all directions was a Humpty-Dumpty collection of two- and three-story buildings, brick, frame, stone, most of them suffering in the stresses of slum existence. An occasional morning glory popped from a window box. Trash fluttered down the curb lines. A red-white-and-blue sign announced the coming of a swimming pool on an empty lot.

But for Sonny Zoo it was home. He claimed to know all its "cracks and crevices," and he said that "if the police is chasing me, he is not going to catch me if I just get a chance to get around a corner." He told us: "I love it. I don't think I will ever leave. My friends are here.

Enemies, too. Even if I went to jail for twenty, thirty years, I am quite sure I would come right back."

He walked in to see us in the office of a ghetto run community agency with two other men. Both were younger, deferential to him, and they sat there, absorbing his words.

Sonny Zoo

Reason I went to jail the first time was to help my mother when nobody she turned to, welfare, city, nobody, would. I was the oldest in the family. I was obligated to helping her and my brothers and sisters. I knew I was too young to get a job, so I did the next best thing: take some money.

One day when I was buying a popsicle, it was like by accident I noticed this white insurance guy was collecting in the neighborhood. I said, "Why you taking in all this money?" He said he was just a bill collector, and I didn't mess with him. Not then. I waited three months. Then it was a spur-of-the-moment thing. Just hit me. I dug it. I didn't see the money on him, but it was the way he was acting that told me he had it, like when a person is trying to be casual as possible, don't want to draw no attention.

It didn't seem like I would be able to do it by myself. There were about six older dudes, twenty-five, twenty-six, something like that, and I told them about the guy having money. I had a shotgun in the cellar, bought it from a drunk, and I went home to get it while the dudes started talking to the insurance guy. When I come back, I hit him in the head. The other dudes snatched his money belt. I grabbed his briefcase. They ran, so I ran.

I cut down an alley. The insurance guy come running to it with a .22 pistol. If I would have come out, he would have seen me, and I knew he would have shot me. I was scared, started to cry, but then I said to myself, "You're here now, and there ain't no turning back." So I pulled out and *boom!* I shot him in the face, but he wasn't killed.

I run around to find the other guys. Briefcase didn't have nothing but papers in it, but there was about $23,000 in the money belt. We split it. I was a little guy, and I know they took advantage, beat me for a lot of money.

When I took my cut home, my mother asked where I got it. I said I saw these dudes robbing this man and I picked up the money on the street. She knew that wasn't true. She fussed me, she beat me, but I told her I wouldn't never say where I got it. It all went to the family. Food, clothes, place to live. And I'll tell you this: That insurance man had been taking from the black people. It was about his time to give something up.

The cops got all the other dudes first. It was like two months before they come to the house for me. My mother said to them, "You can come in." I got my coat and said, "See you later, Mom." Then I walked out with the cops.

I wouldn't have had to do no time at all if I just said these older dudes put me up to it. But my mama had told me, "Never be a snitch." So I said I did it all, and, like, it turned out I was the only one went to jail. I was in court a good five minutes. No lawyer. Stood in front of the judge; man read off my case. Judge looked at me; I looked at my mother. Judge said, "Camp Hill, indefinite." Shocked me. I knew Camp Hill. It was like a junior penitentiary. But there wasn't any reason to cry. I turned around, waved to my mother. That was it.

In jail there is only two kinds of people. The strong. And the weak. Guards don't care if somebody is messing you up; you got to hold your own. If you can't, you are going to be like married to another man. There is always going to be one guy who is going to try you, and you got to hurt him, not just beat him, you got to hurt him! First time somebody challenged me I was in quarantine, like they put you in the first thirty days. Every time I would come down to eat, there was a guy who used to give me more food than anybody else. I didn't dig him. I was a little guy, but I had a lot of heart. One night we had creamed beef, mashed potatoes, and he put it all on my tray, and I took the whole thing and threw it in his face, and I jumped over the counter, and there was a fork, and I used that to stab him in the face. Unless I had done that, I would never had no respect. All my life I knew that you should do unto others as you would have them do unto you—but do it first. If you wait for them to do unto you, you might not live through it.

Anyway, after that, the word was not to mess with that boy Zoo. Warden put me in the hole. That is a joint with two different cells. One got a toilet and a sink. Keep you in that at night. In the day they put you in the other. It ain't got nothing. Nothing! All you hear is tick tick tick tick from the radiators, all day. Another guy was in the hole about ninety-four days. I was in about sixty-three. Everybody thought we was going to snap. But this is one thing I learned about white people. When they think you are weak, they take advantage of you. So I said I was going to walk out just like I walked in—with a smile on my face. Wasn't nothing to it.

When my mother come to jail to see me, she said, "You ain't let them make you no faggot, have you?" I said, "Ain't you got more confidence in your son than that?" I knew jail was not going to be no peaches and cream, but that wasn't the point. The point was, I was there. If you do something, go to jail, you don't expect to lay on a beach. You expect a hard time. If you are so much of a baby you can't take what goes on in jail, then you got no business doing nothing that make you go there.

Odyssey

The bravado of the Street Man is in that story. Sonny Zoo was arrested for a holdup, but the records list no charge of shooting and indicate the loot was $70. The Pennsylvania Industrial School at Camp Hill details him as having been in "segregated detention"—not solitary confinement—for fighting, insubordination and attempting to organize gangs, but records show it was never for longer than fifteen days at a time.

And yet, even with these discrepancies, his story is testament to growing up in the ghetto. Police files say he was eleven when first picked up for disorderly conduct and fourteen when charged with carrying concealed deadly weapons. In both cases he failed to appear for his court hearings, and bench warrants were out for him at the time of the robbery. After his discharge from Camp Hill he was twice picked up for car theft, served time in a maximum security prison, and when we talked with him, he was under indictment for allegedly shooting another youth in the face with a shotgun.

He was then working in a youth program, running a clubhouse just off Thirty-ninth Street, where youngsters could play ping-pong, look at television or have meetings. The job was part of a gang-rehabilitation project, aimed at those in Sonny Zoo's environment.

Sonny Zoo

My mother was thirteen when I was born. Never seen my father, don't want to see him because I made it this far without him and I can make it the rest of the way. Since my mother was so young, my grandmother was responsible for both of us. She was like any old granny, programmed to go to church and be a good nigger. She al-

ways told me, "Never do nothing that ain't right." We was all living in
a house in West Philadelphia. We had one big potbellied stove. Television wasn't here, and we used to have a radio. *Amos 'n' Andy* and
all that. People called me Sonny. I used to run up and down the steps
and play in the backyard. I was always trying to get guys to sneak in
the zoo with me. It was real near. One day a guy named Irving the
Old Folks started calling me Sonny Zoo.

First day I went to school I hookied. My mother took me to the
front door, and I went right on through, and in five minutes I was out
playing in a big ash pile. My mother beat my ass, sent me back. But I
never found a teacher that took any interest in a kid. They was there
to make it out for eight hours, and that was it. Teacher would hit me,
and I would hit right back. Once I was popping gum in class, and my
teacher told me to spit it out. I made like I did, but I wasn't con
enough to fool her, so she got a big yardstick and smacked me across
the face. I took the stick and smacked her. She said she'd have me
suspended and sent me to the principal. I told my mother, and she
come to tell the teacher to keep her motherfucking hands off me.

I went to school into the seventh grade. Didn't mean that much to
me. It was just a thing. Like, they give you a book or a few mathematics problems, but as far as digging down deep, it seemed to me
that if your family didn't press the issue, it just wasn't pressed. Most
kids didn't learn in school.

I was living a hard life. I seen the changes my mother went through
to take care of me. My mother married the man who was father to
the other children in the family. Wasn't too much I could say to him,
wasn't too much he could say to me. He would never hit me; my
mother wouldn't let him. She knew if he hit me, I wouldn't have said
anything, but in the long run I would have hurt him. He was a cook
in a hotel, and when he tried to stop a fight between some other colored cooks, he got stabbed and died. Didn't mean anything to me.

What was important to me was my gang. Hell! Seem like I was always in one. Even as little fellows we had zip guns. I was seven when
I made my first. I knew it could kill somebody. Guess I was about
eleven when I seen anybody get really hurt. Boy got stabbed in the
face. Lots of blood. Didn't make me sick. I didn't think, "What a
shame!" It is just the way it is.

You know, the white race don't think of gang warring as fun, like
they don't consider a lot of things black race do. Some guys up here
will just get out and throw bricks at each other. I mean, it is some-

thing to do. White man put the black man in a jungle where there is only certain things you can do. One day a dude put a big trash can with water on top a door of the clubhouse. When a guy come in, he got it all on his head. Later the dude what put the can up there was asleep in a chair. Some guys put lighter fluid on his chest and lit it. It was fun!

People got to know anyone can get killed in gang fighting. Doing it or not, if you are out there, you have to expect something. Right near here a woman and a little kid was sitting on a porch when boys from one gang started shooting shotguns. Guys from another gang started shooting back. So the woman and the kid got caught in the fire. Killed. But the little guy that shot them, he got shot, too.

This could have been me. I could walk out a door, and somebody could shoot me. I done hurt people, and I know my time is coming. You just got to take what can happen. What the hell! If you go out to gang-war and you come up to a dude and he got a shotgun, what are you going to do, say, "I wonder if this guy is going to shoot me?" You go ahead and shoot him, get it over with. Like I am out on $10,000 bail right now. They said I shot a boy in the face with a shotgun. Just saw him. He spoke to me. I spoke to him. He knows I didn't do it, dig it? I just had a reputation for shooting. He don't hold no grudge against me because he knows he was out there.

There is always going to be gangs. They talking now how anybody get caught gang-warring they going to stand up in the middle of City Hall and whip them publicly. That still not going to stop gangs. They will be when I am dead and my kids is dead. For me, gangs has been my way of surviving this jungle. By joining a gang you fulfill a whole lot of needs, physically, mentally.

Dudes don't realize that only reason gangs is violent is because people in the ghettos is all boxed in. When they try to get out, they can't get housing. That makes ghetto neighborhood nothing but reservations for welfare recipients. You might want things, but you can't get them because your mom only got so much money. If your mom is a drunk, you don't even depend on getting that. So you got to get out there and steal it, and that put you with a group, a gang, because you is not the only dude in that spot. In the gangs you learn to depend on each other; there ain't nobody else. And if you accept the responsibility of killing someone, going to jail or having someone try to kill you as a part of the gang business, then there ain't nothing else. What have you got to be afraid of?

This is a do-or-die society. What you got to realize is that black people is dead, dead as dead, you understand? We been under fire for 450 years. We have tried everything, spiritually, collectively, but we ain't got no other thing but violence. We ain't got nothing to lose.

Odyssey

He said good-bye to us, standing on the outside steps, a little smile on his face, waving almost as if he were giving us his personal benediction.

When we came back, almost a year later, the clubhouse he'd been working in was closed for lack of funds, but he was still around Thirty-ninth Street. He had just finished visiting with the oldest of five children he told us he had fathered by five different girls.

Sonny Zoo

Yeah, the girl brought the kid down for me to see. I had known this girl before I went to Camp Hill, but it wasn't nothing like knocking it off, shit like that. Later she got the wire about my being home, and she wanted to see me, but I forgot what she even looked like. I was carrying a heavy load from being in jail, though, and I wanted a piece of sex. I just got hooked over her, and then over everybody. I got greedy. Two of my kids were born the same week.

I see my kids all the time. Go to the girls' homes, talk with them, meet the guys they're with now, take my kids around to meet each other. I contribute something to their support. If I didn't, I'd be right down in the support court now. Way I look at it all is this: Having kids don't make you a man. Hell! Even faggots can have kids. But if it is meant for me to have five kids or more, then it is just meant for me.

First time I had a kid my mother—and if you was to meet her you would see how blunt she is—my mother told me to, like, get a woman who can do something for you, when you are down-and-out. I know now that in the ghetto the easiest thing in the world is to get cock. Hardest thing is to get cock—and money. That is why it is important to have a woman who can help you if you need money for bail, for anything, when you go to jail.

One woman really surprised me. Got me a lawyer, stuck by me, sent me money for commissary when I was in jail the last time. And me and her wasn't even that tight. I mean, she had a son by me, but we wasn't really that hooked up. When I was busted, I was going with another girl who was pregnant by me, and the first one said to her, "As long as Sonny is in jail, if there is anything you need, just call me." And that made me feel good.

Odyssey

Sonny had never gone to trial for the shotgun-assault indictment. Police records indicated three bench warrants had been issued for him to be arrested and brought into court.

Sonny Zoo

Bench warrants? I didn't know I had any. Wow! Still, they can't be looking too hard for me because I am around the same neighborhood. All they got to do is drop a subpoena with my lawyer or at the house. Besides, I have been going to court on that shooting case. Always gets postponed. Must have been down ten times. Why haven't they dropped the warrants on me in court? Something is a little fucked up.

But I ain't running. Last year I would have said, "Fuck it!" And I would have split. Now, I think, what is the sense of splitting when I know I ain't done nothing? * With the power structure like it is, you know you don't have to do nothing, and you still go to jail. You can be locked up for just one stickup, and they put you in the lineup, and when you come out, all the things they ain't solved is put on you. You are like caught between two things. The world is mean, and it is getting meaner and meaner every day.

Being angry, though, ain't going to get you nowhere. White America and the power structure is very shrewd, very slick. You have to come at them in the same way they come at you. They ain't going to listen to you, to a degree, because you have a deficit against you: You are black. But it is like I am going through a thing. I don't know eventually what I am going to do; still I feel like I am destined for something.

I wanted to go to school, and I wanted a lot of guys like me to go to school, so I went to the Episcopal diocese here and they gave me a

---

* Sonny Zoo later reported he had been picked up by police, brought into court, and then released pending further investigation.

commitment for $10,000 for a leadership program, to work with guys in the gangs, training them to be community leaders. I could have taken the money, and oh, man, bought me a big car. I had the opportunity. I'll never know what made me not do it. But I took the idea for the program to Herman Wrice of the Young Great Society, an outfit in the ghetto, and he turned it over and then told me to pick up about twenty-one other dudes and we would have a program for three months at the University of Pennsylvania. When we would graduate, we would all get to go to Puerto Rico as a present. Not all of us went. One guy was sent to jail for eighteen to twenty-three months.

Last seven weeks of the program I wasn't like going to many of the classes or lectures like the other guys. Didn't think I needed to go. My job was strictly seeing that the payroll was all right, that we got our money on time to pay the fellows. I was showing up mostly on payday. They were talking to me in the Young Great Society about maybe taking the place of a vice-president who is sixty-two years old, so I was traveling with him, learning what he does. But recently I ain't been seeing too much of him because I been like trying to start a dance hall for kids in the community. The other guys in the leadership program was working on starting a laundromat. I didn't want any of that. Any time you get twenty-one guys running something you get twenty-one different ideas what to do.

In that program we did a lot of talking. And I see one thing I never did before. Last year I was still in the gang war thing. Ain't for me no more. I look at all this killing and hurting, and I say, "For what?" We been fighting all this time, for a neighborhood, two, three blocks, to keep other dudes out of it. And it ain't even ours! Just fighting for nothing. Black against black. It is all kind of silly.

Black Cop

Arthur Hill

When I came on the police force, I had a feeling about blacks
who weren't like me, especially those newly arrived from the South.
Their kind of dress, their loudness, their behavior on Saturday night,
brought me down, reminded me of my blackness which I was trying
to forget. So I can recall overreacting on occasion, leaning on them. I
was trying to mimic the mainstream of White America. But I am now
attempting to redirect myself, recognizing people as brothers. It is
very difficult. Whites don't know the psychological damage this system does to black people.

Odyssey

It was Saturday afternoon and Police Inspector Arthur Hill, the
third-highest-ranking black officer in New York, was showing us the
look of Harlem.

Warm, sunny August day. The people were out. The watermelon
men on 125th Street were doing a brisk business. The rib joints exud-
ing their deep barbecue smells, the record shops wailing the blues, the
chicken man hawking his birds and fries—all combined into a pag-
eantry alien to the white world. There was an ease as blacks greeted
one another—laughing, boasting, wheeling and dealing. Dashikis
were for sale in the curbside racks. Muslims offered copies of *Muhammad Speaks!* Long, pointed handles of Afro combs poked from
men's back pockets. Women, wearing minis to maxis, sported tower-
ing naturals. And the kids were all over, taking in everything.

As Inspector Hill moved through the scene, people called out to
him, stopped their cars to shake his hand, asked him questions. Bayard Rustin walked by, and the inspector hailed him, and they talked
for a minute or two. Hill paused to listen to some CORE workers

describing their success in passing out leaflets. Some young men gave him the peace sign.

Arthur Hill

I have never been this involved in any community I've worked, as a patrolman, sergeant or ranking officer. But a policeman has to do that today because of the schism that exists between the police and the community. Once you start, people call on you for many non-police-related jobs, serving on the board of the YMCA, on a youth advisory committee, going to events to indicate that you identify with what is important to them.

I am still not accepted in all groups too openly but pretty much in most of them. Just this morning I went to a meeting with some guys who wouldn't talk to me two years ago, when a few of them were indicted for booby-trapping call boxes in order to "kill a cop a week." Now they have a youth federation for a session called Conference with Black Police Officers. And they invite this kind of dialogue. They know I won't tell them one thing and do another.

In my job you wear two hats—a black one and a policeman's. I am a sworn upholder of the law, but I feel I can do that with some sensitivity. I don't condone lawlessness, yet I think we should understand what's involved in a person becoming a lawbreaker.

We get a lot of calls, people afraid to go out of their homes. At the Y, I was with a group discussing drug addiction, and a guy said that we should sweep the rats into the river. I just couldn't sit by. I said, "Before we start talking like that, let's remember these 'rats' you would dump in the river are human beings. This meeting is at the YMCA, and I thought the *C* stood for Christian."

Odyssey

We had met Hill in his second floor office above a 135th Street precinct station, in a block that is vintage Harlem: grimy four-story tenements; tall windows; people taking the summer air on the cement stoops. Hill, forty-eight, had just been named administrator for a police division patrolling an area jammed with 400,000 people. He wore his hair in a natural on which his cap often seemed to have an uneasy perch. He walked, or half ran, with an athlete's gait. His police eyes rode herd on us.

Arthur Hill

The black existence in our larger cities has always been deplorable and degrading. I was born in a Harlem hospital on 136th Street, and while we lived in Harlem, we moved about quite a bit because we were very poor. Mostly we were in two-bedroom apartments, father and mother in one bedroom, my brother, sister and I in the other.

My father was from the British West Indies. There he had been able to walk with his head up. He couldn't adjust to the role blacks play here or accept the constant reminders of inferiority. Because of this, he became an alcoholic. He was pretty brutal fellow when he was drinking. I saw him strike my mother. And when she was deciding about whether to leave him, we kids encouraged her to cut out.

I judged him very harshly. I thought he had failed me. It wasn't until I was grown, and trying to be a man myself, that I understood what he must have experienced. I am very regretful that he died believing I would not forgive him.

The system never got to my mother. She died happy. Only had but three or four dresses; didn't matter. Just her three kids. If they ate and went to school, that was all she needed. She was from the Dutch West Indies, could hardly write her name. She was a domestic. On welfare, too. She worked hard, scrubbed floors, left home at six o'clock in the morning. Ten o'clock at night, we kids would still be watching the buses, waiting for her to come home. You wonder what kind of a human being would keep anybody out working that late.

I remember that right here in New York City there were certain street corners where the black domestic workers would gather, be like boxed off, standing there for whites to come by and hire them. It reminded me of slave stalls, with the whites sizing up the women and then taking them off. And the going rate was fifteen cents an hour.

My sister was the brightest of us. But as a youngster she was anemic and had to be sent to the dry climate of the West Indies. When she returned, she was behind in school. They put her in what you call an adjustment class, and I think therein lies a great American tragedy. The school never reached her, never motivated her. What they did was train her to operate a sewing machine.

We kids had to pretty much fend for ourselves. And you don't survive in one of these jungles without identifying with your peer group.

Unless you stay inside, don't go out much, maybe only with your parents to church, you have to embrace the street values. I hustled, shined shoes, sold papers, did everything. When I was twelve years old, I was adjudged a delinquent. I was arrested for shoplifting. There were toys in this store which I knew I couldn't afford. There was something about the stuff I stole: telescopes; microscopes; erector sets. Maybe I was trying to look beyond the misery I was in and to build my way out.

Odyssey

He was never again in trouble with the law. After graduating from high school, he went to a local college for two years, served with an ordnance labor outfit during World War II. He came back to Harlem in 1946.

Arthur Hill

For a young man with limited education, civil service offered opportunities, and so I took a lot of the exams. Reason I became a policeman is that they were the first to accept me. In those days a policeman was a very significant individual. If he said "Go!" a black kid went! Didn't stop to ask why, because if he did, he might get arrested. I daresay that many youngsters got a criminal record they might not have had with a dedicated, caring police agency.

I fitted right into the police mold of that time. Unnecessary use of force. Insensitive, especially to blacks. My aim was to be in the mainstream, and if you didn't mimic it, you were rejected. I was black, but I wanted to be white, look white, and the women I was attracted to exhibited white standards of beauty. Wanting that, however, meant I had to hate myself.

I can't exactly pinpoint when the change began in me. I was just moving along in the department. Nine years a patrolman, then up through the ranks.* Going back to college, when I was already a captain, offered me some reading that helped me to understand the less fortunate blacks a little better, the dirty deal they get.

Another boot in the direction of black awareness came in my re-

* Subsequent to our meeting Hill was advanced to deputy chief inspector, the second-highest-ranking black, and made division commander for the Bedford-Stuyvesant, Brownsville and Fort Greene areas in Brooklyn.

turning to Harlem as a precinct commanding officer after the 1964 riots. I had to relate then to people I normally didn't have anything to do with, and I began asking: "What chance had they ever had in this world?" They were no longer discards. I saw them as more human.

I started evaluating things I had always accepted. I remembered people pinching a baby's nose to get it sharp and straight. Why? And why wear my hair to imitate the whites as much as possible? I said, "What the hell! God gave it to me and he must have intended for me to wear it the way He gave it to me."

With the free African nations, I was able to identify with black people as having world status. And I realized how wrong it was to have taught us that in Africa a white man named Tarzan swung from the trees and that black people never made any contributions to civilization.

Malcolm X and the Muslims gave me some cause for believing in the brotherhood of man. I didn't know Malcolm personally, but I get a great feeling of pleasure when I see Muslims, because they really believe in the community in which they live.

However, there comes a point when you blame white people for what they have done to you. Being civilized, you make the point with aloofness, separateness. I know it was observable to my superiors who must have been thinking: "Who the hell did I think I was?" What I was doing was putting the guilt on white people—for what I had done to myself.

But with some thinking, some study, I came to understand as many whites as blacks had been victimized in this system. Doing a paper on sociology while working for my master's degree, I learned what the alcoholism rate is in America, what the suicide rate is. I found out about the white man, and I began feeling sorry for him in some ways.

All this is still coming to me. I don't have it nailed down yet. My wife still straightens her hair. I don't make a deal about it. She and I can have a very positive and good husband-and-wife relationship, but with different feelings for blackness, of social identity. We don't discuss it. Yet we have agreed that we won't straighten our daughters' hair until they are old enough to decide for themselves.

We are living in Queens, but I have just about disassociated myself from that area. I have made where I work my community. My oldest boy will come in to Harlem to be with me and see things he isn't exposed to where we live. Winos, junkies, maybe a guy pulling a knife. He is socially conscious, always asking questions. He wears a natural;

he's fierce about that. I make it a point to discuss with him, and with his younger brother, what has happened to blacks.

I thought it was a great day in our house when I heard them and other kids playing a game in which they said: "Last guy in is a white guy." I said, "What the hell is that?" It's like saying the last one in is a dog. I don't see any signs of hatred toward Whitey, but in their minds—white is not as right as it used to be.

Drugs: A Way of Life

Odyssey

One afternoon we were in the Harlem offices of the Street Workers Program, sponsored by the New York Urban League, talking about dope. With us were Richard Thompson and Bernie Parker, who were then working for the operation, assigned to schools with heavy narcotics problems. They weren't out there to police the students, but rather, by setting an example, to motivate them away from drugs.

Thompson, nicknamed Bouncy, twenty-three, a lanky six three, medium brown, close-cropped hair, with large, expressive hands, was an outstanding basketball player while at Bethune-Cookman College in Daytona Beach, Florida. Parker, twenty-nine, just over six feet, stockier of build, had been a high school basketball man in New York, also played some during his college years.

Bernie Parker

Drugs is killing the youth coming up, killing them dead. They say there is 100,000 known drug addicts in Harlem. They is not even talking about the teen-agers. In one of the high schools I been working in there are 3,000 kids. I could say that almost 1,000 is strung out on drugs, and another 1,000 is curious, saying things like: "Should I get high? It looks tempting. I think I'll smoke a reefer. I ain't going to mess with that other stuff." They say that, but it is only the beginning.

The main thing about black kids is *image*. They come out of a block where they see a guy drive up in his Cadillac, get out wearing 'gator shoes, $100 suit, the rings, talking from the side of his mouth. They think he's made it. He goes into the bar; he's got all the girls. And he has the money to buy cocaine. The kids want to imitate the hustler. They can't afford cocaine, so they sniff the $2 stuff—heroin.

Two, three years ago, all bags of dope was $5 or $6. Then the hustlers got together and said: "If we could sell the kids in high school bags for $2, they could afford them." Average kid gets 50 cents, maybe 75 for lunch. If four of them chip in, they got themselves a deuce bag. The high they get from one of these they figure is so sensational that they go on to other things.

We see what is going on at the schools. We can't do anything about the white man who is supplying the hustler. We can threaten to have the pushers locked up if they don't stop bothering the kids. But it is the kids we have to work with, make them believe in us. Like, we're not cops. We move through the school and the neighborhood. We're black, and we talk their kind of talk. Sure, they try to jive us, even when we catch them taking off on dope. They are still kids, don't want to go to jail. You have got to show them that even though they are on drugs, you respect them as human beings. To do that you have to know about life on the street.

Richard Thompson

We were born and raised here in Harlem. All you see around you is dope. Dope and dirt. You go home, and there might not even be a meal cooked. Kid in the suburbs comes home to a nice place. Ain't like that up here. And it does something to you. When I was in high school, I never even thought I was going to finish it. I didn't feel like school was going to do anything. Only job I knew anybody getting was down in the garment center, lugging things, being a messenger boy. Walk out of the house, come on the corner, see winos laying all over the place, smell the stink of the sewer. I couldn't see no way for me to get out of this.

Bernie Parker

One thing every black kid in Harlem can do is fight. You grow up fighting—and running. Be in the backyard, playing stickball, cutting your legs, fleas biting you. Kids don't care. They want to play. You see a kid in a block with a basket hanging on a fire escape, and to take a shot, he got to jump over stairs or garbage cans. When he gets on a regular court, he goes crazy.

Nobody ever holds up the idea you can also be good at the books. Teachers don't really care if the student learns. They put the work in front of him, and if he doesn't do it, so what? If he does, good. In junior high you get typing, might get a language if you are lucky. When you're fifteen, you graduate because they go by age. In high school you are automatically programmed into a general course. Couple of periods of shop, something they call record keeping, things that will never help you in life at all.

Richard Thompson

The only way a black guy can get to college is if he plays some kind of sport. In my own case, I loved basketball. Made me feel good to hear the girls screaming, hollering my name. In high school the coaches talked to me, kept talking and talking, about going on further. And I started studying a little harder than I had. When I come to graduate, my coach asked how would I like to go to college. I said: I don't have any money. He said, "You can go, full scholarship, everything, four years." And I did.

A black kid knows he's got to do better than a white in sports. In college, guys don't think about doing better in their studies. But there is a good reason to compete for grades, too. If a guy is a very good student, they won't drop him after his eligibility has been used up. If he is just making it or is messing around, they can say, "So long." Like two fellows I knew with this team that won the National Invitational Tournament in New York. Final game over, the school kicked them out. Didn't need them anymore.

In my own case, I graduated. I was the only kid in a family of ten that went to college. I got uncles who never finished fifth grade, and they encouraged me to keep on. College was the first place I started to believe I could get somewhere. And this is the thing I keep telling the kids we work with. But it's hard to express this to a drug addict.

Odyssey

The building just sat there on 123d Street, anonymous in its uniformity with the block: old, tarnished, used up. No sign announced it was the Addicts Rehabilitation Center. The only identification: three letters over the front door—ARC.

The center's director, James Allen, was small, spare, with sharp eyes, hard handshake, quick laugh. The desk in his second-floor office was sprawling with papers, books, note pads. When we sat down, he took off the loafers he was wearing, explaining, "Just relaxing."

James Allen

For years I was on drugs, and I lived the three cycles that control every addict's life: *get money; get dope; shoot up!* Then I discovered the reason for my habit. I was running away from being black, pure and simple. I had decided I would rather be a dope fiend than a nigger.

I have been directing the center for eleven years. I would attribute this token of self-help to others as being God's endorsement. I have only a high school diploma. Foundations hardly know I exist. I have no political connections, yet we are getting $200,000 a year from the state for our program. We are right in the heart of Harlem. We employ 40 people, including 5 PhD's, and provide treatment for an average of 170 persons at a time who spend up to nine months in residence.

It's all voluntary on the addict's part, and we deal with each one according to the stage he is in. If he is high, all we can do is get him into a hospital. When he sobers up, has no drugs in his system, we begin to zero in on him to promote attitudinal change. We go at him at a time when it is very prevalent in his mind that he is black, dirty, greasy, and that he has wasted X number of years out there shooting dope.

The trap that black people have been in ever since slavery is waiting for things to change. What has to alter is the individual so he can conquer and subdue the circumstances around him. Instead of running away from problems or letting them overtake him, he can fight them! And that's what we try to impress on the addict here at the center. He doesn't have to do something just because somebody tells him to, especially when it is going to make him miserable in the long run. We try to get across the notion that he should be working—if it is no more than piling straws—to eliminate the conditions in his own environment. He must realize that it is his responsibility to make life better for the next person, and as he does that, he is making it better for himself.

Odyssey

Allen went to the window, jammed it upward.

James Allen

There are little black boys and girls out there using drugs, being introduced to them at ten and eleven years old, because a black man who can't get a job making $150 a week honestly can make $400 a day selling dope.

Over 100 years ago, a very cruel system grudgingly told the black man, "Here, you are free!" Gave him a suitcase, took him out of the most oppressive conditions, where almost irreparable damage had been done to him mentally, and thrust him into what is considered to be a free society. And said: "Go fend for yourself." So he was supposed to snap into line automatically, live up to new standards, start competing for money. Then the whites looked at him and wondered: "Why don't he pull himself up by his bootstraps?" When he couldn't, they said: "We'll maintain him at an economic level that destroys his incentive to do anything about it, to fight against the system." And they called it welfare.

This is where the black man has been all these years, until all of a sudden he discovered: "I can make it! All I got to do is sell dope, even if it is to my own kids." Was a time when a kid going out on the street to buy drugs would probably get punched in the nose by an old dope fiend or, at least, be ignored. He wasn't supposed to have any business on the street. Not so today.

We had a kid in here who had been selling dope. When they arrested him, he asked the cops, "How much you making? I'm making $200 a day." And that kid was thirteen years old. Half our population at ARC averages in age from fourteen to seventeen years. This is a different breed of addict, not endowed with the same sense of self-hatred I had. The new crop of junkies are just acting out what they have seen and smelled and heard and tasted since the day they were born. They were bred in Harlem, and a lot of them won't get out alive unless they get a free trip to prison.

Odyssey

It was noon, and the long rectangular room where ARC's addicts hold meetings was almost empty. Allen said we were welcome to use it while talking with one of the center's young residents, Ronald, nineteen.

He was tall, hair trimmed short. Shiny black skin, smooth, clear—
except for the scars on his arms. He wore African beads around his
neck, and his khaki pants were sharply pressed.

Ronald

I was in seventh grade. Some guys come around school and
asked did I know anything about reefers. I said No. Black boy lit one
up, and I smoked it. At first I didn't feel any kind of a high. Like
after a while, though, it came.

I smoked reefers for three years. One night, I was going out, me
and my brother. He was sniffing and asked me, "Do you want to get
high?" I said, "Yeah, what off?" He said, "Heroin." And I said
"Okay." I mean, like, he does it, I'll do it. We got $4 together and
sniffed a bag. I went into a discothèque and I was sitting down and
starting to nod. My head said, "This is beautiful."

I began sniffing heroin regular like. Then I was told that if I took a
$4 bag and shot with just half of it, I'd get a high for like three hours,
where you can sniff a whole bag and don't get more than a fifteen-
minute rush. I said, "*This* is beautiful." That's how I started shooting
in the veins.

I was taking money wherever I could to buy dope. But like I never
took any from my mother or my house. I couldn't see this, no way! I
would be home—sick—and my mother's pocketbook be on the table,
and I wouldn't touch it. I'd leave and go do something else to get the
money.

I finally hooked up with this guy I met in school, playing basketball.
We got into this conversation about money, drugs, this and that, and
we were like in a thing together. I leaned on him. I asked how was he
making the scratch and would he do the same for me. I knew he had
a connection, a main man. So he went to this man and said, "I got
this fellow, and he sounds sincere. He wants to make some money."
The connection gave me the drugs. Got to a point where I was dealing $700 to $800 of dope every three days. It wasn't like I was aim-
ing for an Eldorado. What I wanted was a Rolls-Royce!

In school, dope is so prevalent you can get it anywhere. It's like everybody falls into it sooner or later. Worldwide thing, man. I was
shooting three and four times a day, seven and eight bags. Doing it in
the school locker rooms, in the washrooms. After six months, maybe
a year, you reach a peak. You're only shooting to keep down the

sickness. I used to ask God to help me kick the habit. I'd like go to eight o'clock mass, and afterwards I'd go right out and shoot up again. But I'll tell you something: I felt like nobody. I felt like I was dead.

My mother started bearing down. In the beginning, she thought it was only my brother was on it. I had convinced her I wasn't using anything. My brother had come in the center here. He'd be out on a weekend pass and talk to me. I didn't want to hear him. I'd say to myself, "I am a junkie, out on the street, what can he say to me?" Through him, though, and with my mother confronting me, I met Mr. Allen. I told him I wasn't using, and he asked me to take a urine test to prove it. Sure, I said, like I was trying to play it off so he'd say I didn't have to take it in the end. But he kept on, and when the time came, I backed out. He said, "You're jiving me. I can tell right now you're on heroin."

Finally, I admitted it to my mother. She was like deeply hurt. I tried a couple of times to explain why I was using it. You know, I really didn't have a reason for it. I came into the program here. I don't exactly know why. I think what happened was that I got tired of shooting dope, nothing to it for me, anymore.

When you come to the center, you're a probationer for the first fifteen days. You get therapy every morning, seven thirty to twelve o'clock. Sometimes, in the afternoon, too. Otherwise there are group meetings and the work you have to do around here, cleaning up, making quarters straight. After you have been in here awhile, you get time out. But when you leave, you have to have a plan for what you'll do. What you got to do is not go back to the old crowd, stand around talking about the old times. Because somebody is going to say, "Hey, man. You want me to do something for you?" And you might go off and get high, not know what you're shooting, and kill yourself. That could happen. So when I go out, I plan to go to a concert in Central Park, the movies, visit some of my relatives. If my plan don't work, I'll go home, call the center and then just stay in the house, listening to records, until it's time to come back here.

I've been at the center four months now. I'm planning to start New York University next semester, take speech and study music.* Being here is the first chance I ever got to look at myself, think what I want

---

* When we talked with Ronald a year later, he had finished his therapy at ARC and was taking courses getting ready to enter a college. In that time he changed his goal from music to journalism.

to be. Like I never read the Bible. Now I do. And it's just real nice to be able to sit down and know about things that happened thousands of years ago. I can understand about God. I can ask Him for help. He can give me a guiding hand. But it's got to be me that's doing it.

I had tried to see myself before. I couldn't. I had drugs in my head. I know now what I used to be—a greasy dope fiend. Greasy means dirty, no clean habits. You don't have nothing. If I was going to tell somebody what I went through, like making them see a junkie's life, I'd tell them: "Drugs is twenty-four-hour work. All you got to do is work twenty-four hours a day, looking forward to that next fix and getting sick all over again in dirty cellars.

I mean, like it is a waste.

Odyssey

In his office, James Allen was thinking about all the young addicts of Harlem and about himself . . .

James Allen

Soon after I was born in Grand Prairie, Texas, forty-four years ago, my parents decided they couldn't make it together. So I was reared by my grandparents on a farm near Shreveport. It was a most detestable place and as soon as I was able to, I ran away to my mother in Ringgold, Louisiana. In 1942, when I got out of high school there, I had an opportunity to go to Southern University—or to be free by going to California, where my father was.

I chose freedom. And that was the most disgusting freedom you ever heard of. I was part of a black exodus leaving the South, going into ghettos all over the country. I was with my father, except I wasn't. It is kind of strange when you grow up just visiting your parents, because when you later move in with them permanently, your habits, your behavior are already set. There comes a point when you can't tolerate each other. Happened to me. But I needed identification with somebody, and so I fell in with a group in Los Angeles. They were using pot. First time, pot was very disappointing to me. Next time, it felt good. Changed my whole way of thinking, my whole outlook.

Everything seemed different. It hypnotized me into believing I was a good musician. I imagined everything was more pleasant. I searched for ways of extending that. I was really down: pot, pills, alcohol. In three years, I became an alcoholic, had the DT's, went to jail for suspected burglary and then for using marijuana. I was all over the place. Hustling, gambling, stealing, running on the railroad. Thousand things. Just existing.

But you always go home when the chips are down. I went back to Louisiana. I dried myself out, got myself together. Then there was an affair with a girl that set me back. I came to New York—and to heroin. I had fooled with it in Los Angeles, though it was not the popular thing to do. Maybe in California they were afraid they'd be called dope fiends. In New York you could take it on one block and nod on another. People didn't know what you were doing. In that first year in New York I was strung out. I was on dope when I got married. I went the whole bit, saying to myself: "I'm different. I won't get hurt. I'm not really hooked. I'll quit one day. It's all in the mind." Ten years later I woke up in the federal drug hospital at Lexington, Kentucky, trying to do the lindy hop because that was what they were dancing when I first came to New York.

It was a really traumatic experience for me to be in Lexington, surrounded by 2,700 dope fiends. One thing I realized was that I was no smarter. I wasn't no different. We were all just a bunch of bums! And then I started to think how my grandfather had always said that God could solve our problems. Well, that was ridiculous. God was something white people invented to keep niggers in line. Except I was so terribly desperate. There was nothing else I could turn to. I decided I was going to give it a college try, so that once and for all I could prove God was ridiculous.

I read the Bible, early in the morning, late at night, when the other guys couldn't see me. I began to pray and to talk to God. And He's started having some meaning for me.

Things were happening to me that I didn't understand. I kept sending request slips in to see the psychiatrist at Lexington. He told me to write down what I was experiencing and to ask why. I thought this was funny. Because this was all he gave me, I did it, attempting to honestly put my thoughts on paper and analyze them. This is where I came to a full awareness that for thirty-three years I had wanted to be white.

Average black person dissipates his prime-time energies trying to think, act and talk white. He believes that once he does that, he'll be accepted, and then he can do the other things in life that are important. I was aping your manners and being terribly disappointed when I didn't get a lot of jobs I knew I was qualified for. Like on the railroad. I am a doggone good waiter, so why was it I couldn't make steward? When I worked in a tailorshop, I was fired for having a fight with a white guy who didn't get fired although he caused the whole thing by throwing out crooked dice in a crap game. This goes on in a thousand different ways.

Those are the things that I shot drugs and drank wine and smoked pot to get away from. Can you imagine how disappointed I was when I first woke up in Lexington and saw that I was still black? Doggone it! I had learned how to roll my R's, had the best manners, and I had some talents. But I just couldn't be white. And I had to face up to that.

I left Lexington in a month. When I came back to New York, I was shaking in the knees, seeing it for the first time—sober! All those insights at Lexington were on the line. I had learned that I couldn't do it myself. I was going to need help. There was always God, but I had to have people, too. So if I didn't want to take that first shot of dope, I had to call my wife. The most difficult thing is to have basic honesty with your wife. There is always the chance that when she gets mad, she will use it against you.

Before I had always waited until I was high and then said to her, "Baby, I got weak." This time I was going to tell her before I took that shot. She came to Penn Station and brought me home. And instead of saying as I always had, "I'll stall it out until she leaves and then go get a shot," I realistically explored with her how we could abate the urge. We talked, and by night it had died down. It came back, and I did a variety of things. I'd sit with my face to the wall. Other times I'd go out and order pigs' ears. I hate them, but when I was on drugs, sometimes it was the only thing I could afford. So by forcing myself to eat them again, I was reminded of how it had been. Stupid? Well, it worked. I decided the only way I was going to shoot dope was if somebody held a gun on me.

I started going to meetings that the Manhattan Christian Reformed Church was holding on Seventh Avenue. The minister had been caught up by a drug man's question as to whether God cared anything about dope addicts. So once a week he made it possible for people to get together at the church talking about their problem with drugs. The church put me on as a lay missionary. Nobody quite knew what I was supposed to do. I just couldn't sit there and twiddle my thumbs. So I got involved in a lot of things. ARC was one of them.

It is the only thing that has given me peace. I know no other way. I would rather be around a bunch of dope addicts who are seeking desperately to help themselves.

There is something wrong with the way people practice Christianity. Maybe they have misinterpreted it. But to the average black kid it means, Whitey has run a game. And integration isn't the answer. And that is unfortunate because thousands of people died thinking it was the goal. And they died in vain.

My grandfather used to say his concept of freedom was: "Hallelujah! We are all going to go home and walk the streets of glory together, white and black!" I say, "That's a hell of a thing to serve God for, just to be with a white man that has oppressed you all your life."

Black Church

Odyssey

Sunday morning in Harlem. Not much moving: occasional police car, truck or two, here and there a motorist. Saturday's watermelon man is gone, and with him the crowds. Windows are up in the housing projects, but nobody is at them, looking out. The scene is awash in silence. It is as if at some given signal the music stopped, the rib shop fires died, and the people vanished into their private retreats.

We saw—and felt—this as we drove through Harlem in September, 1969, to go to church on 116th Street, called by Malcolm X the worst street in Harlem, with its prostitutes, sharpshooting hustlers, dope peddlers. And when we parked near Lexington Avenue, we saw three young men, all wearing black body shirts, muscular arms bared, plopped on the sidewalk like scarecrows suddenly released from the propping pole. Their backs were against building walls. Spittle dropped from their chins. Nodders, passed out on dope.

A couple of hundred feet away from them on 116th another side of Harlem was beginning to come alive. Women in pink dresses, high-heeled shoes, white gloves, some wearing flower-trimmed black straw hats. Men, with serious faces, in dark suits. White shirts. Ties. They were arriving for services at the Canaan Baptist Church, created in the shell of an old movie house.

We were there at the invitation of the Reverend Wyatt Tee Walker, who had been at Birmingham with Dr. King but now was, as he put it, "doing my thing here in Harlem." Inside, Canaan shut out the mean and ugly from the street, in a service unlike any we had ever known in white churches we had attended. The people in Canaan were filled with joy and freedom. As they sang, they saw the curtains of heaven opening, and they broke from the lyrics to shout their pleasures at being once again in His home. They were ready, as the prayer said, "to love thee more and serve thee better." And when a young woman, Elaine Clark, and the organist, Fred Gripper, raised their voices to sing, they would give everything they had for *just one day in paradise,* they created in that black church, that Sunday in Harlem, an exaltation of life and the Lord that neither of us had ever experienced.

Wyatt Tee Walker

This is the religion of the Galilean Prince, something alien to the white church, which is absolutely impotent to do anything about the social crises in our midst, because it celebrates the religion of America's manifest destiny: capitalistic, imperialistic and racist in character.

Odyssey

There is in the Reverend Mr. Walker a joyousness in being alive—and in being Wyatt Tee Walker. "I am," he said, "aggressive, egocentric, and unafraid." He had a Mephistophelean beard, and his eyes had a compelling, intense quality. He was slender, six feet tall. He said he likes to live well, and his clothes are mod. When we told him we had been traveling the country listening to black people, he said, "The tragic thing is that we have been out there all the time." He is proud of his calling in the ministry.

Wyatt Tee Walker

A lot of people, particularly these loudmouthed so-called militants, miss what the black church is and what it has been. For us it has meant survival. In the beginning, the church was 99 percent of the black man's experience in the South. It was just about the only arena he controlled absolutely; historically the place where we met together. When you work from sunup to sundown at the end of the overseer's whip, you don't have much opportunity for social intercourse. The first black churches were also a form of the underground, with spirituals that detailed code messages, passing the word from plantation to plantation, for those who wanted to take a stab at freedom via the Underground Railway. I tell people all the time,

"Careful how you disparage Uncle Tom; he has been the means of getting us to where we are now, saying one thing, meaning another."

The church has been a vehicle for congealing us as a people. It has been the network of information, the network of leadership, the network of financial resources. It has been our true training ground. In the rural areas of the South, you will nearly always see a public school next to the black church. First there would be a church, and then it opened its school. Until the early 1940's primary education was nearly always in these private schools sponsored by the various black denominations. It has only been in the last twenty to thirty years that public education took over these poorly arranged buildings and made them into public schools.

The church has given black people their first rudiments in parliamentary procedure, in how to conduct a meeting. It is the sanctuary for the community programs. The black church has built senior citizens' homes, federal credit unions, educational plants, and low-cost housing. Then there is the payroll, something the critics overlook. Canaan is a middle-sized church, and the payroll is $50,000 a year. That means we have twelve, thirteen people working, making a gainful, dignified living.

There never could have been a civil rights movement without the church, for only the church could have produced a Martin Luther King whose lesson for all of us was that you could have your manhood—if you wanted it!

Odyssey

When Walker was growing up in Merchantville, New Jersey, just outside Philadelphia, he was, he said, "ashamed to be a Negro because we as a people had absorbed so much humiliation without resisting or striking back." At Virginia Union University, where he was a classmate of the Reverend Channing Phillips, he recalled: "All I entertained in my mind was putting together some kind of underground that would go around assassinating people like Senator Eastland."

He was only twenty-two, newly minted as a *summa cum laude* graduate of divinity school, when in 1952 he began inspiring blacks in Petersburg, Virginia. In this historic town, where General Lee and the Confederacy had fought the last climactic battles before the surrender, Walker had been called to pastor the Gillfield Baptist Church.

Wyatt Tee Walker

I could have settled down in Petersburg for twenty-five or thirty years, living a very pedestrian existence. But that wasn't possible for anyone with my kind of aggressiveness and single-minded purpose. When I came to Petersburg, everything was segregated. When I left, everything was on its way to being desegregated. First thing I discovered was that even the Ministerial Union, which is just a fellowship of pastors, was racially divided. I wasn't even in town one week before I got two other black pastors and went to the white section of the union. So we integrated that, and it caused a furor.

In my eight years there, it was just one controversy after another. I was simultaneously president of the NAACP, state director of CORE and president of the Petersburg Improvement Association. Once we petitioned for the library to be desegregated, went through all the steps, and got a place for our request on the City Council agenda. Instead, they passed an ordinance with a $1,000 fine and a year in jail if you did not leave public property when told to by proper authorities. I was shocked. I said, "We will test it." We went into the library, wouldn't move. They arrested us and put us in jail. We got out on bail, filed an appeal, and the law was thrown out. From our own improvement association, which got nationwide attention, we went on to form a state network of such groups.

In everything we did, we always were nonviolent. I had become convinced this was the most practical road for blacks: If we have to die, have to be the victims of genocide, then we will do so on the basis of principle. Dr. King, who had his SCLC in operation by this time, had been following our work. I had known him for several years, met him first when he was still at Crozer Theological Seminary and came to Virginia Union for a meeting of the Interseminary Movement. I was not impressed by him. I had been told he was a very brilliant fellow. So what? One more brilliant fellow!

Later, when I heard about Montgomery, I was absolutely surprised. Mike King was a thoroughgoing intellectual, born wealthy, and I simply did not expect to see him leading a movement. Like a lot of people, though, I started sending him money. He invited me to meetings of SCLC's board and introduced me as "My dear friend, W. T. Walker." He put me on the Resolutions Committee because he said he knew I had a good mind. And in 1960 I left Petersburg to go to Atlanta as SCLC's executive director. Which meant I was Dr. King's chief of staff.

Dr. King, I discovered, was a fantastic human being, in many ways a mystic. The years with him were the best ones of my life. I always sensed that he was where history was. As a matter of fact, in the role he gave me at SCLC I made one President—John F. Kennedy. I arranged in 1960 for Dr. King to be with the Atlanta students during their sit-in demonstration. When he was jailed for that, I framed two identical telegrams to Nixon and Kennedy, signed by me, asking for some kind of response. To this day I have not heard a word from Nixon, but of course, you know what Kennedy did: called Mrs. King; showed his sympathy; offered help. And Dr. King was released. Millions of brochures telling about that incident were made. These were distributed in the ten largest cities of the North. It was just like an endorsement of Kennedy by Dr. King.

Odyssey

To Walker, Dr. King was "the Leader." But it was Walker who served as the bridge between the movement and White America's reporters, politicians and television cameras. Walker went all through campaigns in Albany, Georgia, where 3,000 people went to jail, and he was there in Birmingham.

Wyatt Tee Walker

As a general rule, my instructions from Dr. King were to avoid getting arrested. During our Birmingham drive I had to take a lot of stuff, but I was usually able to stay out of jail. When he was jailed there, he used a lawyer to send out to us parts of a letter written on toilet paper and newspaper. I stayed up, with another worker, Willie Pearl Mackey, all night for four nights, transcribing it, section by section. We'd send the typed material back in with the lawyer the next day for King to proofread. I felt it was going to be one of the great documents. The Quakers were the first to print it. They titled it *Tears of Love*. But we called it *Letter from a Birmingham Jail*.

In the end, we accomplished in Birmingham what we set out to do. Birmingham turned loose the forces that gave us the civil rights bill. By then, however, I had had it: physically, emotionally, psychologically. In those years I had been jailed. I had been savagely beaten several times. And I had involved my whole family in our struggle. My wife had been brained by an Alabama state trooper. Two of my four kids were in Gaston's Motel the night it was bombed in Birmingham. I was making SCLC's top salary of $10,000, but we just couldn't live on it. So when a publishing company in Yonkers, New York, dangled $25,000 in my face, I decided I had put in enough time, that I could take the job without feeling guilty, because my family had to be my primary commitment.

We moved North, and I became a marketing specialist, began producing a ten-volume series on black history. This meant I had to go all over the country, forty states, fifty major cities, talking with curriculum supervisors about materials telling the true history of black folk. After all the *hell* I had been through, this seemed harmless enough. But the resistance I met on this was greater than any I had found in any lunch counter, the buses—anything! It was so subtle. It was like going for the ghost, discrimination so terribly shadowy you could never know where your enemy really was.

What all of this let me know was that there is a temple they don't want us to enter: the place where minds can be changed. The white world knows that once we blacks undo the brainwashing given us, we are going to be free. So I got out of the book publishing business to return to working for the black community in the arena of the church.

In my first two years at Canaan the congregation has increased to 800. I am a hard-nosed businessman, and of those, 500 give one-tenth of their earnings to the church every week.

I don't separate the Gospel from social concerns. To me, everything that Jesus did was absolutely social. Were He alive today, He probably would be crucified. When you measure it, the world hasn't moved that much ahead. Only the scenery has. Which is why this black church now must be concerned with the flesh-and-blood considerations of our people.

I have a man working for the post office twenty-five years, and they are about to sack him. I called the postmaster and his deputy, and they now say they will not fire him. I have been at the Bronxville detention home to keep a guy together who has been on dope; he's getting out in January, and I have a job lined up for him at a milk company. Our congregation spends about $32,000 a year in relief to people who are in need. And we don't ask questions. We had a woman tell us she had been mugged last week. We gave her money. People who have been burned out we provide with clothes, food, whatever. When a lady in a senior citizens' home couldn't pay her rent because of the state welfare cut, we arranged to get her into public housing.

For some years, I have been special assistant to Governor Rockefeller on urban affairs. I say to him all the time, publicly and privately, that I work for God, but I help him. I refused to take a salary because, as I told him: "When I get ready to tell you something severe, I don't want it choking in my throat."

The church is the strongest, most viable institution we have. It is, in fact, our only stable one. There are black churches in Harlem that are each buying one piece of real estate a year to make sure black folks can stay in this community. Some of us sense a conspiracy to get black people out of Harlem, the most attractive residential real estate in New York.

It is instinctual to know about prejudice. When I meet a white person I can tell, just by the way he says "colored" or "Negro" or "black." I can smell it. It is like I have a railroad track running down my brain. On one side is the Western me talking. The other is the black me, evaluating, watching your eyes, the twitches at the corners of your mouth. It is a hell of a way to live, but it is the only healthy way at this moment. That is why I am a black nationalist. It saves you from going crazy. And what we have to do is use this identity with blackness, this pride in it, to resurrect what is left of the humanity of our people.

We are not in the circumstances we are in because we are black; these are the circumstances forced upon us because of the capitalistic system which always seems to carry with it the oppression of the poor. And I will say this: If in the next four or five years there is not some marked shift in this country that brings more to the black people, I will not stick with nonviolence. If there is shooting in the streets, I will join them. I am not going to walk to the gas chamber.

Who Said It Can't Happen Here?

Odyssey

When we came out of New York we went into Middle America: Omaha, Nebraska, seemingly an epoch away from the nation's urban agonies, a place which once believed it was immune to the sickness of Harlem, Watts and Chicago.

The state sweeps westward from the Missouri River, across the great plains to the sandhills footing the Rocky Mountains. Rich farm and cattle land. More than 3,000 lakes offering some of the country's outstanding fishing and game hunting. Its wheatfields could be birthplace for Grant Wood's painting "An American Gothic," that nostalgic look backward into a time when people fought the land, pitchforks in hand.

But then, as you zero in on Omaha, the eastern border, the twentieth century emerges. Only 15 miles out of the city are the Strategic Air Command (SAC) headquarters where the little red telephone connects the world to the point of no return. Omaha itself boasts of a new downtown. Its periphery has affluent shopping centers, new residential developments. But the city's Near North Side ghetto is mostly unchanged. The heartline of the area is Twenty-fourth Street, sometimes called just plain deuce-four by the blacks whose homes border it.

Since the mid-1960's, Omaha has known what many of the other smaller cities would experience before the decade ran out: racial rioting. In the beginning it was blacks who were shot. But then the targets changed, and police were killed. In Omaha, in 1970, a white policeman was blown to death by a dynamited suitcase. For Dr. Earle G. Person, Jr., black dentist, an official in the Omaha Urban League, the explosion had been predictable.

Earle Person

Most whites and bourgeoisie blacks don't believe this city is in trouble. Yet we do have a racial crisis. This nation does. One definition of crisis is that point in a disease where a decisive change is made, prognosticating either recovery or death. This means to me that somebody should be awful damn busy doing something about the poverty syndrome in the ghetto.

When the whites put together their new downtown area, their slogan was: "Can do." We saw that the slogan for the Near North Side was: "Won't do." The prime movers just say, "Well, we'll try a few little things, form a committee, call in an outside research organization, make a study." And they do survey after survey after survey, and all of them get stuck away in some file.

To me, there is a tragedy in this, because Omaha offers an opportunity we may not have much longer. Here, in this city, we can still get at what ails the patient, racially speaking. This is a town that is not too large, not machine-ridden, where communication between black and white, between the poor and those in authority, should be possible. You *can* isolate the trouble. Trying to look at Chicago is like putting a raw scraping from a man's throat under a high-power microscope. It comes out too thick, too much debris. So in Chicago you don't know what is causing the problem: Mayor Daley, J. Edgar Hoover, the gangs, the police. But Omaha, it is like taking that throat specimen and diluting it on a slide, and my God, suddenly you can see the strep. And what you find in Omaha now, as we have had for some time, is an abrasive situation between police and the Negro community, one carrying the potential for mass violence.

Odyssey

As a case in point, he recalled the Fourth of July weekend, 1966. A steaming hot city. The whites could escape to the lakes, but on the Near North Side, home to something more than 45,000 (about an eighth of the city's population), blacks milled aimlessly on the streets. On the parking lot of a supermarket at Twenty-fourth and Lake streets, young people met, to sit and talk, shoot dice, drink some wine. Mrs. Thomas E. Hayes, black member of the Omaha Human Relations Board, later said that "policemen started parading up and down the street and ordering people around like animals." Whatever the origins, the trouble started there on that lot. Before the weekend of window smashing and rock throwing was over, 122 persons had been arrested, the National Guard called up. Most of the 122 never went to trial, but since then, said Person, the supermarket parking lot, now surrounded by a high wire fence, has been known as Stalag 24.

Earle Person

I had just come in as the president of Omaha's Urban League, and I made the request to get government people in here to observe what was happening. This helped to cool it. I don't care how tough you are, a Hitler, Mussolini, or just a plain bastard. You don't get out the gun or the shiv when you think four or five guys might be looking, that somebody has 50X binoculars trained on you.

I work with the people on Twenty-fourth Street. My office is there. I might die on the Near North Side because, if necessary, I will defend it with my life. But I don't think I will ever have to. Whites aren't going to leave their comfortable homes, no matter how much a vocal minority of them talk about coming down to deuce-four and beating black heads. They have a police majority to do it for them. Whites in Omaha don't stand up and say, "Look at me, I'm a bigot!" But they don't object when unwise police are allowed to overreact at every given thing, come in here saying "nigger!" or "you goddamn black!" and clubbing people needlessly. White racism is articulated through the police force. Without them, the black-white issue would be dead.

Omaha

Alabama's Governor Wallace came to Omaha in March, 1968, to announce formation of his American Independent Party. In the ghetto, his visit was underscored with new violence on Twenty-fourth Street. Among other incidents, a black teen-age boy, spotted in the vicinity of a looted store, was killed by an off-duty policeman who had hired out as a private guard.

Violence returned a year later. Investigating a reported break-in, a white policeman named John Loder came upon fourteen-year-old Vivian Strong and some other black girls playing records in an area behind the housing project where they lived. He chased them, fired his gun, fatally wounded her. Because the shooting happened early on a Tuesday evening, there was time that night for word of it to spread through the black community. Fire bombings, fighting and looting continued for three days, exacerbated when Loder was charged with manslaughter and released on $500 bail, rather than held for murder, which many blacks considered it.*

Odyssey

When Miriam and I came to Omaha, the fires were out, but scars remained: charred, boarded-up structures that had been put to the torch. Twenty businesses and homes had been damaged or destroyed; twenty-two buildings vandalized or looted. Thirty people had been hurt. Sixty had been arrested.

Earle Person

People will tell you that the riot was horrible. Sure it was, in a sense. At the same time, it said something: We have reached a point in time where black people no longer intend to just docilely continue, as the church song goes, "keep on, keeping on." We are tired of suffering. We have had it. And the riot also said: "We've been lying to you."

Very few whites understand blacks or realize that we have hated you for what you have done to us, to our parents and our grandparents. We have had to endure it because it meant our survival. But we have been all the time planning how to get out of our noose. The white man has gone along thinking we were content. But do you know what your black maid, bus driver or mailman is *really* thinking? The black man is essentially cunning. As your doorman says, "Good morning, Mr. Smith, how are you doing?" He is smiling at you, but he is saying to himself, "I could kill you, cut your guts out."

We have gone through the act of being your servant, worked in your kitchens. We have put your daughters to bed when they were ill, taken your sons upstairs when they were drunk. Whites are so dumb! They think the waiter they have in a restaurant, standing behind them, ready to bring them anything, is just another black man. Actually, that black waiter has a vast amount of knowledge. He knows where you live, what company you are with, your status in it. What's more, he has heard other people talking about you. He can tell whose girlfriend is off to Sweden for an abortion or whose pregnancy led to a marriage. And by accumulating this information, even the black

* Loder was acquitted and reassigned to station house duty.

man who has grown up being told he was just nothing feels in his heart that he is more moral than the white person calling him other-wise.

In the past, blacks just communicated with blacks. All the way from jungle drums to the whispers that went cabin to cabin in slavery to the things I hear from those sitting in my dental chair. Stories are handed down generation to generation. Some are true, some fabri-cated, some modified to where they may not be absolutely docu-mented. Doesn't matter. All of them, in the course of a lifetime, give you a feeling: Inside, every black man is waiting for the moment to strike.

Odyssey

Person, who has enormous round eyes, didn't always look di-rectly at us when he talked. Explaining that he wasn't trying to be shifty, he said, "I'm a hypnotist. I use the science in my professional work." A sturdy five feet eight inches, his hairline receding, a light brown in color, he was then forty. He had just finished three consecu-tive terms as the Urban League's Omaha president. He was enthusias-tic, outgoing. Estelle, his pert, pretty wife, who is assistant personnel supervisor for the Northwestern Bell Telephone Company, said her husband "talks, talks, talks, a mile a minute."

"I do what I like and like what I do," said Person, one of Omaha's two black dentists. For him, there had never been any ques-tion but that he would go into some profession. And he grew up con-ditioned to be one of few blacks among many whites. His great-uncle and grandfather were the first blacks to settle in Mount Vernon, a small, basically rural town in the lower third of Illinois, an area often referred to as Little Egypt. At its bottommost tip is the city of Cairo (pronounced kay-roe), longitudinally even with Virginia, and racially as violent as any Southern town where the Ku Klux Klan is still to be reckoned with.

Earle Person

The house where I was born and lived is at least 100 years old, built by Joe Tandy, my great-uncle. A railroader, he went to Mount Vernon, started buying property. Whites, thinking he was just a crazy black man, sold it to him. My grandfather, George Person, a minister, came to the town and started the Pavey Chapel Colored Methodist Episcopal Church.

My father was an orphan at the age of two. His mother died in childbirth, his father in a cyclone. My father carried a bitterness most of his life. Relatives took care of his three older brothers, but because he was just an orphan baby, nobody wanted him. So he was reared by the white doctor who had brought him into the world. My father resented his own family that wouldn't raise him while someone not of his race would. Later on, he quit high school, spent time in California, caught on as a cook with the old Overland Limited. He became a fairly famous chef, and he also started selling insurance to porters and other blacks on the trains. He was a very frugal man. When he returned to Mount Vernon, it was as a self-made, hard-nosed businessman who had the sense to buy the right real estate at the right time.

He was forty-five when I was born. There were just my sister and I. Our home was in a white neighborhood, and because my mother was a great cook, the white kids were always coming around for a meal. Black-white thing didn't mean too much to me. I wasn't allowed in the white grammar school, so I went half a mile to the one for blacks. I was musically inclined, and even though I couldn't attend classes with whites, I performed in their bands. We played football and baseball together, but I couldn't go to the movies with them, couldn't stop and get a malt with them. After a game, I'd just say, "Good night, fellows, got to get home, do my lessons." Or, "I'm tired."

There were several white girls who were very fond of me. My parents would get very nervous if one of them came by. "You are going to get us into trouble," my mother said to me. "This town is going to look down on us." The town could accept us, as being what they would call nice niggers, but you didn't dare date anyone white.

I went to the University of Illinois on scholarships, joined a Negro fraternity, took my degree in bacteriology. Volunteering into the Army, I was trained as an armored cavalry reconnaissance light tank commander, and when I came out in 1953, after three years of duty, I was a first lieutenant. I headed for Omaha because a dentist I'd known in the service told me about a place there called Creighton University, a small Jesuit-run school. The wheels were greased for me to study dentistry. First morning I arrived I had breakfast with Creighton's president. To me that was shocking, because at the University of Illinois I hadn't even been able to get an appointment with the damn graduate student who was supposed to be my adviser. I never saw the president at Illinois. So Creighton impressed me very much.

Odyssey

He had saved $2,200 from the Army. He had the GI Bill for tuition. But he had no job. The wife of a prominent white Omaha dentist insisted Person see a man named Whitney Young (now deceased) at the Urban League.

Earle Person

Being from Southern Illinois, I had never heard of a thing called the Urban League, and the name Whitney Young meant absolutely nothing to me. But because I needed work, I went to the league offices where Whitney was the director. He promised to make some telephone calls. Next morning he told me he had three jobs for me. Two needed a car, which I didn't have, so I took the third, food pathology research at the University of Nebraska's College of Medicine.

Omaha at that time was a desert, as far as intellectual conversation and dialogue were concerned. I guess I represented a fresh thinker, and so, on Saturday nights, Whitney and I would get together with friends at his home on Twenty-fourth Street. It was a big evening when we had two or three six-packs of beer or a couple of bottles of wine. Later Whitney left Omaha for Atlanta University.

While I was still in Creighton, I often bartended for a local white banker. He said he hoped I'd practice in Omaha and that if I ever needed money to come see him. After graduation, I told him I wanted $20,000 to get started as a dentist. "Okay," he said. Just like that, he got me a cashier's check for the amount. I asked, "Where's the passbook for the repayment schedule?" He said, "You don't need one. Bring me whatever you have saved up after six months. In a year, do the same. And so on." This told me that when the white man wanted to make exceptions about credit, he could. Took me two years to pay it off. At the last payment a white man in the bank asked me how I had done it that quickly. I told him I was frugal. "I only wish to hell you were white," he said. "You should have borrowed $100,000 to put up a new building instead of remodeling an old one."

My first wife, my college sweetheart, was with me those early years in Omaha. Then we agreed we had made the worst mistake of our lives. We got divorced. Ten years ago Estelle and I were married.

Odyssey

Person told us, "I'm not rich, but I'm comfortable. I've made $1,000 a day, and I've made nothing a day. I found that money alone just won't make me happy. I have always had some very wealthy patients. They get much less enjoyment from life than many of my workaday people. The rich don't have anything left to drive them on. I suppose this understanding was the beginning for my desire to do something in helping my community."

Earle Person

It was about ten years ago that a member of the Urban League's board here asked if I'd come in as a director, to help it grow. Remembering the warmth of Whitney in getting me a job when I was new in town, I said, "All right!" Since then I've moved around in the organization.

But I am a maverick Urban Leaguer. I love it, I love Whitney, and I hope it keeps on shaking off its barnacles, the old conservatism, and becomes more relevant. Because I am a little old for the Black Panther Party, I consider the Urban League the only organization at this point in time which is equipped to do the job that needs to be done. Every Urban Leaguer is a man trained in the field, able to talk with blacks and the power structure, be comfortable with bank presidents and welfare mothers in the same afternoon. I've been in places where a roach has crawled up my arm. But I wouldn't shake it off while I was talking with that mother in the housing project—because that apartment is the best she can do, and she has learned to live with the roaches.

Here in Omaha, the league has an affiliate that I've been working with to make better homes available to the poor. We buy run-down houses for about $6,000, put maybe another $5,000 into repairing them, and then we can sell them to someone who pays only $60 a month, where he or she had been paying $90, maybe even more, for some hole.

The role of the Urban League is to stand by society's forgotten victims. And to help them create the community structures and organizations to get them their fair share of the pie. There are people who would still have you believe that "everything is all right, freedom is winning." Reminds me of Joe Louis taking on a young white challenger. The guy came back to his corner after the first round, bleeding through the nose and mouth, almost dead. Manager rubbed him down, assuring him, "You're doing fine. Joe didn't put a glove on you." By the fifth round the challenger was sagging on the ropes as the manager soothed him with tender, loving care, saying, "Don't worry, he hasn't hit you yet." Through his swollen lips the white fighter said, "You better take a closer look at that referee, because somebody in there is beating my brains out."

And I think America better take a second look at the referee, because somebody is sure trying to kill the black man.

Odyssey

In the spring of 1968, after Dr. King's assassination had led to many riots, Person got a telegram from Whitney Young, summoning him to a secret league meeting in Washington. From that came the league's New Thrust program, aimed, said Person, "to direct involvement in helping the ghetto, rather than having blacks and whites just sipping tea together."

Earle Person

Later that year, at the annual convention, I was chosen to handle the presentation of New Thrust programs on police-community relations. My theme was that of the dying man who said to his wife, "We die, but you who live must do a harder thing than dying is. For you must think, and ghosts will drive you on." I likened the New Thrust to a baby, for whom Whitney and the 250 of us meeting in Washington had been midwives. I said we tied the umbilicus of the black people to the nation. But, I went on, "We forgot one thing. We forgot that this child we have given birth to has an enemy out there. The greatest foe this child will have is the white police who would kill this child, if we don't do something." And then I challenged everyone in that room to go home and do something about the problem we all have with the police.

Back in Omaha, I called meetings to discuss our police situation.

We had them at seven o'clock on Sunday morning, because I figured that anyone who got up early enough to make the meetings had to be a committed man. And we planned things to do, to talk to the mayor, to get out on the streets. I care about Omaha, and although I know that this town has a bad name from coast to coast—it's got what some call the death mark—I believe it can be turned around.

It is like I told them downtown when they were looking for a symbol to represent Omaha, something similar to the Golden Arch for St. Louis. I said the great thing would be if people in this nation could look to our city as the place that solved its racial problems. The symbol could be an algebraic equals sign on a flag flying over City Hall. That would show every man is a man in Omaha and is treated fairly, and we would be mecca for people coming to see how we did it.

Odyssey

The equals sign didn't go up in Omaha. Nor did blacks profess to see it in many other cities. In the spring and summer of 1969 and 1970, police-black tensions erupted into violence, not just in New York, Philadelphia, Chicago and Los Angeles, but also in: Norristown, Pennsylvania . . . Tucson, Arizona . . . Asbury Park, New Jersey . . . Augusta, Georgia . . . New Bedford, Massachusetts . . . Blytheville, Arkansas . . . Michigan City, Indiana . . . Peoria, Illinois.

In Omaha, it happened the morning of August 17, 1970. Eight policemen responding to a telephone call that a woman was screaming for help in a Near North Side house, entered it. The building was empty, but a booby-trapped suitcase left there exploded. One officer died. Several of his companions were hurt. And when we came back to Omaha the summer of 1970, the talk about the incident was everywhere.

Earle Person

The reaction of the police and of the white part of the city was instantaneous. In the ghetto it looked like Hitler's Germany. The police just cleared people off the streets, went through the housing projects. What really embarrassed them was that for more than a week they were looking for a young boy, who allegedly planted the suitcase, and couldn't find him. They felt 100 to 200 blacks knew where he was. I talked to one lady just after they had gotten through with her in her fish shop. She told me that they came in and said, "Where is he? Where is he?" She said they threatened to kill him on sight and that she had better tell where he was if she didn't want blood all over the place. I asked her why did they question her? She said she had sold him a fish sandwich and somebody tipped off the police that he talked to her all the time.*

To me, the police tactics in rounding up suspects were horrible. Their actions were as bad as the killing of the policeman. His death was not the sickness that I had been talking about in Omaha. Rather, it was the symptom of a bigger one, which is that Omaha, since 1966, had stood around and had done nothing but let black kids get their backs shot out by men I consider "storm troopers in blue."

Odyssey

Person felt that after the policeman's killing, race relations in Omaha had "sunk as low as possible." His wife added, "Earle and I would walk into a place to eat where we have been five hundred times before. And everything would be so cold, just like ice. For example, a white waitress we have known for probably four years just stared at us. The city condemned every black person for this crime."

Earle Person

A patient called me, in tears. She and this other black lady were having lunch in a downtown restaurant. A white fellow stopped at their table and said, "You goddamn black bitches. I bet you'd like to see another white policeman killed, wouldn't you?" And he went on with this tirade for about three minutes when another white guy got up, came over, and said, "Look, I eat here every day, and these ladies do, too. I am sure they don't know a damn thing about what you are talking about. Now get the hell out of here!"

Ohaha has been just that uptight.

I don't believe in war or murder. But today I will kill if I have to.

---

* Subsequently, police and FBI found Duane Christopher Peak, sixteen, asleep on the porch of a Near North Side home. He was arrested and charged with first-degree murder, as were the chairman and minister of information for the Omaha chapter of the National Committee to Combat Fascism, related to the Black Panther Party. As of this writing, none of the three defendants has gone to trial.

I'm a marksman, and I'm now never without my gun. I'm very open about it. People know I'm armed. If it comes to mass confrontation, I'm prepared to go with my people. But I won't get involved in what we in the ghetto call a humbug: Some white guy, policeman or otherwise, says, "Hey, you no-good nigger." I say, "Don't call me that." He says, "What are you going to do about it?" And we both reach for our guns. That's pointless.

Just as the bombing of the policeman was stupid. It simply gave the administration one more excuse for repression, for police to move in on those who are not to their liking. It fed right into the hands of "Tricky Dick" Nixon, his no-knock lawman, Attorney General Mitchell; the venomous Agnew, and Hoover and his FBI boys. The whole bunch is no more interested in attacking the real sources of violence than Jesse James would be in fingering his brother Frank to the sheriff.

In Omaha the booby-trapping meant there is one less policeman. But it moved the white community to raise $53,000 for his widow and five kids. And I submit to you that most of those giving are doing so not because they feel sorry for the family but because it is their way of showing that the black man must be kept in his place. Law and order, or else. Meanwhile, a unified police force is having a field day: asking for raises; demanding the right to ride double, two in a car, and to carry shotguns.

People who used to say, "It couldn't happen here, not in Omaha," don't say that anymore. Events have overtaken all of us.

Chicago: The Arena

It All Hangs Out Here

Ahmed Arabia Rayner

When I was very young, a department store had a black Santa Claus. A little black child was brought in to see him, and when she noticed his color, she spat in his face. "You're not even white," she said. "No black Santa can bring me anything." I guess that's the way this big, ragged city of Chicago is. Raw.

Chicago is where it all hangs out. Anything that happens in the black experience of America can be found here—only more so. Racism is so intense that when the civil rights movement came to this city, it was like Napoleon going into Russia. Only in Chicago did a mayor tell his police to "shoot to kill." Confrontation is omnipresent: blacks against whites; police against blacks; dissenters against the courts. The release of power to blacks is contested everywhere, but in this city the resistance to it is more bitter. Yet if we don't solve the racial thing in Chicago, we're probably forecasting the story of this country, not only for now, but generations to come.

Odyssey

Even on our first meeting, Ahmed Arabia Rayner, who pronounced his middle name air-ah-be-ah, but is mostly known as A.A. "Sammy" Rayner, emerged as his own best example of the black revolution he saw going on in America, because for almost ten years he has been in rebellion. A successful, fifty-two-year-old businessman, he was a friend to Chicago's street gangs. Middle-class, he challenged the conscience of others of like background who he felt had turned their backs on the ghettos. As a political independent, elected one of Chicago's fifty aldermen, he refused to wear Mayor Richard J.

Daley's collar, choosing instead to fight what he called the tyranny of plantation politics.

There was, in Rayner's words about his native city, a bittersweet taste, so that he could love it, yet despair of it. Chicago, in his view, was a place about which it was impossible to be neutral. Especially for blacks.

Fom 1910 to 1970 hundreds of thousands of them poured into Chicago, believing they were going to a land of freedom, where children could be educated, men could get jobs, families could live together in dignity. Instead, they generally were segregated into two major enclaves, finger-shaped areas stretching first to the south and then to the west. Almost from the beginning of this huge black tide, threatening the jobs, schools and neighborhoods of the all-white ethnic groups, Chicago was the benchmark of racial violence. In 1919, when a seventeen-year-old black swimming in Lake Michigan drifted into the area whites had arrogated unto themselves, they rained such a hail of rocks and stones at him that he couldn't get to shore and drowned. From that followed one of the worst of America's race riots: 38 killed, 537 hurt, thousands made homeless in fires. After that, tempers cooled but memories remained.

Ahmed Arabia Rayner

The first house I can remember in Chicago was on the South Side, one bought in the very early 1920's by my maternal grandmother, who was white. She was a German immigrant, a poor girl who started working in Chicago for a family that had a black chauffeur. I don't think she and the chauffeur ever married. She was just a dumb country girl who never did learn to speak English except with a guttural accent, and to the day she died she still said or-ran-jes. Their daughter married my father, who had come up from Texas to become an undertaker in Chicago. If my black father had tried to purchase this house, a two-story building with large windows looking out over the street, the white owners would never have sold it to him, because the neighborhood was then 95 percent white. But when my grandmother made the deal, put up to it by my father, there wasn't any trouble.

I suppose that was typical of my father, who has been the most important man in my whole life. Sometimes I think that just about everything I have ever done has been in at least part trying to prove my manhood to him. He was, and is, a practical man, who knows what he wants and how to go about getting it. He was a good provider for us but never one to show much emotion. His father, a North Carolinian who had moved to Texas, a Negro but as fair as any white man, was probably the last Populist politician in the state, if not in the country. He was a very learned man, whose full name was John the Baptist Rayner, and he called his three sons Ivan, Loris, and Ahmed Arabi. The last he gave to my father, who gave it to me, and I added the *a* to make it Arabia.

Some black people know the exact minute they came to the realization they were something different than other Americans. One of my younger daughters, who has long stringy hair, looks like any red-neck from Tennessee, started out thinking she was white. But on her sixth Christmas we were tape-recording the children, and she said into the microphone, "I am six years old, and I go to Holy Angels School, and I am in first grade, and I am colored." So that was when it happened to her. But for me, I guess I just always knew I was different. When I was a kid, people wrote "nigger" in front of our house, and sometimes they threw rocks into our windows. I was quite frightened.

There were certain areas where blacks, especially youngsters, weren't supposed to be. One of them was in the neighborhood where my white grandmother lived. I started over there one day, but some police stopped me to ask where I was going. When I told them about my grandmother, they took me over there in the police car, not because they were being mean or racist, but to protect me from the white kids.

My grandmother took me to mass nearly every Sunday at Holy Cross Church. My mother never went with us. She had grown up as a Catholic and had gone through a convent school. She was a good student, too. But the day she graduated the sister superior told her, "You can go anywhere in this world, and you can do many things, but you will always be a nigger." My mother walked out, never went back, and today she is an Episcopalian.

Of course, there are priests and nuns with a background of racism; you can't condemn the whole church for that. When I was growing up, I desperately wanted to be an altar boy at Holy Cross, but I couldn't because they wouldn't let me attend their all-white school or even join the church there. I asked my father about it, and he told me "I can't get you in; you just can't go there!" It hurt me, stung me. It seemed so foolish, as Holy Cross was only a block and a half from my home. And it was years before they let any of us into their school.

When I graduated from public grade school, I enrolled at Tilden Technical High School. No more than 2 or 3 percent of the students were blacks, and I supposed because there were so few of us, I didn't have any trouble with the whites. In fact, I was chosen treasurer of the Civic Industrial Club, to which every student belonged. I was the first black ever to have a position of that magnitude and that was quite a feather.

It was about then that I realized I have the patience and the compassion to adjust to people. In our neighborhood, there was a black gang with a guy named Doc as the leader. He was renowned for his viciousness, but I could get along with him better than anyone I knew. Doc used to send for me, and if I could, I would help him, lend him something. My thought was I was a lion tamer, and if I could talk with anybody for five minutes, I could win them over.

Only . . . I couldn't win over a whole system. When I went to the University of Illinois at Champaign-Urbana as a freshman, I found blacks had to live in a certain part of town. The trouble was that after certain hours you couldn't get anything to eat over there. I finally had to take a job in a sorority, not because I needed the money but so that I could eat some decent meals on a regular basis. I went out for dramatics, and when they saw how small I was then they wanted to put me in a bunny costume for this one play. That just didn't seem right, and I wouldn't go for it. My time on the stage ended right there.

Illinois was all just miserable for me. I wrote my mother every day, sometimes twice. When I came home for Thanksgiving, my father was listening to *Amos and Andy*. He looked up and just said hello. My brothers and sisters told me to be quiet, saying I was making too much noise. It was the lousiest welcome I ever had. The only good part of it was walking back to the kitchen where my mother was cooking. It was warm and smelled good. Mama held her arms open to me. Except for that one moment, it was a lonely, sad year.

I didn't flunk anything, but my grades were so low the university suggested I go to junior college for a while. I wanted to go to a black school, as I had an idea my talents could be developed there. My father asked, "How would you like to go to Prairie View College in Texas?" where he had gone. "I'll go anywhere," I said. That's all there was to it.

Things weren't too bad there, but it was away off in no place at all.

I got bored, told everybody I was leaving school to make a million dollars in California. Farthest I got was my aunt's home in Fort Worth. She called my father, and he said: "Tell him if he doesn't get back to school, I'll never put another bite in his mouth again." I told my aunt, "I'm dumb, but I'm not crazy." I went back to graduate.

Since I already knew I was going to work with my father in the funeral business, I took professional embalming training for a year at the University of Minnesota. With the war, I enlisted, tried to make the all-Negro flying unit the Army was putting together. I didn't have the eyesight for it; but after I became a lieutenant in an antiaircraft outfit, the flight standards were lowered, and I was accepted into the Air Corps. Again my father came into my life. I can recall flunking one test at a time when they were washing out black pilots like suds down the drain. For twenty-four hours I thought I might as well quit. But I was more concerned about what my father would say than I was about any flight examiner. I took the test again, passed, and never had any more trouble. And I was touched when my father came down to see me get my wings.

The Army was so busy keeping us blacks segregated that we never did get overseas. What they did was train the pilots first, then follow with the co-pilots, the engineers, the tail gunners, the radio men, and so forth, doing each one separately and in order. While we pilots were waiting for everyone else to be trained, we just took up time with crazy, routine flights to nowhere and back. I have 1,500 hours of flight time, and all I did as a B-25 bomber pilot was go on these endless milk runs. I don't think the Army ever intended to let us get any glory out of the war.

When I came back to Chicago in 1946, I both worked in the family funeral business and went to law school for two years. Finally, I had to choose between them, and I dropped law. I took some business administration courses and settled down to being a mortician. That's all I thought I would ever be.

Odyssey

His background is misleading. Rayner, with whom we talked in 1969 and 1970, was ebullient, feisty, a gregarious 200-pounder, nearly six feet tall. Quite light in color, with a spattering of freckles, thinning, black-gray hair combed straight back.

We told him that just hours earlier there had been a police

shoot-out in the Chicago Black Panther Party headquarters, followed by a fire that burned much of the building. His voice rising, Rayner responded, "Oh, for heaven's sake, you're kidding me! I listened to the radio news, and there wasn't nothing said about it. The Panthers had remodeled the place. It really looked nice. I am the co-signer on their lease. The landlord is going to be so mad! And I just paid the gas bill for them. Oh! I could have saved that eight bucks."

Ahmed Arabia Rayner

I found when I got involved in the black revolution, that to be effective you have to be all out, got to rub shoulders with everybody, even those who sometimes don't smell too good. I have been with CORE, SNCC, the Panthers, as well as with the Black P. Stone Nation and the Disciples street gangs. I feel that if I can be around, with my position, maybe I can help them, give them a feeling somebody is concerned.

Mostly the black who is trying to be affluent is apathetic, sweeps problems under the rug, isn't involved in the race issue. He says, "I got mine, you get yours. I got my home, my deuce and a quarter.* But he is living in a dream world, oblivious to reality. He doesn't realize that as long as the Man has his foot on the neck of the little guy in the housing projects, he's got his foot on the well-to-do black, too. You can be the president of a bank—and you're still black. I saw one straddled over a car the other day while police patted him down for guns. Of course they were apologetic when they found out who he was, but there is no black in this whole city who isn't living under ghetto conditions.

Now, I am middle-class. I admit it, that I never had to want for anything, always been well fed, well clothed, even had a car when I was in high school. I never had what we call the miss-meal cramps, those knots a kid gets in his belly when he has nothing to eat. Just as whites can't imagine what it is to be black, so I can't imagine what it is to be hungry. Because of my education, my training, I can't deny that until recently I had a problem in relating to the life-styles of those who don't have my background. I used to be incensed by a do-rag, the cloth a man wears after he has had a process, to absorb the perspiration, keep the hair from getting kinky, so that when he

* A Buick Electra 225.

takes it off to go out at night, he's real sharp. I thought it was ludicrous, embarrassing. But what the hell! When Rockefeller owns a railroad, he takes out insurance, doesn't he? Do-rag is the poor man's insurance, protecting his $8 or $10 investment, and once I saw it like that, it didn't seem too silly to me.

Before I got involved in politics I wouldn't exactly run away from problems, but when I saw them, I'd say, *"C'est la vie! Comme ci comme ça."* If I went into a strange restaurant and there was a snide remark, a smirking lip, I'd just go into a dreamland fantasy, saying this was not happening to me. Now I may say something, and that is new. When I see what goes on in this city, I am angry.

Odyssey

Looking back on his decision to enter politics reminded Rayner of a story:

"Little black boy whose family had just moved into an integrated neighborhood was out in his backyard, having the best time, rolling in the grass, jumping up and down, when he saw a little white boy peering through the fence at him. 'C'mon over,' said the black boy, but the white boy said *'Nooooo,* my mother says you colored boys fight and carry knives, and you cut people.' Black boy said, 'Aw, your mama don't know what she's talking about.' White boy said, 'My mother wouldn't tell a lie.' But the black boy kept urging him to come over, so finally he did. They got to wrestling, climbing the trees, smelling the flowers, having all kinds of fun when *bam,* something happened and the white boy slapped the black. Black boy reached into his pocket, brought out his knife, and said: 'White boy, you should have listened to your mama.' "

And likewise, Rayner didn't listen to his father's advice not to be in politics.

Ahmed Arabia Rayner

I think my father was remembering all the political heartbreaks his father, the Populist, had suffered in Texas, and he was trying to protect me. But I had basked in his shadow so long that now I wanted to meet my own challenge. I was pretty good at directing funerals because I like people, and I thought I could move on from there to helping them through politics. I believed then, as now, that if everybody dedicated a certain portion of their lives to some public service, we'd all be better off. To me, it was like a duty I had assumed, to spend some part of my time working for my community.

In 1963, I ran for alderman of my Sixth Ward. I came within 170 votes of forcing the Democratic primary into a runoff. That was just about phenomenal for an absolute political unknown. It inspired me to go on, and I wrote a letter to Mayor Daley. In those days I was honestly convinced that the Democratic Party in Chicago was concerned about people, wanted to help them, and I told the mayor I had something to offer, that there were voters who believed in me and that they could be utilized to help the party. I took time with that letter, wrote a good one. I never heard from the mayor directly, but the ward leader, who had been ignoring me up to that point, suddenly began asking me to his committee meetings.

Sure, I went. There were things I didn't like about the party, but I thought that by working from within I could make changes. Everywhere else in Illinois the precinct captains are elected by the people. But in Cook County, which includes Chicago, the ward leaders pick them, not on the basis of who can do the most for the voters, but who can turn in the most votes for the machine. In thinking I could break that up, I was naïve, a political innocent.

The following year I challenged William Levi Dawson, a longtime Congressman from the South Side, Daley's man in the black ghetto. Dawson got 46,000 votes; I got 24,000. Not too bad; in fact, good enough for me to make a real run at getting elected alderman in 1967. I didn't piece it all out at the time, but now I see that the Daley machine didn't really help the man they had put up for the job. In that circumstance, I couldn't lose. I took it as the beginning of a new day. After my election as alderman I told the press, "We have come to realize that the social injustices suffered by black men in America for 348 years will be remedied only by seizing political power denied to us for so long."

What I didn't see, though, was that the Daley machine was letting me win. I hadn't really stirred things up too much, and I think Daley remembered the letter I had sent him four years earlier. They thought that once I was elected, they could control me. It's an old trick in the way they play black politics in Chicago. A young black named Fred Hubbard was elected an alderman over one of Daley's people. First chance in City Council, Hubbard wasn't with us independents who opposed the mayor's Model Cities program. He voted right along with

Daley's machine. Next thing I know the mayor has a prayer breakfast, and who's up there making the speech but Hubbard! It isn't only
the Democrats who do this. When the Republicans controlled the
black vote, they did it, too.

In my early days as alderman some of the people from the ward
headquarters came to see me, saying I should get "on the team."
What I was thinking was that if I did, I wouldn't have any more
troubles about being reelected, could just go on, year after year. But I
couldn't join up, because that is the way they keep their plantation
politics going. In Chicago Mr. Daley is the master of the black plantation, and the so-called black, more likely Negro, politicians are supposed to be subservient to him. They don't think for themselves; they
just act as if they were elected by him, not the voters.

People live with plantation politics because of jobs, patronage, favors. It would be different if they got something worthwhile out of it.
Usually what they get is crumb-ish, dry bones tossed to them. Some
say we blacks now have as much as 40 percent of Chicago's population, yet only about 2 percent of the decision-makers in City Hall are
black. What the machine does is hand out lower-level jobs to keep
people working for the organization. In my ward, forty-eight of the
seventy-five precinct captains are on some kind of public payroll. The
others are just living on the machine's promises, afraid to give up because they think that if they do, they'll lose even the promise.

To me, that's like keeping people in slavery, and I wouldn't have
it. I know that when I was being particularly abusive about the machine, Daley asked a clergyman if he knew me. "Yes, I know him, but
not as well as I know his father," the minister said. The mayor said,
"He gets in my hair." To tell the truth, I wish I could get in there and
give him dandruff!

Odyssey

In 1968 Rayner again challenged Congressman Dawson, who
had beaten him for the First District seat by 22,000 votes four years
earlier. In their second contest, Dawson won by only 10,000, leading
Rayner to think that in 1970 he had a real chance of winning.

Chicago

The First Congressional seat of Illinois in 1928 gave America
its first black Congressman elected in the twentieth century. Sprawling

through nine miles of Chicago's South Side, the district packed within its borders about 400,000 people accounting for 1 of every 3 blacks in the entire state.

In some ways, the district is really two distinct faces of Black America. South of Sixty-third Street are many treelined thorough-fares, tidy homes, well-kept apartment houses. The scene is pure middle-class—to some, the area of the "booghies," the civil servants, the professional people, the blacks who've got it made. To the north of Sixty-third, running to about 2200, the "big first" is home to what-ever is wrong with urban America, anywhere. Rotting tenements, unbridled crime, block after block of welfare families. Thousands oc-cupy the Robert Taylor Homes, a three-mile-long narrow corridor of high-rise public housing projects stretching along South State Street.

Beginning in 1942, the district sent Congressman Dawson, a tough, agile, autocratic black politician, to Washington for fourteen consecu-tive terms, longer in the House than any other black in history. Daw-son had this explanation for his success: "I've just kept my big mouth shut and gone ahead and done the job that needed to be done." In 1955 an incumbent Chicago mayor (as he later said pub-licly) told Dawson and others in the Democratic Central Committee that if reelected, he would never put politics above public service. His speech, he said, was followed by silence, leading him to ask: "I pre-sume, then, it's unanimous?" Dawson was said to have answered: "It's unanimous, all right." The committee's backing went to another Democrat, Richard J. Daley.

By the end of the 1960's, however, Dawson was in his eighties, ill. He died in 1970. In his place, the Democrats endorsed his heir appar-ent, a black alderman named Ralph Metcalfe, who had been loyal to Daley. In the 1970 primary Metcalfe crushed Rayner so badly that Rayner didn't even carry his own ward.

Ahmed Arabia Rayner

In this corrupt city I did the only thing a black man can do in politics: to dream the impossible dream. And they had to stop me, with all the raw power they could put up, because the First Congres-sional District has always been the source of Daley's strength, and he thinks he has the black vote, and if he doesn't, as would be shown had I won, then he might not be able to make another run for the office.

When they beat me, they defeated more than just Sammy Rayner. Other blacks, who might think of fighting them, will now say, "What is the use? What the hell can be done?" So who in the world wants to challenge them now? There won't be anybody like me involved in politics in Chicago, at least not for a long time.

They win because they work on the fears of voters, on what makes a person insecure. The black middle class they make afraid of the gangs; they don't say that in New York dope came in when the street gangs went out, and the bourgeoisie are being raped and robbed by addicts trying to support their habits. The machine lets it be known that the building inspector can find something wrong in a place of business. They manufacture fear, and it is so deeply ingrained, and Mr. Daley's people know what it is, and everything works for them.

The liberal whites who have usually been pretty good to me disappeared this election. One woman wanted to take over a club for a reception, but after first saying Yes, the club then said No. She tried to have it in an art gallery, but when they found out what it was, they turned her down. Finally, she had to have it in her home. She invited 100, thought she would get 50, and 27 finally came. Right after that she got an anonymous phone call, someone saying she was making a big mistake, that I was a Communist, and went on to say things like if she kept trying to help me, something would happen to her. What can you do in a case like that? I told her, when she came to see me, all distraught, that you learn to hang up with the first unkind remark.

When a grocer died after what his family thought was a police beating and Macing, they asked me to get a pathologist for an autopsy. I called one, but he didn't want to do it. "I've had about three or four police cases," he said. "I am afraid to keep doing them." I said, "You are a doctor; you are supposed to do these things!" So for two hours he called other pathologists, not to do the post mortem, but just to be there with him, in case he needed a corroborative witness. He couldn't get anybody to come in. Finally, he did it by himself, talking into a tape recorder as he worked. In the whole city that was about as much corroboration as he could get.

A young black man, up from Tennessee, stranger in the city, stopped his car at a place not too far from the mayor's neighborhood to examine the muffler. People in the area beat him to death. That can happen anywhere in this city.

Many of the young, under circumstances such as these, have written off our society. They're much more defiant, don't give a damn. I was talking with some Black Panthers who don't want to just prepare breakfasts for kids or work in medical centers. They want to die, as heroes or martyrs. They welcome confrontation so they can prove they're willing to lay their lives down for their people.

There are Americans, black and white, who think they are not a part of what is going on, and that they don't have to bother about what they call niggers in the ghetto. Hell! Everybody is involved, whether they want it or not. This country is going to have to change some of its thinking, become more understanding toward the less fortunate, or we are all doomed.

I realize that black people, in fact all minorities, have been double-crossed in this country for so many years that they don't have faith anymore. I thought that maybe I could bring them faith and some hope. The election shows they didn't believe me. I am not going off to Bimini, like Adam Clayton Powell, but I am going to quietly fold my tent, and go back, not to oblivion, but to a place where I can keep helping somebody in my business, in my church, in my community.

I wonder if any of us accomplish what we would like. Look at Malcolm X. Dr. King. Bobby and John Kennedy. Did they do what they wanted? I had to see for myself that I couldn't quite get to the mountain. I have come out of this with my manhood, but in Chicago I've got to ask if good guys win, except in the movies.

Father and Son: From Generation . . .

Ralph Metcalfe

If you ask me for the proudest moment in my life I think it was after I had won the Olympic tryouts in 1932 and I was called over to be measured for my uniform, with the red, white and blue slash across the jersey. I was going to represent the entire United States on the track, and I felt pride in myself, and in my country, because I knew it offered hope to the black man and gave him the possibility of progress. And I will never forget how I felt when I went up to the victory stand to get my medals at the Olympics, and they played the national anthem.

Odyssey

When Ralph Metcalfe, a tall, stringy black kid, was coming up in Chicago's playground track teams, his first coach told him: "If you expect to be declared the winner in any race, you've got to put daylight between you and the white boys." Metcalfe never forgot. Almost from the day he broke from the starting blocks he ran with such determined power that his peers called him "rabbit." He was twenty-two when he was acclaimed "the world's fastest human" because in a single day he tied the world's record for the 100-yard dash (then at 9.4 seconds) and went on to set three new records in the longer sprints. After taking silver and bronze medals in the 1932 Olympics, he came back in 1936 to join Jesse Owens and eight other blacks in shredding Adolf Hitler's claim of Nordic superiority at the Berlin games. Nine of the ten won at least one medal. Metcalfe took both a silver and a gold.

Nearly thirty-five years later, when we saw Metcalfe, he still had, stored away at home, his Olympic jersey. At sixty, time had fleshed

him out. His face had a graveness. Only once or twice, as for example
when he talked about his son, was there any show of emotion. In
every way he was the picture of the establishment black man who
rocked no boats, advancing to levels no black had ever reached in
Chicago's City Hall.

Ralph Metcalfe

My father was a drugstore porter in Atlanta and we lived in a
frame house that was a decent place, not one of those shotgun homes,
as we called them, where the rooms all open into each other and a
shot through the front would go straight out the back. Our place was
up on poles, and my brother, sister and I played under the building or
climbed up and down the steps leading to the front door. After we
kids had been out, my mother made us take a bath and put on fresh
clothes before we could sit down to dinner. We always had food on
the table. Those were happy years.

My father had been born in Atlanta. My mother, up from Macon,
Georgia, was more of a militant, and she just couldn't stand the repression of the South. There wasn't the opportunity to thrive and develop, to feel free. One day when I was seven years old, my mother
told us the family was going North. In Chicago we moved into the first
floor of a two-story brick building on the South Side. From hearing
my mother and father, I knew that in the South the white man was
my enemy, but we drew a line between the southern and northern
white. In Chicago you didn't hear "nigger" as much, and I think I felt
freer. It wasn't until later that I came to see the white man was just as
much my enemy in the North.

Nearly all the people in any authority around us were white. We
lived close to a police station, where I saw that most of the policemen
were white. Teachers and school principals were white. Even the
streetcar conductors were. Having all these whites in the positions of
power, at least in my world, was just an accepted thing. Neither my
mother or father did any talking about the idea of blacks and whites
someday being integrated. We were separate, and we just took that as
the way it was.

What my mother, who had only gone to eighth grade, impressed on
us was the importance of getting an education to prepare ourselves
for making a good, honest living. I came to Chicago with standing as
a third-grade student in Atlanta, but up here they told me I didn't

qualify for that. They put me back in the first grade. I didn't object. Although my mother always insisted I do my homework, I had no motivation for school. Only one or two of my teachers seemed to take any interest in us black students. The classes were overcrowded and frequently kids would be passed along, grade to grade, simply because they had good attendance records.

In junior high school I learned absolutely nothing. The teachers' main concern was keeping discipline. The environment was bad: kids would be shooting craps in the toilet. Even though I was unprepared, I found I could get along in class. It didn't take very much thinking to realize that these conditions were tolerated because of prejudice which kept white students apart from blacks. It's true I didn't know what kind of education whites were getting, but I reasoned it couldn't possibly be worse than mine. I was sure they were progressing, that they were getting the good teachers, and I wanted to share in that.

The neighborhood school districts limited me in Chicago to academic high schools which were nearly all black. My only out was to enroll at a technical school where the boundaries were more flexible. With my mother's encouragement I left junior high for Tilden Technical, which was about 97 percent white.

I have the dubious distinction of never having attended class on any Friday during the years I was in junior high and Tilden. Matter of fact, the Tilden principal objected to my absences, and my mother went over to tell him that she was a taxpayer and that I had to stay out and work, in order for the family to be able to make ends meet. As early as eight years old I had begun working after school. Made $2 a week in a tailorshop, keeping the place clean, pumping water into the old pressing machine, delivering garments. I am very proud of my work record. Starting then, and going on through grocery stores, butcher shops, shining shoes, and into my adult years, in all my life I have never been fired from a job. In junior high I was working for a fish market, and I would be there all day Friday, all day Saturday, part time on Sunday. In the summers I was at the market full time, and I knew the business well enough to run it when the owner was on his Jewish holidays. He offered me $25 a week, a $5 raise from my regular summer pay, if I would stay on during the school year. I was tempted, because our family could have used the extra money. My father and mother had separated when I was about thirteen, and it was my mother, a very strong woman, who kept the family together. I used to look forward to election day because she was a Democratic polls watcher, and when she came home she would have all the food she had bought with her pay. We were on welfare for a time, but she wouldn't let me drop out of Tilden.

I was an outstanding track man. I'd been running since I was on the playgrounds, and by high school I did the 40- and 50-yard dashes indoors, and the 100, the 220 outdoors, and I also ran on the relay teams for the 440, the 880, and the mile. But not even track stopped me from my fish market work. I'd skip practice on Friday, work Saturday morning, go off to the meet, and then come back to finish the day in the market.

Marquette University in Milwaukee gave me a tuition scholarship. I got a job to help me provide my meals and living expenses. I borrowed books from classmates or bought them secondhand. I was scrambling for money all the time. One extra expense was that I had to spend $1 a week for a streetcar pass to commute to school from where I was living. I was running for the Marquette team, but there was no place for me as a black man to stay on campus, so I had to get a place on my own.

I wasn't fighting what they now call the system. I wanted to improve myself so that I could be a part of it, receive the benefits from it. Having to accept separation of the races as the normal course did not make me feel inferior or make me want to be white. I have always been proud to be a black man, because I think that black people have progressed more than any other race in history in such a short time, despite all the repression, the obstacles, the color distinctions.

Odyssey

In his sophomore year at Marquette Metcalfe embraced Roman Catholicism.

Ralph Metcalfe

It seemed more relevant to my needs than the African Methodist Episcopal services of my childhood. In those earlier days I was much concerned about myself, because my minister told me it was sinful for me to dance or to go to a show on Sundays. And yet, with all the work I was doing, Sunday was the only time I had any opportunity for that. I would get a quarter from my mother to see two shows and buy one sandwich. She insisted only that I first go to Sunday school. She gave me a nickel for the collection. So when I saw the shows I felt as though I was violating God's principle, and I didn't feel too good. But Catholicism didn't tell me anything like that. I was at home with it. It was interesting that at Marquette one of my favorite priests used to go with me to the movies on Sunday afternoon. When I came back from the 1932 Olympics, Father Grace, the dean of the university's college of liberal arts, told me that if I wanted to attend graduate school, he would guarantee my tuition.

I got my bachelor's degree in philosophy, then began getting ready for the 1936 Olympics. In the spring before that, a black reporter wrote to some of the outstanding black track men recommending we boycott the games. Without any of us comparing notes, we all answered that we thought it better for us to be on the team, so we could explode Hitler's supremacy theory right in front of him in Berlin. If we hadn't, he could have said we weren't even good enough to represent our own country. We had more blacks on that team than any previous one. That was when Jesse Owens won four gold medals.

We were on that team as blacks, but we were running for the whole country, blacks and whites and everybody who was an American. This is my native land, the only one I know, and it means something to me. I could remember how my coach had told me I'd have to put daylight between me and the whites to win. But in my time I was in many races that were so close not even I could tell who had won. Yet the judges awarded them to me, showing me they could be fair.

After the Olympics, I spent a year in New Orleans, teaching and coaching track at Xavier University, before going to the University of Southern California for my master's degree. When the war came, I went into USO work, first at Anniston, Alabama, then in Louisiana, with the all-black Ninety-third Infantry Division. Whites in that area were fearful because of all the blacks, and the USO wanted to build cooperation by having someone who knew the South and whom the white South knew. When the Ninety-third moved to Needles, California, the commanding general asked that I be assigned with them. Soon afterwards I entered the Army itself.

I thought the draft was fair, and I felt it was my responsibility to be in the armed forces. Going in as a private, I advanced as fast as the table of organization permitted, becoming a first lieutenant, up for a captaincy, and the holder of a Legion of Merit award for my work in physical training. I wanted to be fighting overseas, and I asked for that transfer. My commander wouldn't honor it, explaining he wanted me to stay in this country, directing physical education for all troops, black and white, at Camp Plauche, Louisiana.

While I was in the USO and the Army, I had some unpleasant experiences in the South. In New Orleans one day I went into a garage to have my car serviced. This was the same place I had taken it during my days at Xavier. Then the whites were generally pleasant, and if they didn't call me mister, they at least addressed me as professor. But when I came back in my USO uniform, the same people wouldn't fix anything for me. They sent me to another garage, saying somebody there would do the work, "if you talk to them properly." Another time a white woman in a filling station wouldn't sell me gas unless I said, "Yes, ma'am" to her. I told her I wouldn't, just because she was insisting on it. It was also common that if a white motorist didn't like your driving he would lean out and call you nigger.

When I was discharged, there wasn't any question about where I was going. I left the South and went back to Chicago.

Odyssey

During the fall of 1946 an all-black play, *Deep Are the Roots*, was being performed in Chicago. Metcalfe took a blind date, Fay Young, to it. They were married in less than a year. In 1948 their only child, a son, was born.

Ralph Metcalfe

I wanted my son to have more opportunities than I had had, to be more prepared than I was to make a contribution to the life and progress of black people. And I said to myself that I was going to see to it that he would have the best education he could absorb.

I was working then as director of Chicago's Department of Civil Rights for the Commission on Human Relations. Ed Kelly, the Democrat who was mayor, didn't want us to be identified with politics. He thought our effectiveness in the community would be diminished if people were saying about us, "Oh, here come those Democrats." I stayed away from politics, although I could see how it controlled my total life. The building we're in is governed by a building code. The streets, the traffic, the police, finances, fire, even the air you breathe, are affected by politics.

In 1949 I was hoping to be appointed by Governor Adlai Stevenson to the State Athletic Commission. Congressman Dawson and my ward committeeman* had already endorsed another candidate. I asked if I could be their second choice. The governor, however, passed over their man and said that because of my qualifications he wanted me. It was Dawson who told me I had the job.

A little later I went to Dawson and the committeeman again, this time to ask if I could get started in the Democratic organization. There was never any question about my being a Democrat. My mother had been one in Chicago, in the 1920's, when you would not have more than three or four of them in a precinct, so I knew something about the party's philosophy. After Dawson said to me that I had not done anything politically, I explained how Mayor Kelly had instructed us to stay clear of that. He and the committeeman then checked the Board of Election Commissioners and found I had been with the Democratic Party on every occasion. First they made me an assistant precinct captain, then a captain. The committeeman later got out of tune with Dawson's program. The Congressman moved him aside, put me in. The way he checked on me was to call some Republican friends in my precinct. They said I was a dedicated Democrat and told him to get me out of that spot or else I'd be making them into Democrats. That sat well with the Congressman. I was appointed committeeman in 1951 and elected to the job in 1952.

One of the things I did as the ward leader was to start passing out 1,200 food baskets every Christmas. That's a time when everybody should be made happy, and it ought to be known by the needy that there are people interested in them. I tell my captains to choose the 1,200 families on the basis of need alone. They can be Republicans or Democrats, don't even have to be registered.

When I was elected alderman for the third ward in 1955, one of my goals was to clean up the section along South State Street. There was almost nothing but frame, rat-infested bungalows there, and I was fearful whole blocks could be wiped out if there was a fire. In the Daley administration we got those places eliminated, replacing them with the Robert Taylor high-rise housing projects. Remembering

---

* In the Chicago system, the committeeman is the political leader of the ward. Precinct captains report to him.

what was there before, I am very happy to have them in my ward.

Those projects were built in that location because of the discrimination and prejudices which exist in Chicago. Before the homes were put up, the Chicago Housing Authority had about 5,000 applications from families, most of them black, who needed a decent place to live. The white wards wouldn't accept public housing, so we had to locate the buildings in black areas. Now I am opposed to any more high rises, but it was necessary to have them then because we had only a limited area in which to provide for thousands of families. For most of the residents, the Robert Taylor homes are a 100 percent improvement over where they lived before.

In the same spirit of working for improvements, I voted for the Model Cities program in Chicago because I believe in what it will accomplish for the people. If you serve them, they will keep returning you to office. That is why on the day after one election you start campaigning for the next, and the best way to do that is with a positive action. I was elected alderman three successive times by overwhelming majorities. I became the chairman of the powerful building and zoning committee in the City Council. And I was made the first black president pro tem in the council's history.

I think this attitude of wanting to serve the people is true of the Daley administration. It is an insult to blacks to think that Daley keeps getting the votes because there are ignoramuses out there. The administration perpetuates itself because it is relevant to the needs and provides substantive programs. The people are knowledgeable about that, and as a result, they come out to vote for the mayor.

I think it is unfortunate the mayor made his shoot-to-kill statement.* I can understand why he did. He thought he had good intelligence on this incident and that such a thing should not happen in a city he was proud of. What I remember is what he said two days later, when he modified his position to make it acceptable to everybody and really representative of his genuine interest in Chicago. This is something that those who want to keep emphasizing the negative have forgotten.

There are a lot of people, many organizations, who are determined

* In the Chicago riots following the assassination of Dr. King, 7 persons died, several hundred were injured, 3,000 were arrested, and more than 200 buildings were damaged or destroyed. Daley said afterward that he had ordered policemen in the future to shoot arsonists and looters but later called for using only minimum force necessary in making an arrest or preventing crime.

to change the status quo, change it radically, drastically, and they use terms such as "plantation politics" to arouse emotions. When I am included as a part of this, I answer, like I do to all the other names: My skin is not thin. It doesn't disturb me, but I think it is regrettable, because I want to move away from name-calling and toward unity.

I think I am as militant as anyone—if that is the description of someone who sees a condition and fights tenaciously to correct it. These people who criticize us are not militants; they are dissidents. And who is going to take the place of those they criticize? Somebody's got to be the mayor or the commissioner of police, the controller, to handle all these things they refer to as plantation politics. To state it very succinctly, *they want what we have!* The point is, they haven't earned the right to it because they haven't serviced the people. We do.

When I first came to Chicago there was one black judge. Today there are twenty-four. We had three black aldermen; now there are ten. While there were no black members of the mayor's cabinet, we have four. Garbage, instead of being picked up spasmodically, is collected on a regular schedule, twice a week in the densely populated districts. We have alley lights. The number of black policemen and firemen has increased.

I want to hasten to add that I don't think we have come even halfway of where we should be. That's why in my successful campaign for Congress I emphasized the importance of people getting together to attack the common ills: the lack of proper education; decent housing; enough jobs; preventative medicine; post- and prenatal care. The need for recreation. Overriding all of this is the necessity to be able to walk the streets in the district without fear, and this is what is not true today.

It is not factually correct to say that I am an Establishment black man who rocks no boats. I just don't air my differences with the Daley administration in public. I do my fighting indoors, behind closed doors. But once a decision is reached, I support it. If the black man is going to be in a psychological position to make his contribution to American culture, he has got to have symbols. It is one thing if this is a Ralph Metcalfe, an outstanding Olympic athlete with a good civic record. It is quite another if the symbol is someone who is anti-Establishment, hell-bent on destroying the power structure.

There is in this a lesson for white people. As long as we are looked upon as black, and *not* as human, White America is only working against its own interests. It cannot succeed unless I succeed. You, White America, should stop criticizing black militants, because you have made them. Made me as militant as I am, made my son as militant as he is.

... *To Generation*

Ralph Metcalfe, Jr.

I am a black revolutionary. I support the Vietcong, the Palestinian guerrillas, and I was for Nasser. If I were to be drafted, I certainly would not fight on the side of those I consider to be my enemies. I anticipate socialism as one of the future orders of the world, and therefore, I question whether the United States as we know it today will be in existence at the end of my lifetime. As a matter of fact, I think my role is to work toward eliminating the type of system we have in this country.

Odyssey

All the emblems of resistance were around him in what he called his "thinking room": the pictures and books of Malcolm X. A paper target plate he brought home from pistol practice, showing how he had laid in one bull's-eye and five other bullet holes, all within an area the size of a man's chest. The works of Fanon. Illustrations depicting nine- and ten-year-olds, nonwhite, shouldering rifles. And a National Anti-War and Anti-Draft Union poster saying, HELL NO! WE WON'T GO!

When Ralph Metcalfe, Jr., twenty-two, a veteran of the siege at Columbia University, looked at the symbols in this sparsely furnished room of his home, he was proud. He said to us that as soon as his newly born child was a bit older, the baby's crib would be moved in there. "I want my son to wake up looking at these books and pictures, and I want him to go to sleep with them near him, so that he gets used to the expressions in them and knows from the very earliest who he is, and who we as a people are, and where we must go."

Metcalfe's rented house is on Chicago's South Side, but it is not in the ward his alderman-father represents, nor is it in the First Congressional District. The son chose it because it was available and the rent was low. Only months out of college when we saw him he was looking for a job, surviving off savings and admitting "things were pinching." It hadn't been like that in his childhood.

Ralph Metcalfe, Jr.

We lived in the Rosenwald building, between Forty-sixth and Forty-seventh streets, Michigan and Wabash avenues, and while it was not luxurious, it used to be, among the black bourgeoisie, a fairly prestigious place. It is only about five stories high, with a number of entrances, and the apartments are comfortable. I had my bedroom, my parents had theirs, and we had a living room and kitchen.

I had food, shelter and clothing, and I assumed they were always going to be there for me. By virtue of my father being in politics and having a little money, I was able to attend the Howalton private grammar school, which gave me a better education than I could have gotten in Chicago's public schools. I was there from kindergarten through eighth grade. It was an all-black school, but the only black history thing we got was a single three-week course. I learned that there had been slavery and that we were supposed to be free.

I had a lot of respect for my father, and I still do. I saw a lot of people looking up to him for his doing good in the community. In our family he was always the dominant one. Oh, I did what my mother said, also, but it was like my father had the deciding word. Especially about schools.

I was about to graduate from Howalton and my parents didn't think the high school opportunities in Chicago were comparable to those I could get elsewhere. They wanted me to have the finest education they could procure for me. I thought about the Lake Forest Academy, about an hour out of Chicago, so I would be closer to home. We kids were starting to have parties, and women were creeping into my life in a different way, and I didn't want to completely divorce myself from the city. In the end, though, my father chose Choate School in Massachusetts for me. We took a trip East, seeing about ten private schools. The main thing that impressed my parents was that Choate gave us one of the warmest receptions. Besides, John F. Kennedy had gone there, and it was also the alma mater of Adlai

Stevenson and Allan Jay Lerner. It just seemed a very prestigious place, and they were fairly generous with their scholarship offer.

Choate was where I became aware of white and black worlds. I noticed that the freshmen seemed to develop cliques and friendships. I wasn't concerned about making friends; it was just that I hadn't drawn any. I was the only black in the class, and for three years I was the only one in the school. Of course I didn't have a roommate, at least not for a long time. I couldn't see them asking the other prospective freshmen: "Which one of you wants to room with a black person?" Or "Negro," as they would have said.

As I look back on Choate, I can see many instances of racial discrimination, which because I was relatively naïve I didn't pick up completely at the time. Such as a white boy referring to slavery and saying, "That was in the days when the whites used to have niggers wipe their ass for them." If somebody said that to me now, he would probably be in serious injury for the rest of his life, if he was alive at all. But I was unused to it then. I couldn't confront him about it. I knew that in slavery the master's ass was wiped by his slaves. All I could say then was, "Why would anyone want that done for him?"

I kept telling my parents I didn't like Choate. And at the end of the first year I said I wasn't going to return. They were very slick about it, as parents can be, and they told me, "Okay, you find somewhere else to go and you get it together." I checked out the University of Chicago lab school where some of my friends were. It wasn't really comparable to Choate, which was physically very beautiful and had fine athletic facilities. I did as my parents wanted, continued at Choate.

But it was the beginning of my radicalization. Every time something would happen and the school didn't know who was doing it, they'd look at me—the black one. They figured I'd been out on the street, smoking pot, drinking wine, beating up people, raping women. Except for a little wine and knowing a couple of girls, I hadn't been doing any of those things. By their putting me into that mold, they made it so that I was less able to relate to the people who represented the power structure of the school, like the senior president or the boys on the Altar Guild.

There wasn't anything in their way of life for me to covet. I already had a nice background. But I was looking for something different. I wasn't concerned about the material things, and when I saw at Choate what made those so-called aristocratic whites happy, I figured they were pitiful! One student took me home for a weekend to Connecticut. I met his family, went all around the town with him. None of the girls wanted to talk to me, of course. It didn't bother me none. I just wanted to get laid, and none of them looked that good to me. The whole business seemed to be very empty.

In my senior year a white boy asked me how to get high, cheap. I said, Richard's Wild Irish Rose wine and a quart of beer. He went home to his town in Massachusetts for a big formal dance and he bought the wine and a six-pack of beer. He picked up this little girl who thought he was really hip. On the way, he had half the wine and beer, finished it at the dance. Going home, he passed out at the wheel, ran into a bridge. Fortunately, nobody was hurt. A trooper brought him home, disheveled and drunk.

His parents said: "What were you drinking?" He told them and they said, "My God! Wine and beer! Where did you learn that from?" He told them, "Ralph." Automatically I was to them a bad influence. When he told me about the scene, I just said, "You can't handle the stuff, stay away from it."

At Choate I enjoyed athletics. I played football, wrestled—that's how I got the knee injury that has disqualified me from the draft—and was on the track team. In my senior year I set a record for the 35-pound hammer throw. My athletic ability was largely instrumental in getting me into Columbia. Scholastically, I had only a 72 average. But when the college saw I was the best high school hammer thrower in the whole country, I was accepted. I was going to be Columbia's nigger in the Olympics.

Odyssey

He studied karate, and his huge biceps indicated the power he could wield in a chop. He weighed 215 pounds. He wore his hair in a moderate Afro. He had a large and imposing head; his features were very strong.

Ralph Metcalfe, Jr.

Being on the track team at Columbia consisted of working out four hours a day, six days a week. I did it the first half of the year. But I was like noticing that all the black students were hanging together at Columbia, and I was remembering that in Chicago it was black people I was having all the fun with. Actually the reason I had chosen Columbia, not Dartmouth or Princeton, was that it was in the city among all kinds of people. And I didn't want to live for another four years as I had at Choate—with no girls. That's an artificial, sterile Western custom.

At Columbia, however, I found that track was taking up too much energy. I told the coach one day I couldn't handle it any more. He shed a tear, which made me feel kind of funny, because he was an old man and his whole life was track. I had respect for him as a coach, but I wasn't going to model my life after him.

With my newfound freedom, I asked some of the black dudes what was going on the next weekend. They said they were going to D.C. I said, "Oh, yeah? Can I go?" So that Friday we took the plane to Washington and when we got there I said, "Where the sisters at, man?" Then they told me they were there to go to a black power conference at Howard University. I said, "Well, I am here with you, and even though I wanted to find out what was happening with the girls, I'll go with you."

That was a very significant day for me. Muhammad Ali was one of the two speakers. I had admired him ever since the first Liston fight, when he was so confident, colorful and brash. He had joined the Nation of Islam, which I had never heard of, even though it is headquartered in Chicago. I didn't know if it was good or bad. But when I found out that Muhammad Ali wasn't going to the draft, to fight in Vietnam against people of color, I was confronted with such a fantastic question! I had no way of answering whether he was right or wrong. So I wanted to hear him talk. The other speaker was Dr. Nathan Hare, a professor at Howard. These black people were speaking out so forcefully, criticizing society, that they seemed to present me with a concept of life in which I thought I could function. I wasn't thinking about it in terms of any theory. I was just weighing each individual statement, and they made sense to me.

Back at Columbia the campus humor magazine printed a spoof on a black fraternity. We found it to be very racist and derogatory. We demanded they print an apology and tear out that page from all the copies. When they wouldn't, we blacks marched in, took the copies, set some on fire, locked the others in an office. Somehow they disappeared from there.

That summer I read the *Autobiography of Malcolm X* for the first time. Nobody said, "Hey, man! Dig Malcolm!" I hadn't even heard about him until after he got killed, but everybody seemed to be relating to him as some sort of god. Once I read him, my world was never the same again.

We had at Columbia something called the Students Afro American Society, SAS. Any black person at Columbia could go to the meetings, but it wasn't too advanced ideologically. When they first formed it, the members even had difficulty about whether to let white students in. Our class was the first one where Columbia hadn't just handpicked the blacks it would admit. We had thirty-eight black males in our year, most of them from the streets. We didn't dig the organization of SAS or its leadership, and by the end of my sophomore year we elected one of my classmates, Cicero Wilson, to be the president of it.

The big thing started at school in my junior year, when Cicero went to the rally put on by the Students for a Democratic Society. We wanted to stop Columbia from building a gymnasium in an area that would displace neighborhood blacks. SDS had its own set of demands. After we listened to what everybody had to say, we went down to nail a list of what we wanted on the university president's door. Security guards were there. Me and three of my friends were all set to hit the door and bust on in when SDS's Mark Rudd, with his ignorant self, said, "No, cool it." We figured like, okay, we were going to do it for the dude, but if he don't want us, ain't no point in putting ourselves on the line.

So we cooled out, headed for the gym site around which they had erected a fence. Me and the same three friends got there and were the first to start tearing it down. There was also a black medical student I'd been on the track team with, and while he was quiet and studious —and I liked fun—we respected each other. The police on the scene told him to get back. He did, but not fast enough for this one policeman, who pulled out his club and started hitting him on the legs.

Something inside me just snapped.

I grabbed the policeman, tied his arms all up. He was small and thin, and I am sure I could have broken his back. He kept saying, "I'll kill you, motherfucker. I'll kill you, motherfucker." I was patting the gun in his holster and saying: "Officer, don't make me take your gun."

Fortunately, a police sergeant had the foresight to tell my friends, "You get your boy; we'll get ours," while I was saying, "Why aren't you-all hitting him?" But my friends pulled me back, and the police got their man. And when they did, there was such an intense hate going on between my eyes and those of that policeman!

A white student got arrested down there, but really it was blacks who were getting most of the action. We took the rally back to the campus. Rudd and Cicero decided we'd go into Hamilton Hall, and Rudd said, "Let's keep the dean hostage." So they took him and locked him in his office.

As the thing went down that afternoon and evening, people found out what was happening, and eighty to ninety black people came into the building. We had a black caucus and at three in the morning agreed to barricade the hall, not let any classes go on. The whites still in the building were divided about what to do. One-third wanted to barricade, one-third didn't, and the rest wanted to talk about it some more. So we told them they all had to leave, because we were about serious business. This was the first time I realized that white students are just playing with revolution. They have a whole lot of middle-class guilt feelings to get rid of. They are not fighting for their survival.

We wanted the administration to know that black people were united in the fight to stop that gym. We did let the dean out. We felt it wasn't in our best interests to hold him, inasmuch as we were not prepared to do him physical harm. Then we settled down for a week's stay in the building. We found a shower in the basement and set up times for the men and the women. We had food donations from the community, sisters working in the kitchen. We had a first-aid station. We cleaned up the place twice a day. That hall was cleaner when we finally left it than when we came in.

Meanwhile, I called my father to tell him where I was. He didn't philosophize or moralize about it. He has always been that way. We can talk about our differences. If I ask, he'll give me his considered opinion. If something about me is bothering him he'll let me know. And he didn't say anything about my being in the building. He just said for me to be careful and keep him posted.

After we took Hamilton Hall, the whites went on to five other buildings. Ours was the only place where there was no violence as the police came in to arrest us. We had two or three black lawyers, State Senator Basil Patterson and others, to be sure there was no police brutality. When the police, supervised by a black officer, arrived, we were all lined up along the wall, waiting.

Downtown, we got arraigned on criminal trespass charges, but were released on our own recognizance, no bail or anything. I remember when I came back on the campus, the sun was shining. It was the first day in May. There were no more classes, no finals, and it had been announced Columbia wouldn't build that gym. I was sitting on top of the world.

Odyssey

While saying his Columbia experiences, plus extensive reading, had heightened his own self-awareness and perception of the world around him, he added that they, by no means "lessened the respect I have for my father."

Ralph Metcalfe, Jr.

If you take an external view of America, you must become a black revolutionary. You know that your enemy here is the same one who had Africa in colonial chains for over 100 years and is messing with people of color the world over. The white man is our devil-oppressor, determined to keep the black man powerless and in slavery.

What the white man has never wanted us to know is that we blacks go back to the original man. The remnants of the earliest proto man have been found in Tanzania. When you realize the blacks were the first people on the face of the earth, that we had the earliest of all civilizations, then you have to ask: "How is it that we are held in bondage?" As an answer, you have to make one of two choices. Either develop internally or be forever dependent on the white power structure for survival. The course is clear. You work for the elimination of this racist system.

People of color are waking up all around the world. Twenty-five percent of the population lives in Communist China. Che Guevara was in Latin America. Then there is me in this country, thinking the way I do. I notice how Huey P. Newton and Eldridge Cleaver are thinking, the way Malcolm saw us all, how Stokely Carmichael is going, and it all seems to say the direction in which the world is moving. Nowhere, nohow, can the white man stop it. His system is doomed to collapse and failure.

People always ask, "What happens then?" I don't have any "ism" under which I would like to see this country run. I just want to see a form of government which will function in our best political interests. What has been absent from black people is political awareness, which is due to lack of education. To me, education is the primary factor. That is why, when I saw black students at Columbia learning to be doctors and physicists and chemists, I didn't feel they needed to prove themselves by going out demonstrating. I would rather they went on getting knowledge to be applied back to their own people, just as I hope to follow my undergraduate degree in economics with a doctorate. With education, blacks can reach correct conclusions. Without it, we go on as we were. In Chicago, this means allowing the Daley machine to keep functioning in a way which is not in our best interests.

I can look at the Robert Taylor high-rise housing projects here and say, as I did in an article for Nathan Hare's *Black Scholar,* that they were designed with urban riots in mind:

> The buildings are arranged in groups of three, all facing inward, forming three sides of a square. There are no hallways. The door to each apartment opens onto a common porch, with the elevator shaft in the middle of each floor. Thus, during an insurrection, the sum population of three buildings can be controlled by one piece of heavy military equipment placed on one side of the square and a numerically small contingent of men. No one could enter or exit the buildings without exposing himself. They are strategic hamlets, in other words. . . .

In those projects, a syndrome of dependence is reinforced on the residents by requiring them to submit to a yearly inspection of each apartment, to see if the housekeeping is up to standard. That way, you make a black person think, "I am just hanging on, and if the white man doesn't like it, I won't even be as well off as I am now, so I better cater to him." Which means it is a way of getting votes.

And look at Chicago's Model Cities program. It is a thing where the power structure wants to concentrate black people into less land area than they have now and into more genocidal living conditions. The Daley machine expects to build a reservation and have us happy to live in it. It isn't that I am cynical about the democratic system of voting. It's only that I don't see it in Chicago.

This doesn't put me at loggerheads with my father. He speaks louder in action than in words. He chose another route than me for his contribution to black people. He came up in significantly different historical times than I did. He has been functioning within a structure that was for him the best one through which to operate. It would be ridiculous for him to have spent all his time in one effort and then turn around and say it was all wrong. My father is sixty years old. I love him, and I hope he lives forever. But I am at the beginning of my life as a man, and I don't have to hook myself up in the same way.

No Miracles for Martin

Al Raby

Most of us really had a great deal of confidence in the American dream, and we thought that the difference between the dream and reality was only in the failure of the majority to recognize that there was a disparity. In Chicago we were seeking no more than the legal right to open housing, but when we went into the Gage Park and Marquette Park areas on the Southwest Side and knelt in prayer, the whites threw stones and bottles at us. They yelled "Bitch!" at the white nuns in the march and hit a priest in the face with a brick when he tried to stop them. They stoned Martin Luther King to the ground, shouting, "Kill him! Kill him!" And later Martin said he had never seen such hostility, such hate, in his life.

Chicago

"Who is this man Raby?" Mayor Daley once demanded to know, and then spent the next few years finding out. In that time, Al Raby, black schoolteacher, still in his early thirties, led the North's biggest and most significant civil rights coalition, challenging the power structure, forcing the city to look at its segregated education, and giving a cause to all the black ghetto dwellers suffering from what Dr. King called "the nagging sense of nobodyness."

Al Raby

In the psychology bred by America, lower-class people were taught to regard their circumstances as a product of something inherently wrong with them. The opportunities were proclaimed as being there, and only chance or the lack of fortitude stopped anyone from achieving them, so that you owned your own failures. The corollary is that somehow you could be the master of your destiny, if only you would try, because justice was expected to prevail and there was nothing basically wrong with the country.

The disillusionment from the civil rights movement was in finding that this was not so, that society would not change just because the good folks realized the black man was not satisfied. The movement put America to the test, and it showed people were not willing to give up anything in order to bring about social change. For example: When Lou Harris did a poll, about 65 to 75 percent of those interviewed said they thought schools in urban centers, particularly in ghettos, should be improved, slums should be ended, and welfare recipients should get more money. But when they were asked if they would permit taxes to be increased for these purposes, 69 percent said No. Which is not to say that the working class, which bears the bulk of paying for these changes, is per se racist. While it takes about $10,000 a year to support a family of four in urban areas, the auto workers, as one example, make an average of $8,900, and they are pretty close to being backed against the wall as a source of new taxation.

The movement did very little to illumine this situation because it failed to discuss the economic problems of the working class. What it did do was raise the level of political interpretation by the poor, disabusing them of the idea that they were both the victims and the cause of their own problems. Ten years ago welfare recipients would have been terrified to death to organize or do anything, because they thought that being on relief would be used in a negative way against them. Now they have an organization, and they assert that they have rights as well as anybody else. What happened is that their degree of social consciousness has been heightened to understand how the larger society consciously manipulates and has a lack of concern for the ghettos.

Or consider the Black Panthers. I don't think there could have been a Panther Party in Chicago had not there first been a movement. Their one great program is feeding the poor, and what does that mean? It isn't that the Panthers are feeding every black child who needs to be fed, but it does demonstrate to a certain number of people that our society doesn't give a damn whether children starve to death. It is an educational thrust, revealing the insensitivity of this country to the plight of its poor. I may not agree with all the Panther tactics, but it is coming clearer and clearer to me that they are correct in their analysis: In challenging society's vested interests, they must either be killed or sent to jail. They are forcing the country to expose its determination to protect institutional racism. And all the weight and interests of institutions are pointed this way.

As one illustration, there is in Chicago an apartment complex which had about forty black janitors, making less than $600 a month, and all denied promotions because the head janitors were white. When the blacks struck, a lawyer whom I had known as an official in a church group for racial and cultural unity came to me on behalf of the insurance company-owner. He wanted to use his past relationship to the movement in getting something done for the insurance company. You know how the Kerner Report says one of urban society's major problems is underemployment, undersalary, lack of promotional opportunities? And here was the very symbol of the white liberal community, defending the status quo, using whatever credibility he had in the movement to support institutional racism.

Even a university is part of this maintenance of the present situation. In this city we had: (1) peace marchers beat up; (2) a second peace march in which there was no brutality; (3) the Democratic National Convention where people were again beat up; and (4) a third peace march in which police actually helped demonstrators to cross streets. To me, the conclusion was obvious that political decisions controlled the police actions. Yet the University of Chicago law school raised as the major issue in police-community relations the question of what discretion police should have on an individual basis. That is not the point. The real problem in Chicago is the relationship between the police and the political apparatus. This question the university never reached.

It is hard to appreciate the strength of Chicago's power structure, as symbolized by the Democratic organization. I don't think anyone could have predicted the 1968 convention scene: that a United States Senator could be refused the right to the floor, that Daley could be so arrogant. Before it took place, I could not have believed that in Chicago white folks would be beaten as they were. But if you have an apparatus that can go after blacks, it can also go after whites. And the lesson here was that they'll beat anybody in the head who messes with their thing.

Odyssey

When Raby talked to us about himself, he betrayed no emotions, no matter what violence, what confrontation he told of enduring. "Within me," he explained, "there is a personality sitting back and watching the other part of me out there leading, and maybe there is a kind of contradiction in me being an introvert and a leader at the same time. But I don't find any great value in becoming emotionally involved in what I am doing."

He is wiry-lean, an inch above six feet. He had a heavy black mustache, and his hairline marched steadily to the rear. He had been married three times. His last two wives were white, a fact he called "inconsequential, of very little meaning" in his community work. In 1969 voters in his integrated South Side neighborhood near the University of Chicago elected him, as an independent with no support from Mayor Daley, to the convention writing a new constitution for Illinois. "With my background," he said, "politics is now where I see myself as being most viable."

Al Raby

From somewhere, probably from my mother, I got a certain level of arrogance, a sense of justice and fair play. When I was still very young and living in a Chicago ghetto, a doctor-uncle who had come up from Tennessee for a visit was telling about the problems blacks had in the South. It had been the tradition for the kids in our family to visit his place in the summer, but after hearing me say I wouldn't take those kinds of things, the collective decision was that to save me from being lynched they wouldn't let me go South. Maybe it was braggadocio on my part, but I felt then, still do, an enormous amount of indignity when I am messed over, and I have empathy for others who are.

I was two years old when my father, a postal guard on a truck, died in 1935 after an incorrect diagnosis about his appendicitis. My mother was a seamstress, who at one time supervised about 5,000 people on a WPA project. I can remember her working six days a week and going on Sunday morning to the Cook County Hospital to see one of my brothers who had TB. In the afternoon she went to the parental school where another brother had been sent by the court. My sister and her husband were living with us, and my mother was supporting all of us. When she got sick and couldn't work, we didn't have enough to eat. Trying to figure some way to get food, I suggested we go to another of my uncles in Chicago. My mother, who always had great pride and an almost overwhelmingly strong personality, said she'd rather starve than ask him for anything. So we were on welfare for a while. When she got very sick and had to go into the county hospital, I went to the Cabrini housing project on the North Side, where my sister had gotten a place.

It was about then, age nine, I was hanging in a poolroom on Chicago Avenue. The law said you had to be eighteen to go into places like that, but this one was available to kids. I never got into any trouble with the police, though, mostly because I was a tremendous loner. I was thirteen and back on the South Side with my mother when I started drinking. Before I finished the eighth grade, I dropped out of school. I was living off the street, hustling money wherever I could, shining shoes, doing odd jobs. I'd go along the row of stores on Sixty-third Street, asking the owners if they had anything for me to do. Carol Maynard, who had a photographic shop, gave me the job of washing the bathroom. From then on, he had a very significant impact on my life.

In the ghetto, you usually go into one of two categories. Either you have a middle-class experience, in which there is a certain degree of mobility: Be a doctor, a lawyer, and you strive for that. Or if you are in a lower-class community, your image is generally that of the hustler. I was in the lower class, but I wasn't programmed that way because I met Maynard. He was black, Philadelphia-born, educated, a successful middle-class businessman. He hired me on a weekly basis, and taught me photography. Being able at thirteen or fourteen to take a decent picture was a fairly prestigious thing, and because of the skills I learned from him, I could handle the whole darkroom process. He bought me baseball gloves, encouraged me to play, and we broke a couple of windows together.

We used to have lots of discussions. Generally, from street knowledge or listening to conversations in barbershops or poolrooms, you got a pretty decent sample of the arguments going on, and usually I could carry on a talk with anyone. But with Maynard I found myself in quite a quandary, because there was one area I knew absolutely nothing about: Negro history. It was astounding to me, for example, to hear him talk about Nat Turner or to say that blacks had had slaves. I couldn't reply; I just couldn't enter into any of this discussion.

Maynard and I had this thing going where I would quit, or he would fire me, and we had terrific verbal battles. I guess that before I stopped working for him, we'd gone through this routine six or seven times. When I was sixteen, I was working in the photographic concession at a notorious nightclub reputedly used by a lot of the underworld. I left that and went back to trying to make an existence on the streets. My pitch was just being in poolrooms. My brother, five years older, came home on a Navy furlough, and when he found me, he slapped me, called me a bum. Very next day I called an uncle, and through him I got a job in the paper plant where he was working.

In this place, I was telling some guys one day that this country wasn't so great, that whites had stolen the land from the Indians and had made blacks into slaves. They told me I wouldn't dare tell that to the white foreman. But I did, and from then on, he was always trying to find, or manufacture, reasons to get me fired. He used to tell management, "Either that kid Raby goes or I go." Against this, the only kind of power I could have was through the union. I joined the catchall District 50 of the United Mine Workers. In our local, I was already a vice-president when I was only nineteen.

At twenty, the Army drafted me, but with the end of the Korean War I didn't see much point in playing soldier, like running out into the fields and falling down in water, pretending to shoot things that weren't there. So when an office opening came up at the base, I decided to try for it, because I have a very large ego and think I can do anything. The job called for typing, and I went into town to buy a typewriter. Then I was shocked into a level of reality, realizing I couldn't do everything. I discovered that before you can learn to type you have to know how to spell—which I couldn't. I gave up on that job and started studying. I made up my mind I was going back to school. It was an important turning point in my life. Remembering my time with Maynard, I began reading Negro history. I exhausted the post library, which wasn't great, but I wasn't terribly advanced, either. I recall very vividly a rationale supporting the establishment of the Ku Klux Klan. It struck me as being not quite what it ought to be. I went through it anyway. I was getting some insight into the black experience.

After the Army I went to night school and did enough work to graduate from both grade school and high school within a single year.

I took two years at a junior college, hoping I could go on to major in political science at a university and then become a union organizer. I didn't have the money for that. The only totally subsidized state-supported school around was the Chicago Teachers College. It was free. I went to it.

And that was how, and why, I became a schoolteacher.

Chicago

In the early 1960's an educator named Benjamin C. Willis had a distinction of sorts: As the superintendent of Chicago's public schools, he made $48,500 a year, and of all the millions of Americans on public payrolls, only the President of the United States was paid more.

Chicago had liked the looks of Willis when he arrived from Buffalo, New York, in 1953 to take over a system rotting from years of physical neglect and political interference. Hailed as a no-nonsense administrator, he set about spending billions of dollars to remake the educational plant. He put up or expanded 260 school buildings in less than ten years, and some Chicagoans recalled the feats of an earlier Mayor named Thompson who was called Big Bill the Builder.

But as the Willis years went on, blacks burgeoning in the two big corridors spreading south and west noticed something: At a time when the country was extolling the advantages of integrated education, Chicago's schools were getting more segregated. One survey showed that about 90 percent of the black elementary students were in schools 90 percent or more black. Despite the relentless construction, the overcrowding was often so bad that schools ran on double shifts, and Willis sent in trailers as portable classrooms. Blacks promptly named them the Willis Wagons.

Al Raby

Willis wanted neighborhood schools, which of course maintained segregation, and in order to keep it that way, he built schools as fast as possible or used mobile classrooms. To bolster the rationale for construction in black areas, they even tore down usuable buildings in bordering white communities, where some schools were half-empty. Willis not only failed to promote the maximum use of the physical plant, he diverted money into building that could have been used for quality education.

When I started teaching in a West Side grade school in 1960, there were so few whites around that black kids actually thought they were the majority race. We had gangs then, as now. The only difference is that they hadn't yet been politicized into an issue, and the gang violence was of relatively little concern because the general attitude was: "Let the niggers kill the niggers." In my school there were two kids vying for the presidency of the Vice Lords gang, and one of them came to class one day with a hatchet to hit his competition. He was apprehended and taken off to the principal's office. The next morning at nine o'clock he was back in class. I went to the principal to see what the disposition of the case had been, and the dialogue went like this:

Q. Sir, why is Charles back in class?
A. Why shouldn't he be?
Q. He swung a hatchet at a kid yesterday.
A. He was only taking out his aggression.
Q. We ordinarily don't take out aggression that way.
A. What would you have me do with him?
Q. Send him to a social adjustment school?
A. He's fifteen now and there's a six-month waiting list. And at fifteen and a half they don't take anyone.
Q. What happens if the next time he hits a child on the head?
A. Good point. Go make a report, so that if that happens, the school is covered by showing it knew about the tendency.

And that is the level at which the incident was dealt with. The principal was a very decent human being, and yet the limitations of the system required him to give a response which almost made him inhuman.

By that time nearly every professional group in the city had condemned the segregation in the schools. Except, that is, the public schoolteachers. A junior college teacher named Meyer Weinberg had been trying to get the Chicago Teachers Union to take a stand but was unsuccessful, and then he brought a group of us together, thinking this would be a way of putting pressure on the union. The catalytic agent for the meeting was the firing of a black teacher who had joined a mothers' picket line protesting overcrowding at the school where her child was. We created Teachers for Integrated Education, and I later became its president.

On May 17, 1962, we put out 100,000 copies—going into debt to do it—of a pamphlet we called *Hearts and Minds*. We chose the anniversary of the *Brown* decision to say that eight years after the Supreme Court outlawed schools which were separate but equal, Chicago's system was still segregated—and unequal. The next year the Board of Education, feeling community pressure, adopted a plan permitting students to transfer from overcrowded to underutilized schools, which obviously meant that blacks would be with whites. Willis, even though he was supposed to be bound by the board's policy, refused to allow the transfers. When a court enjoined him from doing that he submitted his resignation. Right away, a group of twenty-eight from the State Street merchants, part of the ruling economic group in Chicago, sent a telegram and took out ads demanding that the board refuse to accept his resignation, and also that it withdraw the transfer plan. It wasn't that the merchants were concerned about quality education. For them, the issue was whether this thing would become disruptive to the city, give it a bad image, and whether the political machine could in fact control the situation. Against that muscle, the board backed down, pleaded with Willis to come back, and threw out the transfer plan after he agreed to return.

This became a big issue for the Coordinating Council of Community Organizations (CCCO) which included some religious and many civil rights groups, thirty or forty all told. As a delegate from Teachers for Integrated Education, I voted with the others to call for a one-day boycott of the schools, in which half of the 500,000 enrollment was black. About 225,000 stayed out. Nothing happened, and in 1964, when I had become the convener of CCCO, we went back for another one-day boycott. This time 172,000 were absent. Again, no tangible results. To give us a spurt we asked Martin Luther King to come in for a rally at Soldier Field that summer. At least 100,000 turned out, and in the whole history of the movement's demonstrations it is still second in size only to the March on Washington. For all of us, it was inspirational, but the rally led to nothing concrete. It had no thrust.

In any big city ghetto of the North you have problems in mobilizing people for action. Some say the civil rights issue isn't one that really concerns them. Others say there is nothing that can be done, the whole idea of "You can't fight city hall." Or that the movement didn't really provide any solutions, any meaningful alternative to strive for. Probably the truth is that you can't organize any crusade, except around some symbolic rallying piece, such as the dogs of Birmingham. In the late spring of 1965 that's what Willis became for us.

He was coming up for appointment to his fourth term. Some newspapers were saying he was not indispensable; 125 professors in local universities and seminaries opposed him, and churchmen appealed to Mayor Daley to come out against him. One board member said the choice of Willis was "most unthinkable, ridiculous, reprehensible." The mayor, who appoints the board, which appoints the superintendent, said he wouldn't intervene. The board gave Willis a new four-year contract but said the understanding was he'd only serve a year or so, until he reached sixty-five. I didn't believe that short-term business. I knew that his reappointment was a tremendous mistake, a political miscalculation. And we thought we could put on enough pressure to force the board to reverse itself.

Through CCCO we supported a two-day school boycott—I had by then resigned as a teacher to give full time to the movement. A court enjoined the walkout. I was for violating the injunction, anticipating support, but when there wasn't any, I had to back off. There was talk of marching down the expressway in the center city, but I didn't think anybody was ready to buck that traffic. Finally I said to our people: "I am going to march June 11 on the streets, and I hope as many of you as can will follow me, and those of you can't, stay on the sidewalks and observe and give what support you can." Assuming that a confrontation was necessary to make our point, I was determined to get arrested. We met that day at Soldier Field and began marching to the City Hall. First we took one lane in the streets, and no arrests followed. Then we took two. No arrests. We went clear across the street in all lanes. Still no arrests, and we went all the way to the mayor's office in that formation. The next time we demonstrated there were arrests. I can remember a group of us were taken to a police station lockup, and there we were in the cells, shouting back and forth about how we would do the next demonstration.

When we were bailed out, we put the CCCO organization to work. We went out on almost daily marches; I guess that there were more than 100. About 700 of us were arrested. I was taken to jail eight times; mostly, I was convicted. We blocked traffic, had sprawl-outs on the street, got Martin to come in and lead a gigantic anti-Willis march of more than 15,000 on City Hall. This was at a time when the political machine had been telling reporters we couldn't muster 200 people. Mayor Daley said he had evidence Communists were involved with us. We put out a pamphlet saying it included all of his "evidence." Inside were sixteen pages. All blank.

Dick Gregory, the entertainer who lives in Chicago and is a civil rights activist, kept insisting we shift our marches from City Hall to Mayor Daley's home. All of us remembered how in 1963, Governor Kerner, whose commission later wrote *that* report, said to an NAACP convention that something had to be done about Chicago's ghettos. Daley, who was on the platform, got up, very angry, and said there were no ghettos in Chicago. Day or so later, at an outdoor meeting of the convention, the SNCC people put on such a demonstration, joined in by the audience, that Daley was prevented from speaking. Against that background, I was apprehensive about what would happen if we marched to the Daley home. When we finally did, the crowd was very hostile. The mayor's neighbors told us to "go back to the zoo." As the New York *Times* reported, some little girls sang:

> I'd like to be an Alabama trooper.
> That's what I'd truly like to be.
> 'Cause if I were an Alabama trooper
> I could kill the niggers legally.

People threw rocks at us, as well as eggs and tomatoes, but the police didn't do anything about that. Instead they arrested us, for our "protection." The courts threw that out, of course. Arresting the victims isn't exactly the idea of police work.

During that summer of 1965 a group of important business and industrial leaders, responding to the Urban League, called on the school board to get busy picking Willis' successor. We filed a complaint with Francis Keppel, the U.S. Commissioner of Education, charging the city wasn't entitled to any federal funds because of discrimination in the schools. After an investigation, Keppel shut off $30,000,000 in school aid for the city. Five days later the money was turned back on, with a very flimsy excuse. We think Daley went directly to President Johnson to get Keppel overruled. And we noticed that eventually Keppel resigned under pressure.

Finally, for us in Chicago, we exhausted the moral force of our thing. From demonstrations that ran into the thousands, we were down to where I was leading nine people and a dog. What we needed was help.

Chicago

The help came from Dr. King, who announced he was moving his SCLC "from the sprawling plantations . . . to the desolate slums and ghettos of the North." Specifically, to Chicago, for a full-scale, sustained assault to get more jobs, housing and education for the city's one million blacks. He explained: "Chicago is the test case for the SCLC and indeed for the freedom movement in the North. Chicago is an experiment in faith. Just as Mississippi stands as the largest bastion of crippling *de jure* segregation in the South, Chicago holds equal status as the most hostile bastion of *de facto* segregation in the North."

Al Raby

All you can do for people is to have some vision of their self-worth and to be willing to fight alongside of them and for them, and Martin did that. When we heard that he was thinking about moving North, I kept calling and calling, asking him to come to Chicago. I think he came for a number of reasons: He had been here, he knew something of the personalities involved, and perhaps he had some confidence in them. He was aware of what had been happening here and realized that we probably had the only coordinated community organization in any city. And I believe he really wanted to come North. Starting with Harlem and Watts, SCLC had been responding to riots, running in, trying to do something after the fighting had started, which made his role very difficult. I am sure Martin had a concern about getting a base in some Northern city so that he and SCLC could offer an alternative to rioting.

Chicago

In early 1966, Dr. King moved into a ghetto apartment on Chicago's West Side and set out to do something about a city in which blacks were then about 23 percent of the population, but 43 percent of the unemployed. He noted that Chicago spent an average of $266 a year to educate a black child but used $366 for a white. And he took direct aim on the city's white neighborhoods, where he said real estate interests barred blacks. That summer, plans were made for marches seeking open housing in the all-white areas around Gage Park and Marquette Park.

Al Raby

On Sunday the thirty-first of July, about 200 or 300 of us, not including Martin, who had to be out of town, drove to Marquette Park. Our plan was to assemble, march through the neighborhood, praying in front of real estate offices and churches, and then go back to our cars and leave. The police assured us they'd be looking out for the cars. It wasn't within the realm of our experience that anything would happen to them.

We had whites and blacks. About half were women. We had recruited members from four street gangs to be the marshals for the march, and it was agreed that every one of us would be nonviolent. Even before we left the park, the neighborhood whites were taunting us. They sat down in the path leading out of the park and tried to block us from leaving. When we got by them and marched out onto Seventy-first Street, there were hundreds of whites waiting for us: men, women, teen-agers. I heard them shout, "Get that bastard Raby." They threw bottles and stones at us, cursed us with every profanity the mind can imagine. From homes, they brought out their garden hoses to wet us down or put out lawn furniture and other things to blockade the sidewalks. The cherry bombs were going off all around us. The rocks started coming faster.

After Jesse Jackson, who later became the head of SCLC's Operation Breadbasket in Chicago, was hit, I called to one of the police sergeants along the line of march. He came over and asked if we would get into paddy wagons to be delivered out of the community. I said No, because this seemed a contradiction of what we were supposed to be doing in the spirit of nonviolence. The sergeant had a policeman with him, posing as a radio reporter, with a tape recorder, and the sergeant kept yelling at him, "Get that down! Get that recorded. They don't want to leave. Get that on tape!" I said, "You'd better get that damn microphone out of my face, because I'm trying to see rocks and dodge them." Next thing I knew the sergeant was hit in the stomach with a rock. This seemed like a kind of social justice.

When we started back toward the park, the whites kept yelling, "Nigger, go home," and waving Wallace for President signs, and throwing anything they could find at us. When we got there, we were totally surprised. Two of our cars had been picked up and thrown into the lagoon. Seven of them had been set on fire. Twenty more were overturned. The potential for violence was worse in the park than it had been outside. From my Army days I knew you shouldn't present a standing target. I gave the signal to march out of the park, down Seventy-first Street, to a church where we could take refuge in the black community on the other side of Ashland Avenue.

No police accompanied us. We marched on one side of the street, while a group of teen-age whites ran up and down the other. The gang members we had as marshals positioned themselves between us and the whites, and often they would catch, barehanded, the stones and bricks thrown at us, so we would not get hurt. Because they were playing a role, they never once turned violence back upon the whites. Every time one of them would make a good catch, we'd applaud. On occasion, even those doing the throwing would cheer.

For eight long blocks we marched that way, getting hit now and then, seeing store windows broken. At Ashland a group of policemen with shotguns was preventing blacks from going west into the white area and stopping whites from going east into the black community. I caught the eye of one young white police officer, and I kept giving him such a dirty look that he could tell I was silently asking him, "Where were you when we needed you?" Finally he yelled over, "Why look at me that way? It's not my fault." Which was absolutely correct. I think that on this day the policy of the Police Department was that they were willing to let us get the hell beat out without dealing with any of the consequences of that. They made only fourteen arrests. But it was all on television, and the national consequence of what they had tolerated was more than they could bear. When we marched the following Friday into Gage Park—this time Martin was with us—there were a number of black policemen on hand, and clearly the conscious determination was to make arrests.

I rode out to Gage with Martin. When we got there, he said, "Let's get out of the car. Nothing is going to happen. These people aren't going to do anything." We left the driver there and walked to the head of the line. Nobody saw the stone that hit Martin. He fell to one knee, and two United Auto Worker guys standing next to him pushed him down, then stood over him to cover him, protect him, while the mob was shouting, "Kill him." We didn't know how badly Martin had been hurt. It turned out he had only really been stunned, and we went on with the march.

Again, there was that terrible noise of people shouting at us. Women were among the most vicious, screaming "you monkeys" at the blacks and "you white trash" at the others. They called all of us *apes* or told the blacks to go back to Africa. When we knelt in prayer in front of a real estate office, the whites threw rocks at us, cursed the nuns, and yelled to the priests that there wouldn't be anything in the collection boxes on Sunday. A nineteen-year-old with us was hit by a thrown knife. The Confederate flag was waved at us. So were banners boosting George Lincoln Rockwell and the American Nazi Party. The police made fifty-one arrests. It must have been a difficult position for the white policemen. Their sympathies were undoubtedly with the community, but they were getting stoned as well as we were. I noticed later that police called our line of march "Bloody California Avenue," and a lieutenant said it had to rate with the worst nights in their history.

Chicago

It was SCLC's last great confrontation in the North. Nobody had any more stomach for violence, Chicago-style. The marches were called off, meetings set up, and finally it was announced that Dr. King, Daley, Raby and community leaders had agreed to the creation of the Leadership Council for Metropolitan Open Housing, with a specific set of goals. It was a hydra-headed face-saver. Dr. King could leave town publicly claiming victory while Chicago was left to decide for itself how much would be done. Raby left CCCO to work on a master's degree.

Al Raby

If we measure ourselves by goals which are unrealistic to begin with, we will always be failures. And I don't think that Martin or any of us realized what a tough town this is and how strong the Democratic organization is. For us, it had to be a learning process in understanding the power structure. What Daley has done is to co-alesce the major economic interests around the question of the center city's survival, making it as palatable as possible for businesses, while, by and large, forgoing most of the other problems. The mer-

348   *Odyssey: Journey Through Black America*

chants and financiers let Daley have City Hall in return for protection of their enterprises.

For the black man, surviving in what Martin called Chicago's ghettos of race, misery and poverty, this means that even if Daley woke with a vision on how to solve the city's problems, he wouldn't be allowed to do it. He became a leader out of a definition of what he was to do with his power, and he cannot stay a leader if he works for the ghettos, because that is not included in the definition. In Chicago they keep on putting up buildings, but they don't think about people in any meaningful way, and always the primary concerns are economic.

So I have no hesitation in saying Martin was not the Second Coming for Chicago. Of course, he didn't accomplish everything. It frustrates me, and it angers me, that people keep looking for instant miracles. The greatness of Martin—and the tragedy of the way in which we perceive him—was that he was nothing but a human being. If we make a martyr of him, we don't have to emulate him, just as we don't try to emulate Christ. Nobody feels it is his responsibility to be crucified.

If you ask me to measure concretely what we achieved in Chicago I have to say, "Very little." We got rid of Willis, but the system goes on as bad as ever. I have very little confidence in the ability of institutions to make changes in society. I am coming to believe that we are in for a much larger and longer fight than any of us thought it was going to be. No one knows how much time is left to solve our racial problems. The death of Martin stepped up the timetable of violence so that our choice now is between a permanent military force on the streets, or finding serious solutions. And what is hard to live with is that even after we have gone through the Martin Luther Kings, the Jim Formans, Al Rabys, Stokely Carmichaels, Fred Hamptons and everybody else, *there may never be an answer!* You are frustrated because your analysis tells you that probably there is no solution in our time, yet you continue to work as if there were one. It is a real, it seems to me, internal conflict.

People do have less hope about this country. And if there is to be, as some say, greater repression of the black community one can only sit it out. What can we do? We accept life and death, right? While we want to prevent it, we know that someday death knocks on our door, and we got to be gone. I don't want to believe it, but my mind tells me that it is inevitable. When the doctor said my brother was dying from cancer, I sat by his bed, and if somebody had walked in and said I could save him by flipping over three times, I'd have flipped over three times. Not believing it was going to save him, but being willing to try. When he died, I accepted it and went out of the room. And I came back to bury him.

So now I'll sit back and help bury America. So what?

Hard Hats and Black Men

Chicago

On the morning of July 22, 1969, Chicago's hard-hat building trades workers got acquainted with the black revolution. About 200 blacks converged on the Loop block where a 59-story skyscraper was being put up for a bank. They stopped a cement truck from making its delivery, then swarmed over the work stations to halt construction temporarily. When asked why, they shouted: "Ten thousand jobs for black men!"

Shortly before nine o'clock, 17 demonstrators, wearing the red and black berets usually designating street gang membership, left the site to walk four blocks to another building. They took elevators to the fourteenth floor, arriving just as a secretary was opening the offices of the Chicago Building Trades Council. After telling the woman to leave, the young men locked themselves in. Police, sent in about an hour later, demanded the youths come out. When they did, they were lined against a wall to be frisked for weapons and then were booked for criminal trespass.

The next day other building sites were picketed, and apprehensive contractors and building owners sent the workers home. There was more picketing the next day, and the day after that, until in two weeks construction had been stopped on more than $80,000,000 worth of work, including a University of Chicago library, two hospitals, a high school named for Martin Luther King, housing projects and one of the country's largest nonprofit low-rent apartment complexes. For the first time, masses of black men, regarding themselves as virtually frozen out of the building trades unions, were saying that if there were no work for blacks, there would be none for anyone.

What began on the streets of Chicago took root elsewhere, so that there were labor demonstrations in Pittsburgh and Seattle and concern in the minds of black men everywhere who felt injustice at the hands of the building trades unions.

C. T. Vivian

We made it plain that it wasn't enough for organized labor to ship $35,000 to the striking hospital workers in Charleston. The liberal actions of yesterday are not adequate for today. To talk of giving us money or organizing us for the unions' benefit, that is out. What we want is in, and on an equal basis in all operations. In Chicago we reached the nitty gritty for black people: survival. In this fight you may not win, but fight you must. Everybody who has ever worked for change in this city has been sharpened by the depth of the opposition to it. To struggle at all in Chicago is to be made wiser and more resourceful and resilient, because this is one tough town!

Odyssey

"I am an activist," said C. T. Vivian. He is also an ordained minister, published writer, teacher, editor, community organizer, father of six. As the coordinator of the Coalition for United Community Action, representing sixty-one groups, the Reverend Mr. Vivian was in the vanguard of the confrontation with the hard hats. He was there, he said, because there was no other place for him to be.

C. T. Vivian

There is a religious devotional that goes:

> Answer back to the love of God,
> In whatever circumstance you find yourself.

That has been most important in my life. I am an activist because I know my duty is to answer back and I do not worry because the same Lord that called me is the one who will take care of the circumstance.

There is a peace that comes from that, one which gives me strength and encourages me to fight on in a country which has always been racist. Against this condition, we common folk, the disadvantaged, the disinherited, the poor black, white, yellow and brown are saying: "Open the doors to us." Revolution is not in our hands to determine. All we can do is take a radical stance, and how much the institutions of this society give us will decide if the people are to rise up in wildness born from frustration. If this system would let masses of people make $4 an hour, those now talking revolution couldn't get an audience anywhere.

White America—we blacks are ready. It is you who are not. All you have wanted was for us to stand here, with our hands out, begging, while you slapped us in the mouth. And then you ask: "Why do we get mean?" It is like somebody is breaking our legs and blaming us for limping.

Odyssey

On the wall in back of Vivian's desk there was a photo blowup showing the almost ethereal figure of a black woman silhouetted against the sun, her hands stretching to the light. For Vivian, she personified "the whole thing of blackness, reaching for the sun, the dream, the vision." When Vivian talked, he populated his scenes with drama and mysticism and power, just by the cadence and imagery of his words. He was then forty-six, tall and angular, a tautly strung man. He was a medium brown, and he kept his mustache immaculately trimmed. Every so often he'd lean back, look up, and as he did so, he closed one eye, like somebody focusing on a distant target.

C. T. Vivian

In the Missouri countryside around Boonville people having picnics used to ask my father's father to get up on a buckboard to make a speech, just so they could hear him talking. He was the black principal of a school, a truly educated man, and he named his son Cordy, saying his inspiration was an ancient orator. In turn, it was given to me, with mother's family names added, so that when I was born in July of 1924, I was Cordy Tindell Vivian. But I didn't even learn how to spell all of that until I was in third grade, because everybody just called me C. T.

My mother and father were divorced. I can only remember seeing him once, many years later. For my first six years I lived mostly with my grandmother in Boonville. A small woman, with long beautiful hair that had been white since she was thirteen or fourteen, she was a pretty thing, deeply religious, devoted to education. My grandmother was very fair, and she had a speech she used to give every so often. The burden of it was: She didn't ask to be born that light.

The wisdom of common folk is something to behold. As far as I am concerned, my grandmother was smarter than I, and my mother had intuitions I will never have. I saw them plan ahead, to create the strategy that has been the salvation of me. The average black family has always honored education, even if the opportunities were often denied them, and my mother and grandmother knew the importance of it. They wanted to go North, where the schools were desegregated. And they wanted to be in a college town, so that no matter what happened economically, I could stay at home and still get a college education. The town they chose was Macomb, Illinois, about 120 miles north of St. Louis, 40 miles east of the Mississippi, and the home of Western Illinois University.

When I came into the Macomb school as a first grader, the classes for that year had already been going on a couple of months; the cliques and friendships had jelled. I was picked on, not only as a newcomer, but also because my mother loved pretty clothes and she dressed me in them. I can still remember how, when class was over, I'd take out through a back door, run right past a lumberyard's big sandpile near the school, and hit up an alley to get straight home. But one night I had to stay late, and when I came out into the yard, I didn't see any other kids. Just as I got to the sandpile a whole bunch of them who'd been waiting for me rose up and circled around. Their leader sent in one kid to fight me. I licked him. He sent in another. I licked him. Then I turned to the leader and I said, "Don't send anybody else—you come in!" Well, he thought that was about enough for the day and there was no more fighting. Next morning the kids who'd heard what happened were all staring at me, one guy in particular. I walked over to him and said, "What do you want?" "Nothing, nothing," he said. Ever since it has been my thing that if something is threatening, go to meet it, don't wait for it.

My best buddy as I went along in grade school was Frank Thompson. White boy, big. We had a heck of a fight one day, knocked each other down six times, got up, shook hands, and from that time on we were together. Wasn't hardly anyone that either one of us couldn't challenge, and we policed that schoolyard. We didn't let no big kids mess over any little ones, white or black. One of my good black friends was trying to take a swing away from a smaller boy when he saw Frank and me coming up. It was only recess, but he got so scared he ran home, didn't come back the rest of the day.

In those years I was living with my mother in a house catty-corner from where my grandmother lived. I grew up with no family beyond the two women in my life. The fact is, when I took an IQ test in the sixth grade, I was rated lower than I wanted to be because I just flunked the whole section dealing with relatives. I didn't know what a second cousin was or an uncle, any of that.

My grandmother went to church regularly, and so did I. From the beginning, as I see it, religion meant something to me. They tell me that when I was very small, my mother had punished me for something by saying I couldn't go to church that night. I ran out to the road and laid down, just waiting for someone to run over me. That's how badly I felt. But my mother, who was more or less in permanent revolt against my grandmother, was always skeptical about religion, at least for her. She said that when I was baptized, I went in as a dry devil and came out a wet one. It was because of my grandmother that I knew the great Scriptures, which helped shape my life. With the Scriptures, no matter how young, you are already in the world of great thoughts, you have the prophets running around in your head, and all the world's wisdom is there for you to know.

People always told me they thought I would be a preacher. Funny, for it never appealed to me. I wanted to be a doctor. Today I can perceive that I was only thinking of helping people, and medicine was my first way of going at that. But I was a flop at high school chemistry, which made me face the reality I was for the social sciences, not the physical. But this time I was also thinking that a doctor patches up a condition and sends the patient back into the world. The idea came to me that maybe it is of first importance to do something about the causal condition. In addition, I was realizing that not all experience has to be explained logically. When I was very sick, unconscious, from an appendix inflammation, my grandmother sat by my hospital bed. She claimed she knew I was dying and that she prayed the devils away. Next morning I woke up, beginning my recovery. I know enough now to not be as skeptical as I was yesterday, just enough not to take anything as stupid. Shakespeare's lines in Macbeth are:

> If you can look into the seeds of time,
> And say which grain will grow and which will not,
> Speak then to me. . . .

First time I read that, it shook me.

One of my high school English teachers, Mrs. Morris, heightened all my sense of literature. She gave us that understanding of how great writing fits with the whole integrity of man. From her teaching, my desire was to be part of the intellectual life that comes only from books and the flow of ideas. I read my first anthology of black poetry. Wasn't a single poem that didn't move me. I came to have some appreciation of the black identity thing; that summer I went natural. Which for me, meant letting my hair grow without using glob on it.

Odyssey

Just as his mother and grandmother had planned, Vivian went through high school and Western Illinois University, all without leaving Macomb. He married, divorced, married again, took a variety of jobs, in youth work, writing, selling. In the fall of 1955, while working for the Helen Gallagher-Foster mail-order house in Peoria, Illinois, he was in the warehouse one day, when . . .

C. T. Vivian

I still don't know whether I said the words or whether they were just so loud within my being that it seemed like I was saying them. They were: "Lord, I don't want to work for anybody but You, ten or twelve hours a day." Up to that point I was always struggling with myself, trying to see the directions of my life. Once I defined what it was I wanted to do, everything became clear, and things happened that I had no way of predicting. I thought the firm's Frank Gallagher would be angry with me for leaving, but as a deeply religious cat himself he could see what I was doing. Both he and my church offered me money, because I had none. My wife was pregnant with our second child, and when I wavered in my determination, she remembered how I was always saying, "Where is your faith?" and then put that thought back to me by asking: "Whose faith is in question now?" I said, "All right, baby!" I hitchhiked to the National Baptist convention, then going on in St. Louis, and there I was offered financial assistance to attend the American Baptist Theological Seminary in Nashville. The incredible thing is that before then I had never even heard of the school; yet within three weeks of telling the Lord I wanted only to work for Him all the arrangements had been made for me to go there.

Events continued to fall for me. When my wife, who had stayed in Peoria, told me she was coming down to Nashville with our two children, I said, "I don't have any way to take care of you here." She said she was coming, and I said, "I understand." Unbelievably, a cottage suddenly opened in the married couple's section at the school. Next, the National Baptist Convention offered me an editor's job on the Sunday School Publishing Board, and every talent I ever had was suddenly at work. For someone to say this was an accidental combination of circumstances, well, let them say it.

Across my desk at the publishing house there began to come the speeches of a young minister who had moved to Montgomery, Alabama. Martin Luther King. I had never met him, but when I read what he had to say, I had a concern that it be preserved. What he was doing was giving us the philosophy of nonviolence. The techniques I had known long before; in 1944 we had used them in opening the lunch counters and restaurants of Peoria, but we didn't see what to do next because we didn't grasp the great body of thought that was behind the action. It took ten years for Martin Luther King to give us that philosophy and to put his body in support of it, so that the Word became flesh and dwelt among us. The first time I actually heard him talk I had to stand in the aisle of a Nashville church, and I took it all on a tape recorder, because his speech had the ring: *This is it!*

It was only natural for me to go into the Nashville movement, which produced more people still known nationally than any other civil rights action in the country. In seminary with me were John Lewis, Bernard Lafayette, Jim Bevel. Our teacher in nonviolence was Jim Lawson. We did the lunch counter sit-ins in Nashville, and I led the march of 4,000 to the City Hall. I was on the first freedom rides. In Chattanooga, where I was called to a church after leaving seminary, I helped open the entire downtown area to blacks, and I was both a board member and on the executive committee for the Tennessee Voters Council. In four consecutive elections our Chattanooga group got as high as 80 percent of the black vote to the polls.

In 1963 Martin Luther King, who by then was "Doc" to me, asked me to join SCLC, which I did, as the director of affiliates. In the action at Albany, Birmingham, St. Augustine and Selma I was shot at, nearly drowned twice, and was jailed half a dozen times. But what I wanted to do most at SCLC was train others for the future. In Alabama I put together a statewide education program in which we took 150 young people who had just graduated from high school but who did not appear to have the qualifications for getting into college. By summer's end we had 107 still with us, and every single one passed college entrance tests and was admitted. When we took the project to Washington for funding, a Johnson administration man said, "This is a college Head Start program." The government wouldn't deal with us; but it took what we had, and the next year they came out with something like our plan, called it Upward Bound.

After Selma, I knew we were headed into a new period. We had to go North, and that was going to take a lot more sophistication, a much deeper understanding of what the American culture really is. For example: When the black revolution moved out of the South, it was no longer fashionable in the North to be for it, and the intellectual, emotional, financial white base for the movement vanished. The superficial talk in explaining this was: "In the South you could get high, but not close. Whereas in the North you could get close, but not high." The truer explanation is that after Selma our issues changed.

When we dealt with voting rights in the South, the North did not object because the North had already given that to blacks. But when we started impinging on the North's economic issues, then we were face to face with the very basics of life. We became involved over housing fit for the twentieth century, not just a roof. We treated education as a fact, not merely a schoolhouse. We dealt with money in a way intended to let families rear children in dignity, not as simply something to do. When you fight at these levels, then society is against you, and those who are the haves are not concerned about whether the have-nots are right or wrong, where the justice or injustice is. They see the others only as competition, and they do not intend to be competed with, because they may lose!

We are confronted with an America that is stuck together by competitiveness, not decency. That's why the level of humanity is so low, the sense of brutality so high. And it is only a fact of history to say that we have this understanding of the country because the movement was the acid that stripped away all the lying, the hypocrisy, and let us see what America is truly like.

Going into this arena, we needed a different kind of guy, one who didn't merely protest, but both protested and programmed. Change could no longer be superficial; it had to be real. In this world of urban confrontation, the issues, by definition, were infinitely more complicated than we had ever dealt with. But as Walt Whitman put it, "Every struggle only makes a greater struggle necessary."

In Chicago at that time the Urban Training Center for Christian Mission had been set up for ministers by Kim Myers, later the Episcopal Bishop of California. The center needed a director for its Ford Fellowship program, and I became that guy. I left SCLC, to become concerned about orientating clergy to go back into their milieu with an understanding of the fight we were undertaking.

Odyssey

Vivian was still directing the fellowship work in 1968, when the coalition of sixty-one community organizations came to see him about a small grocery chain named the Red Rooster Stores.

C. T. Vivian

The coalition wanted me to be executive director, leading the fight against the selling practices of the stores. I said, "No, no, there is a changing style of leadership." I said, "We will all meet in a circle and agree what must be done." Using Christian language, I said I would be *servant*; I would be their coordinator, their spokesman.

Our group included what White America calls street gangs. Why shouldn't they be with us? Their parents were buying from those stores. We wanted prices to be in line with those across the city. In Red Rooster we were paying more than the well-to-do were paying for food. Another thing: Why should any store in the black areas be able to pick up a *nigger,* so to speak, who will work for any amount of money? We deserve the same pay anyone else gets, and we wanted that from Red Rooster. With our picketing, our educational tactics, we got a contract in which the chain agreed to our demands. They kept it for a while, then ignored it, and finally they went out of business.

For a couple of months after that, we continued to sit around in our circle, talking about the next issue to rally the people. It came to us that this had to be Model Cities. When you think about it this could be the Marshall Plan for blacks, if, that is, we run our own communities. If we don't, then the white labor union workers will come in to do the program's construction and take their money to spend elsewhere, leaving us as impoverished as ever. There was a bill in Congress saying indigenous blacks should build Model Cities housing in their own areas, and we spelled out what we wanted to Secretary George Romney in Housing and Urban Development. But when he said the program would be handled by the mayors, we knew that wouldn't give us anything in Chicago.

So we said: "All right, we will attack the labor unions, because we have got to be in the building trades training programs. If we don't get into them, the unions will say they looked for qualified black workers, but couldn't find any and had to use whites. And they will say that there is such a big emergency they have to get going immediately, leaving no time to develop anybody. It's not that big a crisis for us. The emergency we see is that we are not working, which means we don't control our communities, which means we don't decide the priorities of what happens on our own turf."

According to the census, blacks are about a third of Chicago's population. We have only about 3 percent of the 90,000 building trades members. Around that simple fact, black men can unify. They know that men who have been trained can say to their children: "There is nothing wrong with me. I know how to work. The wrong is with a society that won't let me have a job." Not only does this give them a manhood with their children, it also makes them willing participants in creating our social change.

And so in this city, black men went out to the building sites, and they said to the white workers: "Would you fellows please leave until we can negotiate our coming into the unions?" In the whole history of the movement this was the first time where 99 percent of the action was by men. It wasn't women, no mothers carrying babies. It was men who were saying: "Whites will not work on our soil, unless we do, too."

The labor issue was far more profound than any fight for consumer protection or open housing. We have gone from abstractions, like freedom, into specifics. We addressed ourselves to jobs that were fit for the twentieth century, that met the needs of the nation. We didn't want to take work from whites; we only asked to be included when the swelling demand for workers came onto the scene. We asked for 4,000 training slots a year. Nothing vague about that. Just plain mathematics.

Odyssey

However plain, the mathematics added to no easy solution. The trade union people turned down the demands, saying their men were being forced off the job by menacing groups of street gang members. There were arrests, clashes between picketers and police. A court injunction limited the demonstrations. The Reverend Mr. Abernathy, in bringing SCLC's convention to Chicago for an impromptu session, said, "Chicago is the contemporary Rome. It is the Midwest capital of the most imperialistic empire of the world. Racist labor leaders do not represent the only problem in Chicago. Mayor Daley is the Caesar who reigns here in Rome."

The federal government called a hearing on the coalition's charges that the unions discriminated against blacks. When the session opened in a hotel room designed for 150, about 1,000 construction workers jammed the place, forcing Labor Department officials to reschedule it in the U.S. Customshouse. More than 2,000 whites cordoned the building, and while 250 police stood by, taking no action, a solid phalanx of hard hats blocked all doors, denying admission to anyone black or known to be friendly to the coalition. Even government employees assigned to the hearing were turned away.

When Vivian came with his wife, the crowd crushed in around them, shouting, "No coalition!" and "Get out of here, nigger." As this happened, police did wade into to rescue them and lead them to a squad car. Vivian made one more attempt but was again pushed back and returned to the police car which subsequently was pelted with beer cans.

An extra 400 police were sent in, greeted on their arrival by cheers from the construction workers. A government official said he pleaded for ninety minutes with a city lawyer on the scene to have police clear the area so witnesses could get in. The city's lawyer, said the federal man, refused. When some whites rushed toward a small group of blacks, one of the latter fired a gun into the air four times. That touched off a ten-minute black-white-police battle. Five men, four of them policemen, were hurt. Eight arrests were made. It was, said Vivian, "a labor riot, in a city where, during the 1968 convention, there had been a police riot."

C. T. Vivian

Chicago made us see ourselves as the ugly nation we are. Mayor Daley realized that there was going to be outright confrontation between the white laborers of this city and black men. And acting as a conciliator, he called us all together to start the meetings in which we could work out our differences.

We finally got was what some call the Chicago Plan. It specified that every year 1,000 blacks would be upgraded into building trades journeymen, 1,000 would get the finishing training necessary to be journeymen, 1,000 would be admitted into an apprenticeship program, and 1,000 new recruits would be training. In contrast to the government's Philadelphia Plan, which gave the U.S. power to enforce the hiring of blacks, ours was a good-faith proposition, with no enforcement provisions. We knew it was far from ideal, that it had language such as saying the plan would be implemented "given no change in the economic conditions" and other loopholes.

Six months after our agreement was reached I said the plan was not working. Blacks simply were not being admitted into the building trades unions. But this is more than a numbers game. What we began in Chicago was a process, which at its flood tide, could be the Wagner Act for blacks. You can see I am talking about first steps, not about the completion of anything. We are opening doors for the first time. The guidelines of yesterday no longer work today; what we believed then we do not believe now. The beginning of the black revolution was a period of tokenism, when action was dependent on one of our myths. We thought that if only white people would come in contact with us, if we protested and were let in, you'd see how good we are. We thought whites were loving enough to accept a loving people. But what we found was that there isn't enough love in America, there isn't enough of a respect for humanity, for that to happen. We felt you were ignorant, but you weren't. You were vicious! We were really concerned about democracy. The people in charge of this country could be less concerned about that.

I don't know where we are all going. In the 1940's, and '50's, and '60's, we worked very hard to create something which would come to fruition in the 1970's. But now the '70's are here, and we may have to wait until the '80's and the '90's before blacks can go from a situation of survival to one of arrival. I would like to have one decade where I know I am producing, where the fellows around me are doing something about all our lives—black, white, pink and polka dot. It really would be wonderful, just to see that.

There is a line from Coretta King that means something to me. "Maybe," she said, "what America needs is a white Martin Luther King."

There Will Be No Peace, Freddie

Odyssey

The police officers assigned to the state's attorney's office drew out a .45-caliber submachine gun and three 12-gauge shotguns from a police arsenal. Other policemen had their own shotguns or carried handguns, so that all fourteen men picked for the raiding party were armed. They had no tear gas, no lighting equipment, no loudspeaker sound amplifiers to call for a surrender before any shooting began.

At 4:45 A.M. on December 4, 1969, the raiders, who had a search warrant to look for illegal weapons, went to the Chicago apartment of Fred Hampton, Illinois chairman of the Black Panther Party. They shot Hampton to death in his bed. They killed another Panther, wounded four others, then charged the seven survivors of the raid with attempted murder. Sergeant Daniel Groth, who led the police, explained: "There must have been six or seven of them firing. The firing must have gone on for 10 or 12 minutes. If 200 shots were exchanged, that was nothing." State's Attorney Edward V. Hanrahan praised his men for "restraint" in the face of what he called a "vicious" Panther "attack." A report from Police Superintendent James B. Conlisk, Jr., said the raiders "were subjected to deadly assault by firearms" as he announced his department's investigation "shows no misconduct by the police officers involved."

And that, on the surface, left the incident as just another police-Panther shoot-out.

But it wasn't.

For Black America, it became one of those stunningly clear moments when White America stood naked. Even Mayor Daley's friend Alderman Metcalfe could confess to an uneasiness, and he joined others in asking for an investigation. The Panthers said Hampton had been "murdered" as part of a conscious plan to exterminate the party. Scoffing at this, Hanrahan released, but only to the Chicago *Tribune,* pictures of the shot-up apartment. *Tribune* captions said the photographs showed "bullet holes" from Panther shots. In fact, however, the "holes" were nailheads, something the Panthers displayed to thousands who toured the shooting scene.

Months later a 250-page report from a federal grand jury investigating the case said that instead of the Panthers' unleashing "deadly assault" the evidence showed proof of only one Panther shot, while police were said to have fired at least eighty-two times. The jury said the police crime laboratory made serious errors because it set out to find only what supported the officers' version of the incident. The performance of the police Internal Investigation Division, said the jury, was "so seriously deficient it suggests purposeful malfeasance." Superintendent Conlisk described himself as "flabbergasted" when the jury informed him that his own department's investigation included discussing with the raid's leader both the questions to be asked and the suggested answers. The official in charge of the police investigation division said it was the worst inquiry he had ever seen and agreed that it could be called a whitewash.

Hanrahan's office decided to drop all charges against the seven survivors of the raid. The Chicago Bar Association, along with other groups, won court permission for an independent prosecutor and a special grand jury to determine on a local level whether crimes had been committed.

We knew something about the twenty-one-year-old man whose killing led to all that. Shortly before his death we spent a number of hours with Fred Hampton, and what he told us, about himself, his life, his beliefs, amounts to his last testament. When we saw him, we didn't know death had already marked him. He did. "Everybody's got to die," he said. "It's no big deal."

Fred Hampton

If it is the last thing I say, it is that there is nothing but jail, exile or murder for a Black Panther. And until the people relate to this, we are going to have to keep going to jail, keep on being run out of the country, keep on being murdered. It happens to all revolutionaries, and we are going to have to deal from that fact. I'm willing to bet that the people that is jailed, exiled and murdered in this period, 1968, 1969, 1970, and 1966, and all back there, one day these are going to be the people who will be in *Who's Who in America,* because they are going to be the ones who made this country, brought out the issues, forced the people into confrontation, into making a commitment.

That's our job. It's worth it.

I think everybody sees what I see, gets mad about what I get mad about wants to change what I want to change. And I can spell it. It's rats and roaches, it's Red Devils, the pills, barbiturates, the poverty program. It's police brutality, undecent housing. It's seeing people who go to jail because they don't have an understanding of the law. It's watching policemen come into places with their uniforms on and use those uniforms for the same purpose the Mafia used them in the St. Valentine's Day massacre. It's that feeling of realizing people, of whom you are a part, have a lack of education and then understanding that you either have to live with that—to say, "Well, that's just too bad, but I can educate myself; I am not illiterate"—or else you have to make a commitment and say, "It's my job to go into the masses, to try to educate them, and to learn from them."

It's a feeling I have for people. I think you need that, with an understanding of the problem, and you have to have the courage. If I had a son, I would tell him that I would rather see him fight and lose than not fight at all. History is going to show that the ones who were wrong were those who did nothing. People can sit by, while a genocidal situation comes upon them, going to the gas chambers, and so profound and redundant in their bullshit that "it's never going to happen to me." And the last words they uttered while they were choking was: "This couldn't be true." And if we don't get ourselves together, people are going to be shocked, because they will be saying the same words over here.

But so long as there is a Black Panther Party, black people can take a constructive role. We are putting out revolutionary programs people can relate to. We say, "You are hungry—you eat for free. Don't have to stand in line and wait to prove you are poor, don't have to live in a certain community, mile square," and all that kind of bullshit. We're opening a health clinic, because if you are sick, you deserve medical treatment. The Black Panther Party is humanity in movement. People are tired of all the old petitions and hypocritical shit. That's why they relate to the Panthers' programs.

Our job is to make revolutionary black power. In America, you are going to have two, three, many Vietnams, right here, because we are going to have a people's war. The masses are running around now, saying, "All Power to the People," and they understand what that means.

They know that the people need the power.

Odyssey

The Black Panthers, who believe with Mao Tse-tung that political power grows out of the barrel of a gun, came into national prominence with guns, but without firing a shot. During a debate on gun controls, twenty-six Panthers marched into the California legislature on May 2, 1967, openly carrying shotguns, rifles and pistols to demonstrate their objections. There was pandemonium, lawmakers scurrying under desks and taking other cover. But the Panthers let the security guards take the weapons and unload them. When they were returned, the Panthers marched out. No charges were placed against them because they were within the law as long as the guns were not concealed.

Against that backdrop, with a nation suddenly listening, Panther founder Huey P. Newton said his organization was for self-defense. He said the party had chosen the black cat for its symbol because "it is not in the panther's nature to strike first; but when he is backed into a corner he will respond viciously and wipe out the aggressor." There was in White America, however, something menacing about black men with guns, and the Panthers took on the aura of black racists who would kill all whites.

One reason was that the Panthers talked in revolutionary rhetoric; they rarely let White America penetrate that to see the human beings under their leather coats, their black berets, their loaded bandoleers. They either scorned the white press or demanded hundreds of dollars as the price of an interview, the date for which might or might not be kept.

That wasn't Fred Hampton's style. We were in New York when we telephoned him for an appointment. He said he'd be available at noon on a certain day, and when we arrived, he saw us—at noon. We had two more meetings with him, and each time he met us exactly on schedule.

Hampton was big—six feet two, 215 pounds—and wore boot-style shoes. In the second-floor room where he saw us in the Panther headquarters, 2350 West Madison Street, deep in Chicago's West Side black belt, there was a little dais, and he sat up there, motioning us to take two seats in front of him.

Fred Hampton

My parents were working-class, although some might say we were petty bourgeoisie. We were living in Argo, Illinois, about 12 miles out of Chicago, when I was born. My father is a decorator, painter, at the Corn Products plant at Argo. He's been there around twenty-four years. My mother is at the same place, eleven or twelve years, I guess. I've got a brother and a sister. I'm the youngest.

I went to school in Blue Island, Illinois, and then to Maywood, another Chicago suburb. I participated in sports when I was young; I was just like any regular student. First two years of high school I was in wrestling and football, but then I couldn't relate to that, because it was crazy. There is racism in all these sports, and it is pathetic. You'd be playing fullback and a white cat would be quarterback, and they'd have you run and break your leg all the way to the two-yard line. You done did all the running, but nothing got put in the paper, because the white cat scores the touchdown. It wasn't important for me to get in the paper no way, because I didn't want to be no big football player. What Malcolm X is saying in these times is more important than what a Joe Namath is saying.

First time I was arrested, I was about fifteen or sixteen. We had a march in Maywood. See, I had been investigating civil rights groups; it was a feeling I had about the way things were going. Just didn't seem right. I saw a whole lot of shit, people getting brutalized, dogs put on them, on the children. It wasn't only in the South. There was plenty up here, too, things wrong in the community where I lived, Maywood.

In high school we were having demonstrations on most of everything: black studies, the grounds around the building, the black kind of thing. Because I was mostly leading, they would kick me out, especially in my senior year, but I finally did get my degree. In the neighborhood I was out there trying to get a swimming pool for the people, for the children. There was no recreation in Maywood, but the whites in the town could easily get in the pools, the gymnasiums in other communities. When the blacks wanted to do that, the excuse of geographical boundaries was used to keep them out. We demonstrated, and now we have a swimming pool in Maywood.

We also had a situation in Maywood where the police liked to beat up on people. I've been arrested quite a few times. It's not the beatings, because that doesn't last long. But people like to charge you with things you didn't do. In trying to keep the police from jumping on me I've ended up being charged with aggravated assault. And when you see it happening to other people, you see the problem is too widespread to be overlooked.

I was always logical. Ever since I can remember, I was trying to figure things out. My parents tell me that when I was small, I would do that. I never took anything for granted. I used to do a lot of reading, lot of studying, lot of talking, lot of thinking. I saw atrocities committed that I don't know how people could overlook. Every day in the paper there is a case of police brutality, case of false arrest. You see people's houses burning down in oppressed communities because the Fire Department doesn't get there soon enough. Ambulance don't get there; people get asphyxiated. People get sick, and they go to the hospital, and it's like slaughterhouses, and they have to wait hours on end just to get in.

I don't think there is anything overwhelming about my commitment to do something about these conditions. People try to make this out more of a miraculous-type thing than it really is. I think we should go to some Negro who has never been involved, or said anything, and ask him, "When did you make the *miraculous* decision that you weren't going to get involved?" We got some fools walking around here that are so interested in exploiting people to make money that they will do any goddamn thing. These are the motherfuckers you ought to be interviewing and ask them where they get their ideology.

We got a whole lot of old people around who did nothing but cause the problem, and a lot of them need to shut up and let young people tell them some things. Maybe age does nothing but put gray hair on your head, and we can do that with dye! So, if that is all it does for some people, I'll dye my hair and claim to have as much experience as they do. Because all they could ever have experienced is oppression. But I have experience in trying to rid myself and my people of oppression, and what I want to know is what these Negroes are thinking of, you know? I mean, if there is a fire in this room and I get up and run out for some water, but you sit here and be calm, it seems

like to me I ought to ask you: "What are you doing?" Those are the
people who are the walking-around dead.

Malcolm said it a long time ago: "You are going to see horrors
that horrify, terrors that terrorize." That's why young people are beginning to think for themselves. I have been in the struggle a very
long time. Five, six years ago Stokely Carmichael came to town to
speak for SNCC. Bobby Rush, the deputy minister of defense for the
Panthers in Illinois, was at that time in SNCC. They wanted me to
start a SNCC in Maywood, which I did, because they were working
some grass-roots things with the masses. I was also in NAACP, president of its Youth Council, and I was in CORE.

Every time King came to the city I would travel with him. I still
claim the masses never were with him. All the time he would be
marching, the people in the pool hall would be standing inside looking out, and, if you noticed, the charwomen and the people would be
hanging out the windows. *Those were the masses.* Lots of the people
who were with him are the same kind who go to the Kentucky Derby
and don't know a horse from a cow, but they'll come back and say, "I
was there." You find people who, if you talk about the struggle, the
only defense they've got is that "I was at the March on Washington."
And what happened there? Nothing. I remember when Negroes were
first talking about going to Washington they were saying they would
tear the capital down. *Those were the masses.* But the bourgeoisie
thinking of the movement was interjected, and the march did an
about-face in ideology.

You know, the people in riots are not King's people. He would be
asked to explain them, but he couldn't. It is just like if I have eyeball
cancer and somebody else has a common cold, and you go to that
person to ask about my cancer before you operate on me.

The masses of the people are not nonviolent. As a matter of fact, I
believe there was no such thing as a nonviolent Negro until King and
some other people invented him. You never heard of anybody going
on the Ku Klux Klan unarmed. Either I am too scared to go at all or
I'm going with the same weapons they have. So nonviolence was
never in our tradition, among Negroes or black people, or anything
else. I say Martin Luther King discovered the philosophy of Mo-
handas K. Gandhi, and I think it was the wrong application. Don't
get me wrong: King did a lot of good things. I had a lot of respect for
him. But I am telling you that we don't need nonviolence with a vio-

lent people. You don't need to practice religion with people who don't practice it themselves.

When I marched with King here, I would protect myself; I was always a revolutionary, I was never nonviolent. I saw the things that were happening to the other people and after I took an objective look I knew a different-type weapon would have to be used.

Odyssey

The murder of Dr. King in April, 1968, prompted blacks throughout the country into numerous riots. Chicago's was among the worst. If the winds had been strong, the flames that began in the West Side ghettos could have swept, out of control, across the city.

Fred Hampton

It was about May of 1968, and I knew I had exhausted all the available means of dealing with the problem. I had read things that Eldridge Cleaver had written in *Ramparts* magazine about the Black Panther Party, and I started organizing it in Illinois, along with Bobby Rush, even while I was still president of the NAACP's Youth Council. I was coming to see that everything that happens to black people is political, and the Panthers was a political organization, but it was for self-defense, too. The Panthers suggested we read some books, and they helped to change my thinking. Like the *Red Book* of Mao, about the class struggle. Fanon's *The Wretched of the Earth** is another. The third is the *Autobiography of Malcolm X*, which in my opinion is really the foundation for any revolutionary thought. You cannot feel, unless you have read this book.

I had a lot of faith in Malcolm. When I was young, I got a chance to talk to him a couple of times. He wanted to be right, and he prided himself on being right. Malcolm was always honest. The government and all have called these people liars, but he never told the government anything but the truth. His new position on racism† just

---

* Frantz Fanon, black, French-born psychiatrist, best known for his thesis that men of color were dehumanized; he saw them reclaiming manhood only through violence.

† Returning from Mecca, Malcolm X repudiated the Black Muslims' traditional regard of all whites as "devils."

strengthened my stand on him, because I felt he had been learning the racist line so long. Malcolm was that kind of a person, one who could change.

Before I came into the Panthers, I believed there was such a thing as a white world and a black world. I think I first became aware of it, when I was about nine years old, in fourth grade, and I heard stories about lynchings, things like that. So my feelings were antiwhite. I wasn't a racist; if I had been, I would have started an organization to be a black counterpart of the Ku Klux Klan, go out and lynch white people. I am not going to tell you no lie, because we got some white people running around in leadership positions here that need to be lynched, you know what I mean? But I didn't do any of that because of investigation and study. I didn't go like Stokely did, become a child groping in the dark, a person turned around because he got mixed up with some of the wrong people. With his feelings of inferiority, or something, he was scared to deal with white people. He was the type, it seemed to me, that if someone gave him money, just the fact that they gave it to him would affect what he had to do with it. This shows me he didn't have any courage, any faith in himself.

We Panthers don't have any trouble dealing with the white cats. By getting out there, going into poor white communities that were oppressed, I saw what the real problem was. There is a system of people in one class exploiting another. I try to define it as a situation where some people, the capitalists, get together as imperialists, not only against people here but all over the world. We could never rid ourselves of this because the racist seed of division was planted to make the exploited split among themselves, so that Puerto Ricans can't get along with whites, Indians can't get along with Mexicans, blacks can't get along with poor whites. Anybody who has any common sense knows that the poor whites in Chicago's Uptown district are our friends.* They are not exploiting us, nor we them. We haven't been able to meet the problems with any results because we have failed to unite with these friends for the purpose of taking on this one real enemy, the capitalist.

And now it has gotten to a further state than that, because of the

---

* The Black Panther newspaper said its Illinois chapter had a "formal coalition" with Uptown's Young Patriots, identified as revolutionary white Southerners whose berets have a "Free Huey" (Newton) button on one side and a Confederate flag on the other.

repression the Black Panther Party faces from fascism. There are three parts of this. First, the avaricious businessmen, then the demagogic, lying politicians supported by the businessmen, and third, the racist pig cop to enforce the wrongs the others do. You might have greedy businessmen who are slum landlords, and if you go to the demagogic politician, he won't do anything to redress your grievances, and then the pig cop comes in to move you out or force you to pay the rent.

You've got to relate to this shit the way it is. These motherfuckers would never have thought about no black slaves if it hadn't been for money, so racism is based off capitalism, and anybody who sets up a capitalistic system has to be a group of thugs.

Now that I understand all that, I think I would have been a Panther at fifteen, if there was a party then. As it was, when I came in at nineteen, a lot of people had a hangup because I was young. I just took the avenue that I was going to prove myself. I learned the ideology as fast as, or faster than, anybody else could do it. A lot of dogmatism was in the party when it was first started, and there was a question about me coming from Maywood. But these things you just have to deal with. I had to show through social practice what I believe is correct. And I think that ours is now one of the best, fastest-moving Black Panther chapters anywhere in the country.

Odyssey

In Congressional testimony a Chicago police lieutenant said he believed that while the Illinois chapter "may well exceed 100 members," it had only about 25 or 30 of what he called hard-core workers. Usually Panthers don't talk about membership, quoting the line that "those who say don't know, and those who know don't say." However, in a rare deviation, the Panthers' newspaper in 1969 put Hampton's chapter membership at "well in excess of 1,000." The article said this translated into "well in excess of 2,000 guns" because one requirement was that each Panther "own and be proficient in the use of two guns."

According to the newspaper, most prospective members in Chicago "come in here for one reason—to kill. Our job is to educate them in the correct methods of political struggle. To stress education and put new members in their place, the introductory classes are taught by a chubby 14-year-old boy whom everybody calls 'Little Mao.' Little Mao can rip off the 10-point platform and program, and the 26 rules faster than most people can read. He tells new recruits that they will learn the program by heart before they leave, or he will kick their ass." The party, said the newspaper, is not interested in "people who are unwilling to learn," and everyone was required to read two hours a day in "keeping abreast of current developments." Hampton was pictured as "merciless in his castigation of party members who are good 'rally' Panthers but who don't attend political classes" or do "political work among the masses."

The Panther headquarters emphasized security. Miriam and I were first screened by a Panther at the street door, who let us in when we said we had an appointment with Hampton. At the second floor a Panther sitting behind the "Officer of the Day" duty desk told us we'd have to be searched. A girl patted Miriam up and down, then went through her purse, item by item. I was asked to spread-eagle against a wall while I was frisked. Nothing casual about it; the Panther searching me made particularly sure I didn't have a gun hidden in my crotch. I had to take everything out of my pockets. "We don't want anybody planting dope up here," the duty officer explained.

Because we had come somewhat early, we waited in a room near the duty officer's desk. We saw one young Panther take off his jacket to put on a shoulder holster. One gun went into it. He took two more guns to jam under his belt, then put his jacket back on. He didn't say anything to anybody; nobody said anything to him. He just walked out the door, down the steps, onto the street.

Fred Hampton

The Black Panther Party at this stage is self-defensive. We move on that premise because we want to educate the masses of people that we are an armed political propaganda unit. You have to be armed to be out there! From five to twenty-five Panthers are arrested every week for selling Panther papers. Why? They don't want us giving the truth to people. Being willing to protect yourself helps you to survive in the capitalistic world when you are talking about anticapitalism. How are they going to let you talk about socialism, peacefully? They want to destroy the Panthers more than anything. We are the representatives, the protectors, the servants of the people. The pigs definitely do not like us. They protect property while we protect people.

I think it is very clear that the Black Panther Party is going to have to lead the struggle against the power structure. We didn't ask to be the vanguard, but we paid the cost of being boss, paid with twenty-three lives this year, with over sixty political prisoners. So we are very capable of being the vanguard, because we understand oppression. The Panthers are the most disciplined organization I know of. We can't endorse any kind of anarchism. Like with the SDS kids. Don't you think it is insanity when people make a move to get other people wiped out? It is insanity for people to get together and throw bricks and rocks, with machine guns standing around. We told them that with the idea of spontaneity three or four opportunists could move on the police, and they'll get everybody there killed. We defend our homes, our offices. That's all. You never heard of the Panthers attacking police stations, running into schools, pulling people out. We have had more demonstrations than any of the maniacs, but ours have been disciplined, organized, political—educational.

A lot of white people don't get off the expressways enough. They need to come on down here. At three o'clock in the morning there are more people on Madison Street outside the Black Panther office than there are at State and Madison [the Loop's main intersection]. Here is where the masses are. We support them, they support us. One specific sign is that every morning at seven o'clock we feed 4,000 kids in Chicago. When we come to opening a free health clinic, we didn't have to do anything but supervise. People from the community came in and built it almost by themselves. Every program the Black Panther Party has had, on its face, was just a theory, but when we put it out there in a social package the people latched onto it. I don't think anybody could deny that the masses of the people are poor, and our program is for the poor. The masses are oppressed, and our program is for the oppressed. The masses are exploited, and our program is for the exploited. And people want to know why a Rockefeller, a Nixon and some of these other people can't do what the Panthers do. Even with all the oppressions and attacks on our offices, the high bail and astronomical bonds, the Panthers still feed the hungry children, clothe the naked children, treat the sick and the wounded.

So all that raises a basic contradiction. It heightens the political awareness of the masses, and that is what this revolution depends on.

Odyssey

Store windows along West Madison Street near the Panther headquarters were dotted with signs showing Hampton's picture. Some said, "He came down from the mountain to help his people in the valley," while others proclaimed he had been a "political prisoner."

At the time we saw him he had just been freed on an appeal bond after serving three months in a maximum security prison. A street vendor in Maywood said Hampton had robbed him of hundreds of ice-cream bars near a playground. "I am a big dude," Hampton said in protesting his innocence, "but I can't eat no $71 worth of ice cream." He added: "It was a whole group of people who jumped him [the vendor], as I understand. I wasn't even there. I came later on and he picked me out."

During a hearing associated with the case Hampton was asked by a prosecutor from State's Attorney Hanrahan's office: "Do you feel that a legitimate means of obtaining what you are after is armed violence or armed revolution?" Hampton answered: "I believe if we tried anything else, we would end up like Martin Luther King."

On that $71 holdup charge a Chicago judge refused to fix bond pending appeal and sentenced Hampton to serve two to five years.

Fred Hampton

Our appeal is based on excessive and unreasonable sentencing and errors in the trial. After I got out on the appeal bond, the draft sent me a letter and said they didn't want me, wouldn't accept me under any circumstances. If the moon people attacked us, I couldn't get in the Army. I think the basic reason is that I spend too much time with another army, the people's army. I ain't worried about no profit, no money. That's the last thing I would want to steal. As Eldridge Cleaver said, anything that is paper burns. Money ain't no shit; we don't need it. All we need is some people to go out and rap and lay the line down to and tell them about the beautiful thing called socialism. Tell them about how they should live, communal living, tell them that when there is people on the street don't have any place to stay, they are supposed to take them in. These are things anybody with good sense understands.

You know, we aren't dogmatic about anything. We think China is a socialist country run by the people, but we don't just take the *Red Book* and follow it. We follow the things that relate to us right here in America. You have a beautiful example in Hanrahan and others, people that wipe out the young people. What I'm mentioning are things you need to bring about a state of genocide: stop the communications, stop any type of freedom of speech. All these things are fascism. So with me, I don't look for any justice in this system, in the courts,* or nowhere else until the people start feeling this shit themselves, until they start coming out in the streets, coming out in force.

People don't die, if they don't have the love.

The Last Odyssey

Only a few weeks after those words, Hampton lay dead in Chicago. The Reverend Ralph Abernathy, who had been there when the black revolution began with the buses in Montgomery, spoke the epitaph over his body. Looking at the casket, Abernathy said: "I don't think you'll rest in peace, Freddie, because there isn't going to be any peace. We're going to take up your torch, and although my fight will be nonviolent, it will be a militant fight. And there will be no peace in this land. . . ."

* The State Supreme Court upheld his conviction in the ice-cream robbery.

Journey's End

We have come back from our odyssey with no easy conclusions, because to be black in America is many things. It is enduring the savage beating Fannie Lou Hamer took in Winona. It is driving a Mercedes 280-SL in the hills above Los Angeles and realizing, with Richard Allen, that no matter how affluent, a black "can only come out of the ghetto to a certain degree, like moving from one end to the other." It is the pride that a Ralph Metcalfe, Sr., has in wearing his country's colors to the Olympics, although there is no place for him to live on Marquette's campus. It is his son coming through the siege of Columbia University calling himself a black revolutionary and supporting the Vietcong. And it is the tight little island of a Philadelphia slum where a Sonny Zoo could hold out his hand to us and say: "Hope I see you again. Might be under different circumstances. Like, if I ever get married, I'll invite you to my wedding."

What our odyssey thus taught us was that Black America has many faces, says many things, and there are no pat solutions to the problems between the races. All we can do, at journey's end, is to tell you what has been meaningful to us.

In Los Angeles, Miriam and I heard Mary Henry saying, "I have reached the point of believing there is a subtle savagery among white people that will never, ever make them ready to accept people of color. I don't say the Pledge of Allegiance anymore, and when I see red, white and blue, I feel like upchucking." And in New York James Allen mourned the "thousands of people [who] died thinking [integration] was the goal. . . . they died in vain. My grandfather used to say his concept of freedom was: 'Hallelujah! We are all going to go home and walk the streets of glory together, white and black.' I say, 'That's a hell of a thing to serve God for, just to be with a white man that has oppressed you all your life.' "

For Miriam and me it was impossible to listen to words like this all over the country without coming to understand that the gap between

blacks and whites is very deep. It may be getting wider. Time is probably running out on attempts to bridge it.

So, after two years and nearly a million words, we returned discouraged.

But also encouraged, because we have witnessed a revolution.

Instead of shame over blackness—"I wanted to be white, look
white, and the women I was attracted to exhibited white standards of
beauty," said New York's Police Inspector Arthur Hill of his earlier
years—blacks are turning to what Mrs. Henry called the "tenacity of
blackness that brought me peace." The young Metcalfe found his
white peers at Choate "pitiful," and in Mississippi Charles Evers dismissed the whites who once had chased him from the country stores
as "poor, sick individuals." In Atlanta, lawyer Howard Moore saw
that "My liberation doesn't depend on the white man's attitude. It depends on mine. If I have a gun pointed at the white man, I don't give
a damn what his attitude is, as long as I have the gun, it's loaded, and
I have the power to pull the trigger."

That self-reliance is only a generation removed from the fearful
memories of Rosa Parks when the Klan was active near her childhood home at Pine Level, Alabama: "The doors were sometimes
nailed shut, the faces were very tight. . . . It was a struggle, just to be
human." In the span of that generation, however, blacks have come
to see that they can be the agents of change in their lives, and no
longer, in the words of Dr. Nathan Hare in San Francisco, do they
need to "cry and pray and beg for justice from the people who oppress us." Consider an E. D. Nixon, painstakingly working for the
bus boycott that led to the black revolution of our time. In Charleston, where "We Shall Overcome" was born, Isaiah Bennett called the
hospital strike a "freedom movement for black people" so strong that
South Carolina would never be the same. And indeed, in the first
election after he told us that, a racist-oriented campaign for the governor's chair was defeated. In Memphis, Jesse Epps recalled the last
march of Martin Luther King, when, "with the tanks in the street, the
soldiers with bayonets, there came a little man with a sign saying, I
AM A MAN! When you could see that, no matter where you were, you
could take hope."

What our journey did for us was carry us beyond the barriers that
have always seemed to divide white and black and to let us *see* the
men and women whose skin just happened to be black. I know the
exact moment I first "saw" black. It was in Atlanta, in the Vine City

Foundation, with the noise coming in from the street, the voices echoing against the bare walls. Thirty minutes after we began talking with Helen Howard, I suddenly realized I had not been listening to a black woman. *I had been listening to a human being!* As paradoxical as it sounds, I found that seeing black is to become blind to color. It took me a long while to understand why this happened in the time with Mrs. Howard. The clue came when I started to describe her on paper, and the word that emerged was "mother." When Mrs. Howard had been talking about what she wanted for her children, I was hearing my own mother saying what she wanted for me. And it was no longer important that my mother was white and Mrs. Howard was black. We were all people together.

That insight said something else to me. If it happened only after the most intense exposure to blacks, months after we began our travels, then how could I fail to appreciate what an act of will it must take others without that experience to see beyond color? In telling about themselves, blacks showed us something about White America.

Until a Harlem man described the impact of white-bred inferiority on black drug addicts, neither Miriam nor I had been aware of how easily we accepted our birthright heritage from the white world, the idea, as he put it, that "White was best. White Lamb. White Owl. Anything white was right." After the man made the point, we could share in the irony Inspector Hill savored from his sons' game where "the last one in is a white man." As Ann Davis said in the Perry Homes, "The world is sure turning around."

And we with it. In Los Angeles we looked into the mirror that blacks hold up to White America. It doesn't make any difference, Mrs. Henry said, if a flower vase is knocked over accidentally or on purpose; it's still broken. Likewise, it doesn't matter, she said, if racism is tolerated or practiced; the result is the same. Like most white Americans, we had never thought of ourselves as racist. We didn't turn the dogs of Birmingham loose on anyone, and we didn't stone Dr. King in Chicago's Gage Park. But in the mirror Mrs. Henry held up we saw—ourselves, stripped of our comforting illusions. Just by tolerating what she called "subtle savageries"—how close were we in spirit to little Paschal Dubunda, who sat home in West Chester, Pennsylvania, eating his spaghetti, unaware of what he had done to Bayard Rustin by calling him "nigger"? Maybe the worst kind of prejudice is the unconscious kind.

That's one reason we think the South may be pointing a direction out of the racial morass. From their earliest days Southern whites "see" the blacks around them. The Reverend Andrew Young thought it important that in the South blacks and whites "have grown up side by side, they remember each other as kids. The law has estranged the races, but they are not really estranged. In Charleston I said to one of the black hospital workers, whose name sounded very Dutch, 'Where in the hell did you get a name like that?' Everybody in Charleston has these old names, black and white with the same name. All along in the South there has been integration after dark."

We once asked Isaiah Bennett if there was a difference between whites in the North and in the South. "Yeah, there is," he answered. "In the North the white man laugh with you to your face and stick a knife in your back. In the South he stick it in you, right to your face. I like to see my enemy, and I feel better fighting him in South Carolina, because I know who he is." When the Reverend Wyatt Tee Walker went North to disseminate "the true history of black folk," he found it was "like going for the ghost, discrimination so terribly shadowy you never could know where your enemy really was." As Andrew Young pointed out, segregation in the Northern cities bred "distrust, hostility, suspicion" because black and whites were so separate "everybody becomes scared of everybody."

Which brings us to violence.

The single great refrain we heard in Black America was that whites pay no attention to blacks until the cities burn and people are killed. "This is a do-or-die society," said Sonny Zoo. "What you got to realize is that black people is dead, dead as dead, you understand? We been under fire for 450 years. We have tried everything, spiritually, collectively, but we ain't got no other thing but violence." After the Omaha ghetto uprising, Dr. Earle Person could say: "People will tell you that the riot was horrible. Sure it was, in a sense. At the same time it said something: We reached a point in time where black people no longer intend to just docilely continue, as the church song goes, 'keep on, keeping on.'" In Harlem, the Reverend Mr. Walker promised he would join the shooting in the streets "if in the next four or five years there is not some marked shift in this country that brings more to the black people." And Washington's Channing Phillips noted that fifty men can turn a city upside down because "inadvertently the black man discovered the most potent weapon he has is violence."

For blacks, that is all part of getting themselves together, of making more and more of their commitment to black people, and of giving less and less of a damn about whites. They don't see why there has to be any great investigation or debate about what is wrong in this country. "I think everybody sees what I see, gets mad about what I get mad about, wants to change what I want to change," said the Panthers' Fred Hampton. "And I can spell it. It's rats and roaches, it's Red Devils, the pills, barbiturates, the poverty program, police brutality, undecent housing." It is also the frightening loss of human potential because so many blacks have had to pay the price of being black. For years, William Harrison was limited to teaching school in a small Alabama town. But Harrison proved he could run a million-dollar-plus cooperative with such skill that he disarmed even his most segregation-minded critics. And who has been the loser for all those earlier years? White America's welfare dollars went to keep an Irene Martin alive in the Perry Homes. When she broke out of that trap, she showed herself able to earn $7,000 a year. As her friend said, "The real Irene Martin has finally had a chance to come out. What a pity, and what a loss, it had to take so long."

Sitting on her front porch, in her native Mississippi Delta, Fannie Lou Hamer told us a parable: "As long as you have your feet on my neck, you got to stand in the ditch, too. If you move, I'm coming out. I want to get both of us out of the ditch."